Contributions to Management Science

The series *Contributions to Management Science* contains research publications in all fields of business and management science. These publications are primarily monographs and multiple author works containing new research results, and also feature selected conference-based publications are also considered. The focus of the series lies in presenting the development of latest theoretical and empirical research across different viewpoints.

This book series is indexed in Scopus.

More information about this series at http://www.springer.com/series/1505

Léo-Paul Dana • Veland Ramadani •
Ramo Palalic • Aidin Salamzadeh
Editors

Artisan and Handicraft Entrepreneurs

Past, Present, and Future

Foreword by Michelle Brandstrup

Springer

Editors
Léo-Paul Dana
Rowe School of Business
Dalhousie University
Halifax, Nova Scotia, Canada

Veland Ramadani
Faculty of Business and Economics
South East European University
Tetovo, North Macedonia

Ramo Palalic
Sultan Qaboos University
Al Khoudh, Oman

Aidin Salamzadeh
Faculty of Management
University of Tehran
Tehran, Iran

ISSN 1431-1941 ISSN 2197-716X (electronic)
Contributions to Management Science
ISBN 978-3-030-82302-3 ISBN 978-3-030-82303-0 (eBook)
https://doi.org/10.1007/978-3-030-82303-0

This Springer imprint is published by the registered company Springer Nature Switzerland AG.
The registered company address is: Gewerbestrasse 11, 6330 Cham, Switzerland

Dedicated to
Salam Salamzade (1908–1997), Azerbaijani painter
and
Gamar Salamzade (1908–1994), the first Azerbaijani female film director and the creator of the first children's film in Azerbaijan.

Foreword

The famous French sculptor, Auguste Rodin (1840–1917), described his road to success in these words: "In short, I began as an artisan, to become an artist. That's the good, the only method" (Claire 2016). However, especially in the West, the link between craft and art was challenged throughout the twentieth century. First with the Industrial Revolution, and later when much production became outsourced to countries where labour was cheaper. This change in history made it difficult for Western artisans to make a living, and over the following years, much knowledge of craft has disappeared from the countries where it was no longer needed.

Personally, however, I followed Rodin's advice and became a craftsman before I became an artist in the field of fashion. Years ago, I finished my tailoring degree, and I remember people's reaction when I told them about my chosen field. "But where will you find a job?", many would ask me with worry in their eyes. After my apprenticeship, I went to Paris to get experience from the city of *haute couture*, after which I got a job in a small tailor shop in Copenhagen. Here, we would repair and alter clothing which people had bought elsewhere. I later began my studies in fashion design at the university.

People were right about the difficulties in making a living as a tailor or fashion artisan in Denmark because handcraft had become devalued with production outsourcing. At a Christmas market, I sold blouses and tea towels that I had made with my friend Gitte Lægård, a textile designer. At another market, I sold handmade accessories (Fig. 1), but I agree that it can be difficult for the fashion artisan to compete with companies that have bigger marketing budgets; however, a change in the fashion industry has happened over the past few years, which can be advantageous to a fashion artisan. A current trend between Western consumers is to opt for sustainable, handmade, unique, and local-made products, rather than mass-produced, machine-made, and standard ones. Another radical change is how the Internet and social media have changed how fashion companies market themselves and reach consumers. To fully understand this change and how it can be an advantage to the fashion artisan, it is essential to look at how the industry used to work in the past.

Fig. 1 Selling accessories in Kolding; photo © Jørgen Ole Jensen

Long before social media, during the 1980s and 1990s, the fashion industry was more controlled and closed to the public. New collections were shown at fashion weeks twice a year, in major fashion capitals such as Paris, London, New York, and Milano, for a limited pre-selected audience. This audience included industry gatekeepers (influencers), fashion editors, collectors, buyers, and celebrities (Bendoni 2017). Most information about the new fashions presented at these events was not made available to the end consumers just yet.

Reviews of the shows were published in industry trade journals, and collection images were published months later in trade-only publications. These publications were costly and out of reach for the general consumer; however, a few distribution channels gave the public a glimpse into the fashion world at this time and one was CNN's *Style* with Elsa Klench, which aired between 1980 and 2001, and another one was MTV's *House of Style* with Cindy Crawford, which aired between 1989 and 2000, relaunched in 2012 (Bendoni 2017). Since much information was not revealed to the broader public, the people within the industry could maintain much control.

Bendoni (2017) argues that consumers were more passive recipients before social media, and they were more likely to approve than reject what was finally introduced to them in the stores. Consumers were then influenced by celebrities, fashion magazines, and various fashion advertisements, which gave these channels much power. With the introduction of social media, the consumer could now be influenced from anywhere by anyone, making the system much harder to control.

Given the old-fashioned system, it was rather difficult for a new unknown fashion entrepreneur to enter that realm. This person would be very dependent on the few distribution channels there were back then to get exposed. The Internet and social media have now given these people much more opportunities for visibility. Fashion editor from *Hollywood Reporter* and *Pret-A-Reporter*, Booth Moore, says: "*Social media has also created a platform for lesser-known designers to break into the fashion world, which has disrupted the traditional top-down model of designer to media to consumer, and made fashion more democratic and trends less rigid*" (Bendoni 2017).

With the Internet, it became possible for fashion enthusiasts to connect with other enthusiasts. Consumers were now encouraged to engage and take part in various fashion discussions. FashionNet.com (launched in 1995) and theFashionSpot.com (launched in 2001) were some of the first websites to share fashion news directly to the consumer, and forums such as LiveJournal, Blogger, and MySpace enabled anyone with interest in fashion to comment and share fashion news and opinions (Bendoni 2017). In his book about the history of the Internet, Johnny Ryan describes how the Internet from 2001 and onwards created a "mass collaboration between users" (Ryan 2010). From then on, more and more fashion blogs dominated the Internet (Mora and Rocamora 2015). Fashion bloggers were usually not characterised as journalists but rather fashion enthusiasts writing about fashion. They would share their everyday personal stories, present their recent fashion purchases, and write about their fashion opinions. The approach they had to their followers was often more personal and authentic than traditional fashion marketing. This authentic marketing approach became then attractive to the consumer.

As more and more people created many websites, webshops, forums, blogs, etc., chances of getting seen on the vast Internet became lower. This concern inspired Rob Kalin (an artisan himself) to create the e-commerce marketplace etsty.com, which was made to allow artisans and handicraft sellers to sell their crafts. Etsy was launched in 2005 (Althizer 2017); he struggled to get visitors to his website and learned what power community websites could have, such as craftster.org or getcrafty.com, where people would go and interact with other craftspeople. They would discuss topics, ask questions, get inspired, etc. Therefore instead of creating an individual webshop with his own store, he wanted to create a marketplace website with multiple stores (Althizer 2017). Etsy's mission was to be a community where sellers can support each other while offering the consumer an alternative to mass-produced products and facilitate a platform that can help each seller grow their businesses (Pace 2013). You can only open a store on Etsy if you are selling handmade products, vintage products (which are 20 years or older), or craft supplies (Etsy 2021).

Other than Etsy, there are several other online marketplace options for artisans. The American e-commerce company amazon.com launched Amazon Handmade in 2015 (Amazon Handmade 2021). They audit each applicant carefully and the applicant's production methods to make sure products are genuinely handcrafted. Amazon launched this platform because they experienced a growing desire for handmade products made by artisans (Amazon Handmade 2021). In Europe, Amazon has six online marketplaces, which can reach 28 European countries. The artisan will therefore be able to reach many countries (Amazon 2021).

Even though Amazon's reach is impressive, not to mention its popularity with millions of customers worldwide, an artisan needs to find the right marketplace, which attracts the right customers, and contribute positively to the brand feeling. Like the physical world, where it is crucial to choose the right neighbourhood, street, or shopping mall for a physical store, it is just as important to choose the right online marketplace or platform.

Whereas Amazon Handmade is an international marketplace, Folksy.com is a marketplace only for British artisans. To be able to sell on Folksy, one needs to have residency in the UK. They call themselves "The UK's Biggest Online Craft Fair" (Folksy 2021), and this is an example of how a marketplace can create a certain national atmosphere, even though anyone can access it from anywhere.

Some online marketplaces also focus on specific product categories, and within the field of fashion, it is worth mentioning the platform Not Just A Label (NJAL). They focus on emerging fashion talents from around the world, and it is a platform to both gain exposure and connect designers with stylists, buyers, celebrities, and press. If a designer signs up for NJAL+, it is also a marketplace where designers can sell their fashions. It is common to sell made-to-order items on the platform, which means that the designer will only produce the garment once the order has been made. Over 45,000 designers from more than 150 countries have been part of this network (Not Just A Label 2021).

Another well-known marketplace for fashion is ASOS Marketplace, which the online fashion retailer, ASOS, launched in 2010 (Asos 2021). It is made for small independent fashion brands and start-ups and allows them to reach a large international audience. More than 800 brands are selling their designs on the platform. ASOS Marketplace only allows brands who sell their own designs or vintage items, and a brand can start a shop on the platform with just five items. Some brands on this platform also use the made-to-order production method, which can work well with artisans and small brands, who cannot always keep an extensive stock (Asos 2021).

There are many more marketplaces, but these were examples of how fashion artisans can sell their products and get exposure to a large audience by being part of these communities. They give fashion artisans the possibility to reach international customers, rather than just local or national. However, since most people can join these communities, the competition for exposure is very high, and it takes a lot of effort and time to be successful with the platforms.

It is very common for fashion artisans to sell and expose themselves on multiple platforms. Some platforms offer various tools to manage that. For example, the marketplace, Folksy, give their sellers the possibility to import listings from Etsy (Folksy 2021). It is also common for fashion artisans to use social media platforms, redirecting customers to their websites or marketplace profiles. Social media platforms can be helpful for the artisan to get exposure, create a brand feeling, and engage with customers. Much information is passing through social media, and therefore it has also become an effective marketing tool for brands (Groothuis et al. 2020). Studies show that the use of new media can be an effective marketing tool for small businesses. Furthermore, it is possible to advertise on social media with a low budget compared to traditional media (Soedarsono et al. 2019).

Reaching more than 2.7 billion active monthly users in 2020, Facebook is the most extensive social network in the world (Statista 2021). It started as a platform for users to connect with friends and family to share photos, links, news, etc., but has become an effective marketing tool for brands and companies. Because of the large amount of information passing through the platform, Facebook owns beneficial information about its users, such as age, gender, and interests. Via Facebook's advanced applications, this gives companies the ability to reach their target audience when they advertise on Facebook (Djurica et al. 2013). Facebook also states on their own website that these "personalised ads help small businesses get found" (Facebook 2021). However, Facebook is a community of users, and these users can also play an essential role in contributing to free advertisement for a company. For example, if a user comments or uses the "like" button or shares some content from a company, this content is likely to be shared with the user's network of friends. The term E-WOM (electronic word of mouth), which relates to customers' interchange of information, is also something that can be both positive and negative for a company; however, according to research, the engagement of customers seems to have a positive effect on purchasing decisions because customers are more likely to purchase recommendations from their friends (Bernard et al. 2020). Some consumers are also more likely to turn to social media sites for information instead of corporate sites because they believe that the information there can be more trustworthy (Khan 2018).

It is vital for every brand, company, and artisan to know its industry and target group when choosing which social media to be present. Within the field of fashion and clothing, Instagram and Pinterest are popular platforms because they are very visual. On Instagram, brands can share photos and videos with their followers, and because the platform is very visual, it is a great place to give viewers a virtual brand feeling. Although the platform is very competitive, there are different marketing tools, a brand can use to increase its visibility, such as hashtags, Instagram stories, and collaboration with influencers. Both Facebook and Instagram have also applied selling features, so a user can easily be directed to webshops for purchase. In 2019, Facebook Pay was introduced, which gives the customer the option to purchase directly on Facebook or Instagram (Facebook Pay 2021).

Often fashion artisans choose to be present on a selection of online platforms, rather than just one. Some are for selling, some are for exposure, some are very visual, and some are to make a statement. Often one platform has links to others, and it can be argued that they all work together. A fashion artisan might choose to sell his or her products on Etsy or Not Just a Label, build brand loyalty, and also connect with customers on Facebook, present his or her visual universe and everyday authentic stories on Instagram, and show where the inspiration comes from on Pinterest.

The evolution of the Internet, and the fashion system's inevitable change which came with it, has definitely served the fashion artisan with much more possibilities than before. However, more possibilities have also been given to more people, and therefore, the competition for exposure on the Internet is high. With all these more possibilities to reach people, consumers have evolved a skill to navigate through a lot of information, making it even more difficult to grab their attention; however, the new media tools can still be very useful for fashion artisans and small businesses.

The sculptor Auguste Rodin valued greatly the ability to craft. However, the work by hands has not always been valued as much as work of the mind. Therefore, many artisans struggle to make a proper living from their craft, and many need a second income. Terms such as authenticity, handmade, local-made, craftsmanship, and sustainability have become popular terms in the minds of today's consumers. I hope we are stepping into an era where artisans can prosper because of their unique ability to craft, so their creativity can flourish and unfold even more.

Silkeborg, Denmark
25 May 2021

Michelle Brandstrup

References

Althizer KE (2017) 'Meet your maker: the women who create Etsy', a thesis presented to the Department of Anthropology, California State University, Long Beach

Amazon Handmade (2021) Join our artisan-only community of sellers (online) available at https://sell.amazon.com/programs/handmade.html?ref_=asus_soa_rd&, Accessed May 8 2021

Amazon Handmade (2021) Our Vision (online) available at https://www.amazon.com/handmade-about/b?node=17004334011, Accessed May 25 2021

Amazon (2021) Setting up your account in Europe (online) available at https://sellercentral.amazon.com/gp/help/external/G201394300?language=en_US, Accessed May 25 2021

Asos Marketplace (2021) Sell on Asos Marketplace (online) available at https://marketplace.asos.com/my/boutiqueapplication/information?ctaref=mktp|footer|selling|openboutique, Accessed May 25 2021

Bendoni WK (2017) Social media for fashion marketing: storytelling in a digital world. Bloomsbury Publishing PLC, New York

Kingsley BDT, Munasinghe AASN, Premarathne IKRJ, Wijayarathne S (2020) The influence of Facebook marketing on consumer buying intention of clothing: evidence from young adults. Arch Bus Res 8(9): 37–51

Djurica M, Djurica N, Marič M, Jovanović M (2013) Facebook marketing. Conference paper, 32nd international conference on organizational science development, March 2013, Portorož, Slovenia

Etsy (2021) Seller Policy (online) available at https://www.etsy.com/dk-en/legal/sellers/#allowed, Accessed May 25 2021

Facebook (2021) About Facebook (online) available at https://about.facebook.com/, Accessed May 25 2021

Facebook Pay (2021) Simplifying Payments with Facebook Pay (online) available at https://about.fb.com/news/2019/11/simplifying-payments-with-facebook-pay/, Accessed May 27 2021

Folksy (2021) Join the largest UK marketplace for handmade (online) available at https://folksy.com/selling, Accessed May 25 2021

Groothuis D, Spil TAM, Effing R (2020) Facebook marketing intelligence, conference paper, proceedings of the 53rd Hawaii international conference on system sciences

Jones C (2016) Sculptors and design reform in France, 1848 to 1895: sculpture and the decorative arts. Routledge, New York

Khan S (2018) Instagram as a marketing tool for luxury brands. Int J Manag Bus Res 8(2):120–126

Mora E, Rocamora A (2015) Letter from the editors: analyzing fashion blogs – further avenues for research. Fashion Theory 19(2):149–156, Bloomsbury Publishing PLC

Not Just A Label (2021) About NJAL (online) available at https://www.notjustalabel.com/about/njal, Accessed May 26 2021

Pace T, O'Donnell K, Dewitt N, Bardzell S, Bardzell J (2013) From organizational to community creativity: paragon leadership & creativity stories at Etsy. CSCW '13: Proceedings of the 2013 conference on computer supported cooperative work, February 2013, pp 1023–1034, San Antonio, TX

Ryan J (2010) A history of the internet and the digital future. Reaktion Books, London

Soedarsono DK, Mohamad B, Adamu AA, Pradita KA (2019) Managing digital marketing communication of coffee shop using Instagram. Int J Adv Sci Technol 28(10):69–74

Statista (2021) Number of monthly active Facebook users worldwide as of 4th quarter 2020 (online) available at https://www.statista.com/statistics/264810/number-of-monthly-active-facebook-users-worldwide/, Accessed May 25 2021

Preface

Artisans. They have been around a long time, and in every country. Illanes (2003) noted their importance during the nineteenth century. Figure 2 features the home of the *Sociedad Internacional de Artesanos y Socorros Mutuos* (international society of artisans and mutual aid), in Iquique, Chile; its statutes date back to 1896. In India, the Central Cottage Industries Emporium (Fig. 3) has been promoting local crafts and artisans since 1952. Artisanal activities have long contributed to livelihoods—and collectively to the world economy. Yet, so little has been written about them!

Fig. 2 Sociedad Internacional de Artesanos y Socorros Mutuos, Iquique, Chile; photo © Léo-Paul Dana

Fig. 3 Central Cottage Industries Emporium, Kolkata (formerly Calcutta); photo © Léo-Paul Dana

As recently as the 1980s, governments favoured large corporations and artisans were on their way out. Figure 4 shows an artisan tailor in his 1926 establishment—shortly before being forced to close down.

Scase and Goffee (1987) observed that the policy of some governments slowly shifted from discouraging to encouraging independent business. Yet, during the 1990s, there was still little interest in (or government support for) artisans. Greece encouraged artisans and craftsmen, and that was an exception worthy of a publication (Dana, 1999). For the most part, artisans were thought of as individuals using outdated methods to do things that could be more efficient when automated.

A generation later, we see a revival of artisans, and we witness a new artisan, using technology, innovating, and marketing by means of social media. Traditional Inuit sculptors in Canada (Fig. 5) and Greenland (Fig. 6) use power tools to make art that gets sold around the world. No longer are artisans selling exclusively in one community; accessing a global market, platforms have changed the game!

Nowadays, craft is viewed as "a timeless approach to work that prioritizes human engagement over machine control (Kroezen et al. 2021, p. 1)". Hats off to Dr. Prashanth Mahagaonkar, Senior Editor at Springer, for recognising the importance of artisans and much appreciation for his support in producing this book.

Fig. 4 Shop in downtown Montreal, Canada; photo © Léo-Paul Dana

This volume is the result of coordinated efforts by researchers around the world writing during a pandemic—not the easiest scenario. Much appreciation goes to the contributors and to the editorial board for thorough reviews of each chapter. Now sit back, and enjoy!

Fig. 5 Inuit artisan in Coral Harbour, Canada; photo © Léo-Paul Dana

Fig. 6 Carving in Nuuk, Greenland; photo © Léo-Paul Dana

Halifax, Canada	Léo-Paul Dana
Tetovo, North Macedonia	Veland Ramadani
Muscat, Oman	Ramo Palalic
Tehran, Iran	Aidin Salamzadeh
25 May 2021	

References

Dana L-P (1999) Preserving culture through small business: government support for artisans and craftsmen in Greece. J Small Bus Manag 37(1):90–92

Illanes MA (2003) La revolución solidaria. Las Sociedades de Socorros Mutuos de Artesanos y Obreros: un proyecto popular democrático, 1840-1887. Polis, Revista de la Universidad Bolivariana 1(5):1–62

Kroezen J, Ravasi D, Sasaki I, Zebrowska M, Suddaby R (2021) Configurations of craft: alternative models for organizing work. Acad Manag Annals 15:502–536
Scase R, Goffee R (1987) The real world of the small business owner. Croom Helm, London.

Editorial Board

Contents

About the Editors

Léo-Paul Dana is Professor at Dalhousie University and holds titles of Professor at Montpellier Business School and Visiting Professor at Kingston University. He is associated with the Chaire ETI at Sorbonne Business School. A graduate of McGill University and HEC Montreal, he has served as Marie Curie Fellow at Princeton University and Visiting Professor at INSEAD. He has published extensively in a variety of journals including *Entrepreneurship Theory and Practice, International Business Review, International Small Business Journal, Journal of Business Research, Journal of Small Business Management, Journal of World Business, Small Business Economics,* and *Technological Forecasting and Social Change.*

Veland Ramadani is Professor of Entrepreneurship and Family Business at the Faculty of Business and Economics, South East European University, North Macedonia. His research interests include entrepreneurship, small business management, and family businesses. He authored or coauthored around 140 research articles, 11 textbooks, and 18 edited books. He has published in *Journal of Business Research, International Entrepreneurship and Management Journal, International Journal of Entrepreneurial Behavior & Research*, and *Technological Forecasting and Social Change*, among others. Dr. Ramadani is co-Editor-in-Chief of *Journal of Enterprising Communities* (JEC). He has received the Award for Excellence 2016—Outstanding Paper by Emerald Group Publishing. In 2017, he was appointed as a member of Supervisory Board of Development Bank of North Macedonia, where for 10 months he served as an acting Chief Operating Officer (COO) as well.

Ramo Palalic is Assistant Professor at the Management Department, College of Economics and Political Science, Sultan Qaboos University, Oman. His research is in the area of entrepreneurship, leadership, and management. Dr. Palalić has authored and coauthored many articles in globally recognized journals like *Management Decision, International Journal of Entrepreneurial Behavior & Research, International Entrepreneurship and Management Journal*, and the like. Additionally, he has coauthored/coedited several books and many book chapters in the field of business and entrepreneurship published with internationally prominent publishers (Springer, Routledge, World Scientific). Moreover, Dr. Palalić is serving as the reviewer/editor board member in several well-established international journals. Apart from his research, he was involved in business projects in the areas of entrepreneurial leadership and marketing management, in private and public organizations.

Aidin Salamzadeh is an assistant professor at the University of Tehran. His interests are start-ups, new venture creation, and entrepreneurship. Aidin serves as an associate editor for *Revista de Gestão* and *Innovation & Management Review* (Emerald), as well as an editorial advisory *in The Bottom Line* (Emerald). Besides, he is the cofounder of the Innovation and Entrepreneurship Research Lab (UK), and a reviewer in numerous distinguished international journals. Aidin is a member of the European SPES Forum, the Asian Academy of Management, the Institute of Economic Sciences, and Ondokuz Mayis University.

Part I
Traditional Self-Employed Artisans, Home-Made Goods and Markets

Ground Loom Weaving Among Negev Bedouin Women

A. Allan Degen and Shaher El-Meccawi

Abstract It was common to see black tents dotting the Negev landscape in 1948, the year the State of Israel was created. Bedouin women used ground looms to weave tents and carpets from goat hair and sheep/camel wool. However, the tents were replaced by tin shacks when non-sanctioned Bedouin villages sprung up in the Negev in the 1950s–1970s. With urbanization, ground loom weaving continued in the 1980s, but instead of natural goat hair and sheep wool, the women used colourful acrylic yarn to weave carpets and other items. Weaving basically ceased by 2015, and today, it is rare to find a ground loom. Bedouin simply purchase machine-made acrylic carpets for their homes and other purposes. However, in 1991, two Bedouin sisters established a women's cooperative, 'Lakiya Negev Bedouin Weaving', to preserve traditional weaving and provide employment for Bedouin women. Today, there are 30 to 60 Bedouin women employed at the cooperative, most of them working from their homes. A similar pattern of ground loom weaving and its discontinuation among Bedouin women has been described in a number of surrounding countries in the Middle East. Cooperatives were also established in these countries to preserve traditional weaving methods and provide earnings for Bedouin women.

1 Background

Traditionally, Negev Bedouin depended solely on nomadic pastoralism for their lifestyle and livelihood. Sheep, goats and camels provided them with milk and milk products, wool and hair for weaving carpets and tents, transportation and traditional slaughter. Bedouin are patriarchal, and, in the past, men were the providers and

A. Allan Degen (✉)
Ben-Gurion University of the Negev, Beer Sheva, Israel
e-mail: degen@bgu.ac.il

S. El-Meccawi
Achva Academic College, Shikmim, Israel

Kaye Academic College, Beer Sheva, Israel

L.-P. Dana et al. (eds.), *Artisan and Handicraft Entrepreneurs*, Contributions to Management Science, https://doi.org/10.1007/978-3-030-82303-0_1

controlled all sources of income. Women's lives centred on raising children, maintaining the dwelling, preparing food, milking sheep and goats, processing milk, caring for young lambs and kids and collecting wood and water. When flocks were corralled near the homestead, the women, with the help of children, watered and fed the animals. At grazing sites remote from the household, women also helped with the shepherding and shearing of the animals. Besides these activities, women would find time to weave carpets, tents and other accessories and embroider, in particular, dresses. The mobility of women was limited both within the homestead area and at the remote camping sites to preserve the honour of the family (Abu-Rabia 1994, 1999; Degen et al. 2000; Akirav et al. 2021).

Today, there are 250,000–300,000 Bedouin in the Negev of southern Israel, comprising 25% of the Negev population. Approximately 75% of the Bedouin live in planned urban communities and the rest in rural, spontaneous, non-authorized villages (extrapolated from the Negev Bedouin Statistical Data Book 2010). There is evidence that nomadic pastoralism in the Negev dates back to the beginning of the Neolithic period (Sauer 1966). The first Bedouin-type tribes are thought to have reached the region in the seventh century AD with the explosive rise of Islam in the Arabian Peninsula. Bedouin numbers increased considerably during the Ottoman (Turkish) rule of the region (1517–1917) with the arrival of both nomadic peoples and peasant farmers (*fellahin*; فلاحين). The Ottoman rulers tried to consolidate their position in the tribal areas as "they wanted to gain control over the Bedouin tribes to collect taxes from them and to fortify some border areas for strategic purposes" (Alafenish 1987). To stabilize tribal boundaries and to sedentarize the Bedouin, the Ottomans established an administrative centre in Beer Sheva in about 1900. This was the first settlement to be established in the Negev from the Nabatean and Byzantine period that ended in the sixth century. In effect, this attempt by the Turks to curb tribal warfare in the early twentieth century initiated the process of sedentarization among the Bedouin (Goering 1979). Some tribal chiefs moved into Beer Sheva, which, with its market and livestock trade, became the commercial and administrative centre for the Negev Bedouin (Alafenish 1987; Kressel and Ben-David 1995). The Ottoman Empire was conquered near the end of the First World War by the British who were granted a mandate to rule Palestine. During their rule from 1917 to 1947, the British interfered little in the affairs of the Negev Bedouin. By the end of the British mandate in 1948, there were approximately 65,000 Bedouin in the Negev, composed of true-noble Bedouin, *fellahin* and slaves (*abid*; عبيد) (Marx 1967). The exact number was difficult to ascertain because of the mobility of the Bedouin and also because Bedouin are "not favourably disposed towards population counts" (Amiran and Ben-Arieh 1963). Populations of 95,000 have also been reported (Alafenish 1987). The Bedouin were divided into 95 tribes, which were combined into eight Confederations.

Following the war in 1948, there were about 11,000 Bedouin composed of 19 tribes and 3300 families. All Bedouin were placed under Military Administration in a closed area, called the *siyag* (سياج), in the northeastern part of the Negev (Goering 1979). This imposed sedentarization virtually ended the nomadic and semi-nomadic lifestyle of the Bedouin. At this time, formal education, as known in the

Western world, was considered unimportant among the Negev Bedouin. Generally, only boys from wealthy families attended school, usually till grade four or five (Bernstein-Tarrow 1980). As described by Abu-Saad et al. (2007), "[t]he traditional Muslim schools called Kuttab that usually functioned in a tent around the Sheikh's residence were the place of study and classes usually included about 20 boys, roughly between the ages of 5 and 12, who were taught to memorize the whole Quran by sheer repetition. In addition, they learned reading, writing, and the precepts of Islam." No girl attended school till the mid-1960s as Bedouin thought it was more important to prepare the girls for life, rather than formal education. As expressed by Abu-Saad et al. (2007), "[f]or girls, the informal education included cooking, childcare, household management, weaving, embroidery and sewing; lighter agricultural tasks—harvesting crops, taking care of the flock and other domesticated animals; collection, preparation, and preservation of dairy and other food products; making household items such as tents, carpets pillows, mattresses, and quilts; and oral history. Oral history was passed on, as were moral and religious values, through poets, respected elders, and storytellers."

2 Black Tents

Black tents (house of hair; *bayt al-sha'ar*; بيت الشعر) stood out conspicuously throughout the *siyag*. Erecting and dismantling the tent were quick and easy, which was essential as some Bedouin still moved with their livestock. Tents were composed of a rectangular roof and lateral sheets made of woven strips of black goat hair and white sheep and/or camel wool sewn together. The tent also included posts, anchoring ropes and pegs made from local vegetation (Meir and Stavi 2011; Gilbert 2013; Katsap and Silverman 2016). Goat hair is very sturdy, providing good insulation, and once it becomes wet, it expands and prevents water from seeping through (Na'amneh et al. 2008). The end sheets of the tent were perpendicular to the ground, but the lateral sheets sloped at an outward angle from the roof. The roof was raised in the middle by a perpendicular supporting pole, and there were one or more other supporting poles according to the size of the tent. The tent was partitioned by a woven curtain (*ma'anad*; معند) into two sections, one section for men (*shigg*; شق) where male guests were received and the other section for women and her family (*maharam*; محرم) and entertaining women friends. The size of each section was flexible and could be altered according to the family's needs; an increase in family size led to a larger women's section, whereas higher social status and more visitors led to a larger men's size.

Woven carpets covered the ground on the men's side in a three-sided configuration with a fire pit in the middle of the configuration to prepare strong black coffee. Coffee took on a special importance among the Bedouin as it symbolized hospitality and generosity. Bedouin men were and still are very proud of their coffee. Coffee was prepared by the head of the household and included roasting and grinding the beans and adding crushed cardamom. Beans were roasted by stirring and flipping them gently in a frying pan over an open fire and then were ground in a mortar and pestle to a rhythmic beat. The ground beans were added to boiled water in a coffee pot (*bakraj*; بكرج) and was boiled gently until ready. The host would first taste the coffee and only then would serve his guests, usually three small cups (*finjan*; فنجان) each. The women's side of the tent was used mainly for preparing food, traditional bread (*khubz saj*; خبز صاج) and sweet tea, taking care of the children and storing food, equipment for processing milk, and bedding.

The tent was positioned to take the best advantage of the climatic conditions. The two ends faced north and south, with the men's side towards the north and the women's side towards the south. The front sheet in the men's side was often open and relatively short, just reaching the ground, whereas in the women's side, it was generally closed and quite long, folding over on the ground. The openings of the tent faced towards the east, that is, towards the sunrise, so that in winter, rolling up the eastern side in the morning allowed the sun to warm up the inside and dry the interior, whereas rolling up the western side in the afternoon also added some warmth to the tent. In summer, rolling up both the eastern and western sides took advantage of the western winds to ventilate the tent (Meir and Stavi 2011; Gilbert 2013; Katsap and Silverman 2016).

3 Traditional Weaving

Bedouin raised mainly fat-tailed Awassi sheep, a hardy desert breed that produced coarse carpet wool, and Negev goats, a breed well-adapted to deserts. The collection of fibres and processing to yarn underwent a number of steps. First, the sheep and goats were washed, mainly by men, and then hand-shorn, mainly by women (Figs. 1 and 2); however, both men and women participated in both activities. The sheep wool was usually shorn in one piece (*jizzeh*; جزه), but each goat hair was shorn separately and then collected together. Camel wool was removed by simply pulling off clumps during May–June, or the wool was collected from the ground after being shed. The fibres of the three animals were treated differently. The hair and wool were first cleaned by manually removing leaves, burrs and other debris. Goat hair and sheep wool were then washed in soapy water one or two times, but camel wool was not. After drying the sheep wool, it was teased (*tanfeesh*; تنفيش) by pulling it apart (Fig. 3) and, in this way, knots and any debris still present were removed. The teased wool was then carded with a small rectangular carding comb (*kirdash*; كرداش), which had rows of metal teeth. The teeth were dragged over the fleece in different directions, but at the completion, the fibres lay in the same direction. The sheep and camel wool were now ready to be spun; goat hair was spun directly after washing. A wooden drop spindle (*marzal*; مغزل) that had a single hook made from a bent nail was used to spin the fibres. The women made their own spindles by burning a hole in a small piece of butterfly-shaped wood (*farasheh*; فراشه) and then inserting a shaft as a handle and nail as a hook at the head (Willey-Al'Sanah 2013). The wool could be spun directly from a pile of carded wool or could be

Fig. 1 Bedouin woman shearing an Awassi sheep; photo © A. Allan Degen

rolled into a ball enabling the woman to move around while spinning. For a right-handed woman, the shaft of the spindle was held in her right hand at the height of her hip, with the head of the spindle pointing towards the left. Then, with her left hand, she fed fibres to the spindle, which was being twirled at the height of her thigh in one direction away from her body, and the yarn was collected on the handle (*ḥamleh*; حمله) (Figs. 4 and 5). Often, this yarn was rolled into a ball, and then two strands of yarn from different balls were placed together, spun in the opposite direction of the single strand and made into a ball of double strands weighing 4–5 kg (*doḥroje*; دحرجه). Two such double strands could also be spun together so that there would be

Fig. 2 Bedouin girl, with the help of a younger brother, shearing an Awassi sheep. The one piece of wool (*jizza*) is on the ground to the girl's left; photo © A. Allan Degen

Fig. 3 Bedouin women teasing sheep wool (*tanfeesh*; تَنْفيش); photo © A. Allan Degen

yarn of 4 strands. Yarns of different thicknesses allowed the weaving of thicker carpets or a carpet with more than one thickness. The yarn would then be skeined in figure eights (*maslak*; مسلك) between two stakes about a half meter apart (Fig. 6) in preparation for dyeing. Skeined wool was loose, which allowed the wool to be dyed more homogeneously. For dyeing wool, water was boiled in a large vat containing pomegranate peels; the peels were then removed; dye was added; and the yarn was

Fig. 4 Bedouin woman arranging carded sheep wool to be spun; photo © A. Allan Degen

placed into the vat for 12 h. The dyed yarn was removed, dried and the coloured balls were prepared for weaving. The traditional range of colours included natural white, black, green, navy blue, and deep red (Figs. 7 and 8); dyes were purchased in Gaza and Hebron. All Bedouin woman were able to weave, and the skills were passed on to daughters at a very early age. In summers of the 1970s, there were always some Bedouin women weaving in each village (*personal observations*). Women participated in a group in what Willey-Al'Sanah (2013) referred to as an "informal payback system—I help you today; you help me tomorrow." Weaving was an entertaining social event for the women with tea served regularly, songs sung and stories told. Also, young girls observed and learned how to weave.

Weaving was done on a primitive ground loom (*madad*; مدد), which held warp yarn in place, while weft yarn (*lahmeh*; لحمه) was passed between the warp strands and interwoven at 90-degree angles (Fig. 9). Setting up the loom required specific know-how, as it was a very exact procedure that took a whole day to complete. The frame of the loom was marked by four metal stakes pounded into the ground, two at each end, that supported strong wooden or metal rods. A woman sat at each end, and two layers of warp yarn were stretched between the rods by a young girl running back and forth (*jarra yat*; جرايات) with the yarn to each end. Camel wool was generally not used to make tents and carpets because of the low amount collected,

Fig. 5 Bedouin woman spinning sheep wool with the yarn collecting on the handle (*ḥamleh*; حَمْلِه); photo © A. Allan Degen

and it was not as strong as goat hair or sheep wool; occasionally, several warps of camel wool were used for the sides or the divider of the tent. The best yarn was used for the warps, as this was visible in the finished product. A heddle rod (*nireh*; نيره) with loops was placed over the warp so that one warp layer could be fixed by the heddle. The heddle rod was usually supported by empty tin cans of appropriate height. The loom was several meters long, but narrow, so that a woman could easily reach both sides. Two or three strips, each about 3-m-long and attached in a row, could be woven, with a width of 60 cm to 1 m. In this way, two or three carpets or strips of the tent were woven on one loom. The crosswise yarn, weft, was wrapped around a rod (*meshaa*; ميشع) of about 1 m in length, and the weaver would sit at one end, inserting the rod between the warp strands. The tension in the warp was adjusted with a sword beater (*minsaj*; منساج), a heavy, flat stick pointed at both ends, about 65–75 cm long and 70–80 mm wide. The stick was slid under a layer of warp yarns, which were tightened by turning the flat side of the sword beater horizontally and were beaten hard against the new weft yarn. A new opening was made after each

Fig. 6 Bedouin woman skeining sheep wool in a figure eight (*maslak*; مَسْلك) prior to dyeing; photo © A. Allan Degen

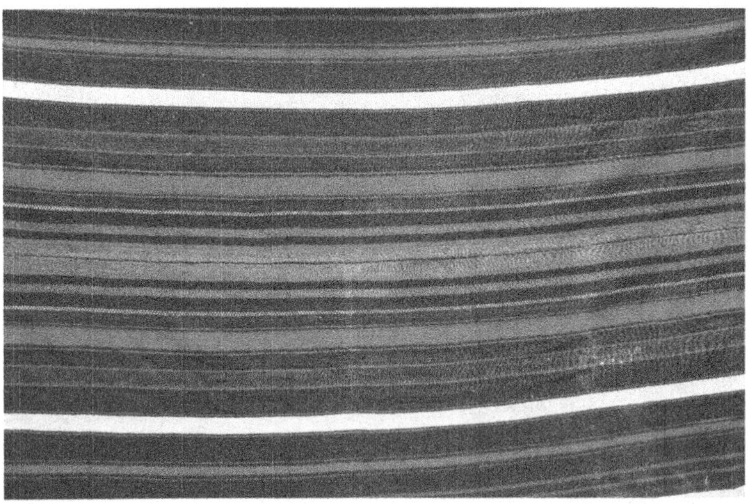

Fig. 7 A sheep wool blanket (*rafrach*; غفرة) with the colours green, black, red, white and blue; the blanket was woven over 60 years ago; © photo Shaher El-Meccawi

pass by forcing the free set of warps up above the fixed or heddled warps and, thus, separating the warp yarns. After the opening was made, the sword beater was placed into it vertically to widen it; the upper warps were then pulled upward with a hook beater (*midri*; مدري) to tighten the warp yarn. The hook beater was a gazelle horn or a bent nail attached to a wooden handle wrapped with soft material (Fig. 10). The next shed was created by pushing the loose warps down past the heddled ones (Figs. 11 and 12). Sewing strips together, if needed, finishing the ends and, perhaps, adding tassels completed the product. At times, two women wove the same carpet at the same time, each one handling half of the width. The addition of tassels for decorations was common and was used even on women themselves (Fig. 13). Long tents

Fig. 8 Spun sheep wool after dyeing (*doḥroje*; دُخرُجه); photo © A. Allan Degen

Fig. 9 Ground loom set-up from the woman's side (*maharam*; مَحَرَم) of the tent. Two stakes at each end of the loom support rods holding the warp yarns. The divider of the tent (*ma'anad*; مَعْنَد) separates the man's side (*shigg*; شِق) from the woman's side; photo © A. Allan Degen

were woven for weddings and other celebrations (Fig. 14). To signify a wedding, a doll (*omariyya*; عومريه) wearing an elaborately embroidered dress, beads and tassels was placed at the top of the tent (Fig. 15). Woven carpets were laid on both sides of the tent with pillows interspersed so that the Bedouin could recline on them. Saddlebags for camels and horses (*khurj*; خرج) were also woven by either cutting the woven material or folding it over (Fig. 16). In addition, camel wool was used to make hats by hand weaving.

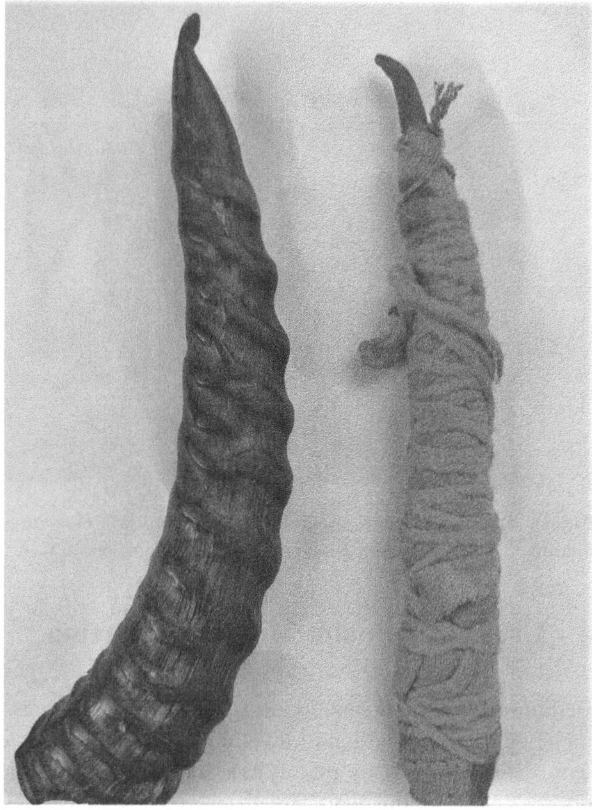

Fig. 10 A hook beater (*midri*; مِدْري) made of a gazelle's horn (left) or a bent nail wrapped with soft material (right); photo © Shaher El-Meccawi

Fig. 11 Bedouin woman weaving a tent. The heddle rod (*nireh*; نيره) can be seen in front of her; photo © A. Allan Degen

Fig. 12 Bedouin woman using a sword beater (*minsaj*; مِنساج) to beat against the weft yarn. The rod holding the weft (*meshaa*; ميشَع) is lying to her right; photo © A. Allan Degen

4 Urbanization and Modified Weaving

Bedouin started non-sanctioned 'spontaneous' villages throughout the *siyag*, which included the construction of dwellings. Authentic tents of goat hair and sheep/camel wool were replaced by mainly tin shacks and, on occasion, by solidly constructed houses. As Bedouin were much less mobile, there was less need for black tents. Also, homes built on a solid foundation were illegal and could be demolished by Israeli authorities. Any tents that did exist were made of jute material or plastic sheets. Today, there are no Bedouin 'black tents' in the Negev Desert. In the late 1960s and 1970s, the Israeli government initiated a policy to settle the Bedouin into towns, ostensibly to settle the problem of land ownership, to integrate them into the national civilian and economic systems and to provide them with public services (Shmueli 1980; Abu-Saad 1996; Abu-Bader and Gottlieb 2008; Tarrow 2008). The transition to urban living drastically changed the lifestyle and economics of the Negev Bedouin (Meir 1997). Men entered the wage labour market (Jakubowska 2000; Abu-Rabia 2001) in or near the big cities, in particular Beer Sheva (Gardner and Marx 2000). Women no longer needed to carry out many of their traditional tasks, but they maintained traditional dress and generally stayed at home, as Bedouin men did not accept women working outside the house. Thus, women lost their traditional roles in the family and had to define new ones (Degen 2003).

The main roles of the women were still taking care of the home and raising children, as in the past, and which was readily accepted by both men and women. More girls were going to primary and secondary schools, and the number of girls completing high school matriculation was increasing each year (El-Meccawi and Degen 2016). Thus, the younger women were leaning towards getting better

Fig. 13 Bedouin woman with tassels of sheep wool for decorations; photo © A. Allan Degen

educated, while the older women (over 60 years) were satisfied with occupying themselves around the house with domestic tasks and taking care of children and grandchildren. The middle-aged women were creating a niche for themselves while coping with 'modern urbanization'. These women could be divided roughly into two groups: (1) married with young children (till age 35); and (2) having older children at the end of childbearing years (ages 35–55). The first group was usually occupied with young children, housework and preparing food for the household. The second group generally had more free time as their children were older and were the main ones continuing traditional activities, however, with modifications. These women, along with the older women, wove carpets (3 m in length × 1 m in width), but only a small proportion, usually the older ones, knew how to set up the loom (Figs. 17 and 18). Synthetic, colourful acrylic yarns that were purchased in the Thursday Bedouin market (*sug*; سوق) in Beer Sheva were used (Fig. 19) instead of natural fibres. Carpets were still needed for the guest room in the house, as it served as a *shigg*, and for weddings and other celebrations (Fig. 20) and for prayers (Fig. 21). In addition,

Fig. 14 Long Bedouin tent being used for a wedding celebration; photo © A. Allan Degen

Fig. 15 A doll (*omariyya*; عومَرِيَّه) wearing an elaborately embroidered dress, beads and tassels is displayed to signify a wedding; photo © A. Allan Degen

Fig. 16 Woven camel saddlebag (*khurj*; خُرْج) of sheep wool and decorated with tassels; photo © Shaher El-Meccawi

women from the *Jerawin* tribe (ألجراوين) wove two carpets for a son and one for a daughter when they were married (*personal data*). Many items were made of colourful synthetic material, including saddlebags, pillow covers and other decorative items such as covering of sticks with added tassels for dancing at weddings, covering of baskets to hold candies at celebrations, and covering of bottles (Figs. 22, 23, 24, 25, 26, 27, 28, and 29). There was little use for sheep wool, and it was often simply discarded. Wool that was kept was used mainly for pillow and blanket fillings. When women were asked why they use synthetic yarn rather than wool, a typical reply was that "it is much easier to work with the material, it has nicer colours, it is softer and it is cheap." When a Bedouin man was asked why wool was not used, seeing it was free, he replied that "it is difficult and expensive to dye the wool since Gaza is closed" (the wool used to be brought to Gaza where it was dyed). Similar sentiments were expressed by Canavan and Alnajadah (2013) when

Fig. 17 Bedouin woman lifting up warps when weaving a carpet (*bsat*; بساط) with colourful acrylic yarn; photo © A. Allan Degen

Fig. 18 Bedouin woman with a hook beater (gazelle horn—*midri*; مِذري) in her right hand and sword beater (*minsaj*; مِنْساج) in her left hand. Another hook beater and the rod holding the weft yarn (*meshaa*; ميشع) are lying next to her right foot; photo © A. Allan Degen

discussing ground loom weaving in Kuwait: "Today much of the traditional knowledge of natural dyeing has been lost and forgotten among the remaining Bedouin women weavers in Kuwait, with cheap and accessible chemical dyes being quick and easy to use. Pre-dyed commercial synthetic yarns are now readily available, the

Fig. 19 Colourful acrylic yarns being sold at the Thursday Bedouin market (*sug*;سوق) in Beer Sheva. Tassels and bags are also being sold; photo © A. Allan Degen

use of which results in a very different quality of product, both in color, feel, and durability. Interestingly, contemporary weavers favor these yarns for their easy availability, inexpensive cost, and bright colors."

5 Bedouin Women Weaving Cooperative

With continued urbanization, traditional ground loom weaving came to a virtual halt in both the urban and rural Bedouin settlements. As expressed by Willey-Al'Sanah (2013), "there was a loss of opportunity for social interaction and ancient weaving skills [were] devalued; tents were no longer needed; the mobility of women decreased; there were no sheep to herd, no water to bring, and no loom to weave." Women simply purchase machine woven carpets for the home, as they are still

Fig. 20 Bedouin man carrying colourful acrylic carpets to a wedding tent; photo © A. Allan Degen

needed in the *shigg* of the house to receive guests and for weddings and other celebrations. This, too, is changing, as furniture is replacing carpets on the floor in homes and an increasing number of weddings and other celebrations are being held in halls or around tables instead of sitting on carpets in tents. In addition, today, tents for weddings are usually rented and made of jute material or plastic sheets supported by aluminium frames (Fig. 30).

In 1991, two sisters, Khadra and Hanan El-Sana, established a weaving cooperative, Lakiya Negev Bedouin Weaving, in Lakiya (Fig. 31), a Bedouin town. The idea for the project originated in 1990 from a member of the 'Sons of Laqiya', a

Fig. 21 Bedouin men praying on woven acrylic carpets. These men were at a wedding celebration; photo © A. Allan Degen

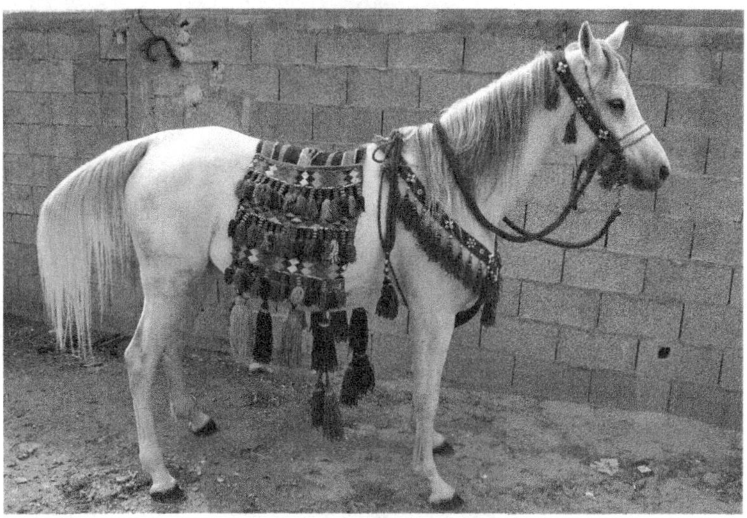

Fig. 22 Woven horse saddlebag (*kharj*; خُرْج) with tassels, all made with colourful acrylic yarn; photo © Shaher El-Meccawi

non-governmental organization (NGO) sponsored by Oxfam. Dr. Charlotte Heath, a British weaving consultant, encouraged the creation of the cooperative and provided technical support, while Oxfam supported the set-up of the cooperative (Willey-

Fig. 23 Bedouin men riding horses at a wedding. Woven saddlebags (*khurj*; خُرْج) and decorative tassels around the neck of the horse can be seen. One man is holding a rod covered with colourful acrylic yarn and tassels; photo © A. Allan Degen

Fig. 24 Bedouin woman finishing a woven pillow cover made with colourful acrylic yarn; photo © A. Allan Degen

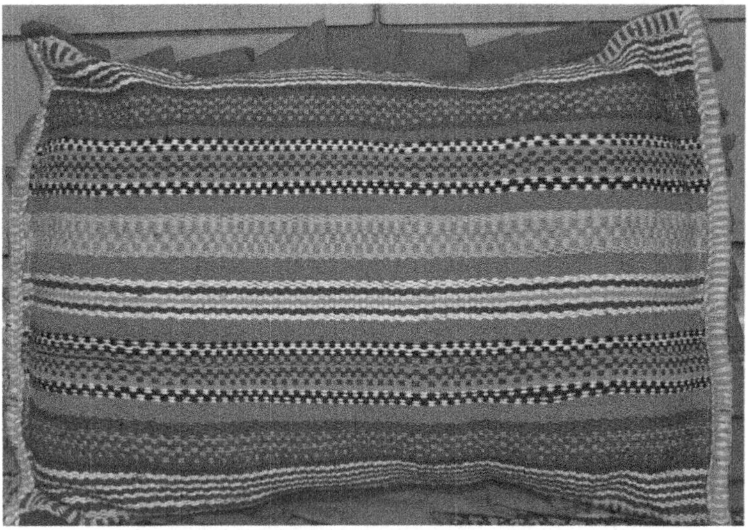

Fig. 25 Woven pillow cover made with colourful acrylic yarn; photo © A. Allan Degen

Al'Sanah 2013). The beginning was difficult as many of the husbands were opposed to an enterprise operated by women and of women being exposed to the public. In fact, the building housing the cooperative was burnt down shortly after it was established (Mustefa 2012), rumoured to be done by men. However, the building was restored, and the cooperative resumed its activities. In 1998, the two sisters established 'Sidreh', a non-profit organization, also located in Lakiya, that supported the cooperative. Sidreh's aims were to improve the status and empowerment of Bedouin women in four fields: "(1) access to knowledge: improving the educational levels of Bedouin women; (2) access to resources: promoting economic resilience of Bedouin women by increasing income and maximizing the use of available resources; (3) gender equality and participation: improving the social position of women and advancing women's rights; and (4) sustainable development: professionalization and organizational development" (Sidreh 2015). One of the sisters, Khadra, became the executive director of Sidreh (Kloosterman 2013).

The goal of the weaving cooperative was to preserve traditional ground loom weaving and to provide employment for women (Fig. 32). This is the only weaving cooperative for Bedouin women in the Negev. Only Awassi sheep wool is used with the traditional ground loom. More colours have been added so that there are 32 in total (Fig. 33); all dyes are purchased in Germany. Today, there are 30–60 women employed at the cooperative, but there were 130 women employed at peak production in the past. The number of women at any one time depends on the amount of work available, with more work at the time of shearing in April–May. Most of the women collect the dyed wool at the cooperative and weave at home. The Lakiya weaving project produces a variety of woven items, including carpets, pillow covers, pouches and bags (Fig. 34). These items are sold on the premises but are also

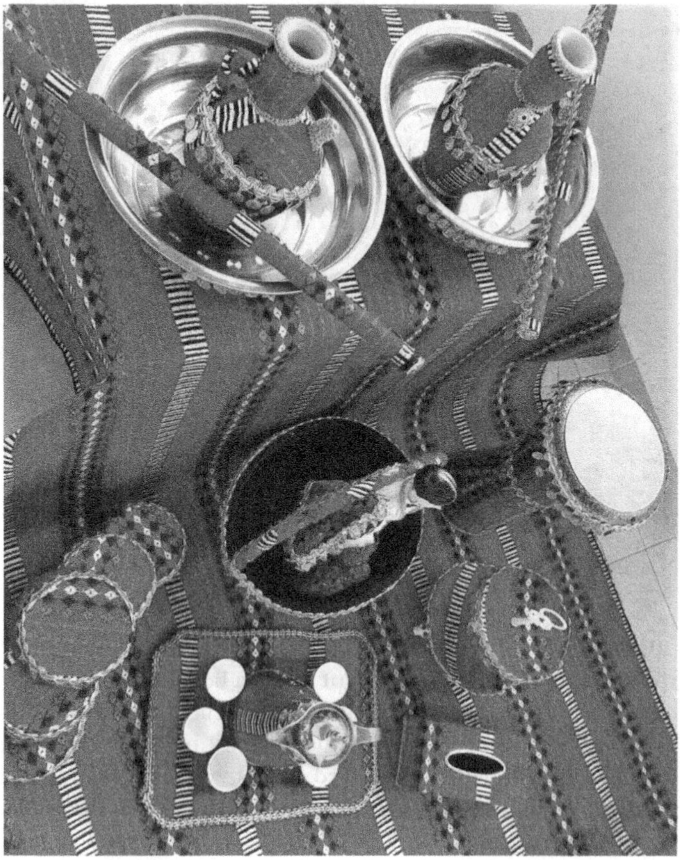

Fig. 26 A woven carpet and different items covered with colourful acrylic yarn that are used for *ḥenna* (حِنّاء) celebrations; photo © Shaher El-Meccawi

marketed in Europe, the USA and Arab states. Products can be bought online, and most sales today are commissioned from Europe. In addition, Hanan and Khadra go on regular speaking tours abroad to discuss Bedouin women and the cooperative. Visitors to the cooperative are provided with tours and explanations and demonstrations of all phases of production.

The cessation of traditional Bedouin weaving is common throughout the Middle East Region. Hilden (2004), in describing ground loom weaving among Bedouin women, stated, "Centuries of tradition in the weaving of the Bedouin, using sheep wool and goat hair, has changed dramatically in the last fifty years. Traditional nomadic lifestyles existed until recently in Saudi Arabia, Oman, Qatar, Iraq, Syria, Jordan, Palestine/Israel and Egypt and North Africa. The decline of nomadism is common to all. As a result of these changes in the society, weaving techniques and products have fallen to disuse or have been transformed with new materials and put

Fig. 27 Baskets that are decorated with colourful acrylic yarn and tassels and are filled with sweets to be offered to guests at a wedding celebration; photo © A. Allan Degen

Fig. 28 Women carrying decorated baskets filled with sweets at a Bedouin wedding celebration; photo © A. Allan Degen

Fig. 29 Bedouin woman holding a rod covered with colourful acrylic yarn and tassels used for dancing at a wedding; photo © A. Allan Degen

Fig. 30 Typical tent for Bedouin weddings today made of plastic sheets supported by aluminium poles and with tassels decorating the entrance. These tents are usually rented; photo © A. Allan Degen

Fig. 31 Road sign pointing to the direction of the Negev Bedouin Weaving in Lakiya; photo © A. Allan Degen

to new uses. Synthetic yarns now predominate, because they are pre-spun and clean. They are also easier to use and do not require dyeing, which is messy. With the decline in the use of wool, the art of spinning is also disappearing." Hilden (2010), in her book Bedouin 'Weaving of Saudi Arabia and Its Neighbors', commented that "[T]he number of nomads in the Arab world has decreased dramatically in the 20th century. Some continue to weave, but the lifestyle that gave birth and purpose to the weaving is fast disappearing, the victim of industrialization, government control and international conflicts." Shelagh Weir (quoted in Jefferies 2013) arrived at similar conclusions, "ancient, beautiful and once essential traditional craft of Bedouin women is probably in terminal decline. For thousands of years the nomads and semi-nomads of Arabia and other desert regions of the Middle East and North Africa

Fig. 32 Sign over the entrance to Negev Bedouin Weaving in Lakiya; photo © A. Allan Degen

have made articles vital for their everyday lives from the hair and wool of their goats, sheep and camels. Now the almost entirely female crafts of spinning and weaving have greatly decreased as nomads settle, or are forcibly settled, animal herding reduces, and mass-manufactured objects and synthetic materials replace traditional articles made from natural products." Scenarios of urbanization, and the establishment of women's cooperatives to preserve weaving, as has occurred with the Negev Bedouin women, were also described in Kuwait (Canavan and Alnajadah 2013; Robertson 2016), Oman (Heath 2013) and Jordan (Salaghor 2007; Saleh 2011; Neiroukh and Jones 2013). The sentiments expressed by Willey-Al'Sanah (2013) fit well for all the Bedouin women in the Middle East when she commented on the importance of the cooperative for the Negev Bedouin: "[t]raditional rug weaving skills were revived and taught and, in this way, preserved for the next generation. Weaving will never again be the central element of Bedouin society that it once was, however, it will be alive and respected in the Bedouin community and provoke

Fig. 33 Samples of the 32 different colours of dyed sheep wool at the Negev Bedouin Weaving cooperative in Lakiya; photo © A. Allan Degen

positive and respectful appreciation." However, the cooperative proved to be a win-win situation for the Negev Bedouin women. Traditional Bedouin weaving is being preserved as women learn how to spin, dye skeins of yarn and weave, and how to finish rugs with decorative stitching and tassels. For the women employed at the cooperative, besides weaving and earning money, they can also learn to read and write Arabic and Hebrew and some basic business skills and can earn a high school diploma. Some women at the cooperative started small businesses or continued to study for higher degrees. The women expressed that they felt more confident in their abilities and more comfortable in leaving the confines of the household without a male companion. Furthermore, their income allowed more daughters to study at universities and women even started driving cars.

Fig. 34 Woven sheep wool carpets for sale at the Negev Bedouin Weaving cooperative in Lakiya; photo © A. Allan Degen

Acknowledgements We are grateful to the Bedouin women, in particular, from the *Jerawin* (ألجراوين) and Tarabin el-Sana (ترابين الصانع) tribes, who provided us with information on weaving and offered us warm hospitality during our data collection. We also thank Maryam Aboud (Negev Bedouin Weaving Cooperative in Lakiya) for information on the weaving cooperative and Khadra el-Meccawi (Tel Sheva) for information on traditional weaving.

References

Abu-Bader S, Gottlieb D (2008) Education, employment and poverty among Bedouin Arabs in southern Israel. Hagar Stud Cult Polity Identities 8(2):121–136

Abu-Rabia A (1994) The Negev Bedouin and livestock rearing: social, economic and political aspects. Berg Publishers Limited, Oxford

Abu-Rabia A (1999) Some notes on livestock production among Negev Bedouin tribes. Nomadic Peoples 3(1):22–30

Abu-Rabia A (2001) Bedouin century: education and development among the Negev tribes in the twentieth century. Berghahn Books, New York

Abu-Saad I (1996) Provision of educational services and access to higher education among the Negev Bedouin Arabs in Israel. J Educ Policy 11(5):527–541

Abu-Saad K, Horowitz T, Abu-Saad I (2007) Weaving tradition and modernity: Bedouin women in higher education. Negev Center for Regional Development, Ben Gurion University of the Negev, Beer Sheva, Israel

Akirav O, Dana L-P, Degen AA, Galperin B, Medzini M (2021) The context for business in Israel, Chapter 20. In: Dana L-P, Salamzadeh A, Ramadini V, Palalić R (eds) Understanding contexts of business in Western Asia: land of bazaars and high-tech booms. World Scientific, Singapore

Alafenish S (1987) Processes of change and continuity in kinship system and family ideology in Bedouin society. Sociol Rural 27(4):323–343

Amiran DHK, Ben-Arieh Y (1963) Sedentarization of Beduin in Israel. Isr Explor J 13(3):161–181

Bernstein-Tarrow N (1980) The education of Arab children under Israeli administration. Can Int Educ 9(1):81–94
Canavan K, Alnajadah A (2013) Material symbols of traditional Bedouin Al-Sadu weavings of Kuwait. Textile 11(2):152–165
Degen AA (2003) Roles of urbanized Negev Bedouin women within their households. Nomadic Peoples 7(2):108–116
Degen AA, Benjamin RW, Hoorweg JC (2000) Bedouin households and sheep production in the Negev Desert, Israel. Nomadic Peoples 4(1):125–147
El-Meccawi S, Degen AA (2016) Higher education among Bedouin of the Negev: Tel Sheva as a case study. Nomadic Peoples 20(1):88–107
Gardner AE, Marx E (2000) Employment and unemployment among Bedouin. Nomadic Peoples 4 (2):21–27
Gilbert H (2013) Trapped by Tatriiz: Bedouin handicrafts and marginalization in South Sinai. Textile 11(2):128–139
Goering K (1979) Israel and the Bedouin of the Negev. J Palest Stud 9(1):3–2
Heath C (2013) Tradition and innovation: social aspects of learning spinning and weaving skills in Oman. Textile 11(2):176–187
Hilden JM (2004) Changes in nomadic Arab weaving due to outside and internal influences. Textile Society of America Symposium Proceedings 486. https://digitalcommons.unl.edu/tsaconf/486
Hilden JT (2010) Bedouin weaving of Saudi Arabia and its neighbors. Arabian Publishing, London
Jakubowska L (2000) Finding ways to make a living: employment among the Negev Bedouin. Nomadic Peoples 4(2):94–105
Jefferies J (2013) Women and middle eastern textiles: globalization and the impact on knowledge and skills—introduction. Textile 11(2):122–127
Katsap A, Silverman RL (2016) Well, waterhole, and tent: the inseparable constructions of Negev Bedouins Desert existence. Water in Negev Desert, waterholes, water wells, tent. In: Katsap A, Silverman RL (eds) Ethnomathematics of Negev Bedouins' existence in forms, symbols, and geometric patterns. Sense Publishers, Rotterdam, Netherlands
Kloosterman K (2013) Weaving Bedouin tradition into their future. https://www.israel21c.org/weaving-bedouin-tradition-into-their-future/
Kressel GM, Ben-David J (1995) The Bedouin market – Corner stone for the founding of Be'er Sheva: Bedouin traditions about the development of the Negev capital in the Ottoman period. Nomadic Peoples 36(37):119–144
Marx E (1967) Bedouin of the Negev. Frederick A. Praeger, New York
Meir A (1997) As nomadism ends: the Israeli Bedouin of the Negev. Westview Press, Boulder, CO
Meir IA, Stavi I (2011) Evolution of spontaneous shelter and settlements of the Negev Bedouin. Nomadic Peoples 15(2):33–52
Mustefa Z (2012) Bedouin women face-to-face with patriarchal culture. https://yourmiddleeast.com/2012/10/02/bedouin-women-face-to-face-with-patriarchal-culture/
Na'amneh M, Mohammed S, Aysegul T (2008) The modern sociocultural significance of the Jordanian Bedouin tent. Nomadic Peoples 12(1):149–163
Neiroukh W, Jones S (2013) Experiences woven, life changed: the influence of the Bani Hamida weaving project, Jordan. Textile 11(2):202
Robertson L (2016) Sadu weaving: the pace of a camel in a fast-moving culture, Textile Society of America Symposium Proceedings, 1005. http://digitalcommons.unl.edu/tsaconf/1005
Salaghor LMN (2007) The re-invention of traditional weaving in Saudi Arabia. Unpublished thesis. Coventry University
Saleh MF (2011) Rebecca Salti: the Bani Hamida weaving project and women's empowerment. Affilia 26(1):83–89
Sauer CO (1966) The agency of man on the earth. In: Wagner PL, Mikesell MW (eds) Readings in cultural geography. The University of Chicago Press, Chicago
Shmueli A (1980) The Bedouin of the land of Israel: settlement and changes. Urban Ecol 4:253–286

Sidreh (2015) Leading social change through development and equality. https://www.sidreh.org/article.aspx?id=16

Statistical Yearbook of the Negev (2010) Negev development authority. Ben Gurion University of the Negev, Beer Sheva, Israel

Tarrow N (2008) Human rights and education: the case of the Negev Bedouins. Hagar Stud Cult Polity Identities 8(2):137–158

Willey-Al'Sanah R (2013) New skills, changing status: the Bedouin women's voice reflected in the Lakiya weaving project, Negev. Textile 11(2):166–175

A. Allan Degen is an emeritus professor at Ben-Gurion University of the Negev, Beer Sheva, Israel. After receiving his PhD at Tel Aviv University, he joined Ben-Gurion University (1980), where he was Head of the Desert Animal Adaptations and Husbandry Unit (1985–2015) and Chairman of the Wyler Department of Dryland Agriculture (2001–2004 and 2013–2015). He was the incumbent of the Bennie Slome Chair for Desert Livestock Production (2004–2015) and served as the Co-Editor-in-Chief of the *Israel Journal of Zoology* (1999–2007). Allan has studied the livelihood of ethnic groups in different countries and, in Israel, is doing research on Negev Bedouin. He has authored or co-authored 24 books or chapters and over 250 publications in peer-reviewed journals.

Shaher El-Meccawi received his PhD in the Department of Life Sciences, Ben-Gurion University of the Negev, Beer Sheva, Israel, in 2007. At present, he is a lecturer at Achva Academic College and Kaye Academic College. He was the Scientific Director of the Negev Regional Center for Research and Development of Bedouin (2007–2010) and was the Head of the Education Program at Achva Academic College (2011–2013). Shaher does research on Bedouin living under urban and rural conditions in Israel and has presented his research in a number of international conferences, has published chapters in several books and has over 15 publications in peer-reviewed journals.

Artisans in Ethiopia

Hafiz Wasim Akram

Abstract This chapter deals with the status and chief occupations of artisans in Ethiopia, including the challenges faced by them. Following an introduction to the chapter, a succinct overview of the country, conditions of the artisans of Ethiopia, and some of their chief crafts in various fields such as pottery production, handloom textiles, basketry, and ground stone are presented in this chapter. In the end, problems and challenges facing Ethiopian artisans have been brought to light along with necessary recommendations to solve their issues for their betterment and the welfare of the country at large.

1 Introduction

The demands of the consumers are met by a good number of stakeholders, and artisans are one of them. The origin of the term "artisan" goes as far back as the sixteenth century from the Italian word "*artigiano*" or Latin word "*artitus*," which means art in English. There are several definitions of artisans. According to Cambridge Dictionary, an artisan is one who does skilled work with their hands. Tweneboah-Koduah and Adusei (2016) call artisans persons with special skills to manually produce products from simple materials. They have the art of creating a unique functional or decorative piece of an item by employing traditional techniques. International Labour Organisation (2003) defines artisans in the following words:

> persons who make products manually. They usually work individually, but can often be helped by family members, friends or apprentices, even limited numbers of workers, with whom they are constantly in close personal contact. This contact generates an intellectual sense of community and attachment to the craft. However, in order to include all business initiatives which contribute to the development of the sector, the use of the term "artisan" should cover those craft entrepreneurs who: (a) although not actively participating themselves in production, specialise in research, market negotiations or product design and

H. W. Akram (✉)
Department of Marketing & Entrepreneurship, CCBA, Dhofar University, Salalah, Oman
e-mail: hakram@du.edu.om

L.-P. Dana et al. (eds.), *Artisan and Handicraft Entrepreneurs*, Contributions to Management Science, https://doi.org/10.1007/978-3-030-82303-0_2

> conception; (b) also make use of machine tools or even machinery, yet not affecting the artisanal nature of the work and the production process; (c) beyond the usual cottage or artisan unit, have associated in cooperatives or any other form of organisation (even informal); and (d) manage or form part of micro-, small- or medium-sized enterprises concerned with artisanal production.

Artisans are tiny producers of goods in monetary terms and live and work in cottages and hutments. With many of them being necessity entrepreneurs, artisanship is a means of survival for a large chunk of the population of a country, more particularly an underdeveloped one. As an art, it is a prop of their living and sustenance. Products produced by them include textile, wooden items, leather goods, pottery, metal, and basketry. The following definition of artisanal products was adopted by the UNESCO/ITC International Symposium on "Crafts and the international market: Trade and customs codification" (Manila, Philippines, October 1997):

> Artisanal products are those produced by artisans, either completely by hand, or with the help of hand-tools or even mechanical means, as long as the direct manual contribution of the artisan remains the most substantial component of the finished product. These are produced without restriction in terms of quantity and using raw materials from sustainable resources. The special nature of artisanal products derives from their distinctive features, which can be: utilitarian, aesthetic, artistic, creative, culturally attached, decorative, functional, traditional, religiously and socially symbolic and significant.

It is very vivid from the above quotation that the scope of artisanal products is very vast and can include complementary categories as well. As per International Labour Organisation (2003), the complementary categories may include various additional materials (mineral, vegetable, animal, stone, glass, etc.) used in craft production belonging to a particular region or country.

The importance of artisans in nation-building has been felt since time immemorial. Their importance grows further in the case of developing and under-developed countries, wherein the livelihood of the common populace is primarily based on agriculture and craftsmanship. They work for their sustenance and contribute to a country's GDP and its export, apart from bringing repute to the nation with their skills. Without a doubt, the quest for fast-paced industrialisation has done a disservice to the artisans the world over. Their existence is at stake, their condition is precarious, and they are being marginalised due to one reason or the other (Scrase 2003). The dwindling employment opportunities in the corporate sector, especially during the current inexorable pandemic Covid-19, make all stakeholders' interest gain currency. Focus is tilting towards rejuvenating this industry again. Though for the last couple of years, the artisan industry has started getting literature positioning from researchers, the research still has been immature, especially related to artisans in a poor country like Ethiopia. It would not be unwarranted to say that this industry owing to its greater significance in nation-building calls for more and deeper attention of the researchers and policymakers so that it can be saved from further deterioration.

2 Ethiopia

Ethiopia, also called the Federal Democratic Republic of Ethiopia, is one of the countries that lie in the Horn of Africa (Meier et al. 2007) (see Fig. 1). The other countries, including Djibouti, Eritrea, Somalia and Somaliland, South Sudan, and

Fig. 1 Map of Horn of Africa. Source: https://www.un.org/Depts/Cartographic/map/profile/horne.pdf

Sudan, are the neighbouring countries. With 112 million people, it is the 12th most populous country in the world (Undata 2019). The capital is Addis Ababa, the largest city in the country (Britannica 2019), having numerous international non-governmental organisations and the headquarter of the African Union. Among a mosaic of around 100 languages spoken here, Afar, Amharic, Oromo, Somali, and Tigrinya are the official languages of Ethiopia (Subhan 2020). Like multiple ethnic groups in other countries of Africa, which affect the political and social environment (Dana et al. 2018), it is a multi-ethnic nation (Adamu 2013), and some of the chief ethnic groups include Oromo, Amhara, Tigrayans, Sidama, Welayta, Gurage, Somali, Hadiya, and Afa. They have a distinctive effect on the political and social environment of Ethiopia (Vaughan 2003). Ethiopia has never been under a colonial legacy (Joireman 1997; Zelekha and Dana 2019). The country has a fascinating and rich cultural and linguistic diversity (UNESCO 2017). It is endowed with a cheap labour force, a pool of artisans, numerous heritage sites, one of the oldest cultures, religious diversity, and pluralism. The peaceful co-existence of many religions such as Christianity, Islam, and Judaism further reinforces the multicultural label attached to this country. The presence of nine world heritage sites, including Aksum, Fasil Ghebbi, Harar Jugol, Konso, Lower Valley of the Awash, Lower Valley of the Omo, Lalibela, Simien National Park, and Tiya (UNESCO 2021), recognised by the United Nations Educational, Scientific and Cultural Organization (UNESCO) gives a lifeline to the economy and is a prop for tourism and the people associated with it including artisans and entrepreneurs. Ethiopia's fascinating biodiversity adds to the country's importance from the point of view of tourism and tourism-related business. With a pursuit of becoming a "Fast Expanding Market" and obvious vistas of economic progression, it has successfully been one of the fastest non-oil-dependent growing economies in the world for the last many years (Shiferaw 2017). However, the current natural catastrophe in the form of Covid-19 seems to be proving a stumbling block. The concept of a Fast Expanding Market (FEM) has been used in the studies such as Tse et al. (2013) and Acheampong and Dana (2017). According to Acheampong and Dana (2017), FEMs have a growth rate of 15% for a minimum of 3 years.

However, it would be unwarranted to turn one's blind eyes to some bitter truths about Ethiopia. For instance, as far as poverty is concerned, it is one of the poorest countries in the world (World Bank 2015a), with a per capita income of less than 1000 US dollars (World Bank 2019a). Around 25% of the total population live below the poverty line, and as high as 36% of people live on just 1.9 US dollars per day (World Bank 2015b, c). Unemployment is skyrocketing, and maltreatment of the low-wage labourers and artisans is rife, with an abysmally low human development index of 0.0485 and a 173rd ranking out of 189 countries (HDR 2020). The country suffers from inadequate infrastructure and institutional capacity for the fast-paced development all around. Due to being a landlocked and resource-scarce country, Ethiopia could not be internationalised to the same extent as other resource-rich landlocked countries (Dana and Ratten 2017). Furthermore, Ethiopia has been facing the worst ethno-political tensions in decades (Yusuf 2019). The series of civil unrests in the Oromia region after the assassination of the renowned musician Hachalu Hundessa in the previous year is just one instance (Ethiopia Insight 2021). The killing resulted in civil disorder in the capital and other places. The recent clash between the national army and the Tigray forces, which ran for many days, has also been unprecedented in the decades (Gebremedhin 2020; O'Grady 2020). To maintain peace and discipline, after the attack on a military base in Tigray by an unidentified mob that was calling for political reforms, the government launched a military attack on the rebellion, which is reported to have resulted in the loss of lives, property, exodus of people, and loss of jobs, among others (Jovanovic 2020). Tourism, FDI, and export are also affected badly if a country faces political disturbances and social unrest (Asmare 2016; Haile and Assefa 2006; Lochner and Dieckhoner 2012). Such developments derail the country's economic progression and leave the innumerable workforce, artisans, and entrepreneurs jobless and in acute distress and agony. The perception of the outside world towards Ethiopia is also deteriorating (Negatu and Hudson 2020), which will indubitably affect the artisans and entrepreneurs of the country. The long inexorable pandemic is adding a nail to the coffin. The fastest-growing country of Africa, like many developing countries, has been experiencing the unprecedented negative impact of Covid-19 (Wondimu and Girma 2020). The impact is socio-economic, with an increase in poverty, unemployment, slow growth, and exorbitant rise in prices of goods. The artisans were already falling prey to these negative shocks; the pandemic has broken their backbones. The efforts by the government backed by financial aids from countries such as European Union and international financial institutions such as World Bank are expected to decrease Ethiopia's agony and bring solace to it, but much has to be done to bring the economy on the path of much-coveted economic progression, which is looking bleak in no time.

3 Artisans in Ethiopia

Artisans, a solution to many economic problems, play a chief role in the socio-economic life of Ethiopia (Abbute 2001; Wayessa 2020). It is rightly perceived that they (artisans), to a large extent, provide a way for financial independence to many in one of the poorest countries of the world. They are involved in pottery making, woodcarving, tannery, basketry, weaving, and beekeeping, among others, which (artefact) they mostly sell in the local markets. Although beekeeping is seen as an agricultural activity, it is nowadays also seen here as a form of artisan entrepreneurship, which plays a significant role in a developing economy (Ramadani et al. 2019). The importance of artisans in Ethiopia increases further owing to the undeniable fact that agriculture in Ethiopia is already burdened as it alone provides employment to more than 80% of people (Broussard and Tekleselassie 2012), and there should be another generator of employment besides agriculture. Moreover, agriculture is plagued by a plethora of problems (Matous et al. 2013), and the association of workers towards the manufacturing industry may bode well for the economy. Thus, the burden on agriculture generally is and must be reduced by artisanship and other forms of menial work that do not require craftsmanship. Where there is a conducive environment for agriculture, artisanship is taken up as a part-time job for earning extra bread for rainy days. For the rest of the places, artisanship is a chief source of income for many. Neither the industry is developed to provide requisite employment to people at par with the demand, nor there is needed education with them (Guarcello and Rosati 2007) compared to other developing countries such as India to get good jobs.

Thus, the last resort for a big chunk of the common people of Ethiopia is to practise artisanship, which has been handed down to them from their forefathers. The artisans, majority women, are predominantly involved in making iron-based, clay-based, leather-based, and wooden products. Apart from them, they are also engaged in clay-mining and weaving, among others. The literature is devoid of any specific date of the origin of artisanship in Ethiopia, and the researchers are divided in their opinions. However, the emergence of need-based partisanship seems to be the valid reason. They might have started making such products for themselves, which later became a symbol for their culture. Nowadays, many products such as kettle made from clay and basketry items are used as symbols of Ethiopian culture. Thus, crafts reflect cultural diversity, creativity, and the heritage of Ethiopia.

4 Key Occupations of Ethiopian Artisans

4.1 Pottery Production

Pottery production, a learned skill, is mainly done by Ethiopian women (Arthur 2014). This craft, not much valued and despised by the society, basically belongs to the low-rank section of the society, which faces extreme poverty (Asefa 2016). Pottery production has been handed down to the generations of low-class people, and children start learning how to produce different items of clay at the age when they attain teenage (Kaneko 2013). The pottery production process starts with the procurement of clay, followed by paste preparation, forming, and shaping. Clay procurement is a very tough task and done mostly by the children who are either adults or about to be adults. The children, usually teenage girls, bring the clay from the source, clean and throw out unwanted pebbles, grind it on the ground-stones, and bring water from the water source, which is a burdensome job due to the huge scarcity of water. Even sourcing of clay, including clay mining and bringing it to the place of production either on the back or on a donkey, is a herculean task and full of danger. Sometimes the clay miners had to lose their precious lives (Arthur 2006). The children also lay their hands in making a paste of the clay, which needs much kneading. As they are young and have needed muscular strength, making a paste of the clay is also done by the teenage children before handing the paste clay to their parents for further processing, which also requires arts. This way, children also attain learning of pottery production. Then, the potters decorate the piece, followed by drying and polishing. Keeping the piece in a fire to harden it is the final stage of

Fig. 2 Artisans selling pottery items in a local market. Photo © 2021 Akram, H. W

pottery production (Asefa 2016). The entire pottery production process starts from the clay kneading till the end finishes in one compound of the potters. The observation of the compound of the potters with firing pits, a large chunk of debris of ashes, fragments of toolkits, and pots is fascinating. It is quite unbelievable to imagine how smartly they do all the processes in one little compound, which does not even deserve to be called a cottage. This profession is not only a means of income for many, but the final product serves utilitarian purposes as well as symbolic values (Sirika 2008). The non-utilitarian function of pottery production may play a vital role in promoting the tourism industry.

There exists an appreciable amount of differences in the ceramic outputs, and these differences are due to differences in the quality of inputs, methods of production, or cultural variations. The main pottery production includes, among others, coffee makers, bowls, pitchers, and plates (see Figs. 2, 3, 4, and 5). The size of all of them, their production methods, and materials used vary from place to place due to one reason or the other.

It is without a doubt that the ceramic work of Ethiopia is bearing the brunt of technological advancement in Ethiopia itself, along with the import of substitute items from other countries such as China. The fast-paced mechanisation replacing indigenous arts is posing a grave threat to their existence, and they are feeling marginalised. The pottery items made by Ethiopian artisans are falling prey to lightweight, cheap, and less-fragile plastic or aluminium plates, bowls, jugs, and cups (Scrase 2003). Acculturation among the affluent class of Ethiopia influenced by western tastes and preferences adds to the woes of artisans involved in clay pottery production. It is high time the government or the ministry of culture did something to prevent this craft from vanishing and promoted it through various media for the welfare of artisans and the country. In addition to it, the ministry should showcase their arts at the national and international platforms in the forms of exhibition and buyer–seller meets. Due to a good number of factors, products produced by them have meagre access to the world market. They have the talents to produce artifacts

Fig. 3 (**a**) A seller is holding bunna maker (coffee maker) in a local market. It is used for making coffee, very famous in Ethiopia. (**b**) Pitcher: It is used for bringing and storing water. It is of different sizes and styles. (**c**) A man is showing one of the varieties of bunna maker (coffee maker) on my request. (**d**) A lady pottery artisan is curiously flaunting her crafted pitcher in a local market. Photos © 2021 Akram, H. W

based on the choice of the world market but need linkages and representations. The emergence of a few shops like "abyssinian craft" and "Savadi Maison" are good developments as they play as a link between artisans and customers.

4.2 Handloom Textiles

Handloom artisans of Ethiopia, especially women, are engaged in making beautiful garments such as shawls and other cultural attires (Haile 2016). According to Chernet and Ba (2019), the establishments of weavers account for around 74% of

Fig. 4 (**a**) Varieties of pitchers, different sizes and styles. (**b**) A girl is selling an injera maker. A type of utensil on which Ethiopians make cultural bread-like round-shaped substances. (**c**) and (**d**) are of varieties of injera makers. Photos © 2021 Akram, H. W

the total number of establishments of the textile industry in Ethiopia, and they provide employment to more than 42% of the total number of workers who are engaged in the textile industry as a whole. Ethiopia, naturally endowed with the finesse cotton (Gudeta and Egziabher 2019), gives these artisans a lifeline to grow and prosper. Ethiopian handloom is dependent on cotton (Zhang et al. 2011). These artisans are involved in tradition-based cotton growing, harvesting, and spinning. Their engagement in fabric making not only meets their household needs and demands for clothing, but it is also a source of income (Chernet and Ba 2019). The modus operandi of their whole process of garments making is very much fascinating and charming. Handweaving by these artisans has been a century old, and they produce both ordinary and unique fabrics for the customers of Ethiopia and abroad. Two well-known castes, Dorze and Konso, are famous for their beautiful crafts, and they chiefly live in a cluster in Amhara and Oromia regions (Temesgen et al. 2018). A good number of Dorze ethnic people also live and work in the capital, Addis Ababa, of Ethiopia.

According to Chernet and Ba (2019), the apparel outputs of these artisans are semi-finished as well as finished ones. The semi-finished garments are further sent to garment factories for the required processing. The finished garments include Netella

Fig. 5 (**a**) A multi-purpose bowl. (**b**) Cups in which Ethiopians take coffee. (**c**) and (**d**) are stoves that serve different purposes, such as cooking and making coffee. Photos © 2021 Akram, H. W

(scarf-like two-layered cloth worn by women), Kuta (scarf-like two-layered cloth worn by men), Gabi (scarf-like four-layered cloth worn by men and women, most of the time, the elderly wear it), and Kemis (see Fig. 6).

Ethiopian handloom artisans play a vital role in Ethiopia's religious, cultural, social, and economic well-being. They meet the religious needs by providing the people with religious clothing, enhancing tourism value with their cultural craftsmanship, growing the country's GDP, and above all, reducing the tension of the government of employment generation. Besides, according to Chernet and Ba (2019), the artisan weavers foster interlinking and mingling of not only regional cultures and languages but also those with the world. Thus, weavers bring about cultural diversities and connect Ethiopia with the outside world. There are many occasions such as weddings, national holidays, birthdays, festivals, church ceremonies, and last rites, where handmade clothes worn by people can be seen. They produce items of wear for particular occasions and communities that exhibit beauties of cultural diversity in Ethiopia. Their engagement in fabric making not only meets their household needs and demands for clothing, but it is also a source of income. Therefore, the socio-cultural value of weaving products is colossal in Ethiopia.

Fig. 6 Sellers selling handmade garments including Netella, Kuta, and Gabi in a local weekly market of Sawla, Gofa, SNNPR. Photos © 2021 Akram, H. W

Like pottery production, this industry is also facing a plethora of challenges (Tadesse 2015). Handloom artisans are prey to the fast-paced mechanisation of garment production, along with the threat from substitute garments from import and power loom. The dominance of western attire like jeans and t-shirt, changing tastes of consumers, and the availability of lightweight and less costly garments are forcing the customers to switch from the traditional ones, which are adding to the woes of weavers and other artisans related to this industry in Ethiopia. It is a matter of the fact that these artisans are cash strapped and at the mercy of loans from the government for the working capital (Zhang et al. 2011). Even loan sanction is subject to so much of paper works and bureaucracy, which deteriorates their condition (Gebeyehu 2002). The handloom artisans are also susceptible to political disturbance in a few areas such as Oromia, Amhara, Wolayeta, and Tigray. The latest national military intervention in Tigray (Paravicini and Endeshaw 2020) to dispel local forces and capture the region from the local leaders has forced many, including artisans, to resort to the exodus from the region to save their lives. Such developments time and again are stunting their growth and their contribution to the nation. They are also prey to the inflationary situation and the exorbitant price rise of the inputs of production, which holds more good during the Covid pandemic (UN Ethiopia 2020). The unabated inflation (Abate 2020; World Bank 2019b) makes it rather unmanageable for them to keep the cost below or at least at par with power loom garments. There is a need to propagate the values of hand-woven garments and the importance of handloom artisans in nation-building. This can be done in the way the Government of India is doing to revive the dying Khadi industry, an industry in which handloom artisans are involved in producing hand-spun and hand-woven cloth using raw materials such as cotton and wool. The latest government push for the Khadi industry (Goel and Jain 2015) in India has brought about a change in the mindsets of the people, and Indians have started using Khadi clothes again. Then, it may prove as a life saviour for the handloom artisans in Ethiopia.

4.3 Basketry

Among rich artisan traditions lies the basketry of Ethiopia. The basketry artisans of Ethiopia produce very eye-catching baskets, mats, bags, fish traps, sieves, and hats, among others, for both the domestics and commercial purposes (Lemma 1998). The artisans, mainly females, need raw materials such as vegetable fibres, wool, leather, plastic, wood, metal, grasses, palm leaves, and bamboo, among others, to produce basketry products (Sterner 2014). In addition to them, depending on the needs, natural dyes, chemically dyed grasses, and awls are also used in the process of manufacture (Asante 2005). The basket makers make products that serve an important function in everyday life and ceremonial activities (Asante 2005). In general, they are used for storing things, sleeping, covering, sitting, fencing, sieving, and so on. The complex pattern and traditional shapes bring reverence to the basketry artisans who accomplish it after a lot of arduous work in giving the products aesthetic qualities and symbolic beauties (Tarsitani 2009; Tedla 2012). Basketry artisanship is a rural-centric job that provides a source of livelihood to scores of Ethiopians. Since this requires less muscle power, mostly females are seen doing the jobs. This skill, like pottery one, is handed down to the female children by their mothers who practise this craft throughout their lives and is known to all women in rural areas (Yeneabat 2007).

Teenage girls learn the basics of basketry skills under the aegis of their mothers and elder sisters. Nevertheless, the basketry artisanship is not confined to any particular location and is spread in the whole of Ethiopia; Harai basket weaving is very famous because of the fine quality products produced with flawless methods (Tarsitani 2009). The basket makers either sell the products to the customers who assemble in the local market or to the shopkeepers who, in turn, sell to the customers (Tedla 2012) (see Fig. 7). At times, they have been found to be selling these items of basketry to the basket brokers. The dissociation of people from cultural legacy, availability of machine-made substitute items, price rise in the inputs of production,

Fig. 7 (**a**) Mix of basketry items on sale in a local market. (**b**) A beautiful tray that serves multi-purpose. (**c**) and (**d**) are used for decoration. Photos © 2021 Akram, H. W

and lack of demand are doing a disservice to artisans who are engaged in basketry production (Kebede 2018). It is a matter of great regret and concern that this profession, despite being so simple and of great cultural and economic significance for Ethiopia, has not been appreciated. It is still confined to local markets and is not commercialised on a big scale to give it an avenue to its export.

4.4 Ground Stone

Apart from pottery production, many low-profile artisans, especially men, are engaged in ground stone production. The craft of manufacturing stones for grinding is complex and burdensome and needs knowledge, design decision, skills, and support and social interactions from fellow artisans (Nixon-Darcus and Meresa 2020). Since stone-works are very heavy and need enormous strength and vigour, they call for the engagement of strong male members (Arthur 2014) (see Fig. 8). Female artisans are also seen supporting the male members, but they lay their hands only in the ancillary works related to ground stone production. The artisans produce a variety of stones for grinding, which are used in different ways for the preparation of foods. The stones for grinding produced by the artisans involved are used in flour-mill, processing of cereal grains, milling dry sorghum, crushing fresh sorghum,

Fig. 8 (a–c) Artisans engaged in ground-stone production. (d) A woman can be seen as using ground stones. Source: Adapted from Arthur, J. W. (2014)

crushing fresh corn, crushing buna (coffee), and crushing spices (Robitaille 2016). These stones also play multi-purpose tools, and the relationship between stones and functions is not always definite. It is rather unwarranted to distinguish grinding stones and point out their very function unambiguously. Among many, grinding-slabs, flat-handstones, grinding boulders, and stone mortars are very ubiquitous products in Ethiopia. These are abundantly found in domestic purposes and are representatives of women's daily lives of Ethiopia by performing an essential task of living and sustenance. Though they are seen as mundane objects, they serve as material items that accomplish numerous goals of the households.

5 Problems and Challenges Faced by Ethiopian Artisans: Discussion and Recommendations

The marginalisation of artisans the world over is being felt, and it would not be a fallacious statement that they are passing through a precarious condition full of ordeals (Scrase 2003). Ethiopian artisans are not an exception to this execrable situation (Cascadden et al. 2020; Lyons and Freeman 2009). The artisans, before the onslaught of Covid-19, were already falling prey to mass production and mechanisation of production systems, availability of cheap factory products and substitute imported products, cash-strapped economic conditions, lack of working capital finance, and soaring prices of the inputs of production, among others, and the long back-breaking pandemic has dug grave for them.

Though the economic and social significance of handiwork is immense (Terry 1999) and the purchasers of handiwork have the feeling of getting connected to traditions, artisans are increasingly confronting struggle, resistance, antagonism, financial persecution, odium, malaise, and commodification of their handiwork in the face of the new wave of global changes mentioned above (Cascadden et al. 2020; Lyons and Freeman 2009; Zhang et al. 2011; Wasihun and Paul 2010). Nonetheless, the National Media and Arts Task Force under the Prime Minister Office of Ethiopia has been established to help out the concerned people with a culture (Dana and Salamzadeh 2021; UNESCO 2020); how much it would give a sigh of relief for the aggrieved artisans only the time will tell. Even the government is silent about how it will compensate the artisans for the loss of those earlier produced items, and now machine production has grabbed that space. The development of a healthy small business sector is a must for the economic welfare and well-being of a country that is passing through a population boom, high unemployment, and rapid urbanisation (Dana 1993). After the Covid pandemic, the government is mandated afresh to strengthen cultural industries, improve the market for cultural products, and empower the artisans and create a conducive environment for them to sell their outputs. At present, both shocks by the execrable pandemic and the civil unrest in many parts of Ethiopia (Belay and Ndiaye 2020; Laillou et al. 2020) are ruining the tourism industry. The continual skirmishes among ethnic groups on account of regional differences have been undermining and weakening its cultural pluralism and diversity. History has seen numerous conflicts in areas such as Ormomia, Awassa, Sodo, and Tigray. All these developments send a negative message to the outside world, which debars tourism from prospering. It is very vivid that the livelihood of a large section of artisans is either directly or indirectly dependent on tourism (Militz et al. 2020; Scheyvens and Biddulph 2018; Teixeira and Ferreira 2019), and the government has to go the extra mile to ensure their livelihood.

In addition to it, ethnic enterprise rules the roost in Ethiopia. In an ethnic enterprise culture, members of some particular ethnic groups possess a higher rate of business formation and ownership than others do (Dana 1997). In the case of Ethiopia, the Gurage ethnic group dominates the businesses in Ethiopia (Mengistae 2001). According to Mengistae (2001), the Gurage owns more or less a third of the business of Ethiopia while it gives employment to only 5% of the workforce. Amhara is the second-largest ethnic group whose ownership in the business is around 40%, and the share of this group in the workforce is the same as that of Gurage. This is not a healthy sign for balanced development, and the workers, including artisans, are badly affected. Apart from it, what to talk of the appreciation which the artisans deserve, some of them such as pottery artisans of the Gamo region are considered ritually impure by a good number of people (Arthur 2014). Mains

(2007) even categorically writes that artisan professions in Ethiopia such as pottery, blacksmithing, carpentry, and weaving are highly stigmatised. Confirming the findings of Mains (2007), the artisans have been seen moving from pillar to post for selling their unique pieces in the local market. Such a negative response to their handwork and craft discourages not only them but also the new generations from pursuing their family profession. Not only this, artisans who are engaged in heavy work such as pottery are paid far below their input of labour. Unless and until society starts paying artisans of such products the price at least commensurate with their labour, we cannot imagine the welfare of those artisans, and they are bound to die sooner or later. Moreover, the unaccommodating and discouraging attitude of the common people towards the contribution of the artisans stunts their growth and need to be changed (Arthur 2014; Mains 2007; Sirika 2008).

It has also been observed that due to the unabated demand for modernisation and urbanisation, the indigenous craft and knowledge receive unfair treatment from the government (Sirika 2008). This has been meted out not only to Ethiopian artisans but those of other developing countries such as India as well. Due to this reason, as per Scrase (2003), many Indian artisans who were famous for their indigenous craft have joined casual wage laborers. The dying sari industry (an ethnic wear) of Banaras, India, is a live example of it, whose artisans (many) had to leave their craftsmanship. The Ethiopian indigenous utensil production is also experiencing the same fate as that of the Banarasi sari of India. The cultural ministry of Ethiopia should pay heed to it and ought to ensure the preservation of cultural identity by keeping indigenous art alive along with the modernisation and urbanisation. The literature indicates that products produced by Ethiopian craftsmen have ample opportunities to be sold in the global market (Sahle 2016), but the problem with it is the glaring fact that they (the artisans) have not moved with the time. They failed to understand the tastes and preferences of the global community, and the requisite modification needed in their products for seeking global attention could not be possible. It may be due to the reason that they lack the necessary funds and infrastructure for any innovation and modernisation of their modus operandi of production.

There is a need to link entrepreneurship with innovation along with sustaining the richness of culture, and this was made possible by the Hellenic Organization of Small and Medium Sized Enterprises and Handicraft (EOMMEX) in Greece (Dana 1999). Innovation and modernisation in the production of indigenous artifacts never imply any kind of deviation from the cultural identity, as is clear from the example of EOMMEX given by Dana (1999). Furthermore, lack of requisite research and development has resulted in a lack of international recognition, which in turn, has an adverse impact on the artisans of Ethiopia to a greater degree. A business-friendly environment needs to be created. Dana (2007) has rightly said that once policymakers understand the significance of the contribution of entrepreneurship and adopt entrepreneur-friendly policies, then developing countries may thrive and prosper. There is a call for the concerned ministry in Ethiopia to integrate the artisans into the world market for the benefit of them as well as the country. For deeper linkages between them and the world demands, the government and the concerned ministry must have more and more buyer–seller meets, international cultural events, exhibitions, trainings, workshops, and incentives for selling to the global community. There should be a minimum support price mechanism for their products if they meet the set parameters of quality and specifications. All of the above-mentioned points will facilitate the empowerment of artisans, make them feel rich, link them with the world, and preserve a strong cultural heritage of Ethiopia.

References

Abate TW (2020) Macro-economic determinants of recent inflation in Ethiopia. J World Econ Res 9 (2):136–142

Abbute WS (2001) The socio-economic role and status of handicraftsmen among the Kambaata of southern Ethiopia. Aethiopica 4:96–120

Acheampong G, Dana LP (2017) Liability of foreignness in fast-expanding markets: evidence from Ghana. Thunderbird Int Bus Rev 59(1):51–61

Adamu AY (2013) Diversity in Ethiopia: a historical overview of political challenges. Int J Community Divers 12(1):17–27

Arthur JW (2006) Living with pottery: Ethnoarchaeologyamong the Gamo of Southwest Ethiopia. Foundations of Archaeological Inquiry, University of Utah Press, Salt Lake City

Arthur JW (2014) Culinary crafts and foods in southwestern Ethiopia: an ethnoarchaeologicalstudy of Gamogroundstones and pottery. Afr Archaeol Rev 31(2):131–168

Asante B (2005) Women's craft guilds and the traditional basketry of Harar, Ethiopia. Afr Study Monogr 29:61–72

Asefa T (2016) An ethnoarchaeological study of pottery production in Tigray: the case of Saharti-Samre and Hintalo-Wajirat districts (unpublished master's thesis). Addis Ababa University, Addis Ababa

Asmare BA (2016) Pitfalls of tourism development in Ethiopia: the case of Bahir Dar town and its surroundings. Kor Soc Sci J 43(1):15–28

Belay T, Ndiaye M (2020) Ethiopia: conflict insights. https://www.africaportal.org/publications/ethiopia-conflict-insights/

Broussard N, Tekleselassie TG (2012) Youth unemployment: Ethiopia country study. International Growth Centre. Working Paper, 12(0592):1–37

Cascadden Z, Lyons D, Paris E (2020) On the surface: an ethnoarchaeological study of marginalised pottery production and the social context of pottery surface treatments in Tigray regional state, northern highland Ethiopia. Azania Archaeol Res Afr 55(1):69–96

Chernet YG, Ba O (2019) Weaving and its socio-cultural values in Ethiopia: a review. Asian J Agric Extension Econ Sociol 37(4):1–11

Dana LP (1993) The trade facilitation model: towards the development of an indigenous small business sector in the Republic of Kenya. Entrep Innov Change 2(4):335–343

Dana LP (1997) The origins of self-employment in ethno-cultural communities: distinguishing between orthodox entrepreneurship and reactionary enterprise. Can J Admin Sci 14(1):52–68

Dana LP (1999) Preserving culture through small business: government support for artisans and craftsmen in Greece. J Small Bus Manag 37(1):90–92

Dana LP (2007) Promoting SMEs in Africa: some insights from an experiment in Ghana and Togo. J Afr Bus 8(2):151–174

Dana LP, Ratten V (2017) International entrepreneurship in resource-rich landlocked African countries. J Int Entrep 15(4):416–435

Dana LP, Salamzadeh A (2021) Why do artisans and arts entrepreneurs use social media platforms?: evidence from an emerging economy. Nordic J Media Manag 2(1)

Dana LP, Ratten V, Honyenuga BQ (2018) Introduction to African entrepreneurship. In: African entrepreneurship. Palgrave Macmillan, Cham, pp 1–7

Ethiopia Insight (2021). Ethiopia: understanding Oromia's mayhem after Hachalu's murder. The Africa report. https://www.theafricareport.com/57957/ethiopia-understanding-oromias-mayhem-after-hachalus-murder/

Gebeyehu A (2002) Loan repayment and its determinants in small-scale enterprises financing in Ethiopia: case of private borrowers around Zeway area (unpublished MSc Thesis), Addis Ababa University, Addis Ababa

Gebremedhin D (2020) Tigray crisis: Why there are fears of civil war in Ethiopia. https://www.bbc.com/news/world-africa-54826875

Goel N, Jain K (2015) Revival of Khadi: an analysis of the state of Khadi in India with supply and demand side problems. Innov J Bus Manag 4(05):100–103

Guarcello L, Rosati F (2007) Child labor and youth employment: Ethiopia country study. The World Bank, New York

Gudeta B, Egziabher AG (2019) Cotton production potential areas, production trends, research status, gaps and future directions of cotton improvement in Ethiopia. Greener J Agric Sci 9 (2):163–170

Haile S (2016) Assessing the determining factors of comptetivness in Ethiopian traditional cloth manufacturing sector (Doctoral thesis). St. Mary's University, Addis Ababa

Haile GA, Assefa H (2006) Determinants of foreign direct investment in Ethiopia: a time-series analysis. In 4th International Conference on the Ethiopian Economy

HDR (2020). Latest Human Development Index ranking. United Nations Development Programme. http://hdr.undp.org/en/content/latest-human-development-index-ranking

International Labour Organization (2003) Promoting the culture sector through job creation and small enterprise development in SADC countries: Crafts and Visual Arts. SEED Working Paper No. 51. https://www.ilo.org/wcmsp5/groups/public/%2D%2D-ed_emp/%2D%2D-emp_ent/%2D%2D-ifp_seed/documents/publication/wcms_117680.pdf

Joireman SF (1997) Institutional change in the horn of Africa: the allocation of property rights and implications for development. Universal Publishers

Jovanovic D (2020) Ethiopia declares victory in fight over Tigray region, but guerrilla warfare likely to continue. https://abcnews.go.com/International/ethiopia-declares-victory-fight-tigray-region-guerrilla-warfare/story?id=74441202

Kaneko M (2013) Transmigration among Aari woman potters in southwestern Ethiopia and the accumulation of experience in pottery-making techniques. Afr Study Monogr 46:81–96

Kebede AA (2018) Opportunities and challenges to highland bamboo-based traditional handicraft production, marketing and utilization in Awi zone, northwestern Ethiopia. Int J Hist Cult Stud 4 (4):57–67

Laillou A, Baye K, Meseret Z, Darsene H, Rashid A, Chitekwe S (2020) Wasted children and wasted time: a challenge to meeting the nutrition sustainable development goals with a high economic impact to Ethiopia. Nutrients 12(12):3698

Lemma A (1998) Raymond A. Silverman, ed. Ethiopia: traditions of creativity. Seattle: University of Washington Press, 1999. Ufahamu J Afr Stud 26(2–3):126–129

Lochner S, Dieckhoner C (2012) Civil unrest in North Africa—risks for natural gas supply? Energy Policy 45:167–175

Lyons D, Freeman A (2009) 'I'm not evil': materialising identities of marginalised potters in Tigray region, Ethiopia. Azania Archaeol Res Afr 44(1):75–93

Mains D (2007) Neoliberal times: progress, boredom, and shame among young men in urban Ethiopia. Am Ethnol 34(4):659–673

Matous P, Todo Y, Mojo D (2013) Roles of extension and ethno-religious networks in acceptance of resource-conserving agriculture among Ethiopian farmers. Int J Agric Sustain 11(4):301–316

Meier P, Bond D, Bond J (2007) Environmental influences on pastoral conflict in the horn of Africa. Polit Geogr 26(6):716–735

Mengistae, T. (2001). Indigenous ethnicity and entrepreneurial success in Africa: some evidence from Ethiopia (Vol 2534). World Bank. Development Research Group, Macroeconomics and Growth

Militz TA, Kershler D, Southgate PC (2020) Informing artisanal pearl and pearl-shell handicraft production for the cruise tourism market through analysis of intended purchase behaviour. Tour Mar Environ

Negatu G, Hudson G (2020) Experts react: understanding the conflict in Tigray. https://www.atlanticcouncil.org/blogs/africasource/experts-react-understanding-the-conflict-in-tigray/

Nixon-Darcus L, Meresa Y (2020) Men at work: grinding stone production by the experts and others in northern Ethiopia. J Lithic Stud 7(3):1–24

O'Grady S (2020) What is behind the conflict in Ethiopia? The Washington post. https://www.washingtonpost.com/world/2020/11/17/ethiopia-tigray-conflict-what-is-happening/

Paravicini G, Endeshaw D (2020) Ethiopia sends army into Tigray region, heavy fighting reported. https://www.reuters.com/article/us-ethiopia-conflict/ethiopia-sends-army-into-tigray-region-heavy-fighting-reported-idUSKBN27K0ZS?il=0

Ramadani V, Hisrich RD, Dana LP, Palalic R, Panthi L (2019) Beekeeping as a family artisan entrepreneurship business. Int J Entrep Behav Res 25(4):717–730

Robitaille J (2016) The ground stone industry of the Mursi of Maki, Ethiopia: Ethnoarchaeological research on milling and crushing equipment (technique and function). J Lithic Stud 3 (3):429–456

Sahle E (2016) Ethiopian traditional artisans appealing to the global market. https://africabusiness.com/2016/02/10/ethiopian-traditional-artisans-appealing-to-the-global-market/

Scheyvens R, Biddulph R (2018) Inclusive tourism development. Tour Geogr 20(4):589–609

Scrase TJ (2003) Precarious production: globalisation and artisan labour in the third world. Third World Q 24(3):449–461

Shiferaw A (2017) Productive capacity and economic growth in Ethiopia. CDP background paper no. 34 ST/ESA/2017/CDP/34, Department of Economic & Social Affairs, United Nations

Sirika B (2008) Socio-economic status of handicraft women among Macca Oromo of west Wallaga, Southwest Ethiopia. Ethiopian J Educ Sci 4(1):1–15

Sterner J (2014) Basketry in Africa. In: Selin H (ed) Encyclopaedia of the history of science, technology, and medicine in non-Western cultures. Springer, Dordrecht

Subhan ARA (2020) One to five: Ethiopia gets four new federal working languages. Africa News. https://www.africanews.com/2020/03/04/one-to-five-ethiopia-gets-four-new-federal-working-languages//

Tadesse B (2015) Socio Ecnomic role of clustering and government constructed working premises on traditional handloom weavers (Doctoral dissertation). St. Mary's University, Addis Ababa

Tarsitani BA (2009) Revered vessels: custom and innovation in Harari basketry. Afr Arts 42 (1):64–75

Tedla TH (2012) Empowering women through home-based work and institutionalized threats in Ethiopia. http://citeseerx.ist.psu.edu/viewdoc/download?doi=10.1.1.851.9139&rep=rep1&type=pdf

Teixeira SJ, Ferreira JJ (2019) Entrepreneurial artisan products as regional tourism competitiveness. Int J Entrep Behav Res 25(4):652–673

Temesgen AG, Tursucular OF, Eren R, Ulcay Y (2018) The art of hand weaving textiles and crafting on socio-cultural values in Ethiopian. Int J Adv Multidiscip Res 5(12):59–67

Terry ME (1999) The economic and social significance of the handicraft industry in Botswana (Doctoral dissertation). SOAS University of London, London

The Editors of Encyclopaedia Britannica (2019). Addis Ababa. Encyclopedia Britannica. https://www.britannica.com/place/Addis-Ababa

Tse T, Esposito M, Soufani K (2013) Fast-expanding markets: where new growth can be found. Eur Bus Rev 2:11–14

Tweneboah-Koduah I, Adusei C (2016) Entrepreneurship determinants of artisans/craftsmen in Kumasi Metropolis, Ghana. Am J Ind Bus Manag 6(02):163

UN Ethiopia (2020) Socio-economic impact of Ethiopia Covid-19 in Ethiopia. http://www.undp.org›content›dam›undp›library›covid19

Undata (2019) World Population Prospects: the 2019 Revision. United Nations Population Division. https://data.un.org/Data.aspx?d=PopDiv&f=variableID%3a12%3btimeID%3a83%2c84%3bvarID%3a2&c=2,4,6,7&s=_crEngNameOrderBy:asc,_timeEngNameOrderBy:desc,_varEngNameOrderBy:asc&v=1

UNESCO (2017) Ethiopia 2017 report. https://en.unesco.org/creativity/governance/periodic-reports/2017/ethiopia

UNESCO (2020) ResiliArt - Ethiopia: strengthening the resilience of artists and cultural professionals beyond Covid-19. https://en.unesco.org/news/resiliart-ethiopia-strengthening-resilience-artists-and-cultural-professionals-beyond-covid-0

UNESCO (2021) Ethiopia, properties inscribed on the World Heritage List. https://whc.unesco.org/en/statesparties/et

Vaughan S (2003) Ethnicity and power in Ethiopia (PhD Thesis). The University of Edinburgh, UK

Wasihun R, Paul I (2010) Growth determinants of women operated micro and small enterprises in Addis Ababa. J Sustain Dev Afr 12(6):233–246

Wayessa B (2020) Whose development? The dilemma of rural artisan women in southwestern Ethiopia. Anthropol Today 36(4):20–23

Wondimu W, Girma B (2020) Challenges and silver linings of COVID-19 in Ethiopia– short review. J Multidiscip Healthc 13:917

World Bank (2015a) Ethiopia Poverty Assessment 2014. https://openknowledge.worldbank.org/handle/10986/21323 License: CC BY 3.0 IGO

World Bank (2015b) Poverty headcount ratio at national poverty lines (% of population) - Ethiopia. https://data.worldbank.org/indicator/SI.POV.NAHC?locations=ET

World Bank (2015c). Poverty headcount ratio at $1.90 a day (2011 PPP) (% of population) - Ethiopia. https://data.worldbank.org/indicator/SI.POV.DDAY?locations=ET&name_desc=false

World Bank (2019a) GDP per capita (current US$) - Ethiopia. https://data.worldbank.org/indicator/NY.GDP.PCAP.CD?locations=ET

World Bank (2019b) Inflation, consumer prices (annual %) - Ethiopia. https://data.worldbank.org/indicator/FP.CPI.TOTL.ZG?locations=ET

Yeneabat M (2007) Pottery production an asset for women livelihood (Master Thesis). Addis Ababa University, Addis Ababa

Yusuf S (2019) What is driving Ethiopia's ethnic conflicts? ISS East Afr Rep 2019(28):1–16

Zelekha Y, Dana LP (2019) Social capital versus cultural capital determinants of entrepreneurship: an empirical study of the African continent. J Entrep 28(2):250–269

Zhang X, Moorman L, Ayele G (2011) Infrastructure and cluster development: a case study of handloom weavers in rural Ethiopia. J Dev Stud 47(12):1869–1886

Hafiz Wasim Akram is a faculty at the Department of Marketing & Entrepreneurship, College of Commerce and Business Administration, Dhofar University, Salalah, Oman. He holds his Bachelor of Business Management (BBM) from Magadh University, Bodh Gaya, and Master in international business (MIB) and PhD in Commerce and Business Studies from Jamia Millia Islamia, New Delhi, India. He has been a recipient of Junior Research Fellowship (JRF) and Senior Research Fellowship of the University Grants Commission, Government of India. His particular areas of research interest are entrepreneurship, logistics, international business, and international marketing.

Craft Artisans in Namibia's Okavango Tribe

Wilfred Isak April

Abstract This chapter is a result of an exploratory experiment conducted with the Namibia Okavango women on the river banks of Northern Namibia at the Far East Angola/Namibia border. The academic literature link entrepreneurship to innovation and creativity. With this in mind, this chapter explores the role of women in Namibian small businesses in crafts and art in preserving culture while improving the livelihoods of the Okavango Tribe. Without a doubt, this experiment will inform another cultural layer that the world has never experienced before. The ground-breaking works of Joseph Schumpeter linked to culture as an essential component of innovation. Numerous scholars after his works had a very similar viewpoint. Using these insights, the Namibia government has come with various initiatives (such as policies) to promote entrepreneurship among small businesses, but the crafts and arts market has been neglected, or the sector is not deemed as critical. This chapter will interview 30 local women from the Okavango tribe in Namibia. In addition, secondary data will be explored through books and oral histories, and this chapter serves as one of the springboards for many more experiments to be conducted in this space in terms of women entrepreneurs in crafts and arts in Namibia from an African context.

1 Introduction

Artisan entrepreneurship has been regarded as one of the key initiatives in entrepreneurship that can significantly contribute to the economy and society. This has indeed generated sustained interest from scholars, practitioners and those in charge of various economies making policies (Al Dajani et al. 2015; Ramadani et al. 2019; Dana and Salamzadeh 2021). Moreover, according to Bruni and Perrota (2014), prior research has indicated that artisans find creative ways to discover and exploit opportunities in the market, which will at times involve turning hobbies into a passion, which eventually generated sustainable businesses.

W. I. April (✉)
Maltas Club Namibia, Windhoek, Namibia

L.-P. Dana et al. (eds.), *Artisan and Handicraft Entrepreneurs*, Contributions to Management Science, https://doi.org/10.1007/978-3-030-82303-0_3

Numerous international studies highlighted and showcased the essence of artisanal products and their impact on regional competitiveness and tourism development. It is, however, critical to understanding that the aspirations and vision of artisan entrepreneurs are diverse, and their practices are very different depending on the context in which they are embedded. It is, therefore, pertinent for the author to delineate the existing body of knowledge and research. Therefore, this chapter seeks to advance the body of knowledge regarding artisan entrepreneurship from the Namibian context (Dana 1993), with specific reference to the Okavango women in the Zambezi Region.

In order to facilitate this exploration, the chapter first looks at the history and origin of the Namibian Okavango women. Thereafter, a review of related literature within the knowledge domain will be explored (with specific emphasis on the practices and products of artisan entrepreneurs—rooted within the field of cultural entrepreneurship). Furthermore, the methodology adopted for this chapter will be discussed, followed by a discussion of findings. Subsequently, conclusions are drawn, and suggestions for future research directions are made.

2 The Republic of Namibia (Okavango Women—Okavango Region)

The Republic of Namibia, formerly known as South West Africa, gained independence on 21 March 1990, from a very long South African rule under the League of Nations. Prior to that, Namibia was colonised by Germany (April 2021). This chapter looks at the entrepreneurial drive of a very unique group of women in the Okavango Region in the northeastern corner of Namibia. The Okavango people initially arrived in Namibia via Angola and are part of the Bantu-speaking group of people who later separated across the various Northern regions of Namibia, according to their tribes. The people of the Okavango Region follow a matrilineal system, where succession and inheritance follow the mother's bloodline. This implies that women within the royal family have the right to take over the throne from a deceased ruler. This contrasts with many indigenous communities where women are excluded from power or figurehead positions (Moses Hippo, Personal communication, 17 March 2021).

Zooming back to the Okavango history, at least five women became chiefs among the Vakwangali, four among the VaShambuya and two among the VaGciriku. These leadership positions occupied by women did not come without challenges, as some were assassinated by male rivals. There are also many other women leaders in the Okavango people, such as VaMbunza and Hambukushu communities. Women are remembered to be the most prominent leaders because they do not believe in only accumulating wealth like their male counterparts, but they believe in a life of service and contributing positively to their communities. Male chiefs tend to claim the wives of other men as their own. It is evident that the women leaders of the Okavango

Region give hope to inspire the women of today to the highest leadership positions, even to a position of Presidency in the Republic of Namibia (Elifas Dingara, personal communication, 15 March 2021). We will explore the role of culture in entrepreneurship in the next section of the chapter.

3 The Role of Culture in Artisan Entrepreneurship

Without a doubt, the study of culture and the role it plays in small businesses have gained prominence (Chua et al. 2015). This has also resulted in a number of theoretical perspectives (Gehman and Soubliere 2017; Giorgi et al. 2015). Thus, cultural entrepreneurship can be defined as the carrying out of a novel combination that results in something original and appreciated within the cultural space—this is so distinctive yet links to artisan entrepreneurship (Pret and Carter 2017).

DiMaggio (1982) looked at the "making culture" approach, which looks at the production and the way cultural products are distributed. In fact, cultural products are defined as the commodities, which are directed to public consumers, for whom they are usually aesthetic or expressive, rather than a clearly utilitarian function (Hirsch 1972). The thrust of artisan entrepreneurship is creating and selling crafts items. It is important to highlight that arts and crafts entrepreneurship are terms that can be used interchangeably.

There have been new trends in some developing nations that the industrial economy is developing into a very unique yet new type of economy. This new economy is based on creativity, skills, experience and a continuously growing demand for goods and services, which are authentic, with a high intangible value. The craft and the art sector is very significant and unique in the sense that it has a unique combination of aesthetics, creativity, emotions and the personalised labour of craftsmen, which create very significant values for the economy, although the maximum potential might not have been reached yet. The next section of this chapter defines craft entrepreneurship and looks into the various typologies.

4 Defining Art Entrepreneurship and Typologies

There is no common definition used when we look at the craft sector, but evidently, it is related to craft, which is defined as an activity that has to do with making items by hand or one can also refer to them as work objects that are made by the hand (LEXICO 2019). In the Merriam-Webster (n.d.) dictionary, craft is defined as an occupation or trade requiring manual dexterousness or artistic skill. There are very specific features of this sector when items are made by hand, although the degree of the handmade items can vary from country to country (Zulaikha and Margot 2011). In this case of Namibia, one will be exploring the craft made from wooden items. The broad definition of entrepreneurship will be combined with the definition of crafts for this exploratory study. In addition, when we look at craft entrepreneurship, it is critical to view it also as the creation, organisation and the way within which the business venture is managed. This involves the application of human skills which leads to the design of products and handwork, which pertains to it look at the creation of utilitarian products or services, which has a certain degree of aesthetic value. Given the latter mentioned, we define "craft entrepreneurs" as individuals who earns his/her living by creating something that has a significant value, partly using handwork. Artisan/craft entrepreneurs have a very high level of technical mastery and possess specific practical skills. As specialists in their respective field, they are industrious and also very patient individuals. As inventive as they are, they tend to display a certain level of assertiveness. In the next section of this chapter, we will look at the typologies of entrepreneurship, namely *Entrepreneurial Opportunity and Entrepreneurial Identity:*

4.1 Typologies of Entrepreneurship

4.1.1 Entrepreneurial Opportunity

Schumpeter (1934) viewed the typology of entrepreneurs as the categorisation of traditional entrepreneurs as those having "the desire to win," to fight and to conquer; and the joy that comes with solving a particular problem that the society is confronted with. However, it is the assertion of Aldrich and Wiedenmayer (1993) that not all entrepreneurs are driven by the same goals and that, in fact, the personal characteristics of the entrepreneurs are barely able to explain the outcomes of the entrepreneurial endeavours. Furthermore, a number of studies were looking at particular characteristics of entrepreneurs separately from one another, and this could only partly explain the behaviour and the actions of entrepreneurs (Baum and Locke 2004; Erikson 2001; Pret and Cogan 2019).

It is important to reiterate that the central construct in entrepreneurship is about recognising and developing opportunities (Summatatvet and Mervi 2015) and the individuals who can develop those. It is thus pertinent that when we look at craft entrepreneurship, we should not only be able to answer the question of who is an entrepreneur but also how he/she behaves? What are the decisions which have to be made? And how do entrepreneurs establish their ventures? There is indeed a dire need for further exploratory research in developing economies such as Namibia in terms of the number of opportunities in the entrepreneurial process to understand what entrepreneurs actually do and the process involved.

Opportunities for entrepreneurship consist of several parts, namely the type of opportunities, the process of discovery and enactment, and individuals who do so. It is critical to explore why certain opportunities are taken, while certain people take up opportunities and not necessarily others. Opportunities should be viewed in the light of a process of *discovery, evaluation and exploitation*. It also has to do with one's creation, discovery and recognition (Wright et al. 2008). It is also important to understand the discovering that an opportunity has also got to do with all the processes in opportunity development, which are interchangeable and overlapping. The debates as to whether opportunities are created or discovered continues; however, one thing is certain that opportunities need to be seen and enacted by entrepreneurs. The outcome of this enacted opportunity largely depends on the entrepreneur and the business environment within which he or she operates. Furthermore, it is possible to see opportunities through the lens of the original value and the various stages of development. This includes four types, namely starting with dreams, progressing the transfer of technology, problem solving and finally how businesses are formed.

4.1.2 Entrepreneurial Identity

For any entrepreneur to succeed, he/she must be able to pursue opportunities and create an organisation. This will usually be influenced by a number of factors, such as the role and identity of the entrepreneur, which is a basis for the cognitive framework of reference, and it also encompasses traits they are required to possess. When we talk of the role which entrepreneurs play, it has to do with how they interact with other people, realise their motivations and shape their actions while they are part of the social milieu (Alsos et al. 2016). This is rooted in the identity theories, which is based on the premise that individuals become entrepreneurs because they want to validate important social concepts, and they are also viewed to have a certain position within the society. Social identity in this chapter has a lot to do with the perceptions and meanings individuals hold about themselves, others, and how they interpret the external environment, and why they behave and act in a certain way. It is critical to understand that social identity has a much broader meaning than role identity because it has to do with social motivation and influence and also the influence of the contextual factors (Powell 2008; Brewer and Gardner 1996; Hogg and Terry 2000). It is thus important to highlight in this chapter that entrepreneurship is a social phenomenon, and one can look at it through the lens of the social identity theory, whereby we differentiate between craft entrepreneurs based on the way they view themselves and also, at times within a particular social group (Hogg and Terry 2000). We explore the role of Small Medium Enterprises in the next section of this chapter.

5 The Role of Small Medium Enterprises in the Artisan/ Craft Entrepreneurship

Zooming into the international literature, there are a number of organisations such as the Hellenic Organization for Small and Medium Enterprises (commonly referred to as EOMMEX). EOMMEX is funded by the Greek government and European sources and is a non-profit organisation. Through its Ministry of Industry, Research and Technology and Trade, the organisation was created by laws passed in 1977 and amended in 1984 and 1991. The core mandate of EOMMEX is to maintain an environment favourable for the long-term development of small- and medium-sized enterprises, with an emphasis on handicrafts. Amongst the many activities spearheaded by the organisation include minimising entry barriers and enhancing the business climate in ensuring that the chances of success are achieved or attainable. EOMMEX is also actively involved in ensuring that artisans are provided with a wide range of services, including training, financial assistance and marketing. Interest on business loans is also subsidised through this organisation, and letters or guarantees are also issued to clients. Approximately 650 specialists are employed through this organisation in Athens alone, with 26 regional offices. Other offices are in Brussels, Frankfurt and New York (Dana 1999).

Noteworthy to mention is the fact that the craft centre preserves traditional craft and products. The specialist is provided with artistic and technical assistance. This includes the marketing and the promotion of items. This sector in Greece is regarded as a priority as it is regarded as the cultural pride of the Greece economy and is integrated within the policy of the government. What is so special and significant about this sector is the fact that the rural population is kept within the countryside while ensuring that there is a healthy and conducive craft sector.

The handicraft sector in the Republic of Namibia falls under the Ministry of Trade and Industrialisation under the Small Medium Enterprises. All organisations have the opportunity to register their enterprise in the form of ownership they choose to (Pty Limited, Non-Profit Organisations, etc.). If we look at the organisations that sell traditional craft and art, these, amongst many others, include the San Women in the Nyae Nyae Conservancy, the Namibian arts and craft centre and Oba Arts Trust selling craft too. The craft and artisans' sector in Namibia is chosen as a context for this chapter as it plays a significant role in the economy and also the current state of economic development, which has been to a certain extent affected by COVID-19.

Craftsmanship is without a doubt a critical economic accelerator, and an interaction with other industries will indeed help to enrich not only the architectural but also the urban heritage of Namibia. In addition, it will enhance the Namibia tourism sector not only locally but also globally. Numerous organisations and individuals are interested in a handicraft; however, this chapter looks into the art and the craft of the Okavango people in Namibia. This chapter specifically deals with the Okavango people as they make most of their items from timber wood, which they collect from the field. These items, amongst many others, include furniture, cutlery and canoes. Other benefits these individuals benefit are subsiding of rental space from the Ministry.

This specific market is located on the river banks of the Namibian/Angolan border. There are approximately close to 70 entrepreneurs doing business in this open market. See Figs. 1, 2, 3, and 4 with the various descriptions of the products sold at the market. There are a number of items made from timber wood, namely clay pots, dishes, spoons, buckets for milking, and canoes for fishing, and these canoes are also used as a means of transport to carry water across the river. It is noteworthy

Fig. 1 A variety of craft items for home decoration at the Okavango Market; © Wilfred Isak April

Fig. 2 Pottery at the Okavango Market; © Wilfred Isak April

Fig. 3 Tables and chairs at the Okavango Market; © Nantana Elago

to highlight that the communities have a number of perennial rivers. In addition, it is noteworthy to mention that the women collect fruits from the veld, namely the Maguni fruit, which is eaten and also used in the making of wine. The timber wood is also collected by the women. Women are also very much involved in cooking meals on a daily basis for the family. In addition, the women ensure that the traditional huts are built, the land is cleared, and hunting is mostly done by the husbands. Young girls are also groomed to be leaders from a relatively young age as they are on a daily basis dealing with the pounding of mahangu, collecting of water and also firewood. The making of traditional mattresses is also done by women, as can be seen from some of the items in Fig. 2. The communities have a lot of traditional skills and knowledge, which can be enhanced through further exposure

Fig. 4 Canoes, wooden plates and side coffee tables at the Okavango Market; © Karu Njarakana

and training. These are the knowledge of crop production, dance songs and so on. Storytelling also forms an essential part of these communities as there are special songs for each of the cultural events in local languages. The communities also have a very deeply rooted promotion of Afrikaans in the region. As a nation, there are many lessons to be learned from the Greek economy.

6 Methodology and Data Collection

Considering the limited amount of research in the craft and the artisan sector and given the ill-defined boundaries of the sector, this chapter uses a qualitative research method and the grounded theory data collection approach. Using the qualitative approach to research enabled the researcher to analyse the phenomena that have not yet been studied, understood and also explained in their totality (Dana 1987 and Dana 1996).

In Namibia, a study looking at Okavango women as artisans has not been conducted before. According to Henry and Foss (2015), even though the core aim is not a statistical generalisation, it generates data that will be very valuable for generalisations. In addition, it creates the possibility or the foundation to develop new theoretical concepts and theories (Korsgaard 2011; Neergaard 2007). Grounded theory, in turn, gives the possibility to remain theoretically flexible while using a combination of research that has been done before while sensitising new research concepts emerging from the current data. This will also add new dimensions and concepts to the already existing theoretical foundations. This chapter uses interviews and observation as techniques to obtain data from the respondents. A total of 30 craft entrepreneurs were interviewed to obtain the data. In order to understand the nature of opportunities offered, it is critical that the crafts entrepreneurs tell the stories themselves and how best they understand their personal sense of experiences when they pursue opportunities (Dimov 2011). One can best learn about the pursuit for entrepreneurial opportunities through storytelling as how their businesses unfolded can shed more light on artisan entrepreneurship research. This study will therefore apply the storytelling narrative with interviews.

Initially, it was important to carry out interviews with craft entrepreneurs using semi-structured interviews, which enabled the respondents to elaborate on questions while giving them the freedom for expression. If possible, examples were also provided. Interviews usually started with a brief introduction of the aims and the objectives of the chapter. The determinants of the chapter were also outlined.

In addition, respondents were afforded the opportunity to highlight the determinants of craft entrepreneurship and also why the opportunity is important. The following indicative questions were asked: How would you describe yourself as a craft entrepreneur? Why is craft entrepreneurship important for Namibia? What makes Okavango craft entrepreneurs unique? What are some of the challenges and opportunities you have experienced in this sector? Based on the responses, the researcher will expand on the topic, which could guide with giving good data. The interviews lasted for an hour and were carried out in English. Where possible, translation and precision services were used. The interviews were recorded, analysed and manually coded. During the coding process, themes that were similar were grouped together.

It was first important to look at the general experiences of entrepreneurs and their personal experiences in the wood sector. It was noticed during this phase that there are several themes that have to be grouped together. When looking at issues pertaining to entrepreneurial opportunity and identity concepts that had to deal with self and perceptions were grouped together under the social identity themes, which resonates with the work of Brewer and Gardner (1996), who highlighted that social identity has a set of three critical variables, namely social motivation, assessment of self and also the frame of reference. It is also critical to highlight that these craft entrepreneurs also have their personal value and belief system and aspirations of what they view as success. It is at the core of this chapter to identify the opportunity Okavango women entrepreneurs experienced in the craft entrepreneurial sector. We look at the findings and discussion in the next section of this chapter.

7 Findings and Discussion

A total of 30 women entrepreneurs from the Okavango tribe in the Republic of Namibia were interviewed. The women were between the ages of 15 and 65. It was interesting to note that young entrepreneurs had children, who were mostly younger than 3 years. Teenage pregnancy is rife in this region. None of the entrepreneurs hold a bachelor's degree, and 50% of them have finished grades 10–12; 20%, grades 7–9; 15%, grades 3–8; and the remaining 15% have only basic literacy skills but were very comfortable in trying their best to speak English, and when the questions appeared to be challenging, precision services were used.

The Okavango entrepreneurs who are mainly making their goods from craft can be regarded as craft entrepreneurs. They perceive a business opportunity as the possibility to break through to be recognised as a creative star. Some of the craft entrepreneurs said that they received the opportunity through luck, and that is how everything came together. Others were of the opinion that they are where they are today as a result of observing what their forefathers and mothers were doing. As women, they have learned a lot from women who went before them. Starting a craft business, although in an informal basis, is not something we anticipated; it was as a result of encouragement to give a chance to try out something new. This can be seen from the excerpts from the interviews below:

R Denotes Respondents

> After failing Grade 10 I did not just want to stay at home, so through informal contacts I managed to start working at this market with my cousin. At first I was stressed as I could not cope, but with time all was better than expected (R2).

> For me personally working here is by luck, I never expected to be in the position that I am today, given that I only completed primary education. We use a lot of our personal value and skills (R17, R18).

> My friends were the ones, who have pushed me into this craft business ventures. Given my average creativity, I was hesitant at first, but they kept seeing the potential in me, which I never knew I had (R12, 13, 16, 17, 20).

It is important to indicate that the source of opportunity always lies in the own creativity of a person. It is about the unique value the person is able to convey in an authentic nature through their products and services. With opportunity, it is critical that people practice their craft to get a sufficient return on investment. For the case of the Okavango women entrepreneurs, it is a matter of an internal feeling as to whether they really wanted to start a business. The direct quotes from the interview indicate this:

> I just have this internal sense of peace and satisfaction that this was the right thing to do (R2,5,8,9).

> We believe that we have the required skills to bring value to our businesses with the skills we possess (R1,3,7,9).

It is clear from the quotes above that these women are expressing their freedom and a sense of ownership through engaging in craft entrepreneurship. It indeed takes tremendous effort and creativity to be part of craft entrepreneurship. These entrepreneurs believe that art makes their life better, positive and collect people to have a very open mind. Adding value to businesses, that is, encompassed within the initial definition of craft entrepreneurship, is evident in the quotes above.

> Designing craft and various shapes carved out from wood is the most rewarding experience. I create very positive emotions while keeping in touch with our culture. It makes us believe that we want to make a better life for our own people (R11, 13,15,25.26,28,19).

As craft entrepreneurs, we are driven by our own imagination, creativity and the need for experimentation and self-expression. Our identity is also enhanced through craft entrepreneurship; thereby, the products we produce has a lot to do with our identity and convey a very personal experience of our life stories, experience and how we make meaning out of certain situations. Our identity gives us a sense of personal pride, fulfilment and enormous satisfaction, especially when we sell the items to tourists who are not from our own culture.

> Our success and how we identify ourselves in the market is what makes us going. If we are able to design, create and make new items, we enjoy the creative process. Our customers appreciate that? (R16,30).

Furthermore, the value of a sense of belonging was highlighted by the craft entrepreneurs. It is the viewpoint of the Okavango women entrepreneurs that practising craft can also be viewed as a hobby or having an interest in cultural heritage. Although they would love to make a living through selling craft, in the back of their minds, there is an emphasis on traditions and history and the belief in safeguarding the richness and uniqueness of traditional knowledge and skills deeply embedded in their cultural heritage, and this must be passed down through generations. This is evident from the quotes below:

> Through producing our commodities, we are trying to tell the people how far we have come and how far we still intend to go. It is up to us to pass on our cultural generation to our immediate community and also our children. Through our carved wooden item, we are certain that we will tell the stories of our female women leaders, stories, fairy tales and everything which carry a significant meaning not to us as individuals but also the community at large (R23,24,26,29,30).

As entrepreneurs, we are faced with a tremendous number of challenges. Issues pertaining to tribalism are one of the key challenges amongst many others we experience in our own country. Additionally, we experience issues of financing, rental space, an unconducive working environment and also sexism as we are women who are standing up for themselves and try our best to make a difference. The quotes below illustrate the challenges Okavango women experience on a daily basis.

> Namibia is relatively a small nation, but tribalism is the order of the day. We are challenged daily and experience tribalism on a daily basis. Comments such as the Okavango tribe is backword, nepotism and professional jealousy is the order of the day (R12,14,16,17,18,23).

> As Okavango women running the markets, we have a shortage of financing. We have applied for a couple of loans, but it appears to fall on death ears. We complement our craft with the support and assistance we are able to receive from our farming (R1,4,5,6,9,10).

> The cost of renting space is extremely expensive, and we always do not have money. We are really challenged with paying rent; thus, we prefer to sleep in the open space. Although not the best option we are left with no choice (R15,17,18,19,23,25,29).

> We do not have proper rental space, as we sometimes sleep in the open market. The rain, dust and the challenges we experience as a result of the coronavirus is also a critical factor (R12,13,16,18,19,23,26).

> Sexism and gender-based violence is rife in our community; we are being killed on a daily basis and no one seems to care. We have been demonstrating, but continue to suffer and are killed on a daily basis (1,7,9,10,15,18).

These experiences above continue to leave us helpless most of the times, although we push extremely hard to be our better best. Our local government has tried to intervene, but we do not receive national support from the central government, and with the coronavirus, the support has become even poorer.

There are a number of success factors we believe are crucial for the survival of this sector. These, amongst many others, are the drive and determination of Okavango women and their tenacity to succeed no matter what. The Okavango women also have the belief that their unique national identity makes them a huge success story for any community. They are aware of their oral histories, and as was introduced in the beginning, they have female chief leaders, which is something very rare to find in the Republic of Namibia.

The Okavango women also have the firm belief that craft has indeed become a "philosophy" of their lifestyle. Our success indeed lies in the way we view life and what we intend to get out of life in the long run. We also have an Okavango traditional museum that we wish to expand and share with the rest of the country, but we will need support from the national government. To support their business on the site, the women are also involved in selling Maringa traditional beer. The beer is a key highlight for our identity, and we take absolute pride in it. We believe that the drink defines us as a people, and it is our story of success one can find nowhere in Namibia or the world. This latter mentioned is evident from the quotes below:

> It was the eureka moment when my own philosophy of a lifestyle as an Okavango woman "my business—my pride." For some of the respondents this was the perfect opportunity to change their (customers) life and fulfil their dreams (R2,6,9,10,11,12,18,30).

The traditional museum is the heart of our success and cultural identity. In addition, our traditional costumes and the special dances items are displayed in this museum in addition to craft which is our key product (R,12,17,19,20,29).

7.1 Discussion on Okavango Craft Entrepreneurs

There are indeed several factors, as can be extrapolated from this chapter, that motivate the Republic of Namibia Okavango women to venture into craft entrepreneurship. In this first instance, the issue pertains to social motivation, which enables them to remain intact with their cultural identity and also gives them the drive to sports opportunities. Craft entrepreneurs are individuals who create something of value, and this fits the definition as was defined in the theoretical section of this chapter. It is evident from this research that craft entrepreneurship in Namibia tends to be an intersection of traditional values and national heritage, current contemporary trends and also practices. What these opportunities provide is a unique value, and it is indeed based on a particular meaning or the story of the craft practitioner, which entails the identity of the local community and the nation at large. The Okavango women entrepreneurs create value not only for themselves but also for those around them.

It is evident from the results that craft sector entrepreneurs are intrinsically driven, and many of them have been pursuing goals that are idealistic and also give room for entrepreneurs to express themselves. It is clear from the results that the Okavango women are intrinsically driven, and many of them pursue individualistic idealistic goals, and they have complete control over their ability to implement their personal ideas and concepts. There is tremendous passion in what they do on a daily basis, and they certainly wish to preserve their culture. They would like to pass on this knowledge for many more generations to come. Craft entrepreneurs also look up to experts and new ways to improve their products so that they are quality driven. Ensuring that they are well represented in their respective fields and expertise, the Okavango women place a significant meaning on impact and quality. As they spend a tremendous amount on input quality, it is very critical that they are regarded as change-makers in their sphere of operations.

The study also revealed that the success factors play a prominent role for the Okavango women entrepreneurs as they link their success to personal aspirations, which is linked to professional development and also the inherent entrepreneur potential they possess. There are a number of challenges, such as finance, the working environment and space, which has an impact on their operations. They also run the risk of being infected with the coronavirus as they do their operations outside in an open space. Issues pertaining to gender-based violence and sexism were also some of the challenges craft entrepreneurs face on a daily basis, and they want these to be addressed as soon as possible. Growth to these women entrepreneurs has a significantly different meaning compared to how it is defined on a daily basis. The chapter also clearly revealed that finance alone cannot be regarded as a success factor but is a combination of many other factors. It is the ascertaining of the author that the primary wish for this women is to contribute to the overall well-being of the children and a better future. Overall, craft entrepreneurs are inclined to develop their businesses, big or small, to achieve the long-term growth and sustainability of building their personal brand.

8 Conclusion

Artisan/craft entrepreneurs serve different purposes to their communities, but undeniable, it contributes to preserving and fortifying national ethos (Livingston and Parry 2005). This also serves as the ethos for Okavango women. It has become clear that craft entrepreneurship is not only about heritage and traditions, it is also about the untapped inherent entrepreneurial potential of these women, which yet need to be noticed by the global world. It was important to first explore the role of culture in entrepreneurship, followed by the various typologies of entrepreneurship. It is evident that these women have strong entrepreneurial drives, and they have a sense of how important decisions are made in the business. It is clear from the theoretical literature that craft entrepreneurs pursue opportunities with the intention to create a better insight into the theory and practical reality. This chapter confirms that craft entrepreneurship is very diverse and important for the development of the Namibian economy. With the growing interest in craft entrepreneurship around the world and the high level of unemployment, studies of this nature are critical to act as a springboard for many more experiments to be conducted in Namibia. Looking at Africa, this chapter will indeed act as an inspirational perspective for those individuals who are thinking of venturing into this sector in entrepreneurial actions and thinking about how they can offer a unique product not only to Namibia, but the entire globe. There are a number of limitations that this chapter is confronted with because qualitative research in its nature can include a very subjective interpretation of data upon which one can build theories and concepts now and in the future. This is because it involves perceptions of self and also the environment at large. Qualitative studies such as this one of the Okavango women in Namibia do not provide a theoretical generalisation normally required in the academic discourse, but they provided a deeper insight into this particular phenomenon under investigation. Therefore, it was very critical from the onset to look at the role of culture in craft entrepreneurship, the typologies to see how best they are suited in the Namibian context. For future studies, it would be interesting to study how different types of craft entrepreneurs develop the opportunities for the kind of decisions people wish to make in the future. This is very critical for internationalisation purposes. Future research should closely look at the various indigenous groups and tribes that exist within Namibia. Additionally, it is our premise that longitudinal studies could help to study whether the social identity of entrepreneurs evolves and the impact they can make on entrepreneurial decisions.

References

Al Dajani H, Carter S, Shaw E, Marlow S (2015) Entrepreneurship amongst displaced and dispossessed: exploring the limits of emancipatory entrepreneuring. Br J Manag 26(4):713–730

Aldrich H, Wiedenmayer G (1993) From traits to rates: an ecological perspective on organizational foundings. In: Katz JA, Brockhaus RH Sr (eds) Advances in entrepreneurship, firm emergence, and growth. Jai Press, Greenwich, CT, pp 45–195

Alsos GA, Tommy HC, Ulla H, Solvi S (2016) Entrepreneurs social identity and preference of casual and effectual behaviours in start up processes. Entrep Reg Dev 28(3–4):234–258

April WI (2021) Youth entrepreneurship and SME challenges Namibia in the COVID19 scenario. In: Handbook of research on sustaining SMEs and entrepreneurial innovation in post COVID-19 era. IGI Global Publisher of Timely Knowledge, Pennsylvania

Baum R, Locke E (2004) The relationship of entrepreneurial traits, skill, and motivation to subsequent venture growth. J Appl Psychol 89(4):587–598

Brewer MB, Gardner WL (1996) Who is this "We"? Levels of collective identity and self representations. J Pers Soc Psychol 71(1):83–93

Bruni A, Perrotta M (2014) Entrepreneuring together: his and her stories. Int J Entrep Behav Res 20 (2):108–127

Chua RYI, Roth Y, Lemoine JF (2015) The impact of culture on creativity: how cultural tightness and cultural distance affect global innovation crowdsourcing work. Adm Sci Q 60(2):189–227

Dana LP (1987) Industrial development efforts in Malaysia and Singapore. J Small Bus Manag 25 (3):74–76

Dana LP (1993) An analysis of the strategic interventionist policy in Namibia. J Small Bus Manag 31(3):90–95

Dana LP (1996) Small business in Mozambique after the war. J Small Bus Manag 34(4):67–71

Dana LP (1999) Preserving culture through small business: government support for artisans and craftsmen in Greece. J Small Bus Manag 37(1):90–92

Dana LP, Salamzadeh A (2021) Why do artisans and arts entrepreneurs use social media platforms?: evidence from an emerging economy. Nordic J Media Manag 2(1):263

DiMaggio PJ (1982) Cultural entrepreneurship in nineteenth century Boston: the creation of an organisational base for high culture in America. Media Cult Soc 4(1):33–50

Dimov D (2011) Grabbling with the unbearable elusiveness of entrepreneurial opportunities. Entreprneurship Theory and Practice 35(1):57–81

Erikson T (2001) 'The promise of entrepreneurship as a field of research': a few comments and some suggested extensions. Acad Manag Rev 26(1):12–13

Gehman JC, Soubliere JF (2017) Cultural entrepreneurship: from making culture to cultural making. Innovations 19(1):61–73

Giorgi S, Lockwood C, Glynn MA (2015) The many faces of culture: making sense of 30 years of research on culture in organization studies. Acad Manag Ann 9(1):1–54

Hirsch PM (1972) Processing fads and fashions: an organisation-set analysis of cultural industry systems. Am J Sociol 77(4):639–659

Hogg MA, Terry DJ (2000) Social identity and self-categorization processes in organizational contexts. Acad Manag Rev 25(1):121–140

Korsgaard S (2011) Beyond discovery: a review of critique of the discovery view of opportunities. In: Paper presented at the Academy of Management Conference, August 7–11, in Chicago, Ill

LEXICO (2019) US dictionary. https://www.lexico.com/en/definition/craft. Accessed 15 March 2021

Merriam-Webster (n.d.) "Craft". https://www.merriam-webster.com/dictionary/craft. Accessed 12 February 2021

Neergaard H (2007) Sampling in entrepreneurial settings. In: Neergaard H, Ulhøi JP (eds) Handbook of qualitative research methods in entrepreneurship. Edward Elgar, Cheltenham, UK, pp 253–278. https://vivauniversity.files.wordpress.com/2014/02/neergaard-parm-ulhoi-2007-handbook-of-qualitative-research-methodsin-entrepreneurship.pdf

Pret T, Cogan A (2019) Artisan entrepreneurship: a systematic literature review and research agenda. Int J Entrep Behav Res 25(4):592–614

Pret T, Carter S (2017) The importance of fitting in: collaboration and social value creation in response to the community norms and expectations. Entrep Reg Dev 29(7–8):639–667

Ramadani V, Hisrich RD, Dana LP, Palalic R, Panthi L (2019) Beekeeping as a family artisan entrepreneurship business. Int J Entrep Behav Res 25(4):717–730

Schumpeter JA (1934) The theory of economic development: an inquiry into profits, capital, credit, interest, and the business cycle. University of Illinois at Urbana-Champaign's Academy for Entrepreneurial Leadership Historical Research Reference in Entrepreneurship. https://ssrn.com/abstract=1496199. Accessed 4 November 2009

Summatatvet K, Mervi R (2015) Cultural heritage and entrepreneurship inspiration and novel ventures creation. J Enterp Commun People Places Global Econ 9(1):1–44

Wright M, Liu X, Buck T, Filatotchev I (2008) Returnee entrepreneurs, science park location choice and performance: an analysis of high-technology SMEs in China. Entrep Theory Pract 32 (1):131–155

Zulaikha E, Margot B (2011) Innovation strategies for developing the traditional souvenir craft industry. In: Proceedings of the first international conference on engineering. Designing and developing the built environment in sustainable wellbeing. Queensland University of Technology, Brisbane, Australia, 53–58

Wilfred Isak April is a seasoned entrepreneurship academic in the Republic of Namibia. He is passionate about community development, indigenous entrepreneurship and cultures. Wilfred holds a PhD (Entrepreneurship) from New Zealand, Master of Commerce (Business Management) in collaboration with European Business School (Frankfurt) from the University of Stellenbosch in Cape Town, HonsBComm (Industrial Psychology and Human Resource Development) from the University of Stellenbosch and Business Administration undergraduate degree from UNAM and recently completed a Postgraduate Diploma in Higher Education at UNAM. Currently, he is pursuing a professional German as a Foreign Language qualification B2 and C1 Certificates at the Goethe Insitut Namibia, with the aim of teaching German from an entrepreneurial dimension in Namibia and around the globe.

Artisan Enterprise in the Rural Economy: Drystone Walling in North Yorkshire

Gerard McElwee

Abstract The chapter sets out to explore the significance of 'creative enterprise' and 'the cultural industries' in the rural economy. It does this by providing a case study of two drystone wallers, based in North Yorkshire, a region of the UK. By so doing, it demonstrates how creative enterprises in the rural economy can be conceptualised to aid understanding, further research and development.

It can be argued that the discourse of 'the cultural industries' is centred primarily around clusters of production and consumption in urban centres. In contrast, cultural enterprise in the rural economy is less well understood and researched. Yet, creative enterprise has contributed to the living culture of rural society throughout history, and as the rural economy changes, creative enterprise has an increasingly significant role to play, both economically and in renewing the cultural life of rural communities. The chapter briefly considers prior research on rural and farm-based enterprise (DeRosa et al. 2019; McElwee 2008), illegal enterprise (Smith and McElwee 2020) and creative enterprise (Henry 2007). The chapter summarises the state and limitations of existing research on artisan enterprise in the rural economy.

The significance of artisan enterprise in the rural economy in terms of its contribution to employment, wealth creation and visitor attraction is explored. Indeed, it appears that after Covid, it may be more significant, particularly as out-of-country travel will be limited for the foreseeable future. The chapter provides a case study based on interviews with two rural artisan entrepreneurs, which illustrates and develops a conceptual framework from which insights and questions relating to the start, development and limitations of such businesses can be formulated.

Dedicated to Calum James McElwee died aged 31 on 29th August 2021. A free spirit.

G. McElwee (✉)
University of York St John, United Kingdom

L.-P. Dana et al. (eds.), *Artisan and Handicraft Entrepreneurs*, Contributions to Management Science, https://doi.org/10.1007/978-3-030-82303-0_4

1 Introduction

There has been increasing interest in the study of 'artisan industries', especially since the publication of, in the UK, the first creative industries mapping study (DCMS 1998) and the development of related thinking and policy (e.g. Leadbeater and Oakley 1999). The creative industries are recognised as being of global economic significance (Henry 2007) and often are embedded in the local economy (Tregear and Cooper 2016). However, the discourse of 'creative industry' has been located very much in an urban context, and in comparison, the role of creativity in the rural economy has been neglected. Moreover, the study of rurality, and of rural development, has also developed significantly in parallel with that of the creative industries over a similar timescale, yet there have so far been surprisingly few points of connection between 'the rural' and 'the artisan'. Pret and Cogan (2019) suggest that artisan entrepreneurship can be defined as individuals who produce and sell products or services that possess a distinct artistic value resulting from a high degree of manual input. Arguably, the drystone waller fits this definition.

My own interest in this area is that I have written about rural entrepreneurship for many years, and I have built and repaired drystone walls for over 30 years.

In the context of the rural economy, enterprise has a vital role to play in enabling creative activities to thrive, and that whilst artisan enterprise is not well understood, it is increasingly significant in rural life. The chapter provides a case study of two drystone wallers, Calum McElwee and Neil Harland.

The chapter is structured as follows. First, it defines what constitutes 'the rural' and artisan entrepreneurship in a rural context. Second, it provides a brief description of drystone walling. Third, it describes the methodological approach taken and offers the case study of two entrepreneurs.

2 Does Rural Exist?

There are multiple constructions of both the rural and rurality (Philo 1992). Rural has been depicted as 'global mediascape' (Appadurai 1996) and social construct (Little and Austin 1996) or cultural (van der Ploeg 1997) construct. Thus, the 'rural' exists but is conceptualized for different purposes according to the agenda of those who so label it. So, for me, nothing is rural—naming it makes it so. Similarly, as I have argued elsewhere (Henry and McElwee 2015; McElwee 2012; McElwee et al. 2018), there is no discrete phenomenon as rural entrepreneurship. Rural entrepreneurship is entrepreneurship that happens in rural environments. However, by and large, there are some types of artisan entrepreneurship that can only occur in rural environments. Drystone walling is one such example.

3 Prior Work

Where enterprise and entrepreneurship are explored in a rural context, studies have tended to focus on the dynamics and behaviours of individuals as entrepreneurs within a rural setting (e.g. Carter 1996; Kalantaridis and Bika 2006; McElwee 2006). Carter and Rosa (1998) and McNally (2001) argue that the methods used to analyse business entrepreneurs in other sectors can be applied to rural businesses such as creative industries entrepreneurs. This chapter does this.

4 The Artisan Rural Enterprise

The artisan enterprise can be defined as a business venture based on ideas in the broadest sense, founded on the production and sharing of artefacts and experiences originating from knowledge, imagination and cultural resources.

The creative and cultural industries are said to be amongst the fastest growing sectors of the UK economy, accounting for 8% of national GDP in 2004 (UKTI 2007), rising to over 11% in 2018. DCMS (2006) defines the creative industries as including the following 13 industries: advertising, architecture, art and antiques, craft, design, designer fashion, film and video, interactive leisure software, music, performing arts, publishing, software, and television and radio. Naylor (2007) reports how these can be grouped into four generic types of creative business: creative services, creative content, creative experiences and creative originals. Little is said to be known about the impact of the creative industries on the wider economy, particularly their impact on other firms, although there has been extensive research on the scale of the sector (DCMS 2006). What does seem remarkable is that, whilst there is increasing knowledge of rurality and of rural enterprise, just as there is of the creative economy, very little is known about the interface of these two subjects: the significance of artisanal enterprise in the rural economy.

It is apparent that increasingly in the aftermath of Brexit and the end of CAP support for UK farmers, the economic implications of so-called public good will be significant. The representation of the idyllic landscape of a good deal of rural Britain is the drystone wall—in itself a public good. Paradoxically, the role of the artisan craft entrepreneur in the rural may well become once again significant.

No figures for the number of people employed in the creative industries in the rural economy nor for the number of creative enterprises that exist were given in the State of the Countryside report (2006). This stated that 'Rural England is host to a range of recreational activities' and cited outdoor leisure pursuits such as walking, fishing and riding, but no mention was made of cultural or creative activities (2006, p. 124).

It can be argued that the discourse of 'the cultural industries' is centred primarily around clusters of production and consumption in urban centres, whilst in contrast, cultural enterprise in the rural economy is less well understood and researched. Yet, creative enterprise has contributed to the living culture of rural society throughout history, and as the rural economy changes, creative enterprise has an increasingly significant role to play, both economically and in renewing the cultural life of rural communities. Naylor (2007) is one of few writers to have explored creative industries and rural innovation, observing that

> the presence and role of the creative industries in rural areas needs to be both more widely acknowledged and better understood in order to pursue innovation policies aimed at developing rural economies. (2007, p. 45)

Individual artisans work as arts and crafts makers, jewellers, painters, potters, instrument makers and other crafts makers. There are designers and specialists who run niche, creative businesses from farmhouses, communicating with clients in urban centres via broadband. There are independent retailers and people running art galleries and tourist destinations dependent for their attraction on cultural production and consumption. They are there, in almost every village, yet we know little of them.

Of course, the rural creative economy is not new in most countries of the world. The creation and production of cultural artefacts and media have existed for thousands of years. The creation and production of rock art, textiles, jewellery, music and song, and many other aspects of cultural industry have long roots in the countryside. As well as giving meaning and pleasure to people's everyday lives, their production opportunities for their makers demonstrate their skill and creativity and give them cultural identities as a musician, craftsman and artisan, for which they were rewarded with recognition, sustenance, and in due course with currency, at which point the 'creative economy' came into formal being.

5 Drystone Walling

The industrialisation of the rural economy, since the late nineteenth century in particular, has affected and often acted to threaten or impoverish (sometimes literally) the creative rural economy. Drystone walling is one such activity that was once a managed and industrial process. Drystone walls have been a feature of the British rural landscape for thousands of years, and those that are still standing are generally well over 200 years old; indeed, little large-scale new build has occurred since about 1850 (Garner 2018). There are significant regional differences in the type of drystone walls, dependent on the stone, but the principles of construction and function are broadly similar. Walls tend to last but longer than manufactured barriers such as fencing and wire and are as iconic to the rural landscape as the hedge. Drystone wallers are either professional wallers or skilled volunteers, who usually combine this activity with other rural activities as will be seen in our two case examples.

Walls are built using local stone, so different regions and countries use whatever stone is locally available. In the case of North Yorkshire, it is predominantly sandstone.

Fig. 1 Drystone walls scenery in North Yorkshire (Source: The author)

Figure 1 shows a typical scenery depicting drystone walls in North Yorkshire.

6 Methodology: The Research Problem

The research question is 'what is the nature of the creative industries in the rural economy?' McElwee et al. (2006) demonstrate that there is extensive literature on entrepreneurship and the related field of rural enterprise. However, as discussed, there is very little written, which combines the three topics of the rural, the creative industries and entrepreneurship. There is little on drystone walling as artisan work.

Following Weber (1968), I am interested in the tradition of interpretative understanding or *verstehen* in this context related to the 'life worlds' of the creative industries entrepreneurs, their culture and their ways of 'being in' and 'looking at' the world. A qualitative perspective has been used in this study to develop an interpretative understanding of the 'life world' of creative industries entrepreneurs. The notion of 'emergence' is a useful concept, in that people may be said to 'make' their enterprise within a rural context through undertaking creative activities. They may not have set out to 'become' a creative entrepreneur, and they may have had different starting points of creative, business, vocational and rural lifestyle intents or motivations, and the creative enterprise may have 'just happened' (Watson and Harris 1999).

The aim is to understand the 'subjective' experience of the creative industries entrepreneur by listening to the ways in which they make sense of the world and ascribe and attribute value to their experiences.

McElwee et al. (2006) report that there is little research using phenomenological, social constructionism or interpretative approaches in the rural entrepreneurship literature.

Indeed, it appears that there is some hostility to qualitative research into rural entrepreneurship; however, Dana and Dana (2005) so articulately suggest, '[Some] research which needs to be done cannot be conducted using mail questionnaires, surveys or brief interviews'. Interviewing artisans such as drystone wallers cannot be done in 'conventional settings'.

For Smith and McElwee (2015), such entrepreneurs are at the margins of conventional research and qualitative research streams are often the most appropriate methods to gain insightful and interesting information about their ways of seeing the world.

Translating and understanding the interpretive accounts of creative industries entrepreneurs, about their experiences, is of course a complex process, as Denzin and Lincoln (2000) indicate that

> individuals are seldom able to give full explanations of their actions or intentions all they can offer are accounts, or stories, about what they did and why. No single method can grasp the subtle variations in ongoing human experiences (2000, p. 14)

The primary aim of this study is to explore the nature of the entrepreneurial creative industries entrepreneur, using a phenomenological approach to understand the lived experience of the creative industries entrepreneur.

Regarding the research process, collecting data implies '[getting] inside situations by empirically generating qualitative data through interaction with a number of key respondents', as Burrell and Morgan suggest (Burrell and Morgan 1979, p. 7). Actually identifying key respondents was not a problem as the wallers are my beloved son Calum, and Neil a good friend. Moreover, I work alongside both of these wallers and occasionally take on walling contracts of my own.

The interviews took place in February 2021.

6.1 The Conceptual Framework: Classifying the Rural Creative Enterprise

As the literature review has shown, creative industries entrepreneurs are a highly diverse population. They possess a wide range of interests, skills and outlooks, which enable them to operate as multi-functional businesses. This section focuses on the economic or business aspects of the enterprise business.

In this chapter, I suggest three broad ways of classifying the economic activity of the artisan entrepreneur, whom I define as a person who starts and aims to grow and develop a creative enterprise that is not easily replicated.

Artisans can be considered as entrepreneurially active individuals; however, like other creative practitioners, they may view their enterprise simply as a means of supporting their creative lifestyle and would not be considered as entrepreneurs. Therefore, for example, someone who makes artisan cheese may be an artisan but not necessarily see themselves as an entrepreneur.

The two concepts are different but may overlap; that is, creative industries entrepreneurs may be more or less entrepreneurial in their role as business managers, whilst individuals may be more or less creative in the way in which they develop their businesses.

Björkegren (1996) proposed that both a creative and a business strategy are required for the successful development of a creative enterprise.

7 Case Studies

The two case studies presented aim to illustrate two different types of creative workers, Neil and Calum. Neil is a farm-based entrepreneur who engages in drystone walling as a necessity-based activity. Securing long-term contacts enables him to generate a regular income source to supplement his core business of sheep farming. Calum is an opportunity-based entrepreneur. Drystone walling is merely an opportunity to generate income from an activity that he also enjoys doing and finds rewarding. Both play a vital role in the notion of 'place-making' where creative entrepreneurship acts as a means of constructing a distinctive identity, attracting visitors, and staging events and experiences which convey the 'sense of place' (Naylor 2007). In this sense, the drystone wall becomes an integral part of the attraction. Without its presence, the landscape would lose an integral aspect of its beauty.

7.1 Case 1: Neil Harland

7.1.1 The Farm-Based Entrepreneur

Neil lives on a farm in Danby North Yorkshire, based in the North York Moors national park. He is 56 and trained as an electrical engineer.

His holding is a 65-acre upland farm, and he raises sheep. In his 30s, Neil realised that he would have to diversify his business activities in order to stay in business. He retrained as a computer technician and did some teaching and training. He established a computer business and a social enterprise. Being a farmer necessitates a wide skill set. So like most farmers, Neil is multi-skilled. One of those skills is drystone walling, which he learned as a youth. Living on an upland farm in North Yorkshire means that there is always walling work to be done as they are in constant need of repair. Damage is done by livestock, moles, rabbits and trees. Malicious damage is also caused by humans who climb on walls and even steal stone for their urban rockeries, or demolish walls to gain access to fields for illegal activities such as sheep rustling (McElwee et al. 2017; Smith et al. 2017).

Increasingly, Neil is taking on more walling work, which usually consists of taking down and rebuilding walls. Much of this work is grant funded as there appears to be an increasing awareness of the value of the drystone wall to the rural landscape and the rural economy.

Contracts for walling work can be for short stretches of wall repair and rebuild or for long-term labour-intensive jobs of over a kilometre.

Neil is becoming more and more adept as a waller.

He recognises the value of what he is doing for the environment saying 'I am conscious that this type of craft will become more important to the rural economy and may possibly be the future'.

'I may be farming the environment!' he says.

Not only is time working on a wall, very weather dependent, but drystone work can also be a lonely activity, the results of which are only noticed by occasional walkers or shepherds. On one job in Fryup dale access can only be gained by quad bike or motorbike, a 15-min ride from the nearest dwelling. See Fig. 2.

Other jobs are located where there is a significant number of walkers, such as the Cleveland Way. It is here where the impact of a wall is noticed and commented on by the general public who love to take photographs and ask questions.

'Unless you are careful you can be chatting to someone for 20 minutes', jokes Neil.

Some photographs of Neil and the author working on a wall near Gribdale gate North Yorkshire can be seen at https://scott-beveridge.photography/dry-stone-wallers?fbclid=IwAR18k_p0ChTt1DlLE5FSvYAcYHMLPSOJChnLeeaxBohlZAuGC1nW1S9nQHk (Scott Beveridge photography).

Scott is also a rural artisan entrepreneur based in North Yorkshire who specialises in rural photography.

Somewhat self-depreciatingly, Neil says, 'I have lots of ideas but not the skills to put them into practice and of course if I become more commercial it would no longer be the lifestyle business I like'.

Neil sees the walling business as a rural business, although he describes what constitutes a rural business as 'a thick broad grey area. My inspiration is taken from the environment in which I live and that's what makes me creative'.

As a farmer, Neil is truly embedded in his own community and enjoys social capital (Tregear and Cooper 2016) amongst a number of rural agencies.

Fig. 2 Access is difficult for some walls. Fryup North Yorkshire (Source: The author)

7.2 Case 2: Calum McElwee

7.2.1 Opportunity-Based Entrepreneur

Calum is 30. Like Neil, he has been repairing walls since a young age. He started working alongside Neil and took on larger and more complex work. He comes from a creative family. His brother Jack is a sculptor and also works in rural environments and has set up his own business.

Myatt-McCallum myatt-mccallum.co.uk

Calum is a trained arborist and is most happy when he is outside working. He is a sole trader—the most precarious form of employment. Like tree surgery, walling is very weather dependent. Walling is best done when the days are longer and it is warmer. Fortunately, tree work is best done in the winter months when trees are dormant.

Calum's creative skills are increasing all the time. He is a very competent waller.

Calum does not perceive himself as an entrepreneur: 'I don't see myself as an entrepreneur because I'm not always looking for opportunities. I think I'm good at networking but don't look for opportunities—I stumble across opportunities'.

Rural Business Development

In terms of developing a rural business, he commented, 'That grey area is changing because of virtual and physical accessibility. Some rural creative businesses: sculptors, garden furniture makers, for example, need to attract the customer to the rural [location] as the customer is not local. My business is different'.

Creative Development Orientation

Most of the drystone walling that Calum and Neil do is generally boundary wall. For Calum, it is not always as stimulating as he would like. 'I'd like to do more creative work, which lets me apply my skills more and brings in more income'.

Business Development Orientation

Calum is becoming more aware of the extent to which he needs to use social media to develop his business. 'Word of mouth is ok, but with a specialist business, like drystone walling, it is not enough. I do need to be more proactive'.

The right-hand side photograph in Fig. 3 shows a completed wall. The left of the batter boards is a wall that needs to be taken down and rebuilt. Batter boards enable the wall to keep the level of the wall as it is being constructed. Laying foundation stones is very physical and requires the use of strong iron bars, as shown in Fig. 4.

'If you want the truth, it is really easy to romanticise it (walling). The first thing you think about is the wall—how straight it is, what stones to use to make it look right etc. Of course when you are at the wall, you can't help but think about its history. All sorts of things pop into my head. Who built it and why?'

'You can look at a wall and imagine the mentality of the original waller and maybe someone will feel something like that about my work in the future'.

The 'batter' is the slope on either side of the wall. Generally, a wall is about four feet wide at the base and narrows to approximately one foot at the top of the wall.

Fig. 3 Batter boards in place on a section of wall in Goathland, North Yorkshire (Source: The author)

The top of the wall is finished with coping stones, called 'Toppers'. Without batter boards, the slope cannot be easily gauged. Figure 5 shows a hand-made batter board.

'It's actually a lot similar to when I was sailing [Calum had sailed the North East coast of Australia]. You experience every emotion when building a wall. Frustration and irritation and then the joy when it all comes together and you have put up something which looks fantastic. Of course it's a dying skill, but I do feel as if I have created something rather iconic'.

Calum does not enjoy the same social capital as Neil. He is not embedded in the local community as much as he would like to be and also he will go whereever he can gain the most money. Covid and physical distancing requirements have also limited the development of business opportunities, many of which occur in social locations such as the village pub. Neil has to work less at attracting new business as he is more well known.

These cases are illustrative of many other craft-based artisanal rural creative businesses that operate at a relatively informal level. The motivation is both personal creative fulfilment and making money, but it is acknowledged that there may be relatively little potential for growth, and both Neil and Calum eschew the role of entrepreneur. The enterprise provides part of a wider portfolio of land-based skills rather than a principal income. Whilst modest in scale and ambition, such businesses are likely to be numerically significant in the creative rural economy, thereby shaping its character and culture (Fig. 6).

Fig. 4 Calum at work on a wall in Goathland, North Yorkshire (Source: The author)

8 Conclusions and Implications

Whether the walling business is strictly speaking a creative enterprise in relation to the DCMS (2001) criteria may be questioned as it is foremost a *part* of a visitor experience; people do not, as a rule, travel to see drystone walls, unless they are built as land-based artwork created by artists such as Andy Goldsworthy. Interestingly, such artists provide more work to specialists and other artisans. His (https://hangingstones.org/) project in Rosedale, North Yorkshire, is one such project.

Fig. 5 Calum tying a batter board to set the level of the wall (Source: The author)

The chapter proposes that there are both similarities but also important differences between urban and rural creative enterprises. Drystone walling is a complex craft that requires great skill. Such artisanship is an integral part of the landscape.

Fig. 6 A completed section of wall (Source: The author)

As remarked, very little academic research and few policy-related studies have explored the topic of creative rural enterprise, and so it is suggested that this chapter has advanced the limited knowledge available and can initiate further exploration. The following three conclusions are offered.

First, the chapter demonstrates that there are different types of creative enterprise in the rural context, in which the interests, motivations and lifestyles of the entrepreneurs play a fundamental role in orienting the enterprise. It is important to recognise that not every rural creative person running a business is an entrepreneur when it may well be that only a minority should be so described. Rural creative businesses are heterogeneous and hence understanding these variable factors is essential in researching as well as examining ways to encourage and support rural creative entrepreneurs, as there is no uniform approach that meets the diverse needs of these different types of business.

Second, creative enterprises and the cultural industries are increasingly important and dynamic aspects of rurality, although their relative significance varies across rural areas. They are significant in a number of respects. They valorise both cultural and economic capital through 'measures of happiness' and through their economic contribution to GDP. They generate employment, recruit from local labour markets and in some cases employ graduates, thus contributing to graduate retention in rural areas. They attract people to the countryside, forming an important aspect of the tourism economy, and generate income for other businesses both in the service and hospitality sectors. Culturally, they contribute in no small part to the 'placemaking' and cultural regeneration of the identity of rural communities. They may also contribute to the knowledge-based, higher value-added and innovative aspects of the economy through high technology, information services and the manufacturing sectors. And yet, there is little official measurement of this activity, and hence they tend not to receive the financial and socially networked support that the creative industries in more rural environments receive.

Third, there is a 'blind spot' in both academic and policy-related research in relation to the creative rural economy, with a few exceptions such as Naylor (2007), and both the Countryside Commission and DCMS appear to overlook its actual and potential significance. Possibly the rural creative economy has 'slipped down the gap' between government agencies?

We suggest that further work therefore needs to be carried out to determine such factors as these:

(a) What is the scale of creative enterprise in the rural economy?
(b) What policy support is available and is required to establish and develop rural creative enterprises?
(c) What barriers and drivers face creative enterprise development in the rural economy? Exploration via primary research with networks of rural creative enterprises should ascertain the challenges, opportunities and optimal forms of business development support they require to sustain and grow their businesses. This should inform the development and provision of business support available to the cultural practitioners and entrepreneurs who want to establish rural creative enterprises.

Finally, artisanal entrepreneurship has the potential to keep endangered rural crafts and skills from extinction.

References

Appadurai A (1996) Modernity at large: cultural dimensions of globalization. University of Minnesota Press, Minnesota

Björkegren D (1996) The culture business: management strategies for the arts related business. Routledge, London

Burrell G, Morgan G (1979) Sociological paradigms and organisational analysis. Heinemann, London

Carter S (1996) The indigenous rural enterprise: characteristics and change in the British farm sector. Entrep Reg Dev 8(4):345–358

Carter S, Rosa P (1998) Indigenous rural firms: farm enterprises in the UK. Int Small Bus J 16 (4):15–27

Dana LP, Dana TE (2005) Expanding the scope of methodologies used in entrepreneurship research. Int J Entrep Small Bus 2(1):79–88

DCMS (1998) The cultural industries mapping document. Department of Culture, Media and Sport, London

DCMS (2001) The cultural industries mapping document. Department of Culture, Media and Sport, London

DCMS (2006) Creative industries economic estimates statistical bulletin, September 2006. Department of Culture, Media and Sport, London

Denzin NK, Lincoln YS (2000) Introduction: the discipline and practice of qualitative research. In: Denzin NK, Lincoln YS (eds) Handbook of qualitative research, 2nd edn. Sage, Thousand Oaks, CA, pp 1–28
DeRosa M, McElwee G, Smith R (2019) Farm diversification strategies in response to rural policy: a case from rural Italy. Land Use Policy 81:219–301
Garner L (2018) Dry stone walls. Shire Press, Oxford
Henry C (ed) (2007) Entrepreneurship in the creative industries, an international perspective. Edward Elgar, Cheltenham
Henry C, McElwee G (2015) Defining and conceptualising rural enterprise. In: McElwee G, Henry C (eds) Rural entrepreneurship. Emerald, Bingley
Kalantaridis C, Bika Z (2006) Local embeddedness and rural entrepreneurship: case-study evidence from Cumbria, England. Environ Plan 38(8):1561–1579
Leadbeater C, Oakley K (1999) The independents: Britain's new cultural entrepreneurs. Demos, London
Little J, Austin P (1996) Women and the rural idyll. J Rural Stud 12(2):101–111
McElwee G (2006) Farmer's as entrepreneurs: developing competitive skills. J Dev Entrep 11 (3):187–206
McElwee G (2008) A taxonomy of entrepreneurial farmers. Int J Entrep Small Bus 5(6):465–478
McElwee G (2012) A sustainable rural? Local Econ 27(2):1–10
McElwee G, Anderson A, Vesala K (2006) The strategic farmer: a cheese producer with cold feet? J Bus Strateg 27(6):65–72
McElwee G, Smith R, Lever J (2017) Illegal activity in the UK halal (sheep) supply chain: towards greater understanding. Food Policy 69:166–175
McElwee G, Smith R, Somerville P (2018) Conceptualising animation in rural communities: the village SOS case. Entrep Reg Dev 30(1–2):173–198
McNally S (2001) Farm diversification in England and Wales – what can we learn from the farm business survey. J Rural Stud 17(2):47–257
Naylor R (2007) Creative industries and rural innovation. In: Rural innovation, Chap. 4. NESTA, London, pp 43–58
Philo C (1992) Neglected rural geographies: a review. J Rural Stud 18(2):193–207
Pret T, Cogan A (2019) Artisan entrepreneurship: a systematic literature review and research agenda. Int J Entrep Behav Res 25(4):592–614
Smith R, McElwee G (2015) Developing qualitative research streams relating to illegal rural enterprise: reflections on researching qualitatively at the margins of entrepreneurship research. Int J Entrep Behav Res 21(3):364–388
Smith R, McElwee G (2020) The 'horse-meat' scandal: illegal activity in the food supply chain. Supply Chain Manag Int J. 2020:1–29
Smith R, McElwee G, Somerville P (2017) illegal diversification strategies in the farming community from a UK perspective. Rural Stud 53:122–131
Tregear A, Cooper S (2016) Embeddedness, social capital and learning in rural areas: the case of producer cooperatives. Rural Stud 44:101–110
UKTI (2007) Creative industries UK, UK Trade and Investment July 2007, London
van der Ploeg JD (1997) On rurality, rural development and rural sociology. In: De Haan H, Long N (eds) Images and realities of rural life.Wageningen perspectives on rural transformations. Van Gorcum, Assen, pp 39–73
Watson TJ, Harris P (1999) The emergent manager. Sage, London
Weber M (1968) Economy and society: an outline of interpretative sociology. Bedminster Press, New York

Further Reading

The excellent handbooks on artisan rural crafts produced by the conservation volunteers in the UK (https://www.tcv.org.uk/) are an excellent resource for both professionals and volunteers alike

Scott Beveridge photography. https://scott-beveridge.photography/work

Gerard McElwee is an independent scholar. His particular research interests are village sustainability, illegal rural enterprise and rural animateurs. He is the founding editor of *The International Journal of Entrepreneurship and Innovation* published by SAGE. He sits on numerous editorial boards in the area of entrepreneurship.

Traditional Food and Self-Employed Artisans in Druze Villages

Osnat Akirav and Gil Cohen

Abstract Food tourism or culinary tourism is attractive around the globe. It can represent the culture of a nation, region or community. It offers to travellers and tourists delicious food and relaxation, and to researchers, it provides a great reflection of a people's life. In this context, this chapter depicts potential in Druze villages in culinary tourism that is currently facing challenges and obstacles to get its full potential. New women entrepreneurs appear on the horizon, highly motivated to contribute to the region's development and attractiveness. As culinary tourism is growing and attracting people from all around the world, in this regard, an interview was performed to get fresh insights about culinary tourism that is considered part of cultural tourism and the culture in this region. Other insights into this business potential are highlighted and further discussed.

1 Introduction

In 2021, the Israeli population was about 9,291,000 people, including 143,000 Druze, a unique, monotheistic, Arabic-speaking religious group that grew out of Islam—but these people are not Muslims. The Druze population live mainly in two districts: the Northern District with about 81% of the Druze population and the Haifa District with about 19%. Of the total, 98% of the Druze in Israel live in 19 municipalities that are mainly homogeneous, 17 of which are in the Northern district and 2 in the Haifa district. The municipalities with the highest number of Druze are Dalia al-Carmel and Yarka. The estimated average household size is at 4.0 persons, higher than Jewish and Christian households (3.1), and smaller than Muslim households (4.7). About 80% of Druze families have a traditional structure, which includes a couple with children (children of all ages). Of these, 61% of all Druze families include a couple with at least one child up to the age of 17, slightly lower than

O. Akirav (✉) · G. Cohen
Western Galilee College, Akko, Israel
e-mail: osnatak@bezeqint.net

L.-P. Dana et al. (eds.), *Artisan and Handicraft Entrepreneurs*, Contributions to Management Science, https://doi.org/10.1007/978-3-030-82303-0_5

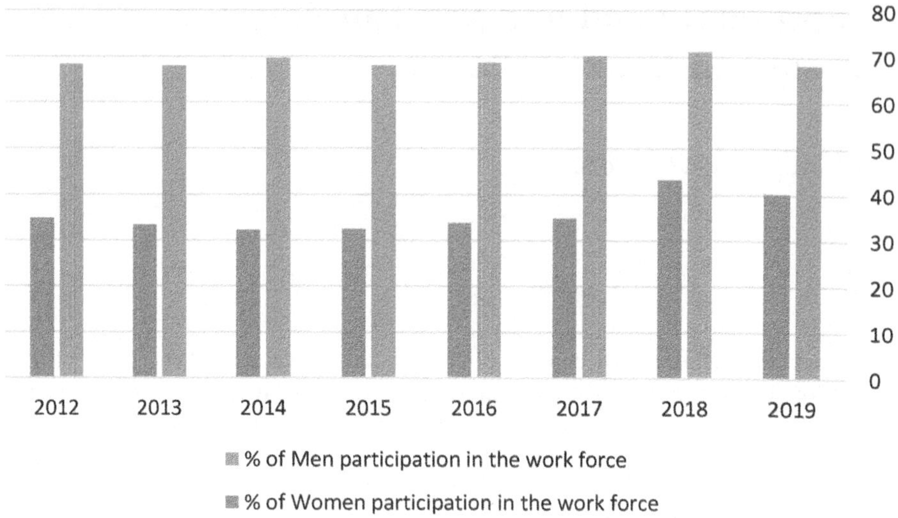

Fig. 1 Percentage of participation in the workforce by gender

Muslim families (66%) and higher than Jewish and Christian families (46% and 45%, respectively).

Zooming out to the Galilee population, it consists of 53% Arab citizens and 47% Jewish citizens. Based on the Galilee index,[1] developed at the Galilee Research Institute at the Western Galilee College, both religions suffer from a high unemployment rate, low longevity, low performance in education and a high percentage of crime. Previous studies indicated that the Arab potential workforce in Israel has not reached its potential, hence considered one of the future growth engines of the Israeli economy, and the government should invest resources in it (Dana 1999; Schnell and Shdema 2016). Two indicators regarding the Druze population strengthen the data yielded from the Galilee index: percentage of participation in the workforce by gender and Druze education system. Both present a picture of high potential for the qualified workforce of Druze women with a high unemployment rate.

Figure 1 shows that the percentage of participation of Druze men in the workforce is 69%, with not much fluctuation during the years, but of Druze women is only 35.5%, which is lower than the average women participation rate in Israel, which stands at 84%.[2]

Figure 2 shows that 31.8% of Druze pupils are eligible for matriculation, while the average in Israel is 69.7%. Moreover, the average percentage of eligibility for university degrees is only 14.5%, while the average in Israel stands at 46%. Finally,

[1] https://online.fliphtml5.com/jsbsl/fofz/#p=1

[2] https://www.boi.org.il/he/NewsAndPublications/PressReleases/Documents/%D7%94%D7%9E%D7%A6%D7%98%D7%A8%D7%A4%D7%99%D7%9D%20%D7%9C%D7%A9%D7%95%D7%A7%20%D7%94%D7%A2%D7%91%D7%95%D7%93%D7%94.pdf

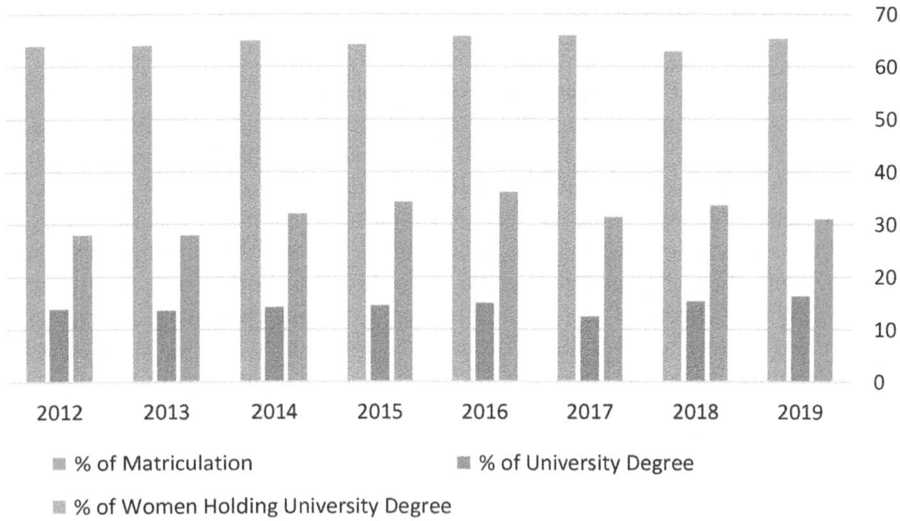

Fig. 2 Druze education system

an interesting piece of information that can be noted in Fig. 2 is that out of the Druze holding university degrees, 64.6% are women, while the average in Israel is 58%.

Arab women in Israeli society are a minority within a minority in a male-dominated society and face discrimination in four areas: as women, as a national minority, as part of traditional Arab society and as women in Israeli society (Sasson-Levy 2002; Pataki et al. 2017). A previous study on Druze women explored the obstacles that Druze women face in both their traditional society and Israeli democratic society when they want to become entrepreneurs. And second, how do they overcome these obstacles? (Akirav 2019). The research used a case study analysis—the story of Savta Gamila (Savta means grandmother in Hebrew), a religious Druze woman who manufactures and sells herbal soaps worldwide.

Akirav (2019) maintained that as the story of Gamila shows, the most significant obstacle Druze women face is the immediate Druze tradition community in which they live. Even though Druze society in Israel has changed a great deal and recognizes the importance of education and work opportunities for its women, traditional barriers still remain. To overcome them, women must be driven and determined. However, the increasing number of young female Druze entrepreneurs indicates that they are meeting the challenge.

In order to change part of the vicious circle Druze women are part of, in recent years more Druze families invite tourists in the Galilee to dine and learn how to cook their traditional Druze food. Indeed, this type of entrepreneurship does not create job opportunities for Druze women holding university degrees, but it enables less educated Druze women to participate in the labour market on their own terms. Previous studies called it culinary tourism (Richards 2018; Robinson and Getz 2014).

2 Culinary Tourism

Food (culinary) tourism represents a topical concern for destination managers, academics and marketers, especially as food is one of the indispensable aspects of the tourism industry (Henderson 2009; Robinson and Getz 2014). Food tourism is part of cultural tourism in general, which Richards (2018) defined it as a type of tourism activity in which the visitor's essential motivation is to learn, discover, experience and consume the tangible and intangible cultural attractions/products in a tourism destination. Recent data from the United Nation World Tourism Organization (UNWTO)[3] indicated that cultural truism is a major element of international tourism, accounting for over 39% of tourisms. Gastronomic tourism is one dimension of cultural truism. Millán et al. (2017) argued that cuisine is part of the cultural identity of the territory, and, as other studies indicated, traditional food can be the element that differentiates a place (Renko and Bucar 2014; Alonso and Krajsic 2013). Researchers have concluded that food is a central driver of tourists' memorable experiences (Kivela and Crotts 2006; Wolf 2006), can influence travellers' satisfaction (Robinson and Getz 2016) and can also predict their future travelling plans (Choe and Kim 2018; Cheng and Huang 2015). Because of its importance, tourism marketers must determine every possible strategy for improving the value of tourists' local food (Tsai and Wang 2017; Mak et al. 2012). In order to achieve effective markets, it is important to understand travellers' food-related behaviours that include consumption values, destination food images and the overall experience (Michael and Hall 2004; Cheng and Huang 2015). Choe and Kim (2018) argue that because food perception is influenced greatly by tourists' own food culture, the impact of tourists' local food values must be examined in terms of travellers' cultural background. Ottenbacher and Harrington (2013) explained that food could be seen as an artefact representing the local culture and giving visitors a flavour of the destination's peculiar lifestyle. Moreover, according to Robinson and Getz (2016), food also reflects the specifications of a locality.

3 Governmental Programmes and Resolutions

In Government Resolution no. 959[4] from 2016 named "Plan for the development and empowerment of Druze and Circassian villages 2016–2019", the government designated areas and localities as national priority areas, including most of the localities subject to this decision (except Daliyat al-Carmel and Isfiya). The set of circumstances that distinguish the Druze and Circassian sectors and the distinctive characteristics of these sectors led to the creation of understandable gaps between the

[3] https://www.unwto.org/

[4] https://www.gov.il/he/departments/policies/2016_dec959

Druze localities and their residents and the other localities in Israel, including those defined as national priority areas.

In 2007, the ministry of tourism initiated a tourism and hospitality venture named "Kfar Bikratem"[5] (have you visited the village) that was aimed to promote local and foreign tourism to Druze and Circassian villages. "Kfar Bikratem" is the largest and oldest tourism project for promoting Druze and Circassian tourism in Galilee, led by the ministry of tourism, the ministry of regional cooperation and the Directorate of Socio-Economic Development of the Druze and Circassian sector. The programmed targets were to deepen acquaintance between different communities in terms of culture, perceptions and way of living. This venture offers guided tours by local certified guides in a different village and focuses on the cultural traditions and unique sites. Travellers got to know the heart of the ancient villages and visited ancient cloth houses, historic springs, impressive churches, lookouts and natural sites unique to the area. Travellers were invited to visit the authentic homes of local Druze and Circassians. They watched traditional dances, got to know the village artists and visited local workshops including music, Druze and Circassian cuisine, cheese making, olive pressing and honey production, coffee-making workshops, and art and flower workshops.

Additional initiation to promote the Galilee in general and the Druze population, in particular, was established by Western Galilee Now,[6] which is an NGO dedicated to promoting the Western Galilee's multicultural, historical and geographical richness and to highlighting the region's boutique wines and beers, local delicacies, organic produce and traditional handicrafts, along with its natural beauty and the magnificent sights connecting the Mediterranean Sea and the mountains. Western Galilee Now is mostly funded by JNF-USA donations.

In order to tell the narrative of the traditional self-employed in food tourism in the Druze villages, we interviewed the establisher of the Strawberry Tree Restaurant Nearby the Spring, a Druze woman named Nazha. In addition, we conducted content analysis on the website of Druze villages in order to see the characteristics of food tourism.

4 Food Tourism in Druze Villages

The Strawberry Tree Restaurant Nearby the Spring, situated in the heart of the old village of Peki'in, serves authentic and traditional Druze food for more than 20 years. Nazha El-Din (see Fig. 3) cooks fresh Druze food as her ancestors did

[5] https://kfar.galilgov.co.il/

[6] https://www.westgalil.org.il/en/article/about-western-galilee-now/

Fig. 3 Nazha El-Din and her husband at the restaurant; photo © Peretz Avitan

for hundreds of years.[7] Nabil Abu Asraf, Nazha's father, assists her and tells visitors the story of Peki'in, the Druze people and their connection to the Jewish people before and after the establishment of Israel. For example, near the restaurant, there is the memorial site for the Druze soldiers from Peki'in who were killed during the

---

[7] https://www.ozrothagalil.org.il/poi/%D7%9E%D7%A1%D7%A2%D7%93%D7%AA-%D7%A2%D7%A5-%D7%94%D7%AA%D7%95%D7%AA-%D7%91%D7%9E%D7%A2%D7%99%D7%99%D7%9F/

Fig. 4 Memorial for Druze soldiers of Peki'in; photo © Peretz Avitan

wars since the establishment of Israel. The Druze people lost more soldiers as a percentage of their Israeli population (0.31% Druze soldiers) than other soldiers (0.23%). Figure 4 shows a memorial.

Nazha El-Din has three children. When her youngest son turned 4.5 years old, she decided to cook traditional food she learned from her mother as a part-time employment. It was 20 years ago, she noted, "we were the first family that opened an outdoor restaurant. We started with four tables outside the restaurant and served just olives, labane (kind of cheese), Druze pita, humus and falafel". The turning point was when a couple from Tel Aviv visited the restaurant and wrote a review of the restaurant in one of the popular newsletters at that time. They described the place as the strawberry tree restaurant nearby the spring with the best *humus* in Israel. Since then, the name of the restaurant became the Strawberry Tree Restaurant Nearby the Spring. A similar story happened to Savta Gamila in Peki'in, as described in Akirav's (2019) study: "after a visit from a group of tourists from Tel Aviv, the tour leader asked her (Gamila) why she did not advertise her excellent soap products. Gamila answered that she did not have money for advertising and was happy with the money she made from selling the products in her store. The tour leader asked Phyllis Glazer, an American-born food journalist based in Tel Aviv, to write a newspaper article about Gamila's soap. Phyllis came to Gamila's shop to see the products and interviewed her. When asked how old she was, Gamila's husband said that she was a grandmother (Savta). Phyllis wrote a newspaper article about Savta Gamila and created the trademark of Gamila's soaps, which Phyllis called miracle soap. She also included Gamila's telephone number in the article and indicated that the products could be sent by mail. After the article was published, Gamila received requests from all over Israel for her soaps" (Akirav 2019, p. 241).

Nazha needed to spend more time at the restaurant, and her youngest child used to return from his kindergarten to the restaurant to eat and then play. Some of the regular customers knew him by name. In order to increase the number of customers, Nazha's husband contacted tour guides, school principals and soldiers and invited them to taste the traditional Druze food. When big groups arrive, Nazha's whole family helps to serve the food she cooked.

Nazha's father said that "*when it is the first time for a group to visit a Druze village, we tell them the story, traditions and customs of the Druze people. For some of them, the Druze people is an enigma*".

Again, Nazha's story is similar to Safta Gamila's story, as described by Akirav (2019); both present traditional items (food or soup) of the Druze people to tourists as their main employment and became small business entrepreneurs, even though both did not have formal high school education.

Previous studies maintain that Arab women in Israel face socio-cultural obstacles, have only informal power and struggle to influence their surroundings without challenging the existing patriarchal order (Abu-Rabia-Queder and Oplatka 2008; Shapira et al. 2010). Furthermore, Arab women are expected to limit their interactions outside their family and community; their primary focus is on the home and family. Arab women are discouraged or even forbidden from seeking employment and education outside their villages, and there are strong norms and prohibitions against spending time with a male who is not a family relative (Weiner-Levy 2009; Offer and Sabah 2011; Abbas and Court 2013).

When Nazha established her small restaurant, there were few tourists that came to the area; most of them stopped at Ra′aya[8] to eat Druze pita. But, she noted: "*in the last 10 years there was a significant increase in the number of tourists that came to the Galilee and specifically to Peki'in. Hence, more Druze restaurants opened, and some of the owners came to me to learn what tourists like in the Druze food*".

We looked at the website that the tourist ministry created in order to present information for tourists about the Druze villages at the Galilee.[9]

We found another interesting story of traditional Druze food that a Druze woman prepares for tourists. The woman Ebtesam[10] invites people to her private home, cooks traditional Druze food for them and lets them feel comfortable in her home.

> She took some cooking courses and made cooking her professional. She even participates in TV shows and demonstrates the traditional Druze dishes. When the tourists eat her Druze food, she tells them about the Druze traditions and her husband tells the history of the Druze people.

---

[8]Ra′aya was the first woman in Peki'in who sold Druze pita to tourists.

[9]https://kfar.galilgov.co.il/

[10]https://ebtesam2504.wixsite.com/hospitality

We can see that in both cases, Nazha and Ebtesam initiated their own small business of food tourism; they do it in their own village, with the cooperation of their husband and family.

5 Epilogue

Druze women used traditional Druze food to create an occupation, which can be an accelerator for financial success and can empower them to be independent women. Such employment enables Druze women to help with the family finances and to fulfil personal aspirations. Culinary hospitality combines business with traditional hospitality and family Druze customs. The Druze population has succeeded in integrating into the general population in Israel. However, their participation in the workforce is lower, especially for women, than the general population. The self-employed artisan business helps to bridge that gap. Moreover, managing a business needs specific knowledge and expertise that can be acquired through academic studies, which can further advance the Druze society towards full integration and equality with the people in Israel.

References

Abbas R, Court D (2013) We cannot move forward unless we preserve our traditions: women principals as leaders in Israeli Druze society. Educ Soc 30(2):67–82

Abu-Rabia-Queder S, Oplatka I (2008) The power of femininity – exploring the gender and ethnic experiences of Muslim women who accessed supervisory roles in a Bedouin society. J Educ Adm 16(3):396–415

Akirav O (2019) The lioness from Peki'in. Int J Entrep Small Bus 37(2):232–249

Alonso AD, Krajsic V (2013) Food heritage down under: olive growers as Mediterranean food ambassadors. J Herit Tour 8(2–3):158–171

Cheng Q, Huang R (2015) Is food tourism important to Chongqing (China)? J Vacat Mark 1:13

Choe JYJ, Kim SS (2018) Effects of tourists' local food consumption value on attitude, food destination image, and behavioral intention. Int J Hosp Manag 71:1–10

Dana LP (1999) Small business in Israel. J Small Bus Manag 37(4):73–79

Henderson JC (2009) Food tourism reviewed. Br Food J 111(4):317–326

Kivela J, Crotts JC (2006) Tourism and gastronomy: gastronomy's influence on how tourists experience a destination. J Hosp Tour Res 30(3):354–377

Mak AH, Lumbers M, Eves A, Chang RCY (2012) Factors influencing tourist food consumption. Int J Hosp Manag 31(3):928–936

Michael C, Hall R (2004) Consuming tourists: food tourism consumer behaviour. In: Food tourism around the world. Routledge, Abingdon, pp 72–92

Millán G, Arjona-Fuentes J, Amador-Hidalgo L (2017) Olive oil tourism: promoting rural development in Andalusia (Spain). Tour Manag Perspect 21:100–108

Offer S, Sabah M (2011) Individual and familial determinants of married Arab Israeli women's labor force participation: trends of change and stability. Marriage Family Rev 47(5):326–343

Ottenbacher MC, Harrington RJ (2013) A case study of a culinary tourism campaign in Germany: Implications for strategy making and successful implementation. J Hosp Tour Res 37(1):3–28
Pataki S, Abbas R, Carey SR, Clayton J (2017) Balancing work, family, and community roles among Arab women living in Israel, unpublished manuscript, Bridgewater State University
Renko S, Bucar K (2014) Sensing nostalgia through traditional food: an insight from Croatia. Br Food J 116(11):1672–1691
Richards G (2018) Cultural tourism: a review of recent research and trends. J Hosp Tour Manag 36:12–21
Robinson R, Getz D (2014) Profiling potential food tourists: an Australian study. Br Food J 116 (4):690–706
Robinson R, Getz D (2016) Food enthusiasts and tourism: exploring food involvement dimensions. J Hosp Tour Res 40(4):432–455
Sasson-Levy O (2002) Constructing identities at the margins: masculinities and citizenship in the Israeli army. Sociol Q 43(3):357–383
Schnell I, Shdema I (2016) The role of peripheriality and ethnic segregation in Arabs' integration into the israeli labor market. In: Socioeconomic inequality in Israel. Palgrave Macmillan, New York, pp 207–224
Shapira T, Arar K, Azaiza F (2010) Arab women principals' empowerment and leadership in Israel. J Educ Adm 48(6):704–715
Tsai CTS, Wang YC (2017) Experiential value in branding food tourism. J Destin Mark Manag 6 (1):56–65
Weiner-Levy N (2009) When the hegemony studies the minority – an Israeli Jewish researcher studies Druze women: transformations of power, alienation, and affinity in the field. Qual Inq 15 (4):721–739
Wolf E (2006) Culinary tourism: the hidden harvest: a dozen hot and fresh reasons how culinary tourism creates economic and community development. Kendall/Hunt, Dubuque

Osnat Akirav is a Professor of political science at the Western Galilee College, Israel, the head of the department of political science and the head of the Galilee research institute at the Western Galilee College. Her specialisation is in legislative studies, setting the agenda, candidate selection methods, local government, gender and politics, minorities and politics, research methods and the Israeli political system. In 2010 and 2015, she received a prize for outstanding teaching in political science from the American Political Science Association, and in 2012, she received Edmond Safra award for outstanding achievement and excellence. In 2012 and 2016, she received a prize for best article from the Israeli Political Science Association. In 2015, 2018 and 2019, she received a prize for excellent researcher from the Western Galilee College. In 2019, she was elected as the vice president of the Israeli Political Science Association.

Gil Cohen is a Professor of Finance, Chair of the Management Department, Western Galilee College and a member at the Galilee research institute at the Western Galilee College. His research has been concentrated on two fields of finance: corporate finance and financial markets. He has researched the behaviour of managers in different situations trying to contribute to managers' knowledge in order to improve their decision-making process at different finance dilemmas such as investment, finance and dividend. He has also researched the behaviour of the financial markets around the globe, searching for anomalies and explanations to investors' behaviours.

Part II
Entrepreneurial Innovation in the Artisanal Sector

Artisan Food Production: What Makes Food 'Artisan'?

Sophia Lingham, Inge Hill, and Louise Manning

Abstract Artisan food is characterised as being made through creativity, passion and traditional methods and with traditional ingredients. John McKenna describes this as the quartet of place, product, passion and personality of the producer, with tradition being implicit rather than explicit in this description. This chapter considers the contemporary framing of artisan food and artisan producers, how the use of the term 'artisan' has evolved over time, and the emergent trends within the artisan food sector. The research question arising from these ideas is, *Can artisan food be both innovative and traditional at the same time?* The chapter discusses three food producers and critically evaluates the extent to which they fit within existing definitions of 'artisan food'. The term 'artisan' can be said to be socially constructed; that is, the meaning is constantly reconstructed as new innovations are adopted and associated with place, product and producer. Artisan food needs to stand out in some contemporary way from more mass-produced food, especially as it often has higher costs of production or includes an embedded environmental or social value that the purchaser must be willing to pay for.

1 Introduction

Consumers are becoming increasingly aware and differentiated in their food choices, with characteristics from organic to 'ethical sourcing' to 'local' production featuring increasingly highly in their consumption choices across Europe and beyond (Dunn and Wright 2017). In the academic literature, there seems to be no clarity, and instead a conflation of the concepts of 'artisan', with 'good food', 'speciality food' (Wyshak 2014; Collinson 2018), 'traditional', 'farmhouse', 'natural' (FSAI 2015; Collinson 2018), and 'farm-produced' (Oledinma and Roper 2021). Artisan has also been linked to notions of the craft aspects of food, i.e. 'cottage industry' (Murray

S. Lingham · I. Hill · L. Manning (✉)
Royal Agricultural University, Cirencester, Gloucestershire, UK
e-mail: Louise.Manning@rau.ac.uk

L.-P. Dana et al. (eds.), *Artisan and Handicraft Entrepreneurs*, Contributions to Management Science, https://doi.org/10.1007/978-3-030-82303-0_6

1987), 'craft food' (Ashkenazy et al. 2018; Darnhofer and Strauss 2015; Oledinma and Roper 2021) and 'handmade' (Collinson 2018).

The concept of artisan food has been studied as a driver of tourism (Collinson 2018; Smith and Xiao 2008; Testa et al. 2019), in the maintenance of social networks (Grimes and Milgram 2000), the difference between local production for local consumers and local production for distant consumers (Fonte 2010), and in the wider context of global food trends (Desmarais 2003). Artisan food has also been considered in relation to its embedded nutritional value (Ruiz-Cano et al. 2013), high quality (Quinn and Seaman 2019), gender opportunities and equality (Maidment and Macfarlane 2011; Escurriol Martinez et al. 2014), and the tensions between factory and artisan producers (Oledinma and Roper 2021). Another aspect is that of artisan being linked to autonomy and independence in terms of business and regional identity (Quinn and Seaman 2019).

According to the School of Artisan Food, 'artisan' food has the following qualities (The School of Artisan Food 2021):

- It is food produced via 'non-industrialised methods, often handed down through generations, but now in danger of being lost'.
- Embeds producer knowledge, understanding and respect for their raw materials, and is made by people who have an 'historical, experiential, intuitive and scientific understanding' of the production process and have social and environmental awareness.
- Producers who make artisan food never stop learning and improving their craft.

This definition proposes tradition, but also the elements of being experiential and improving as a craft suggest elements of innovation. Innovation is quite simply the process of innovating, i.e. the introduction or adoption of new ideas, new technology or new ways of thinking. McKitterick et al. (2016) differentiate between incremental (small changes that lead to innovation over time) and radical innovation where adoption of new ideas or technology happens quickly and state that many artisan foods demonstrate radical elements of innovation. Leroy et al. (2013) comment on the difference between tradition (authentic, local) and innovation (improving, unconventional, novel, global) and the contradictory aspects of innovation in a traditional food product. However, they state that innovation can be associated with the re-emergence of the traditional in a market where this has not been a contemporary focus and where authenticity is an implicit characteristic of the food driven by characteristics and a sense of familiarity for consumers. This suggests that the familiarity can indeed be innovative in a re-emergent market.

Thus, the term artisan food can be positioned in terms of the food itself, the way the ingredients have been sourced, processed and the innate features of that method, the people and their values, beliefs, and ethical perspectives, the degree of formalisation of the businesses involved, the interaction between craft and markets (McKitterick et al. 2016), and the story of the product and aspects of transparency, authenticity and roots (Ashkenazy et al. 2018). These aspects will be considered in turn. Artisan food has been described as luxurious, elitist, exclusive and expensive (Thompson and Kumar 2018). Indeed, artisan food may need to stand out in some contemporary way from more mass-produced food, especially as it often has higher costs of production or includes an embedded environmental or social value that the purchaser must be willing to pay for. Artisan could be said to describe a food product produced in limited quantities or means of production, with a socio-traditional value, generally associated with a specific location, culture or heritage, which may go some way to re-connecting consumers with multiple aspects of their food. The case studies later in this chapter will be evaluated according to the FSAI definition of artisan:

- Being made in limited quantities.
- By skilled craftspeople.
- Where the processing method is not fully mechanised and follows a traditional method.
- The food is made in a micro-enterprise at a single location.
- The characteristic ingredient(s) used are grown or produced locally, where seasonally available and practical.

To complement this definition, the evaluation will also consider the more abstract definition by the Irish food writer, John Mckenna, who defines it as 'a synthesis of the *Personality* of the producer, the *Place* it comes from, the *Product* itself and *Passion* in the manner it is produced' (Teagasc 2017). Neither of these terms address innovation as an inherent aspect of a food being artisan and yet creativity and craft is at the heart of artisan food production. This leads to the research question:

Can artisan food be both innovative and traditional at the same time?

The next section considers the evolving nature of the term 'artisan' over time and the innate aspects of innovation that this demonstrates.

2 Artisan as an Attribute: Product, Production and Producer

The academic literature on artisan production of food is rather limited (Azavedo and Walsh 2019), with varying uses of the term 'artisan'. Pre-1990s, the terms 'artisan' and 'cottage industry' (Murray 1987) were fairly synonymous, and in some areas, this remains the traditional view (e.g. in parts of Spain and Greece). 'Artisan' seems throughout the last 20 years to have had an historic element, with those promoting artisan wishing to protect local history, heritage and traditions. The late 1990s saw the start of the artisan food movement as we recognise it now, with producers, consumers and other stakeholders wishing to protect and market 'smaller regional food producers . . . make foods concurrent with local history' (Quinn and Seaman 2019, p. 4), whilst strengthening links to the locality and preserving traditional production practices (Bowen and De Master 2014; Lotti 2010; Oledinma and Roper 2021). Whilst this motive is still strong, more recently perhaps, there is a

Table 1 Aspects of artisan food production

Theme	Description
Mastery and craft	Mastery and craft production involving an historical, experiential and intuitive understanding, acquiring skills . . . from experienced practitioners, emphasising hands-on and tacit knowledge rather than learning by rote or from the book (Jackson 2013).
	Craft production, having an economic/social and cultural environment embeddedness (Escurriol Martinez et al. 2014).
	Skilled craftspeople where the processing method is not fully mechanised and follows a traditional method (FSAI 2015).
Place (locality, seasonality)	Civic Agriculture: Caricofe (2011) emphasises the strong desire of artisans to operate 'locally embedded businesses.'
	Characteristic ingredient(s) used are grown or produced locally, processed in a given location and where seasonally available and practical (FSAI 2015).
	Food that forms part of the established tradition of its local area, usually produced on a relatively small scale (Quinn and Seaman 2019).
Values and beliefs	Products 'embody the processor's values and beliefs'(Gralton and Vanclay 2009).
	Artisans were found to be 'values-based individuals emphasizing product quality through their careful sourcing of ingredients and the use of traditional, time consuming production methods' (Caricofe 2011).
	Producers are driven by a mix of lifestyle-oriented goals and commercial growth ambitions (McKitterick et al. 2016).

rising emphasis on local community, knowledge (Escurriol Martinez et al. 2014), and its use in alternative food networks.

Whilst the general indicators of what it is for a food to be 'artisan' may remain constant, the reach in terms of how the term is used has widened and diversified. This means that the term 'artisan' is becoming more relevant to a wider circle of consumers and becoming a tool allowing smaller producers to compete with large-scale producers/supermarkets by creating a 'niche' parallel market. The creation of new markets can in itself be described as innovation, especially where such market opportunities have not existed in the past. Iterative themes arise from the literature with regard to artisan food production (mastery and craft, values and beliefs and place in terms of locality and seasonality); see Table 1. Thus, the definitions focus on product, place and producer as aspects of production where methods are traditional and time-consuming.

What production systems are classed as 'artisan' is complicated. In some countries, what constitutes *artisan* changes depending on the area and product. For instance, in Spain, there are varying regulations throughout the country regarding where the raw materials originate from, the number of workers producing the artisan product etc. (Escurriol Martinez et al. 2014). In the UK, there is no specific artisan food law; artisan producers must abide by the same rules as larger food producers. In the United States, the Food and Drugs Agency (FDA) ruled in 2014 against the historic tradition of aging cheese on wooden boards (Danby 2015); some Spanish regulations also forbid the maturing of cheese on wooden shelves (Escurriol Martinez et al. 2014) on hygiene grounds. If this was the traditional method of production, can cheeses matured in other ways be classed as 'artisan'? Conversely, should 'artisan' be able to disregard health and safety legislation on the grounds of authenticity or scale? Is this a form of innovation where the product still exhibits the characteristics of craft and creativity, but when a new emergent form of 'artisan' production does not, to comply with contemporary legislation, follow historic practices?

In the mid-1990s, a dichotomy within food production was recognised as standardised/generic versus specialist/dedicated food systems; the former related to industrialised food production, mass market production, and economies of scale, whilst the latter described artisanal food production with labour-intensive production methods to produce products for specific groups of consumers (Oledinma and Roper 2021; Storper and Salais 1997). This binary segregation of production is echoed in the present-day dichotomy of food networks, between conventional and alternative; however, this distinction, many argue, is too rigid, with artisanal and alternative food networks co-existing and interacting with conventional networks on multiple levels (O'Neill 2014). Within these new networks is the perception of an artisanal food economy, which has been described as 'artisan entrepreneurs'/farmers . . . influential in developing a new economy which 'selectively uses technology, couples it with traditional elements and addresses societal and consumer needs' (Darnhofer and Strauss 2015, p. i). This peer-to-peer networking to provide an artisanal ecosystem has also been highlighted by others (Blundel 2002; Felzensztein et al. 2010), driving social innovation, niche markets, and new, innovative and creative business models, centred around skills and knowledge merging the old and the new (Darnhofer and Strauss 2015). Thus, artisanal food economies can make traditions relevant to a modern society. Culinary tourism may also be perceived as its own emergent economy, with regional foods strengthening an area's place on the map as a tourist destination and also rejuvenating culinary traditions, which, but for the tourist market, may have been lost in history due to lack of local participation or awareness. Thus, food can be used as a tool to rebrand an area and create a sense of social community. Culinary tourism has been defined as when eating, tasting, buying and appreciating local food products is an important component of visits to the area (Hall and Gössling 2016; Smith and Xiao 2008), with an emphasis on culture, authenticity and local, three vital components of being artisan. This raises an interesting question as to whether innovative entrepreneurship can focus on regional taste and food culture, i.e. local gastronomy (Dann and Jacobsen 2009). Metaxas and Karagiannis (2016) report that culinary tourism driven by gastronomy represents examples of innovative entrepreneurship. Extending the context of culinary tourism is the development of artisanal products as 'cultural goods.' This is not a new phenomenon. Indeed, eating the product may not necessarily be the primary aim, instead the focus being on creating the cultural experience, seeing or even keeping the product as a keepsake, and creating a food memory, e.g. seaweed in western Ireland (Collinson 2018). Can this experiential aspect of artisan food be used as a marketing tool for tourists or within food businesses that develop innovative brands that are differentiated from the existing market by being pitched to appear as artisan?

What is meant by local is in itself a debate wrought with diverging opinions (O'Neill 2014), especially the question whether, by 'food', we mean the final product or also include the ingredients within it. Some studies in southern Europe have shown more of an emphasis on the locality of ingredients (Escurriol Martinez et al. 2014). However, others have considered the scaling up of Italian alternative food network schemes and suggest fluidity in the notion of local (Martindale et al. 2018), meaning producers can purchase ingredients from beyond their local area but within a direct chain. This approach is in contrast with UK viewpoints on alternative food networks, which Martindale et al. (2018) assert have a more rigid idea of local. As many of the notions of artisan mention an environmental awareness, it may be that artisanal producers use ingredients obtained in an environmentally friendly way/close by or that the processes cause minimal environmental damage. The idea of seasonality and traditions of an area may also point to a more local ingredients base, although changes in traditional cultivations and economics may have influenced this.

Generally, when considering artisan products in the UK, one might think of cheese, bread, preserves, chocolates, pies and cured meats, ales and ciders. Obviously, some of the ingredients, such as cocoa, are not locally grown. However, as Escurriol Martinez et al. (2014) show, artisan food can be anything: alcohol, dairy, poultry, meat, fruit and vegetables, condiments, and flour. In such areas as rural Spain, traditionally grown foods are seen as artisan but without necessarily commanding the higher price that may be associated with artisan in the UK; however, as debated by many traditional/home producers wish to disassociate themselves with the term 'artisan' due to larger commercial producers using the term to describe competing products. A UK equivalent example is that described by Quinn and Seaman (2019), who highlight the 'Oakham' chicken range from M&S not being from Oakham as an authentic place of provenance, but instead from a range of poultry farms across the UK. Whilst this product is not marketed by the retailer as artisan, it can affect the sales of other businesses positioned as artisan if consumers feel their product experience has been fulfilled by buying a product from the Oakham range. The above leads to the following considerations: In the UK, would we call locally grown vegetables 'artisan'? Is the consideration of what is artisan more complex? Are some foods determined as artisan in the UK seen as mainstream foods in other cultures, e.g. local honey, milk, cheese, olives etc.?

In summary, determining what artisan food, artisan production (Ramadani et al. 2019) and artisan producers are is difficult to do from the existing literature. Tensions exist between different producers of craft/artisanal products. For instance, although factory production of craft cider is not artisan, it directly competes with artisan-produced ciders. Farm producers of artisan cider argue that the allowance of non-traditional production methods during factory production of craft cider reduces the value of the geographic indication (GI) and provenance in terms of protecting food heritage and artisanal production (Oledinma and Roper 2021). Legal and social tensions that develop are the difference 'between supporting artisanal production and protecting the potentially more economically significant, factory-based production of traditional products'. For example, as organic food products become more mainstream and are produced on more industrial farming and manufacturing scales making them less alternative, does this create an alternative consumer demand for foods that are differentiated from the mainstream, beyond organic? (Fonte 2010). Wider permissiveness in the scope of Protected Geographic Indication (PGI) allows factory-made products to benefit from being linked to local tradition and heritage, with any associated marketing gains, without adhering to traditional production techniques. This may crowd out artisan producers from the market. The mechanisms for implementing protected food names related to food heritage in the UK following Brexit mean that national UK legislation will be revised and refocused. It is interesting to consider how they should be positioned given the narrative in this chapter. With a view to the craft aspects of artisan food and the making of food with specific organoleptic qualities, or made with creative passion, is something inherently lost during the mass production of products or with new techniques and innovations, i.e. *Can artisan food be both innovative and traditional at the same time?* This question is now considered in a series of case studies.

3 Entrepreneurial and Innovative Ways to 'Stand Out' and Yet Still Be Defined as 'Artisan'

Standing out from 'the crowd' in a given market place drives a food producer's unique selling proposition (USP). However, for consumers to recognise a new product (or service) and engage with it, they need to be able to identify some common features of the new product while at the same time need to see how a new product is different from other options they have available. This difference needs to be big enough to differentiate a product and yet not too big to be distracting and allowing comparisons with existing products (De Clerq and Voronov 2009). The three case studies now considered exhibit different characteristics of what it is to be 'artisan' and inform the discussion section of the chapter. Information about the case studies is sourced from company websites and social media accounts, as well as personal experience of the authors.

Elements of the FSAI definition are used to consider these three producers and whether they can be said to produce artisan foods and how any innovation associated with the producer can be determined:

- 'Limited quantities': FSAI states that total production by the food business operator should be less than 1000 kg/L of food per week on average over a year.
- 'Skilled craftsperson': someone who has special expertise in making food in a traditional manner.
- 'Traditional': 'proven usage on the domestic market for a period that allows transmission between generations; this period is to be at least 30 years'.

- 'A micro-enterprise': an enterprise that employs fewer than ten persons … and whose annual turnover and/or annual balance sheet total does not exceed EUR 2 million.
- 'Characteristic ingredients': include milk in cheese, pork meat in ham, strawberries in strawberry jam, and oats in porridge. The characteristic ingredient(s) are those that would normally require a quantitative ingredient declaration (QUID) under the food information regulations.
- 'Locally': within 100 km of the manufacturing/food service establishment.

3.1 Wild Irish Seaweed (Wild Irish Seaweed 2021)

This is a family-run business, run by the Talty family, in its fourth generation, in Southern Ireland. The seaweed is naturally grown and certified as organic (https://wildirishseaweeds.com/).

1. **Limited quantities**

They state that they are the global leader in the supply of natural, wild organic seaweed for the food ingredients, pharmaceutical, nutraceutical and cosmetic industries. This statement does not suggest small scale/limited quantities.

2. **By skilled craftspeople**

Wild Irish Seaweed is a family-run business who have special expertise in their craft via following traditional harvesting and production methods passed down through generations.

3. **The processing method is not fully mechanised and follows a traditional method**

For four generations, the same family has for over 100 years been collecting seaweed via hand-harvesting sustainable techniques, which qualifies, both in terms of the time period and the transmission through generations, suggestions by the FSAI as being 'artisan'. On their website, they state, 'We have kept the same hand harvesting techniques handed down over 4 generations' and 'Our harvesters like our ancestors use sustainable harvesting methods to ensure our seaweed will regenerate for the generations to come' (Wild Irish Seaweed 2021). However, they have also built a 'state of the art' drying and processing facility, allowing for innovation.

4. **The food is made in a micro-enterprise at a single location**

Their website suggests that the seaweed is processed at one location, although this is not expressly stated. However, the business is not a micro-enterprise.

5. **The characteristic ingredient(s) used are grown or produced locally, where seasonally available and practical**

The seaweed is harvested from the West coast of Ireland, in County Clare, close to where their business is situated. It is grown naturally and harvested sustainably, suggesting working with the seasons.

In summary, Wild Irish Seaweed seems to fulfil some of the FSAI requirements of being artisan, with the possible exceptions of business size and limited quantities of production. They more readily fit the description of an 'artisan entrepreneur' by embracing technological developments and new market opportunities, whilst preserving traditional methods and heritage. Much emphasis is placed on their identity as a family business being handed down the generations and the importance of sustainably sourcing local good quality seaweed; the locality and harvesting of the raw ingredient is as important to them as the processing of it. Thus, the intrinsic value they give to the natural product, as well as the economic opportunity, embodies their beliefs in working with the environment, characteristics not seen in the FSAI definition. Mckenna suggested that artisan food reflects *Personality* of the producer, the *Place* it comes from, the *Product* itself and *Passion* in the manner it is produced. This example would fulfil all four Ps. Wild Irish Seaweeds Ltd. describes itself as 'where tradition meets innovation' (Wild Irish Seaweed 2021). That is, whilst four generations have harvested seaweed, it is the use of this seaweed as a raw material for food ingredients and pharmaceutical, nutraceutical and cosmetics sectors that make the business innovative. It could be argued that the artisan entrepreneur is innovative in how the food products are positioned and packaged and is able to extend the customer base beyond existing markets.

3.2 *Cotswold Kid Meat—Just Kidding (Just Kidding 2021)*

Cotswold Kid Meat started in 2013 and has achieved the Great Taste Award Gold Star for three of their kid cuts (an accreditation scheme for artisan and specialty food producers). They are a two-man band, employ sustainable practices and are part of the Slow Food Movement[1] (https://cotswoldkidmeat.com/).

1. **Limited quantities**

Cotswold Kid Meat sell with Farm Drop[2] to London and direct to consumer via events, online retail, local pubs, Michelin starred restaurants, and clients such as Jamie Oliver and James Martin. Considering the breadth of their customer base and the quantities needed to fulfil their orders, the quantity produced is difficult to determine from the data available.

[1] https://www.slowfood.org.uk/

[2] https://www.farmdrop.com/shop

2. **By skilled craftspeople**

They use a local family-run abattoir, Broomhall,[3] and a local artisan butchery, Woodchester Meats. This butcher has been in operation since 1994, and along with Just Kidding, does not yet qualify as 'traditional' in terms of age of business. One of the business owners of Just Kidding is from a farming background, and the other was a chef, which are both undoubtedly skilled professions. They have been rearing kids since 2013, producing high-quality, award-winning meat. Recipes are available on their website promoting the creative use of the kid meat. The artisan and creative element of the business are further promoted through the circular use of skins to produce rugs, wall hangings and cushions. It could be argued that embracing circularity in this way is to be an innovative entrepreneur.

3. **The processing method is not fully mechanised (industrialised) and follows a traditional method**

The goats are kept as free range, allowing for as natural/ 'wild' a life as possible. Whilst it is not traditional to rear goats for meat in the UK, keeping animals free to roam qualifies as not being 'industrialised'. The abattoir is local and family run, suggesting that it is small; the wholesale butchery is described as 'artisan', and from an internet search, it appears to serve the area local to Stroud only. However, what would qualify them as 'artisan' is harder to decipher as there is little information about their butchery practices or techniques, but online reviews do call them 'high-quality ... true artisans'. The FSAI specifies that the traditional method used in production must be from the domestic market. Thus, whether or not their method of goat rearing is traditional for global farmers makes defining the production system as artisan in the UK context more difficult.

4. **The food is made in a micro-enterprise at a single location**

The final meat product is not generated from a single location, with four locations in the supply chain: the original dairy enterprise where the kids are sourced from, the rearing farm (where they are fed on grass in the summer and cereals grown 10 miles away in the winter), the abattoir and the butchery. Just Kidding is run by two people, which is micro-scale in terms of the FSAI definition.

5. **The characteristic ingredient(s) used are grown or produced locally, where seasonally available and practical**

The kid billy goats are sourced from a 'high health status dairy farm', but the location is unspecified.

In summary, using the FSAI definition of what it is to be artisan, Just Kidding does not meet all these criteria; however, if the emphasis is on processing and using traditional/unmechanised/skilful methods and craftspeople, then the producers could be said to be artisan. Perhaps, with the rising importance of animal welfare,

[3] http://www.jbroomhallltd.com/

environmental sustainability and the interest in local food, the artisan entrepreneur, the processes they use and the products produced should reflect these characteristics; although, this would mean what it is that makes a food artisan is more consumer-centric than product-centric. Just Kidding focuses on the aspect of giving the billy goats a purpose and a value that they never previously had, to avoid euthanasia, and also to practice sustainable, circular practices on the farm. These are characteristics intrinsic to the identity and personality of the producers and the product. Therefore, some questions arise from this case study:

(a) Should such characteristics of identity and personality be valued in artisan food, or do identity and personality merely describe niche products?
(b) Should the definition of artisan continually adapt so aspects of the process sustainability or circularity can redefine what it is to be artisan? If multiple changing criteria are used to define what it is to be artisan, does this risk losing the identity of what it is to be an artisan product or producer altogether?

So, whilst not conforming to traditional ideas of artisan, Just Kidding are creating their own emergent version of artisan. This entrepreneurial and creative approach has developed a market through an emotive story and sustainable practices, attractive to a new movement of foodies and consumers interested in traceability, animal welfare, sustainable farming and good quality produce. They are, as a result, more in line with the 'four Ps' version of artisan, whilst also symbolising authenticity, short supply chains and a respect for their raw materials. A small business but with increasing reach, they have contributed to and created their own local food network by using small businesses in processing their product, which in itself would characterise them as innovative entrepreneurs. This gives rise to another question:

Should the definition of artisan include a requirement for community involvement as an extension of tradition?

3.3 *Black Mountains Smokery (Black Mountains Smokery 2021)*

The final example is Black Mountains Smokery, a family-owned smokery business with 12 core staff in Wales (https://www.smoked-foods.co.uk/). They have received the Gold Star Great Taste Award for many of their products and have had much press coverage, including with Kate Humble and the Guild of Fine Foods. They use language on their website to create an image of artisan, such as 'Welsh artisan food,' 'traditional' and 'we now work closely with many like-minded artisan family producers, mostly Welsh, many local'.

1. **Limited quantities**

They use sustainable fish and high-quality meat; the narrative on their website would suggest that they supply quantities sufficient for wholesale and retail: they supply chefs, caterers, cafés, farm shops and delis, the local rural community and a 'very loyal, ever-increasing customer base further afield'. They also work with other artisan producers in the area, demonstrating community value, a characteristic not mentioned in the artisan definition, but highlighted in the cases. However, these facts suggest that their production is not in limited quantities, and again no specific data was available.

2. **By skilled craftspeople**

Black Mountains Smokery highlights how the quality of the products is reliant on the skill of the smoker, describing the importance of timing and temperatures, care taken, and the traditionality of the craft, therefore demonstrating skilful expertise.

3. **The processing method is not fully mechanised and follows a traditional method**

The craft of smoking and curing itself is traditional, but instead of being for preservation, the narrative on the website explains that it is for taste enhancement. They do, however, use modern custom-built kilns; whilst the traditional craft has been active in the area for over 30 years as a preserving technique, the use of modern kilns does not satisfy the definition of traditional in its purest sense, again questioning the description of artisan in the context of requiring innovation in processing.

4. **The food is made in a micro-enterprise at a single location**

The fish and meat come from other areas, but processing is completed at the smokery. With just over ten employees, they exceed the definition of a micro-enterprise.

5. **The characteristic ingredient(s) used are grown or produced locally, where seasonally available and practical**

Whilst the producers have detailed product provenance, the salmon are sustainably farmed in Shetland, the sea fish are Marine Stewardship Council (MSC) certified from the North Sea, and the Red Tractor duck and chicken can come from anywhere in the UK; only the sausages are from Crickhowell, a local butcher, the cheeses from Wales, and the oak shavings used for smoking are Welsh. Thus, many of the characteristic ingredients come from more than 100 km away. The question is whether it would be practical to source these raw ingredients more locally, but as they are not traditional products for Wales, this may be tricky. As they have local ingredient options that would arguably provide a more authentic product, such as John Dory, Mackerel, grey mullet, and lamb, fulfilling this part of the artisan definition is possible without compromising the niche feeling of the product. Again, the FSAI criteria cannot be used to define what it is for food to be artisan here, but the four Ps fit this business well.

In summary, as the business has innovated their business model to provide a wider choice for their customers, this creates a challenge to provide artisan food in totality. Other businesses they work with are creating innovative foods that blend the traditional with the 'gourmet'. For example, their shop includes Welsh Tea, where the tea is sourced from Assam and China. Products in their shop, which would be commonly described by consumers as artisan (their products are niche, expensive, not everyday food consumables), and their identity as a family business, with an emphasis on flavour and sustainability, support this blending. Their emphasis is also on 'service', developing relational trust with the customer. This idea of value creation by storytelling, creating a relationship of trust, both systemic and personal, surely also kindles this feeling of traditional values, and perhaps what it is to be artisan. Questions arising from this case study include the following:

(a) How necessary is it for the raw ingredients to be sourced in the local area for a food or the producer of that food to be termed artisan?
(b) Should the relationship created with the customers be a criterion within the artisan food/producer definition?
(c) Should wider community value be a consideration for artisan food/producers?
(d) Should the definition also include luxury goods/niche products as suggested by some authors, even if they are not local?
(e) Does the producer have to be a micro-enterprise to be termed artisan?

These three case studies show the innovative ways in which these businesses have positioned themselves, their processes and their products to 'stand out'; yet, can the businesses themselves all be defined as 'artisan'?

4 Concluding Thoughts

In the literature, there is evidence of increasing demand for artisan food as consumers search for the 'authentic', through 'a desire to purify and to cleanse—the body, the mind and the soul' (Collinson 2018, p. 39). The profligate nature of western societies, i.e. a situation of "peak stuff" in the early 2000s, has been in decline (Goodall 2011), and there is a greater emphasis on health, planet and experiences. Artisan food, therefore, has a role beyond nutritional access in many countries and provides a strong driver for food economies and emergent requirements for addressing concerns over resource use and environmental impacts of products. One of the case studies, kid meat was an innovation that came from this concern, and the business model focused specifically on innovative ways to improve circularity.

In Europe, artisan food is a vital part of the rural economy and culture in some countries, e.g. Spain (Escurriol Martinez et al. 2014). Artisan food is available in European towns through the development and embedding of alternative food networks (Martindale et al. 2018), with emphasis on local food specialities and identity (Parrott et al. 2002). In the UK, the contemporary role of artisan food is more limited. As well as being seen through an economic lens, the local food movement can be seen through a political focus. Part of the strength of the local food movement is rooted in notions of artisan food being more environmentally friendly and anti-capitalist, favouring small producers and marginal areas, promoting food sovereignty and creating greater connection between locality and food quality (Fonte 2010). The support for local food can redefine food consumption as an expression of citizenship that speaks of collective rights and responsibilities (Lockie 2009). This suggests a form of neoliberal consumer action where consumers use their consumption choices and food decisions as expressions of social agency or citizenship (Fonte 2010; Guthman 2007).

Attributes such as 'authentic' can be real or constructed stories or narratives (Collinson 2018) that are based on aspects of food heritage and, in part, can prove misleading. The case studies show the narratives that frame the foods, reflecting the traditional, luxury and gourmet. None of the case studies fulfil all the FSAI requirements for being traditionally artisan, with the increased scale of production and their markets developing being a common theme. The three case studies here show businesses that have arguably grown beyond the micro-scale, drawing a wider customer base by word of mouth, social media, food festivals and marketing. This demonstrates how rigid the FSAI criteria are, leading us to question whether such rigidity is necessary for describing what it is to be artisan. What is evident though is that it is the aspects of product quality and tradition (whether an historic tradition or a developing, new emergent perception of tradition) rather than the production methods that are more prominent in the narrative associated with artisan food production. The case studies also explore flavour and taste as essential elements of artisan food, as well as the building of food networks and community involvement with that network. This is interesting with the emphasis on tradition and heritage.

Considering the craft aspects of artisan food and the making of food with specific organoleptic qualities or with creative passion, artisan food can be said to be both innovative and traditional at the same time. The innovation can be in recipe design, processing techniques or business model. The traditional aspect is in the storytelling associated with the food and the embedded authenticity associated with the product, place, people, processes, personality and passion. The passion can be intrinsic in the food and can address multiple features of the product.

In order to be 'artisan', the local production and attachment to people and time, often summarised as heritage, need to be visible and addressed in the narrative around the artisan food. This narrative can be delivered on the packaging, in associated leaflets, or on the company website and social media. This narrative adds to the physical eating experience with a cognitive experience associated with the food's source and producers. What it is to be 'artisan' can be objectively defined in part, but other aspects are subjectively linked to the creative and often gourmet aspects of the food. Returning to the chapter's question, '*Can artisan food be innovative and traditional at the same time?*', we can conclude that this is not only possible but also necessary as emerging ideas and consumer requirements frame and reframe what it is to be an artisan food or producer.

References

Ashkenazy A, Calvão Chebach T, Knickel K, Peter S, Horowitz B, Offenbach R (2018) Operationalising resilience in farms and rural regions – findings from fourteen case studies. J Rural Stud 59:211–221

Azavedo M, Walsh JC (2019) A comparative study of artisanal food producers' motivations in Western Australia and Thailand. Acta Universitas Danubius 15(3):76–89

Black Mountains Smokery (2021). https://www.smoked-foods.co.uk/ Accessed 01 June 2021

Blundel R (2002) Network evolution and the growth of artisanal firms: a tale of two regional cheese makers. Entrep Reg Dev 14(1):1–30

Bowen S, De Master K (2014) Wisconsin's "happy cows"? Articulating heritage and territory as new dimensions of locality. Agric Hum Values 31(4):549–562

Caricofe EE (2011) Handcrafting the change they want to eat in the world? An inquiry into the who, what and why of artisanal food production in Central Ohio. Master's Thesis. Ohio State University, Ohio

Collinson P (2018) Consuming traditions: artisan food and food tourism in Western Ireland. In: Medina AFX, Tresserras J (eds) Food, gastronomy and tourism social and cultural perspectives. Universidad de Guadalajara, Guadalajara, pp 31–48

Cotswold Kid Meat (2021). https://cotswoldkidmeat.com/. Accessed 01 June 2021

Danby G (2015, May 28) 'Artisan' and 'natural' defined – but is Ireland taking a step in the right direction? | Artisan Food Law Blog. Artisan Food Law. http://www.artisanfoodlaw.co.uk/blog/brand-protection/'artisan'-and-'natural'-defined---but-is-ireland-taking-step-in-right

Dann GMS, Jacobsen JKS (2009) The tourist as a metaphor of the social world. In: Dann GMS (ed) Leading to tourist by the nost. CABI, Wallingford, pp 209–235

Darnhofer I, Strauss A (2015) Rethink: rethinking the links between farm modernization, rural development and resilience in a world of increasing demands and finite resources: Organic farming and resilience case study report. http://citeseerx.ist.psu.edu/viewdoc/download?doi=10.1.1.705.7470&rep=rep1&type=pdf

De Clerq D, Voronov M (2009) Toward a practice perspective of entrepreneurship. Entrepreneurial legitimacy as habitus. Int Small Bus J 27(4):395–419

Desmarais A (2003) The via Campesina: peasant women at the Frontiers of food sovereignty. Can Woman Stud 23(1) https://cws.journals.yorku.ca/index.php/cws/article/view/6372

Dunn M, Wright A (2017) Irish local and artisan foods: multiples make space! Cogent Bus Manag 4:1–16

Escurriol Martinez V, Binimelis R, Rivera-ferre MG (2014) The situation of rural women in Spain: the case of small-scale artisan food producers. Historia editorial Abstract

Felzensztein C, Gimmon E, Carter S (2010) Geographical co-location, social networks and inter-firm marketing co-operation: the case of the salmon industry. Long Range Plan 43 (5–6):675–690

Fonte M (2010) Introduction: food relocalisation and knowledge dynamics for sustainability in rural areas. In: Fonte M, Papadopoulos A (eds) Naming food after places: food Relocalisation and knowledge dynamics in rural development. Routledge, New York, pp 1–38. https://www.book2look.com/embed/9781317090762

FSAI (2015) Guidance Note No. 29: the use of food marketing terms, p 3. Food Safety Authority of Ireland. https://www.fsai.ie/news_centre/press_releases/marketing_terms_14052015.html

Goodall C (2011) "Peak Stuff" Did the UK reach a maximum use of material resources in the early part of the last decade? 1. http://static.squarespace.com/static/545e40d0e4b054a6f8622bc9/t/54720c6ae4b06f326a8502f9/1416760426697/Peak_Stuff_17.10.11.pdf

Gralton A, Vanclay F (2009) Artisanality and culture in innovative regional agri-food development: lessons from the Tasmanian artisanal food industry. Int J Foresight Innov Policy 5(1–3, 193):–204

Grimes K, Milgram L (eds) (2000) Artisans and cooperatives: developing alternative trade for the global economy. The University of Arizona Press, Tucson. https://uapress.arizona.edu/book/artisans-and-cooperatives

Guthman J (2007) Commentary on teaching food: why i am fed up with Michael Pollan et al. Agric Hum Values 24:261–264

Hall M, Gössling S (eds) (2016) Food tourism and regional development: networks, products and trajectories, 1st edn. Routledge, New York. https://www.routledge.com/Food-Tourism-and-Regional-Development-Networks-products-and-trajectories/Hall-Gossling/p/book/9781138592414

Jackson P (2013) Food words: essays in culinary culture, 1st edn. Bloomsbury Academic. https://www.bloomsbury.com/uk/food-words-9780857851956/

Leroy F, Geyzen A, Janssens M, De Vuyst L, Scholliers P (2013) Meat fermentation at the crossroads of innovation and tradition: a historical outlook. Trends Food Sci Technol 31 (2):130–137

Lockie S (2009) Responsibility and agency within alternative food networks: assembling the "citizen consumer.". Agric Hum Values 26(3):193–201

Lotti A (2010) The commoditization of products and taste: slow food and the conservation of agrobiodiversity. Agric Hum Values 27(1):71–83

Maidment J, Macfarlane S (2011) Crafting communities: promoting inclusion, empowerment, and learning between older women. Aust Soc Work 64(3):283–298

Martindale L, Matacena R, Beacham J (2018) Varieties of alterity: alternative food networks in the UK, Italy and China. In: Sociologia Urbana e Rurale, vol 115. Franco Angeli Edizioni, Milan, pp 27–41

McKitterick L, Quinn B, McAdam R, Dunn A (2016) Innovation networks and the institutional actor-producer relationship in rural areas: the context of artisan food production. J Rural Stud 48:41–52

Metaxas T, Karagiannis D (2016) Culinary tourism in Greece: can the past define the future? Dimensions of innovation, entrepreneurship and regional development. J Dev Entrep 21 (03):1650018

Murray F (1987) Flexible specialisation in the 'Third Italy.'. Cap Class 11(3):84–95

O'Neill KJ (2014) Situating the "alternative" within the "conventional" - local food experiences from the east riding of Yorkshire, UK. J Rural Stud 35:112–122

Oledinma A, Roper S (2021) Tradition (re-)defined: farm v factory trade-offs in the definition of geographical indications, the case of three counties Cider. J Rural Stud 84:12–21

Parrott N, Wilson N, Murdoch J (2002) Spatializing quality: regional protection and the alternative geography of food. Eur Urban Reg Stud 9(3):241–261

Quinn B, Seaman C (2019) Artisan food production, small family business and the Scottish food paradox. In: Nutrition and food science, vol 49. Emerald Group Publishing, Bingley, pp 455–463

Ramadani V, Hisrich RD, Dana L-P, Palalic R, Panthi L (2019) Beekeeping as a family artisan entrepreneurship business. Int J Entrep Behav Res 25(4):717–730

Ruiz-Cano D, Pérez-Llamas F, López-Jiménez JÁ, González-Silvera D, Frutos MJ, Zamora S (2013) Caracterización y valor nutritivo de un alimento artesanal: El pastel de carne de Murcia. Nutricion Hospitalaria 28(4):1300–1305

Smith SLJ, Xiao H (2008) Culinary tourism supply chains: a preliminary examination. J Travel Res 46:289–299

Storper M, Salais R (eds) (1997) Worlds of production: the action frameworks of the economy (Illustrated, revised). Harvard University Press, Cambridge. https://books.google.co.uk/books?id=tFLBbGgE8TsC&lr=&source=gbs_navlinks_s

Teagasc (2017) Artisan food industry in Ireland - Teagasc | Agriculture and Food Development Authority. Artisan Food Industry in Ireland, Teagasc. https://www.teagasc.ie/rural-economy/rural-development/artisan-food/artisan-food-industry-in-ireland/

Testa, R., Galati, A., Schifiani, G., Di Trapani, A. M., & Migliore, G. (2019). Culinary tourism experiences in agri-tourism destination and sustainable consumption—understanding Italian Tourists' motivations. Sustainability 11(4588). file:///C:/Users/sophi/Downloads/sustainability-11-04588-v2.pdf
The School of Artisan Food (2021) What is Artisan Food | The School of Artisan Food - The School Of Artisan Foods. What Is Artisan Food? https://www.schoolofartisanfood.org/page/what-is-artisan-food
Thompson CJ, Kumar A (2018) Beyond consumer responsibilization: slow food's actually existing neoliberalism. J Consum Cult
Wild Irish Harvest (2021). https://wildirishseaweeds.com/. Accessed 01 June 2021
Wyshak S (2014) Good food, great business: how to take your artisan food idea from concept . . . - Susie Wyshak - Google books. Chronicle Books. https://books.google.co.uk/books?id=d-kAp7tw0lYC&dq=artisan+food&lr=&source=gbs_navlinks_s

Sophia Lingham is a PhD researcher at the Royal Agricultural University, UK. Her research focuses on the socio-economic aspects of food networks and food SMEs.

Inge Hill is Senior Lecturer in Business Strategy and the Royal Agricultural University and lead for contributions to NICRE, the National Innovation Centre for Rural Enterprise. Her research interests are entrepreneurship-as-practice research and creative industries.

Louise Manning is Professor of Agri-food and Supply Chain Security and Director of Knowledge Exchange at the Royal Agricultural University, UK. Her areas of research are the socio-technical, environmental and economic aspects of food supply.

Enterprise Culture in Art: Artist-Entrepreneur Graham McKean

Robert Smith

Abstract There is a growing appreciation of the 'aesthetic' dimensions of enterprise culture and the power of artisanal entrepreneurship as a driving force in local economies and enterprise cultures, but despite a growing body of research on the topic, there is little research on how 'artisans' operationalise their business models to extract value from their environments. This is important because many artisanal businesses do not at first glance appear to follow the classic entrepreneurial business model and aesthetics, nor do 'artisans' adopt an obvious entrepreneurial identity. We see them as artists, artistes and creatives, not as entrepreneurs, because we focus on the artisanal aspects of their businesses. In this chapter, I examine the business model of the Scottish artist Graham McKean and establish that as well as being an artist he is also a shrewd artist-entrepreneur attuned to the nuances of his localised enterprise culture and that his art also captures and commodifies the unique enterprise culture of 'Glasgow' and the 'South of Scotland' area and its masculine characterisation. The men are portrayed as heroic individuals and resonate with corporate and entrepreneurial mythology. Using semiotic analysis, this study examines a selected strand of his artistic output and identifies how artistic tropes such as caricature, meme and parody can be used to depict and sell visual aspects of 'success' and 'enterprise culture' and how enterprise becomes infused into the artisanal business.

1 Introducing the Illustrative Case Study of Graham McKean

There is a growing appreciation of the 'aesthetic' dimensions of enterprise culture and the power of artisanal entrepreneurship as a driving force in local economies and enterprise cultures (Rivetti and Migliaccio 2018; Andrews 2020; Roberts 2017; Elias et al. 2018; Mitra 2020), but despite a growing body of research on the topic, there is little research on how 'artisans' operationalise their business models to 'extract value' from their environments (Anderson 1995). This is important because many

R. Smith (✉)
Aberdeen, UK

L.-P. Dana et al. (eds.), *Artisan and Handicraft Entrepreneurs*, Contributions to Management Science, https://doi.org/10.1007/978-3-030-82303-0_7

artisanal businesses do not at first glance appear to follow the classic entrepreneurial business model and aesthetics, nor do 'artisans' adopt an obvious entrepreneurial identity. Instead, we see them as artists, artistes and creatives, not as entrepreneurs, because we focus on the artisanal aspects of their businesses. Indeed, the overarching characteristic of the 'artisan entrepreneur' such as artists, actors, authors and musicians is that they 'work with their hands' and are masters of their 'craft'. Although the topic of the 'craftsman entrepreneur' (Smith 1967) has featured in entrepreneurship studies, the artisanal entrepreneur, like other creative types such as the 'Impresario' (Inverne 2001), has not been given the research profile they deserve.[1]

The genesis of this chapter began, in the summer of 2017, when I first encountered the art of Scottish artist and entrepreneur Graham McKean (see https://www.graham-mckean.co.uk) via viewing his celebrated painting '*A Captain of Industry*'. It was hanging in a meeting room in an Aberdeen hotel appropriately entitled the 'Board Room', and the portrait dominated the room, demanding attention. The painting obviously parodied the genre of conventional 'CEO Portraits' (see Guthey and Jackson 2005; Davidson 2010; Acevedo 2014; Schnugg and Lehner 2016). This viewing made an immediate aesthetic impact on me and led to subsequent internet searches locating McKean's website and the decision to download other examples of his work and led to the compilation of the gallery presented below and the subsequent analysis. Graham McKean is one of Scotland's most celebrated living artists whose work is immediately recognisable and eminently collectable. His works capture the essence of 'working class' Scotland, and critics have praised it for its humour, romanticism and chivalry and because it captures the 'feelgood factor'. As well as being an artist and artisan of renown, he is also a shrewd businessman, entrepreneur and charitable philanthropist, as will be demonstrated in this chapter. This chapter is intended both to highlight a talented artisan and as a case study of how an artisan can also legitimately be regarded as a serious entrepreneur. As such, it is an illustrative case study (Yin 2014). A secondary problem is to illustrate the complexity of artisanal entrepreneurship, where the entrepreneurial identity of the artisan is closely connected with their craft and outputs.

There is also a theoretical element to this study, and to situate the study within the appropriate entrepreneurship literature, a brief theoretical discussion is articulated to underpin and inform the analysis of the images. This is followed by a discussion of the visual semiotic methodologies of photoelicitation and photomontage, used to analyse and make sense of the portraits and gendered entrepreneurial identities. The analysis of the images is separated into masculine and feminine themes. The findings demonstrate that the gendered representations of men and women in the art are markedly different in nature. The men are portrayed as heroic individuals, and the imagery resonates with corporate and entrepreneurial mythology. This research illustrates how artistic tropes such as caricature, parody and meme can be used to depict visual aspects of entrepreneurial identity that cannot be captured via the written word.

---

[1] Indeed, they are entrepreneurs by another name.

2 Introducing the Context and Literature of 'Artisanal-Entrepreneurship'

In this section, I consider three separate aspects of the literature, which are important in relation to understanding and theorising artisanal entrepreneurship and the specifics of the embedded case study of the artist Graham McKean. The three relevant areas are (1) the expanding literature on artisanal entrepreneurship; (2) arts entrepreneurship and the aesthetic dimension; and (3) the aesthetics of entrepreneurial identity. An understanding of these is necessary to better understand McKean as an artist and entrepreneur.

2.1 Exploring the Literature of Artisanal Entrepreneurship

There is a growing appreciation in the academic literature of the sub-genre of 'craft-based entrepreneurship' (Smith 1967), the 'artisan-entrepreneur' and 'artisanal entrepreneurship' (Hoyte 2018; Ferreira et al. 2019; Pret and Cogan 2019; Ratten et al. 2019; Crowley 2019; Solomon-Blake and Mathias 2020), and accordingly, there is an expanding literature with special issues and calls such as this on for book chapters on the topic. Indeed, in terms of entrepreneurial identity, the 'artisan-entrepreneur' has a specific identity normally based on their particular art form and industry standards and as a result they usually identify themselves as artists, sculptures, potters etc., and not entrepreneurs per se. Many actively reject entrepreneurial identity in favour of one more aligned to the creative sector. This is exacerbated by the fact that in the past artisanal entrepreneurship has been associated with subsistence type entrepreneurship and small/micro business (Pret and Cogan 2019) and with a specific creative personality type centred around four personality-based identity positions or dimensions: cultural heritage, community entrepreneurship, craftsmanship and innovation (Hoyte 2018).[2] According to Ratten et al. (2019), this interest is based upon an appreciation of the role artisan entrepreneurship has in revitalising economies and in placing emphasis on cultural heritage and traditions. However, Solomon-Blake and Mathias (2020) stress that artisan-entrepreneurs can grow their businesses through adopting recent technological and social changes such as the internet and e-commerce platforms, which have the potential to empower them and render them highly entrepreneurial and also by embracing their counter-institutional entrepreneurial identities. For Solomon and Mathias, artisans' counter-institutional identity contains two sides—promoting the exclusion of 'who we are not' (and thus oppositional identity) or providing support for 'who we are' (and thus relational identity). For Crowley (2019), 'artisanal entrepreneurship'

[2] Indeed, we are all of us familiar with the stereotype of the tragic, impoverished artist who inhabits their studios and who cares more for their art than for fame or fortune (Rivlin 2018). The artist as a tragic hero resonates and feeds into the heroism of entrepreneurial mythology.

involves the marketing of creative assets and products closely linked to manual creation and to place and tradition. Crowley argues that much research to date on artisan entrepreneurs has focused on micro and meso levels and not on macro behavioural aspects. In a similar vein, Hill (2020) argues that successful artisans engage in context-dependent collaborative business solutions, which emerge from the interplay of the materiality of buildings, social relations management and personal resources such as their entrepreneurial social capital. From the literature, two contrasting types emerge—'the artisan-as a-tragic hero' and the 'artisan-entrepreneur'. I now turn to consider the topics of arts entrepreneurship and its aesthetic dimension.

2.2 *Arts Entrepreneurship and the Aesthetic Dimension*

Also, of interest are the concepts of 'arts entrepreneurship' and the 'aesthetics of entrepreneurship' (Rivetti and Migliaccio 2018; Andrews 2020; Roberts 2017; Elias et al. 2018; Mitra 2020). These form recognisable sub-literatures. According to Rivetti and Migliaccio, the literature of arts and entrepreneurship require to be disentangled for practitioners to make the most use of them in practical art-based settings. According to Elias et al. (2018), customers play a fundamental role in the entrepreneurial creation processes, particularly for artisans, but little is known about how value emerges from interactions and collaborations between entrepreneurs and, importantly, their customers. Nevertheless, there is a relational, embodied process whereby entrepreneurs and their customers interact to co-create 'aesthetic value'. For Elias et al. this entails three interrelated processes: imagining, contemplating and consensus building. Although customers play a vital role throughout the entrepreneurial creation process, neither the entrepreneur nor the customer has the final say; rather, their embodied experiences combine with an evolving product to co-create a particular commodified, 'aesthetic value' (Elias et al. 2018). According to Mitra (2020), an inexorable pursuit of economic gain has ushered in fashionable, entrepreneurial manoeuvres in the arts resulting in an increased awareness of the creative industries and of the process of 'creative industrialisation' that encourages a new market logic and notions of entrepreneurial value to an otherwise dependent culture of the arts. Entrepreneurship is imbued with the heroism of being able to 'rescue' the 'failing' arts. Such applications of market logic can ignore the multivalence of entrepreneurship or the rich textures of meaning provided by the arts, different forms of value creation in entrepreneurship and the creative entrepreneurial dimensions in the arts.

However, there are constraints in adopting a market logic approach. Mitra suggests that creative latitude can be found in the meaning of entrepreneurship as '... the mobilisation of the resources of imagination' (Mitra 2020). For Roberts (2017), there are no clear definitions of entrepreneurship and art, albeit there are definite processual connections. This makes it difficult to theorise arts entrepreneurship education. Roberts argues that many artists lack business skills but can learn and acquire these via 'arts entrepreneurship education' programmes. Such programmes combine business and aesthetic skill sets that are needed to make a living as an artist.[3] Other skills gaps identified include financial, business management, and entrepreneurship skills. For Roberts, artists (such as McKean) who acquire business skill sets have a higher probability of success making a living practicing their art form whilst benefitting from its commodification. There is also a practical, pragmatic basis in the literature. For example, Andrews (2020) in his handbook 'Arts Entrepreneurship' has drafted a hands-on guide to entrepreneurial success for those involved in the 'arts' and the 'creative' sectors. It offers a valuable resource for students and early-stage business founders in the creative sector looking for guidance on how to create and sustain their own successful venture, including chapters on arts entrepreneurship, planning and assessment, marketing, fundraising, legal issues, money management and entrepreneurial finance, organisational design and career development. It provides the essential tools, techniques and concepts needed to invent, launch and sustain a business in the creative sector. This is important because the artist can learn entrepreneurial and business skills in a similar manner to how they learnt their artistic skills. I now turn to consider how the 'arts-based' aesthetics can influence entrepreneurial identity.

2.3 *Considering the Aesthetics of Entrepreneurial Identity*

Among entrepreneurship scholars, it is now becoming accepted that entrepreneurial identities are understood to be differentiated by context and gender (Bruni et al. 2004; Mavin and Grandy 2012; Marlow 2014). Importantly, these entrepreneurial identities can be broadcast visually via artefactual and sartorial imagery, including art and in particular portraits. According to Davidson (2010), visual portraits of the business élite are widely disseminated and form significant sites for communicating messages associated with intellectual, symbolic and social research. Indeed, CEO portraiture conveys and communicates a sense of authenticity, charisma, identity and status that we associate primarily with masculinity. It could be argued that this masculine aura even extends to parodies of such art bringing artistic tropes such as caricature, meme and parody into play re-creating idealised, stereotypical representation (of gendered corporate imagery as depicted in the art).

It is widely accepted that masculinity and in particular masculine identity, behaviours and values are the dominant norm (Lewis 2006; Hamilton 2013) and thus dominant aesthetic. So much so, that entrepreneurship is primarily equated with the masculine leading Hamilton (2014) to refer to the '*discourse of entrepreneurial masculinity*'. Nevertheless, feminist attributes can be expressed within

[3] For example, consider the 'Coleman Fellows Program', which provides an opportunity to test the arts entrepreneurship theory constructs.

entrepreneurial identity (Orser et al. 2011), albeit entrepreneurship and its ideals resonate with some women, but not others. Indeed, Orser et al. (2011) argue that some female entrepreneurs try hard to avoid being identified as different from the masculine norm of entrepreneurship. Moreover, the discourses of womanhood and motherhood (and also artisanship) may conflict with the ideology of entrepreneurship (Díaz García and Welter 2013). As a result, women (and indeed artisans) may and do construct their identities differently depending on the context in '*doing gender*' (Bruni et al. 2004; Mavin and Grandy 2012; Palalic et al. 2017). Gender is 'done' through simultaneous, multiple enactments of femininity and masculinity, which are often exaggerated, idealised expressions of both masculinity and femininity (Mavin and Grandy 2012). Also, it is accepted that men and women do gender differently, as gendered practices are influenced by different symbolic places and practices, including gender commodification (Bruni et al. 2004). For Hamilton (2014), there is a double epistemological and ontological shift in play whereby differentiated gendered identity is co-constituted and located in repertoires of historically and culturally situated narrative (and arguably imagery).

Additionally, Marlow (2014, 2020) made a call for research that challenges the status quo, including gendered representations of female entrepreneurs and for research that advances our understanding thereof. Moreover, Marlow (2014) stressed that there is scope to add to existing knowledge, particularly by employing discrete gender critiques to inform a broader and far-reaching appraisal of the entrepreneurial project dominating the contemporary socio-economic context. I argue that this includes the artistic and visual. Additionally, Marlow also stressed the over-emphasis on studies relating to the business domain. This is important because, according to Max and Ballereau (2013), the gender aspect of entrepreneurship is essentially socio-psychological in nature, and as such, it transcends the domain of work and thus, it could also be argued consideration of representations in art. Also of interest is that the methodologies used have invariably been content and narrative analysis, which rely heavily on the written word, not the visual. Notwithstanding the points discussed above, there have been no studies focusing specifically on representations of entrepreneurial identity in visual mediums, including paintings and/or portraits. In imagery associated with masculinity, entrepreneurship and success, the business suit predominates as a signifier of hegemonic masculinity, success and status (see Barry 2018; Barry and Weiner 2019). Modern Western society has framed fashion in opposition to hegemonic masculinity (Barry 2018) and fashion and (re)fashioning function as a principal means by which men's visible gender identities are established, situated and thus differentiated.

3 Methodology

The choice of methodological approaches in researching gendered representations of entrepreneurship is important (Henry et al. 2016). Moreover, the methodologies used to date have been primarily qualitative in nature and can be categorised as 'discrete forms of critique'. By its very nature, because it is based on a single case, the choice of approach was guided by case study methodology. For Groenland and Dana (2019), a core element of case studies lies in the explaining of a phenomenon from the context in which it takes place. It is clearly an empirical inquiry that investigated the works of McKean as a contemporary phenomenon in-depth and within his real-life context, as articulated by Yin (2009, p. 18). In addition, it offers a contextualised explanation of a specific artisanal business environment (Tsang 2013). It also adopts a comprehensive approach located in an inductive, constructivist paradigm (Dana and Dumez 2015). According to Jännäri and Kovalainen (2015), the research methodologies adopted in '*doing gender*' mostly deal with interview data and their analysis. Thus, interview data is used most often as the primary source for ethnographic analysis. This can limit the potential interpretations available for the analysis of the conceptual idea in question. Jännäri and Kovalainen made a call for under-represented studies using naturally occurring data, which must obviously include visual data such as art. Consequentially, the purpose of this study is not to conduct an overly theorised study of the portraits presented but to use the art and imagery itself to illustrate extant themes in the gendered literature of entrepreneurship in a novel way, via semiotics as a discrete form of critique. This necessitated presenting the images using photoelicitation (Harper 2002) and photomontage techniques (Berger and Mohr 1975, 1982; Dillon 2004; Zervigón 2012) to identify common stereotypical representations, archetypes, memes (Dawkins 1976) and themes to expand the body of archetypal gendered entrepreneurial (and often pejorative) stereotypes. Photoelicitation permits the recording of responses to images, attributing their social and personal meanings and values (Harper 2002). It also permits a collective story to emerge from and across the montage images.

A search of the internet located the images presented below. Permission was sought and granted from the artist himself to use the images presented. The images were subjected to a semiotic analysis and examined for visual cues and in particular gendered artefacts and clothing (Chandler 2001) including the sartorial. These were then subjected to a coding process (as per Table 1). Following the methodology of Davidson (2010), a framework consisting of four sets of rhetorical codes in portraiture, namely, *physical, dress, spatial and interpersonal*, were applied to organise and analyse the data as visible visual rhetoric (Davidson 2014). Davidson also utilised a framework incorporating four types of visual repetition—identity, similarity, accumulation and series. The two frameworks were merged to help interpret the data. It must be stressed that the analysis and interpretations that emerged from this visual reading as presented below are those of the author and do not represent any perceived intentions of the artist Graham McKean. Readers are strongly encouraged to peruse the images and form their own interpretations and to check out other images and outputs produced by McKean.

4 Presenting the Case for McKean as an Artisanal Entrepreneur

Graham McKean is an established, renowned and respected, contemporary Scottish Artist who lives and works in the Scottish seaside town of Ayr, out of his business premises—WASP studios. Ayr is a seaside town in the county of Ayrshire and is situated in the South West of Scotland, which is part of the wider Strathclyde Council Area. McKean has a long connection to business and particularly with male-dominated working-class industries and was also formerly employed as a commercial graphic artist prior to becoming a freelance artist and as such is no stranger to the corporate business world. Indeed, there are evident, overarching themes of commerce and work running through his impressionistic body of art. The artworks of Graham McKean form part of the contemporary Scottish art scene / Scottish School of Artists and as such are very collectable in their own right. The Scottish School includes other famous artists such as Jack Vettriano.

McKean's unique style is influenced by the tropes of caricature, meme and parody. He draws inspiration from street scenes and his surroundings. His paintings are also artistic products that are sold, exhibited as valuable, collectable items. It could be argued that McKean himself is an entrepreneur in his own right, making his artistic interpretations authentic and valid. As an art entrepreneur, McKean co-creates '*aesthetic value*' with his customer base (as suggested by Elias et al. 2018). Thus, his portraits as products must be viewed as interactions and collaborations between himself and his customers, achieved via the processes of imagining, contemplating and consensus building (ala Elias et al. 2018). McKean articulates that he draws inspiration from everyday street scenes in his 'hometown' of Ayr and in the wider Glasgow/Strathclyde area. His artistic process is to sketch ideas in pencil on lined-graph paper before painting them in oils or pastels. His paintings could be said to possess a 'South-West-of-Scotland cultural aesthetic'. It is of note that the 'West of Scotland' and 'Central Belt' areas of Scotland have a history and heritage of being part of industrialised Scotland. His paintings could therefore be said to possess an industrialised/urbanised aesthetic. In analysing McKean's business model, it is necessary to consider him as McKean the man (with all the gendered nuances that entails because his art is framed in a masculine gaze); McKean the artist (his collective body of work/portfolio); McKean the artiste (in respect of his public and media appearances); and also McKean the businessman/entrepreneur. These could all be used as separate strands of analysis. He is often commissioned by businesses to paint themed portraits for their boardrooms and makes a living by selling original pieces and signed prints. His original works fetch thousands at auction and are featured in numerous art galleries. The images discussed possess an aesthetic dimension and an 'aesthetic value'. As this article relates to a semiotic analysis of his selected works, there is atypically no guiding research question, only a resultant critique. The 'artisanal' business model adopted by McKean is important in identifying him as an artist-entrepreneur. See Fig. 1.

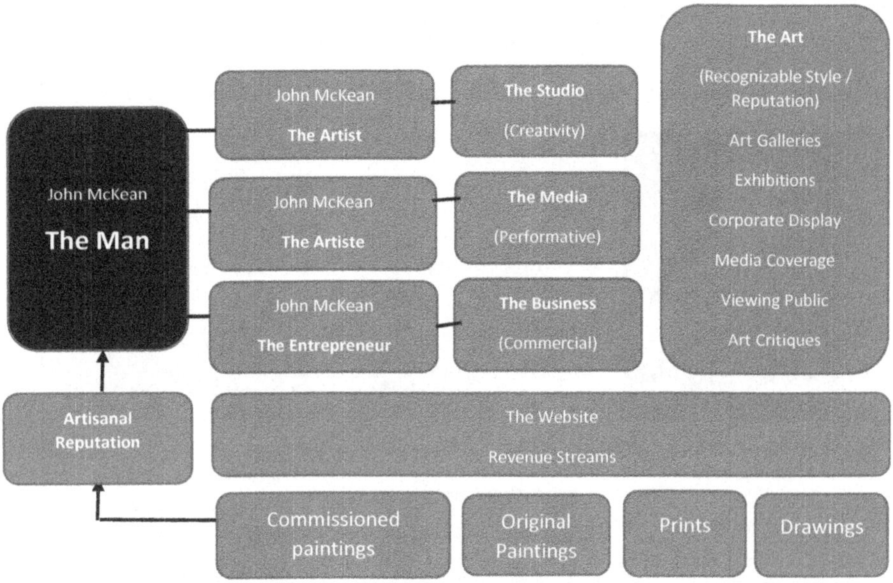

Fig. 1 The artisanal business model of Graham McKean

It is clear from the figure that McKean's business model is a highly nuanced entrepreneurial model and not the typical laissez-faire, artisanal model. McKean's body of work covers several major themes of which the corporate aesthetic is but one. His other themes include the characters from the whisky industry and feminine forms, and it is important to note that being an artist and entrepreneur he will inevitably paint what sells.

5 Findings (from the Empirical Data)

The gallery presented below contains 21 selected images. It is pertinent that the portraits presented are not normally viewed in such close proximity to each other and are usually hung individually or in small lots at exhibitions, art galleries or private collections. Collectively these portraits of business life paint a powerful imagery. The analysis is conducted in the form of a semiotic critique (Chandler 2001).

5.1 Analysing the Masculine Imagery

M1 "A Captain of Industry".

M2 "Another Captain of Industry".

M3 "Architect of Dreams".

M4 "City Banker".

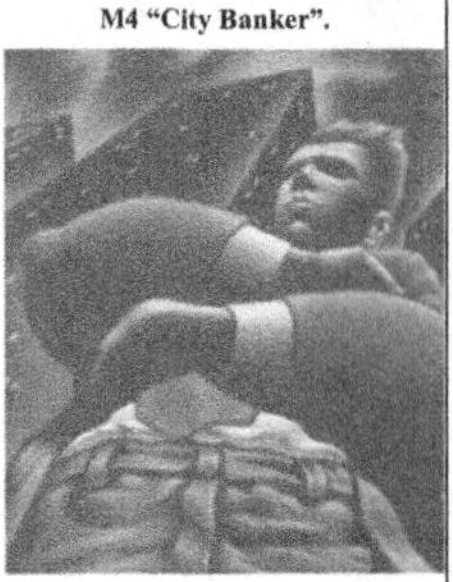

M5 "Nine till Five".

M6 "20th Century" or "Dignity".

M7 "The Road Ahead".

M8 "From Humble Beginnings" or "The Tree of Good Fortune".

M9 "The Man Who Made It".

Gallery 1 Appreciating the masculine aesthetic and entrepreneurial success

M10 "Life in the Fast Lane". 	**M11 "The Speculator".** 	**M12 The Bread Winner".** 
M13 "Desperadoes". 	M14 "Slaves to the Dollar". 	M15 "Chasing the Dream". 
M16 The Man Who Tried To Turn The Tide". 	**M17 "The entrepreneur" or "The Apprentice".** 	**M18 "Pillars of Destiny".** 
M19 "The Man Who Always Looked Forward". 	**M20 "The winning share".** 	M21 **"Financial Times"/"No Regrets".** 

It is obvious that the male figure chosen by McKean is representative of the typical male and that it is the same basic image in each portrait that takes on the form of the heroic clean-shaven corporate man. Image M1 is an obvious satirical/stereotypical parody of the genre of figurative '*CEO Portraits*'. As such, it is a heroic representation of '*Heroic Entrepreneurship*' (Drakopoulou and Anderson 2007) in visual form. Note the folded arms, the sombre confident facial features, square set jaw, the focused stare and the well-groomed hair. The folded arms represent a masculine confidence. The semiotics of the clothing with the ubiquitous corporate dark coloured suit, white shirt and red coloured tie depicts a serious corporate gravitas. It is a perfect parody of the real genre. Image M2, another captain of industry, is presented in an outdoors setting and continues the heroic theme. Image M3 depicts a corporate man in an urban city setting. The overall presentation in images M1, M2 and M3 is of corporate power. In image M4, the gaze comes from below and the city banker is presented against the backdrop of a stormy night sky, signifying overcoming adversity. The images are very much of men in power. Image M5 depicts a man marching purposefully towards his future and resonates with the theme of hard work and long hours as well as weariness. Image M6 resonates with the industrial superhero imagery metaphorically and symbolically. In image M7, we see a corporate employee running purposefully towards his future. Image M8 shows a dreamy-eyed male holding a small tree and symbolises the metaphor of entrepreneurial growth, as does the verdant foliage behind it. Images M9 and M10 signify the poor-boy-made-good with the fruits of their labour and the ubiquitous sports car. In Image M10, the male is dressed in a brown suit and has dark sunglasses signifying entrepreneurial difference and perhaps a 'bad-boy' persona, whereas image M9 denotes corporate compliance. Both images signify wealth, access to resources and conspicuous consumption (Veblen 2010). Image M11 depicts entrepreneurial guile and faceless corporate greed. Conversely, image M12 signifies the earning power of man as a heroic provider. Images M13, M14, M15 and M16 all set against urban city backdrops depict related 'action orientated corporate scenes of chaos and struggling to make-good'. They depict a grasping, ruthless side of human nature as corporate workers compete to climb the corporate ladder and achieve financial success. Note the looks of hope on the subjects' faces. In image M13, note the sexist undertones as the female workers are depicted in short skirts and black stockings despite carrying briefcases and displaying gendered corporate attire and the male colleague apparently pushing her out of the way. The money floating in the wind signifies grabbing opportunities as they come along. In image M14, we see a different symbolism of desperation and the corporate edifice of bricks crumbling. Note the empty bottles of alcoholic spirits depicting underlying stressors and an undertone of hedonism. This is the recession illustrated as the males compete to save a briefcase. Image M15 is powerfully symbolic of the entrepreneurial dream showing men and women rushing dream like to work whilst cooperating to create their shared fortunes. Image M16 depicts the theme of corporate adventuring and of struggling forlornly yet hopefully against the inevitable tide of defeat. Image M17 signifies going it alone, facing danger and adversity bravely whilst battling against the fortunes of life's tide. It is about facing new beginnings. Image M18 depicts a calm and patient corporate worker seated casually on the steps of a large building iconic and symbolically powerful building with other workers rushing past. Note the shirt sleeves and the jacket folded across his knees. This signifies waiting for one's destiny to unfold.

Image M19 shows a corporate man looking to his future through binoculars, denoting planning and environmental scanning. Image M20 symbolises corporate success and serendipity as the winning share is held aloft in the boardroom with the four males staring triumphantly at it. Note the backslaps, masculine camaraderie and the juxtaposed corporate high-rise buildings behind it. Image M21 depicts a 'laid back' worker resting on a park bench with a bottle of spirits.

The images utilise and present recurring artefactual and sartorial memes (Dawkins 1976) as presented in Table 1.

Individually and collectively, these iconic masculine memes act as symbolic props of masculinity and to McKean's ideal typical representation of his subjects. The purpose of this ideal typification is to create an instantly recognisable imagery associated with himself as an artist and with the cultural aesthetic his customer base 'identifies' with. It is also of note that in using clichéd phrases associated with enterprise culture McKean will recycle the same captions in different portraits. In all, the masculine images depicted in these stylised, parodied, stereotypical and often satirical portraits are consistent, with the '*heroic male entrepreneur*' (Drakopoulou and Anderson 2007) or '*heroic corporate warrior*' (Morris 1986) imagery evident both in the academic literature and in popular media representations. Granted, the imagery is highly stylised and often 'caricatured' towards idealised gendered and genre expectations. The judicious use of repetitive memes coalesces and combines to create an accepted reality. Moreover, the images have a certain cultural resonance with the author and those who buy McKean's art. It is visualised '*hegemonic masculinity*' (Connell and Messerschmidt 2005) replete with chauvinism and chivalry. The heroic meme portrays a dominant, action-orientated man. This is an idealised, visual form of hegemonic masculinity.

6 Some Concluding Thoughts

This chapter has highlighted a talented artisan Graham McKean presenting an illustrative case study of how he can be both an artisan and an entrepreneur (Yin 2014) as well as illustrating the complexity of artisanal entrepreneurship where the entrepreneurial identity of the artisan is closely connected with their craft and outputs. This case has also presented a contextualised explanation of the works of Graham McKean (Tsang 2013), particularly as a viable artisanal business model, and has done so in a holistic manner illustrating the complexity of the artisanal model. The case has captured the real-time dynamic processes. It can be argued that McKean as an artisan has co-created a particular enterprise base aesthetic that resonates with Scottish 'working class culture'. This particular strand of McKean's body of work not only conforms to the form of corporate art (Tyson 2005) but also conforms to the notion of a co-created aesthetic. It does contain masculine themes of chauvinism and chivalry. As an artisan, McKean is quite far removed from the subsistence model of entrepreneurship practiced by many artisanal entrepreneurs (ala Pret and Cogan 2019). Nor does he lack the business skills that many artisans

Table 1 Recurring visual memes in the masculine portraiture

Recurring meme	Significance and recurrence in constructing a masculine entrepreneurial identity
Physiological	
Folded arms	Signifying masculine strength of purpose. This appears in four of the portraits.
Purposeful fixed gaze	Again, signifying masculine strength and a sense of purpose. The gaze appears in 18 of the portraits. The gaze is either upwards towards heaven or staring into the distance/future.
Stern face	This meme is present in 19 of the portraits accompanied by a raised chin.
Artefact and clothing as symbols of corporate power	
Dark coloured suit	The ubiquitous dark coloured suit appears in 33 of the portraits and signifies conformity but also becomes a meme for urbanised masculinity itself. It comes in a variety of shades of grey, blue or black including pin stripes worn with or without a tie.
White coloured power-shirt	The white shirt appears in 25 of the portraits and signifies conformity and tradition. In three of the portraits, this is substituted for a blue coloured shirt, which also signifies corporate conformity. The shirts when worn open necked denote the male at rest or play.
Red coloured tie	The ubiquitous red tie signifies conformity and appears in 19 of the portraits.
Fluttering ties	This meme is present in 13 of the masculine images and perhaps signifies action, activity and a sense of adventure.
Brief case	This ubiquitous business meme appears in seven of the portraits.
High valued cars/marques	These appear in four of the portraits and are Bentleys or sports cars.
Physical objects	
High-rise buildings, pillars and industrial chimneys	These iconic symbols of urban industrialism appear in 19 of the portraits, and the heroic male is presented in juxtaposition to them. This depicts power, and some commentators may argue phallic power, although that may be an analysis too far. The high-rise buildings may be intended to signify the financial district of the city. In the images, the subjects are often seen walking away from the buildings as if leaving work.
Outdoor settings	These are both urban and rural, but urban imagery predominates. Only 5 of the images are rural whilst 25 are urban.
Rhetorical/linguistic	
Rhetorical codes—clichés, metaphors and storylines	The titles of the portraits themselves are of significance because they are loaded with symbolic and metaphoric meaning, which triggers our perceptions of the art and how we think and react to the images. Some of the titles are based on cliched masculine metaphors such us 'Daily Bread', 'The Bread Winner', 'Bringing home the bacon' and 'A good day at the races'. Another category is that of mythic metaphor as

(continued)

Table 1 (continued)

Recurring meme	Significance and recurrence in constructing a masculine entrepreneurial identity
	in 'the man who tried to turn the tide' with its obvious inference to King Canute and 'The Tree of Good Fortune'. A third category relates to stereotyped corporate or business job roles—'The Banker', 'Security', 'The Bookie', 'The Speculator', 'The Entrepreneur' and the 'Apprentice'. Work-related clichés form another category such as 'Nine till Five' and 'The Night Shift'. The most significant of the categories are entrepreneurial storylines such as 'A Captain of Industry', 'Chasing the Dream', 'Architect of Dreams', 'The Winning Share', 'From Humble beginnings', 'The Man who made it' and 'Life in the fast lane'. These signify different aspects of the entrepreneurial dream of the poor-boy-made-good.

allegedly do (Roberts 2017; Mitra 2020; Crowley 2019; Solomon-Blake and Mathias 2020). Indeed, he embraces the world of e-commerce and marketing platforms.

A fundamental limitation of this study is that despite being a comprehensive case it cannot capture the artisanal situation as experienced by McKean and is therefore influenced by the situation as perceived by me, the researcher (Dana and Dumez 2015). Nevertheless, despite potential accusations of 'circularity', it has comprehensively captured the artistic actions and outputs of McKean as an artisan by allowing readers to become viewers of his richly descriptive (and depictive) artistic expressions. Another major limitation of this study is that it reports an analysis of the impressionistic art of one male artist only. Another limitation is that it only reports selected images and not the whole corpus of his works that contain other stylised themes. Clearly, further studies into the visual presentation of representations of gendered entrepreneurial identity in the art of others would be helpful in building upon the ideas presented in this study. One must remember that the portraits are first and foremost art and that McKean only paints what sells. McKean's customers play a vital role in this artistic, entrepreneurial creation process to create aesthetic value (Elias et al. 2018). The female images in McKean's work border on being sexualised corporate images (Egan and Hawkes 2008), but the other contextualised and parochial elements point to being representative of a specifically, contextualised and perhaps peculiar urbanised 'South of Scotland' culture. Nevertheless, from an aesthetic perspective, the portraits are compelling as products of an arguably masculine entrepreneurial culture and are visually '*authentic*' (Guthey and Jackson 2005) because the heroic symbolism of the masculine portraiture imagery resonates with male viewers, albeit for different aesthetic reasons unrelated to entrepreneurial identity. McKean's artistic body of work with its inherent cultural symbolism confirms that entrepreneurial identity is gendered differentially. I conclude that Graham McKean is a classic example of the growing genre of the 'artisan-entrepreneur' who possesses 'business nous'.

References

Acevedo B (2014) Portraiture and the construction of 'charismatic leadership'. In: Bell E, Warren S, Schroeder JE (eds) The Routledge companion to visual organisation. The Routledge Companion to Visual Organisation, New York

Anderson AR (1995) The Arcadian Enterprise: an enquiry into the nature and conditions of rural small business. University of Stirling, Stirling

Andrews A (2020) Arts entrepreneurship: creating a new venture in the arts. Routledge, London

Barry B (2018) (Re)Fashioning masculinity: social identity and context in men's hybrid masculinities through dress. Gend Soc 32(4):638–662

Barry B, Weiner N (2019) Suited for success? Suits, status, and hybrid masculinity. Men Masculinities 22(2):151–176

Berger J, Mohr J (1975) A seventh man: migrant workers in Europe. Penguin Books, Harmondsworth

Berger J, Mohr J (1982) Another way of telling. Pantheon Books, New York

Bruni A, Gherardi S, Poggio B (2004) Doing gender, doing entrepreneurship: an ethnographic account of intertwined practices. Gender Work Org 11(4):406–429

Chandler D (2001) Semiotics: the basics. Routledge, London

Connell RW, Messerschmidt JW (2005) Hegemonic masculinity: rethinking the concept. Gend Soc 19(6):829–859

Crowley C (2019) Artisan entrepreneurial behaviour: a research agenda. In: McAdam M, Cunningham JA (eds) Entrepreneurial behaviour: individual, contextual and microfoundational perspectives. Springer Nature, Cham, pp 261–280

Dana L-P, Dumez H (2015) Qualitative research revisited: epistemology of a comprehensive approach. Int J Entrep Small Bus 26(2):154–170

Davidson J (2010) [In]visible [in]tangibles: visual portraits of the business élite. Account Org Soc 35(2):165–183

Davidson J (2014) Visual rhetoric and the case of intellectual capital. Account Org Soc 39(1):20–37

Dawkins R (1976) The selfish gene. Oxford University Press, Oxford

Díaz García M-C, Welter F (2013) Gender identities and practices: interpreting women entrepreneurs' narratives. Int Small Bus J 31(4):384–404

Dillon GL (2004) Montage/critique: another way of writing social history. Postmod Cult 14(2). http://faculty.washington.edu/dillon/rhethtml/crmontage/

Drakopoulou DS, Anderson AR (2007) Mumpsimus and the mything of the individualistic entrepreneur. Int Small Bus J 25(4):341–360

Egan D, Hawkes G (2008) Girls, sexuality and the strange carnalities of advertisements: deconstructing the discourse of corporate Paedophilia. Aust Fem Stud 23(57):307–322

Elias SRSTA, Chiles TH, Duncan CM, Vultee DM (2018) The aesthetics of entrepreneurship: how arts entrepreneurs and their customers co-create aesthetic value. Organ Stud 39(2–3):345–372

Ferreira J, Sousa BM, Goncalves F (2019) Encouraging the subsistence artisan entrepreneurship in handicraft and creative contexts. J Enterp Commun People Places Global Econ 13(1/2):64–83

Groenland E, Dana L-P (2019) Qualitative methodologies and data collection methods: toward increased rigour in management research. World Scientific Publishing, ProQuest Ebook Central. http://ebookcentral.proquest.com/lib/dal

Guthey B, Jackson B (2005) CEO portraits and the authenticity paradox. J Manag Stud 42 (5):1057–1082

Hamilton E (2013) The discourse of entrepreneurial masculinities (and femininities). Entrep Reg Dev Int J 25(1–2):90–99

Hamilton E (2014) Entrepreneurial narrative identity and gender: a double epistemological shift. J Small Bus Manag 52(4):703–712

Harper D (2002) Talking about pictures: a case for photo elicitation. Vis Stud 17(1):13–26

Henry C, Foss L, Ahl H (2016) Gender and entrepreneurship research: a review of methodological approaches. Int Small Bus J Res Entrep 34(3):217–241

Hill IR (2020) Spotlight on UK artisan entrepreneurs' situated collaborations: through the lens of entrepreneurial capitals and their conversion. Int J Entrep Behav Res 27(1):99–121

Hoyte C (2018) Artisan entrepreneurship: a question of personality structure? Int J Entrep Behav Res

Inverne J (2001) The impresarios. Oberon Books, London

Jännäri J, Kovalainen A (2015) The research methods used in "doing gender" literature. Int J Gend Entrep 7(2):214–231

Lewis P (2006) The quest for invisibility: female entrepreneurs and the masculine norm of entrepreneurship. Gender Work Org 13(5):453–469

Marlow S (2014) Exploring future research agendas in the field of gender and entrepreneurship. Int J Gend Entrep 6(2):102–120

Marlow S (2020) Gender and entrepreneurship: past achievements and future possibilities. Int J Gend Entrep 12(1):39–52

Mavin S, Grandy G (2012) Doing gender well and differently in management. Gender Manag 27 (4):218–231

Max S, Ballereau V (2013) Theorising about gender and entrepreneurship: bridging the gap with social psychology. Int J Gend Entrep 5(1):97–110

Mitra J (2020) On regarding the value of aesthetics for entrepreneurship. In: Formica P, Edmondson J (eds) Innovation and the arts: the value of humanities studies for business. Emerald Publishing, Bingley, pp 73–90

Morris DJ (1986) Theory "W": the corporate warrior. Perform Improve 25(7):22–25

Orser B, Elliott C, Leck J (2011) Feminist attributes and entrepreneurial identity. Gender Manag 26 (8):561–589

Palalic R, Ramadani V, Dana LP (2017) Entrepreneurship in Bosnia and Herzegovina: focus on gender. Eur Bus Rev 29(4):476–496

Pret T, Cogan A (2019) Artisan entrepreneurship: a systematic literature review and research agenda. Int J Entrep Behav Res 25(4):592–614

Ratten V, Costa C, Bogers M (2019) Artisan, cultural and tourism entrepreneurship. Int J Entrep Behav Res 25(4):582–591

Rivetti F, Migliaccio M (2018) Arts and entrepreneurship: disentangling the literature. Accessed 21 February 2021. Arts and Entrepreneurship: Disentangling the Literature | IntechOpen

Rivlin BB (2018) The artist as tragic hero: the creative process of playwright. Director Michael Gurevitch. Thesis - Wayne State University

Roberts J (2017) Arts entrepreneurship: education, theory, and practice. Bus Manag

Schnugg C, Lehner J (2016) Communicating identity or status? A media analysis of art works visible in photographic portraits of business executives. Int J Arts Manag 18(2):63–74

Smith NR (1967) The entrepreneur and his firm: the relationship between type of man and type of company. University of Illinois at Urbana-Champaign's Academy for Entrepreneurial Leadership Historical Research Reference in Entrepreneurship

Solomon-Blake SJ, Mathias BD (2020) The artisans' dilemma: Artisan entrepreneurship and the challenge of firm growth. J Bus Ventur 35(5)

Tsang E (2013) Case study methodology: causal explanation, contextualisation, and theorising. J Int Manag 19(2):195–202

Tyson K (2005) The illegal art exhibit: art of exploitation - a look at the fair use doctrine in relation to corporate degenerate art. Comput Law Rev Techn J 9(425):453

Veblen T (2010) The theory of the liesure classes. Dover Publications

Yin RK (2009) Case study research: design and methods, 4th edn. Sage, Thousand Oaks, CA

Yin RK (2014) Case study research design and methods, 5th edn. Sage, Thousand Oaks, CA

Zervigón A (2012 November) John Heartfield and the agitated image: photography, persuasion, and the rise of Avant-Garde photomontage. University of Chicago Press, Chicago

Robert Smith is currently an independent scholar, operating from Aberdeen, Scotland. Rob gained his MA in Management at Aberdeen University and his PhD by research at Robert Gordon University before entering academia. He was formerly a reader in entrepreneurship at Robert Gordon University and a professor of enterprise and innovation at the University of the West of Scotland. Rob's research interest includes the social construction of entrepreneurship, gender and enterprise, rural entrepreneurship and small business including artisan entrepreneurship. He is an eclectic and prolific author and has published over 200 peer-reviewed journal articles and book chapters.

Arts Entrepreneurs in an Emerging Economy

Mohamad Taghi Toghraee, Ali Ahmadi, and Aidin Salamzadeh

Abstract Artists who bring creative products to the market in the innovation economy, such as handcrafters and others, mostly do not make it to a more prospering entrepreneurial venture and bring economic rent from their talent. In order to shed light on this issue, the role of an entrepreneurial mindset and the use of business tools such as social media by creative workers in the cultural innovation economy cannot be neglected. In this chapter, we bring an overview on how entrepreneurial mindset in such players plays a crucial role inside the innovation economy, how arts entrepreneurship can bring profound results, and how, as the aftermath of COVID-19 prevailed, gaining entrepreneurial skills and use of business tools have surged, more specifically, the use of social media for promoting products and branding the artists themselves.

1 Introduction

Although the innovation economy has not received serious attention in most of the developing countries, many of these countries have a rich cultural capacity, playing the role of a hidden, untapped national treasure. This extraordinary capacity has not seen much chance to grow and flourish due to a lack of financial resources, cultural infrastructure, and institutional capabilities of the innovation economy. Many artists do not even know how they can have access to the market for their works (Barrowcloug and Kozul-Wright 2008).

M. T. Toghraee
Department of Museum and Tourism, Art University of Isfahan, Isfahan, Iran
e-mail: m.toghrayee@aui.ac.ir

A. Ahmadi
Department of Strategic Management, Industrial Management Institute, Tehran, Iran

A. Salamzadeh (✉)
Faculty of Management, University of Tehran, Tehran, Iran
e-mail: salamzadeh@ut.ac.ir

L.-P. Dana et al. (eds.), *Artisan and Handicraft Entrepreneurs*, Contributions to Management Science, https://doi.org/10.1007/978-3-030-82303-0_8

Nevertheless, specialists believe that activating and flourishing culture industries can significantly contribute to developing countries' economies and sustain traditions and cultural values. Thus, a vast segment of investigations and scientific research is pursuing a way to improve the art sector effectively. They have suggested providing suitable loans and teaching management skills to artists. One of the widely known suggestions in this field is training cultural entrepreneurship interns. The main goal of this suggestion is to teach entrepreneurial skills to artists to improve their innovative products successfully (Salamzadeh and Markovic 2018). A cultural entrepreneur has the vision to establish a cultural organization and a passion for obtaining the resources, people, and customers to develop it (Seilern 2013). The art sector is mostly lacking this link, which is why they cannot start their own creative business. Until now, no one has studied the essential and significant effects of entrepreneurship and entrepreneurial methods in supporting the innovation economy in developing countries (Salamzadeh and Arbatani 2020).

One of the side objectives of this research is to study the role of entrepreneurship in the relation between artists and innovative organizations to make them sustainable. How much can entrepreneurial capacities contribute to developing artists and art sectors as crucial role players? Furthermore, how artistic (cultural) values can be comprehended by entrepreneurial capabilities? These are among the main theoretical contributions of the authors in this chapter.

The chapter is structured as follows. First, the authors will review the literature on the innovation economy, creative, and arts entrepreneurship. Then, the authors will discuss the impacts of the COVID-19 pandemic and how arts entrepreneurs use social media during this period. Finally, the chapter will conclude with some remarks and directions for future research.

2 Innovation Economy

According to the 2010 Innovation Economy report, international trade of innovative products has seen a 14% growth from 2002 to 2008. Even in the 2008 financial crisis, the demand for these products has stayed on the rise. It is well within the mark that they have decided to consider the innovation industries the most growing and agile sector of the international economy. Furthermore, the value and significance of innovative industries have been increasingly noted in scientific communities. They exploit the results of innovation to create new wealth, local talents, innovative capitals, employment, improving competition, and new exporting markets (Cunningham 2004). On the other hand, art develops social capacities, cultural diversity, and human development from a human perspective. This constant growth assumes that cultural trade increases in developing countries and can result in wealth creation and development. However, a considerable part of developing countries' potential of cultural industries is still untapped and not appropriately noted in terms of financial profitability (Dana et al. 2021). The most important factors that create an unsuitable competitive environment for creative sectors in developing countries and need to be solved in vast cooperation mainly consist of education, poverty, and lack of institutions. Access to capital, sponsors, and financial support are among the limitations of growth in this industry.

Moreover, the cultural products' value chain is fragile. The steps and processes that a cultural product has to get through before being offered to the market, such as promotion, branding, distribution, and patenting, are mostly weak, not only due to the fact that these steps have been neglected to begin with but also because artists lack the necessary knowledge about these processes (Klamer 2011). This lack of an entrepreneurial mindset is affecting the growth rate of the whole industry as well. Fillis and Rentschler (2010) noted that an entrepreneur breaks the conventional rules and pushes the boundaries for unprecedented economic success when he/she contributes to creative works.

One of the other main issues is that art and culture are not simply related to the monetary conditions of these countries, and the relationship with the market is not formed entirely yet. Artists do not consider their profession as a business but instead consider it a continuous tradition (Kamara 2004). For example, young musicians mainly focus on their performance while attending festivals, discarding opportunities to make new connections and find new revenue streams. Thus, one of the main hindrances for which these industries do not grow as much as they should is different mindsets among individuals. The absence of an entrepreneurial mindset eventually results in a lack of other capacities as well. This is why artists do not possess managerial skills, business professionalism, networking, confidence in risk-taking, and a common knowledge of markets. In general, there are no explicit cultural policies that promote funding and educate the art sector's actual capacity. One of the major factors to developing the art and creative sector is understanding and comprehending the longing for art in the view of the people. It is when we know how art is presented and its value comprehended that we have the right to study ways and methods to promote and improve it.

3 Creative and Arts Entrepreneurship

Entrepreneurship in these sectors means creative ideas and following them until the point of commercialization in order to gain profit from them. Nonetheless, profit cannot be the only stimulant for individuals. There are other motives such as creativity, the capacity to build something, satisfaction, or the ability to follow creative interests. Therefore, a combination of the creative and entrepreneurship sides is possible (Aageson 2008).

Although there is no general agreement on how we can define entrepreneurship, it can be defined as a holder of risk, creator of venture activity, or invoker of innovation, but there is even less concurrence on how it can be defined between the creative and cultural sectors. Furthermore, according to the solid economic share of the cultural and creative sector in countries' GDP, defining the entrepreneurial aspect of this sector is of paramount importance. Therefore, this issue is crucial to be attended because it can discuss how the two aspects can be supported in the best way possible and also in order to discuss the various factors that affect cultural and creative entrepreneurship.

The definition of cultural entrepreneurship has been generally accepted in the past decade. In this field, various models have been presented as a tool to understand the systemization of the structural specifications of cultural and creative industries, and in this way, it has been tried to create a common definition of cultural and creative entrepreneurship (Kituyi 2020).

While the products that artists create for the sake of art are changing, there is a clear boundary between the cultural and creative aspects on the one hand and the entrepreneurial aspects on the other hand. Motivations for a tendency toward creative and cultural entrepreneurship vary based on individuals and the segment of the industry that they work at. The tension between a cultural product creator and an entrepreneur works peculiarly. Among the cultural and creative entrepreneurs, the emphasis is on prioritizing the value of cultural creativity and less motivation for creating economic value (creativity-based view). On the other hand, entrepreneurship prioritizes economic efficiency in comparison with cultural value (growth-based view). These tensions suggest that any support should be provided based on the nature of the organization and the sub-parts in which they perform (Granger and Hamilton 2010; Salamzadeh 2021).

There is a meaningful relation between creative and cultural entrepreneurs and the texture of their entrepreneurial activities. Hölzl (2005) claim that "the process of new product creation in creative industries is mostly located in networks and clusters. Knowledge-sharing is one of the most important traits of this process, called the creative process cumulation." As a system of relations between employees and networks, it can be seen that entrepreneurs perform in unofficial frameworks, flexible behavioral norms, free access, and no attachment to a single location. "As a result of that, they work in multiple places and time" (Granger and Hamilton 2010). This argument may head up that entrepreneurship works in contrast with other activities and strategies of networks that create aesthetic products, but it is the genuine factor that shapes them (van Heur 2010).

External positive and negative factors such as globalization, improvement of technology, or, in this chapter's primary concern, global pandemics affect creative entrepreneurship. These factors influence members in attaining an innovative culture (Fillis and Rentschler 2010). Building on the previous statements, Fillis and Rentschler (2010) also suggested that concepts such as profitability have dimensions other than the financial solvency in these industries, such as social wealth and social capital.

4 COVID-19 and the Effects of Social Media

The use of social media as the new "mega-trend" is a great help for business performance (for small and medium enterprises) for its impact on competitiveness. It also enables targeting specific geographies around the country and provinces. Social media can even increase customer loyalty when they have prior information about the product and make sure it is fit for them, leading to trust and loyalty (Palalic et al. 2020; Salamzadeh et al. 2019, 2020; Salamzadeh and Tajpour 2021; Susanto et al. 2021).

Entrepreneurship literature considers entrepreneurs as the role player to bring disruption to markets, while in the case of COVID-19, the disruptive force is external, and the role of entrepreneurs can be to establish a new normal. Shepherd (2020) brings up the "the high fluidity of the market" as a current phenomenon and suggests that by redefining the "new better situation," entrepreneurs will shape the future equilibrium as the widespread pandemic dissipates.

Research on the importance of social media for home-based business (HBBs) development in Kuwait City under the shadow of COVID-19 showed that they are using Instagram, WhatsApp, Snapchat, email, and their websites to establish communication channels with their customers and grow b2b relationships. They have also suggested that home-based businesses continue their venture for independence, more revenue than usual, inheritance, hobby, or unemployment rate in companies (Ramadani et al. 2019; Saleh 2020). The results of another study in Indonesia suggest that the use of SM boosts the performance of small to medium enterprises. It further implied that more professional use of SM could improve their sales, customer relationships, and productivity (Syaifullah et al. 2021). Social media allows small businesses (including home businesses) to outperform their previous marketing and sales activities because it brings a much larger (and primarily global) customer base for cheaper advertisement (Susanto et al. 2021; Dana and Salamzadeh 2021). These qualities make SM the first option for small and home businesses to look forward to whenever the offline or traditional market is disturbed by something.

In the wake of the COVID-19 outbreak in early 2020, pressure on artists and creative workers for a steady flow of income has brought many to online marketplaces. They have brought years of silent creative work to offer with a price that customers would not imagine finding on the market. Nevertheless, the challenge has always been the same for the artists, direct channels to market with minimum finder's fees. In the case of creative workers in Iran, seasonal, monthly, and weekly handicraft exhibitions in parks, crowded places, and subway stations along with a relatively invisible presence in daily markets, widely known as "Bazaar" in Iran, were all that this particular sector of creative workers used to deal with as possible channels to offer their supply of products. There are indeed exotic markets for handicrafts, both as ornaments and souvenirs, that provide a plethora of high-quality products from a vast range of diversity, though they tend to be much more expensive and so out of everyday buyers' reach. It has to be noted that the unfair value chain from the artist to the store shelves leaves a short percentage of the price tag for the

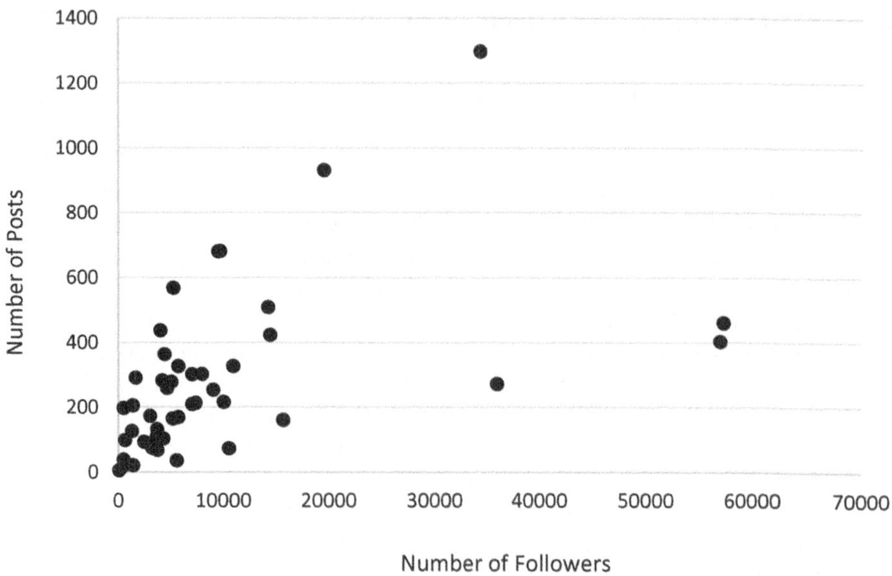

Fig. 1 Selected pottery workshops on Instagram, in term of number of posts and followers

artist, while the store has to push for a constant supply of the same objects. People who own and run these stores are not necessarily artists, and the constant friction between the two mindsets makes it even more challenging to bring about synergy. In every sense, when offline selling went off the table due to national lockdowns, the artists had to use whatever entrepreneurial skills they have had to reach the market, and the most available channel in 2020 was social media which is widely used and highly effective in Iran.

According to Hootsuite 2021 report on Iran's digital structure, Iran has 59.16 million Internet users (70% of the population) and 36 million active social media users, with a growth rate of 10%. As for the financial inclusion factors, 94% of people aged 15 or higher have an account with a financial institution, and 46.5% make online purchases or pay bills online (Moghadamzadeh et al. 2020).

We have analyzed the joining date for Iranian Instagram pages related to pottery (both sellers and content) and conducted online interviews with six creative artists who mainly worked in the area of pottery. The snowball method was used to randomly select them, resulting in three men and three women working privately and at home in the capital city of Tehran (access to eight million potential offline customers) (Fig. 1). The interviewees were all 27–35 years of age and had previous relevant arts and handcrafts backgrounds (comparable e-readiness). They had worked in the pottery industry before the pandemic began and had their offline channels (Fig. 2).

The most noticeable pattern about the effects of COVID-19 on these creative artists was the necessity and inevitability of showing up on social media (Salamzadeh and Dana 2020) (Fig. 3). Thus, learning a set of new skills, such as

Fig. 2 A local pottery workshop. Photo © Ali Ahmadi

Fig. 3 Using social media platforms in a local pottery workshop during the COVD-19 pandemic. Photo © Ali Ahmadi

networking with other players, content and advertising, customer relationships, and even more complex accounting. As the constant revenue from offline streams was cut, online presence seemed more vital and even more fruitful. Searching the keyword "pottery" in Farsi, "Sofal—Sofalgary," brings 62 individual pages on Instagram working specifically on the pottery and ceramics merchandise market. The pages are either individuals who showcase their handicrafts or dealers and stores

Fig. 4 Scatterplot of Instagram posts—Instagram followers for the active Instagram pages related to pottery (source: authors elaboration)

that have an online site and occasionally pages that discuss ceramics and pottery in an educative way, and most of them are newly created. Mapping the number of posts with many followers for the active pages (the ones that posted in the last 24 h) shows a considerable majority of these pages are located on the bottom left of the scatterplot (Fig. 4).

The interviewees all had their own set of private furnaces and other equipment. As for the infrastructures in the industry, it is reasonably possible to find any quality of equipment on the market, though the prices are too high and require to kick off funding to begin. Furthermore, the national post service is widely accessible around the country, with reasonable price and somewhat reliable quality of transferring fragile objects. On the other hand, the supply of raw material for their professional works is limited and subject to price volatility, leaving their pricing system in constant change.

The market environment has seen some change during the pandemic; a surge of players on the Internet social media tightened the competition, resulting in more high-quality content and presentation, promotions, branding plans, and special offers. The market players seem not to have prior business and entrepreneurship knowledge or training; thus, everyone has a relatively stable situation. "There is a constant struggle to do something that attracts people to our pages on Instagram or Twitter," one of the interviewees stated. In terms of marketing efforts, the most dominant action is using Instagram opinion leaders or celebrity figure attractions. Page owners, whom we entitled with the "artist mindset," now try to find popular celebrity pages with the most compatible follower decks so that the marketing investment they make brings better returns, which is an "entrepreneurial mindset" in its way.

Other senses, such as product and service management, care about service experience from Instagram direct messaging to the final product packaging and later aftersales. They instead push transparency on how the products are developed, make more innovative actions on their design routines, and even use specific points on a calendar for promotions and sales.

In general, the difference between artistic and entrepreneurial mindsets in developing countries starts to shrink in the face of real competition on the market. Therefore, online social media can become the universal arena for individuals working in the innovation economy to face the market and gradually begin to learn managerial and entrepreneurial skills, which will later be of their use to create their organizations and art companies.

5 Conclusion

A large part of entrepreneurship investigations and scientific research is pursuing a way to improve the creative sector effectively. From the innovation economy perspective, developing countries exploit the results of innovation to create new wealth and enable local talents, innovative capitals, and employment while improving competition and new exporting markets. The main hindrance in this goal is that art and culture are not simply related to the monetary conditions of the developing countries, and the relationship with the market is not formed entirely yet. Artists do not consider their profession as a business, but instead a sort of continuous tradition, leading to a significantly different mindset among individuals. The absence of an entrepreneurial mindset eventually results in a lack of other capacities as well. This is why artists do not possess managerial skills, business professionalism, networking, confidence in risk-taking, and a common knowledge of markets. In the wake of the COVID-19 outbreak in early 2020, pressure on artists and creative workers for a steady flow of income has brought many of them to the online marketplace. After showing up on social media and more direct exposure, creative workers have developed entrepreneurial skills by engaging in content creating, marketing, customer relationship management, packaging, and logistics. By interviewing six creative pottery artists using the snowball method, this study suggests that the surging use of social media by creative workers in the aftermath of the COVID-19 pandemic has helped them gain managerial and entrepreneurial skills, leading to more effective performance in the market. It can be implied that despite the devastating outcomes of COVID-19 on the business environment and the loss of a significant section of the market, it has improved the entrepreneurial mindset for artists by bringing them to the online platforms of social media.

References

Aageson T (2008) Cultural entrepreneurs: producing cultural value and wealth. In: Anheir HK, Ray Isar Y (eds) Cultures and globalization: the cultural economy, vol 2. Sage, London, p 92

Barrowcloug D, Kozul-Wright Z (2008) Creative industries and developing countries voice, choice and economic growth. Taylor & Francis

Cunningham S (2004) The creative industries after cultural policy. Int J Cult Stud 7(1):105–115

Dana LP, Salamzadeh A (2021) Why do artisans and arts entrepreneurs use social media platforms?: Evidence from an emerging economy. Nord J Media Manag 2(1)

Dana LP, Salamzadeh A, Ramadani V, Palalic R (2021) Understanding contexts of business in western Asia: land of bazaars and high-tech booms. World Scientific, Singapore

Fillis I, Rentschler R (2010) The role of creativity in entrepreneurship. J Enterp Cult 18(01):49–81

Granger R, Hamilton C (2010) Creative spaces: the role of the underground and the prospect of lock-in in the creative industries. Regions Magazine 277(1):13–15

Hölzl W (2005) Entrepreneurship, entry and exit in creative industries: an exploratory survey. Austrian, Institute of Economic Research (WIFO)

Kamara Y (2004) Keys to successful cultural enterprise development in developing countries. The Global Alliance for Cultural Diversity, Division of Arts and Cultural Enterprise. UNESCO, Paris. https://citeseerx.ist.psu.edu/viewdoc/download?doi=10.1.1.541.9863&rep=rep1&type=pdf

Kituyi M (2020) Trade and development report 2020. https://unctad.org/webflyer/trade-and-development-report-2020

Klamer A (2011) Cultural entrepreneurship. Rev Aust Econ 24(2):141–156

Moghadamzadeh A, Ebrahimi P, Radfard S, Salamzadeh A, Khajeheian D (2020) Investigating the role of customer co-creation behavior on social media platforms in rendering innovative services. Sustainability 12(17):6926

Palalic R, Ramadani V, Gilani SM, Gërguri-Rashiti S, Dana LP (2020) Social media and consumer buying behavior decision: what entrepreneurs should know? Manag Decis

Ramadani V, Hisrich RD, Dana LP, Palalic R, Panthi L (2019) Beekeeping as a family artisan entrepreneurship business. Int J Entrep Behav Res 25(4):717–730

Salamzadeh A (2021) How artisans and arts entrepreneurs use social media platforms? J Org Cult Commun Confl 25(2):1–2

Salamzadeh A, Arbatani TR (2020) Developing a framework for understanding how media entrepreneurs act: an actor-network perspective. In: Williams I (ed) Contemporary applications of actor network theory. Palgrave Macmillan, Singapore, pp 77–98

Salamzadeh A, Dana LP (2020) The coronavirus (COVID-19) pandemic: challenges among Iranian startups. J Small Bus Entrep:1–24

Salamzadeh A, Markovic MR (2018) Shortening the learning curve of media start-ups in accelerators: case of a developing country. In: Evaluating media richness in organizational learning. IGI Global, pp 36–48

Salamzadeh A, Tajpour M (2021) Identification of the challenges of media startup creation in Iran. J Entrep Dev 13(4):561–580

Salamzadeh A, Radovic Markovic M, Masjed SM (2019) The effect of media convergence on exploitation of entrepreneurial opportunities. AD-Minister 34:59–76

Salamzadeh A, Tajpour M, Hosseini E (2020) Exploring the impact of social networks on entrepreneurial intention. Media Stud 15(48):111–124. https://mediastudies.srbiau.ac.ir/article_16051_en.html

Saleh Y (2020) ICT, social media and COVID-19: evidence from informal home-based business community in Kuwait City. J Enterp Commun People Places Global Econ

Seilern N (2013) The role of cultural entrepreneurship among impoverished artists in Africa in becoming more sustainable. http://hdl.handle.net/2105/15171

Shepherd DA (2020) COVID 19 and entrepreneurship: time to pivot? J Manag Stud 57 (8):1750–1753

Susanto H, Fang Yie L, Mohiddin F, Rahman Setiawan AA, Haghi PK, Setiana D (2021) Revealing social media phenomenon in time of COVID-19 pandemic for boosting start-up businesses through digital ecosystem. Appl Syst Innov 4(1):6

Syaifullah J, Syaifudin M, Sukendar MU, Junaedi J (2021) Social media marketing and business performance of MSMEs during the COVID-19 pandemic. J Asian Financ Econ Bus 8 (2):523–531

van Heur B (2010) Creative networks and the city. In Creative networks and the city. transcript Verlag

Mohamad T. Toghraee is currently a faculty member of the Art University of Isfahan, faculty of excellent research in art and entrepreneurship, Department of museum and tourism, Isfahan. Iran. Before this, he had done his PhD in Entrepreneurship at the University of Tehran, Faculty of Entrepreneurship. His main research interest focuses on art and cultural entrepreneurship, entrepreneurial marketing, and entrepreneurial schools and education.

Ali Ahmadi studied MBA in strategy at the Industrial Management Institute of Tehran, Iran. Ali is interested in strategic management and innovation in high-velocity contexts. Coming from a mechanical engineering background, he is interested in technology and emergent business models and their consequences for market turbulence.

Aidin Salamzadeh is an assistant professor at the University of Tehran. His interests are startups, new venture creation, and entrepreneurship. Aidin serves as an associate editor in *Revista de Gestão, Innovation & Management Review* (Emerald), *Entrepreneurial Business and Economics Review*, and *Journal of Women's Entrepreneurship and Education* as well as an editorial advisory in *The Bottom Line* (Emerald). Besides, he is a reviewer in numerous distinguished international journals. Aidin is a member of the European SPES Forum, the Asian Academy of Management, and Ondokuz Mayis University.

Stone Carving in India and the Need for Process Innovation

Sriparna Guha, Anirban Mandal, Pranam Dhar, Sandeep Poddar, and Léo-Paul Dana

Abstract In the developing and third world countries, in particular, a sustainable livelihood approach to poverty reduction has become a prime concern worldwide, where livelihood depends largely on the outcomes of conventional farming. On the other hand, the handicraft sector traditionally plays an influential role in improving people's livelihood conditions. It is a growing challenge to conserve and preserve the knowledge and skills of traditional crafts. Handicraft by local craftsmanship and materials are special manifestations of a specific culture or society. However, growing globalization leads to more commoditization of goods, and artisans find their products competitive worldwide. It is also necessary to secure a sustainable livelihood for the artisans who work in this traditional craft. This chapter will explore the traditional art form of stone carving, which is widely practiced among a group of people of the Susunia region of Bankura district of West Bengal, India. This research will look at the limitations and weaknesses associated with stone-carving operations and also aims to investigate the numerous livelihood results obtained from stone-carving activities by stoneworkers through entrepreneurial activities. Entrepreneurship is known as an antidote to poverty and unemployment. This research aims to promote and explore the influence of entrepreneurship on the sustainability of artisans.

S. Guha (✉) · A. Mandal
Brainware University, Barasat, West Bengal, India
e-mail: am.mgmt@brainwareuniversity.ac.in

P. Dhar
West Bengal State University, Barasat, West Bengal, India

S. Poddar
Lincoln University College, Petaling Jaya, Selangor, Malaysia
e-mail: sandeeppoddar@lincoln.edu.my

L.-P. Dana
Rowe School of Business, Dalhousie University, Halifax, NS, Canada
e-mail: lp762359@dal.ca

L.-P. Dana et al. (eds.), *Artisan and Handicraft Entrepreneurs*, Contributions to Management Science, https://doi.org/10.1007/978-3-030-82303-0_9

1 Introduction

Traditional skills and experience as an intellectual property are respected for the future contributions of local people to ecosystem protection and livelihoods (Pandey et al. 2007). Connecting technology, skill, and conventional knowledge offers the ability to support local livelihoods and environmental sustainability. It is important to reinforce the art and craft sector while preserving traditional handicraft products (Dana 1999). The handicraft and artisan sector is considered as an essential priority of any country as it carries principal features of national culture and national heritage (Dana 1999). The recent value of stone carving in India offers a chance to explore how traditional stone-carving awareness contributes toward improving livelihoods and household incomes.

A livelihood is environmentally sustainable if it preserves or strengthens the local and global assets on which the livelihood relies and provides a net profit for other livelihood sources (Kabir et al. 2012). A livelihood is a collection of skills, assets, and activities that provide the means for people to respond and to support their fundamental needs. The development of livelihoods represents material and experiential needs and seeks to satisfy those (Pret and Cogan 2019). Livelihood is not just a localized phenomenon but linked to a broader national, regional, and global arena through environmental, economic, political, and cultural processes (Castro 2004). In India, a wide range of activities encompassing sustainable livelihoods, goals, and impact strategies were implemented across different societies. The sustainable livelihood sector in India has been, and is, mainly based on agricultural and related industries for many years. A variety of farming and non-farm operation may provide different livelihood strategies (Igwe et al. 2019). The presence of artisans is a remarkable thing in the informal sector. This informal sector has immense potential for opening new jobs and income generation and purchasing power for the rural population (Solanki 2008).

Artisanal and other non-farming practices are an important part of livelihood options in the developing world (Pret and Cogan 2019). Traditionally, craft companies have been primarily connected to places and locations and are often identified in the cultural types of businesses (Brown 2015). In one section of literature, craftsmen distinguish themselves by their form of business, while in another, they are specified based on distinct purposes or values (Tregear 2005). Over the years, craftsmen have created useful products in their communities to meet social demand. Now, artisanal culture had to change under the influence of external players to new goods (Markwick 2001). Crafts, which were often traded in the community as products or everyday items in the past, are now increasingly being sold off outside the local markets (Swanson and Timothy 2012). Artisan entrepreneurship plays a considerable role in the economy and culture (Luckman 2015). Research has shown that craft entrepreneurs find innovative ways to explore and leverage opportunities that often turn their interests and hobbies into profitable businesses (Bruni and Perrotta 2014).

It is important to understand that small business can contribute to different economic and social developments such as employment, the balancing of disparities, income generation, and distributive justice (Dana 2000). This paper aims to explore the literature available, define the gaps in information, and set research goals that lead to functional models to improve livelihoods by linking local stone-carving knowledge to global markets through entrepreneurship.

2 Methodology and Significance of the Study

This being a qualitative study, a case study of artisans, we follow the case study protocol (Dana and Dana 2005; Groenland and Dana 2020; Yin 1984). The chapter will highlight major issues and problems relating to the training, marketing, direct selling, and livelihood conditions of the stone-carving artisans in the village of Susunia. The study would highlight the facts on making the stone crafts profession more attractive and enriched for a sustainable rural livelihood by preparing them as entrepreneurs. The study aims to identify the need for stone-craving artisans of the village of Susunia to sustain their livelihood and assess the role of entrepreneurship toward sustainable business practices.

3 Stone Carving as the Oldest Traditions of Art in India

The tradition of stone carving is the richest in India among the world. Stone was one of the first materials used to make tools by prehistoric man. While stone-constructed artifacts gave way to metal products, stone remains one of the favorite sculpture materials. Mason guilds and carvers of stone were found here from the seventh century BC (India-Craft n.d). The skills were passed on from father to son as a family affection, a tradition which still predominates in some parts of the world. The stone-carving practice was closely related to architecture. The rich heritage of Indian stone carvings is demonstrated in every major temple in India such as Puri, Konark, Khajuraho, Kailasha Temple, and Mahabalipuram (India-Craft n.d). An enormous amount of very colorful marble materials of various textures can be found in India. Many of these are easy to run, such as Italian marble, but the quality shifts to the same block to such a degree that it becomes more difficult to complete the work of art (Bocchi 2008). The stones in India are not only adorned with sculptures of deities or temples but are also used to render artifacts such as carved panel, panels, sheets of paper, stalls, patterns of historic buildings, and animals' and humans' sculptures (India-Craft n.d).

In India, craftsmen make use of different types of stones such as marble, soapstone, sandstone, etc. Lengthy blocks of stone are picked up and brought to different art centers. The fundamental nature of the stone has a crude form. Then the final sculpture is made, and the objects are polished. The heritage of Madhya Pradesh is rich in the stone craft. Gwalior is famous for work on jali. In Jabalpur and Tikamgarh, animal and human figures are created. Bastar's tribal area is renowned for its tribal gods and pillars in the monument. Durgi, Allagadda, and Tirupati are the principal centers of stonework in Andhra Pradesh. These centers exemplify the elaborate sculpture of gods and goddesses (Bocchi 2008). The artisans obey strictly old rules concerning the production and manufacture of sculpture. Gujarat is famous for Ambaji's marble sculptures. Rural areas in Bihar are renowned for black stone utensils. Uttar Pradesh has several craft centers devoted to the manufacture of various stone products. The district of Hamirpur is renowned for statues of red soft stone made locally available. The Banaras Riding Group produces a wide range of marble products, including tableware, pots, glass bowls, food containers, candlesticks, etc. Agra is well known for the complex marble inlay influenced by Taj Mahal. Rajasthan is still one of the largest stone-carving centers in the world. The city of Jaipur is the center of Rajasthan's marble carving. At Ajmer, Udaipur, Jodhpur, and Bikaner, we can see some beautiful examples of the intricate jali work performed on royal palaces' screens and panels (India-Craft n.d). Simulpur in Midnapur is the main center for traditional stone carving in West Bengal, and the carvers are called Sildah. Burdwan is another major place in West Bengal for stone carving with Patun and Dainhata, and this region's stone carvers are often referred to as Bhaskars or Sutradhars (The Craft and Artisans 2010). The place *Susunia*, an archaeological site of the Bankura district of the state West Bengal, is famous for its echo-tourism spot at *Susunia Hills* and exquisite sand stone handicrafts made by the local artisans. This article will discuss the livelihood of the stone-carving artisans of the Susunia region of Bankura district (Mukherjee et al. 2016).

The art of engraving stone into beautiful sculptures was pioneered by Mr. Sahadeb Karmakar only 60 years back and attracted many local aspirants for their livelihood option. But interestingly, till date the methodology of teaching-learning of the art is largely *Guru-Sishya Parampara* where master craftsman teaches the novice on hand using traditional tools and devices (Bocchi 2008).

Product varieties of the stone crafts in the industry are nearly 500 with a price range from Rs. 20 to 2.5 lakhs depending on the size, delicacy, stone material, and labor-power invested in the product. A retail market of the stone carving is available at the Susunia foothill, where nearly one lakh tourists and pilgrims visit throughout a year (Bocchi 2008).

4 Literature Review

Susunia hills of Bankura draw visitors all year round. However, many of us probably do not know that this place also contains one of the oldest types of stone carving from Maurya and Gupta. Susunia is a renowned archaeological site with stone articles made and used for thousands of years here. In fact, the first stone carving was conducted in Bengal in this region by experts (Get Bengal 2020).

Stone-carved elephant, peacock, and model of Radha-Krishna. Source: Photography by Author-S. Guha

The handicraft sector traditionally plays an influential role to improve the livelihood conditions of the people associated with the trade, but so far, most of the trades are neglected because of various issues. If the problems are addressed properly, then a greater dependency on the agricultural sector alone may be reduced. Most of the past research focused on specific skills and trades of the handicraft sectors of West Bengal and addressed the issues related to it. Gangopadhyay and Sen (2019) addressed the issues of craftsman of Bankura district of West Bengal and also highlighted the challenges that they are facing in their profession. Hazra and Barman (2017) worked on the clay pottery of Krishnanagar and identified that young generations are ignorant about the age-old native product as a result of which it is losing its real market value.

Mukherjee et al. (2016) try to identify the new-age promotional tools to increase the visibility of the handicraft products in their work so that the products can get potential buyers. In one such work, Ghosal and Prasad (2019) try to identify the scope of the digitalization of handicraft products so as to increase visibility and sales. Sahoo et al. (2016) worked extensively on the Bankura terracotta products and found the market potential of the products was mostly underutilized due to lack of capitals and marketing orientation. They mostly depend on tourists to sell the products. Ghosh (2014) also worked on the terracotta products of Bankura districts and developed an econometric model to address the economic viability of the products.

In Susunia, the art gradually decayed amid a rich history of stone carving over thousands of years. The current generation is reluctant to participate in a time-consuming, laborious form of art. Acute poverty prevents many from taking stone carving as a stable occupation. Many traditional stone carvers are obliged to look for other careers due to a lack of sufficient facilities and financial assistance (Get Bengal 2020).

Source: Photography by author-S. Guha

The reviews give us an understanding that the handicraft sector has the potential, but the same is affected by various issues at the local level as well as at the regional level. One of the main concerns is the finance and marketing of the products. If these issues are addressed, then it will help to improve the socioeconomic conditions of the artisans.

5 Problems Faced by the Stone-Carving Artisans in the Study Region

National awardee and owner of Mr. *Nayan Dutta* of Susunia village reports that there is a huge demand of the majestic stone crafts, including statues/idols of Hindu God/Goddess and eminent personalities. But, there is a crunch of right manpower since most of the learners do not have the artistic aptitude, strong enthusiasm, and the ability to work hard.

Stone carving by an artisan. Source: Photography by author S. Guha

Due to the eco-preservation mission at Susunia, collecting stones from the local hill sources is banned. Craftsmen are now buying the raw materials from the Odisha (sand stone) and Rajasthan (marble). Naturally, the cost of production becomes higher. Unfortunately, to make the price competitive, few craftsmen are manufacturing fake products made of stone dust, especially utensils. Counterfeit stone products are damaging the brand image of the *Susunia* handicrafts, and genuine products are getting a backlash.

Sculptors who would like to build the modern workshop of stone crafts are lacking loan funds from the banks and other financial institutions due to terms and conditions imposed upon them (Hazra 2017). However, West Bengal Khadi and Village Industries Board (WBKVIB) has rather extended its hand to large workshop owner providing subsidized loan to eligible craftsmen. But, for small artisans, accessing financial assistance is a major challenge.

Artisans are highly dependent upon merchants and vendors who collect their product to sell in the domestic and international market and supply raw materials for their products. Therefore, a considerable profit is appropriated by the middlemen in the crafts market, depriving the poor artisans.

6 Opportunities to Strengthen Livelihoods Through Entrepreneurship

Many stone-carving craftsmen of the study district maintain their livelihood by making aesthetic and functional crafts from natural materials from a local source, using simple handheld tools with the skills and expertise transferred from generation to generation. Often distributors (most wholesalers) order these handicrafts by verbal agreement covering the details such as the design and size of the product, quantity, quality level, date of completion, and the prices per part as defined by the distributors. The ordered handcrafted products are not to be labeled or signed by the artisan in any way. Some craftsmen make handicraft in small batches without such an order and then try to market them directly to visitors, merchants, or consignment agents (from their own homes or at local small shops). However, the sector is troubled by several problems and cannot meet its real potential in an equitable way. These include the sector's unorganized nature, a fragmented value chain, lack of quality raw materials, weak facilities for manufacturing, restricted marketing capabilities and insufficient knowledge and asymmetry in relation to the markets and the consumer.

Micro, small, and medium enterprises (MSME) of India dealing with the artisans' industry have gained considerable prominence for their large role in economic growth such as job creation, revenue generation and distribution by using the local capital, entrepreneurial talent incubation, market dispersal and socioeconomic development (Kazungu and Njau 2018). Artisans in the Susunia region need a favorable and welcoming atmosphere, including business facilities, funding, and affordable training in entrepreneurship. In addition, training in entrepreneurship and management skills and business development services like details on credit institutions in banks must be offered at the required stage. The production of livelihoods needs various types of investment to maintain traditional art, strengthening the sector and growing the incomes of craftspeople. For several decades, many well-meant social enterprises (profit, nonprofit) have been working for these challenges in the handcraft sectors and ought to be assisted in a decisive way to increase the scope and effect of their activities in a sustainable manner. A coherent and focused effort is important at the policy level to address the challenges facing the craft ecosystem through financing and programs. At the same time, the private sector has an important role to play in inspiring stone-carving artisans through the numerous business drives of chain stores, high-tech designers, and a more recent surge of social enterprises.

7 Conclusion and Recommendation

Training and development should be improved through quality education and diverse skills that foster small enterprises' growth. The challenge is to shift the mentality of the artisans, who are predominantly engaged in business and oppose technology adoption (Ramadani et al. 2019; Dana and Salamzadeh 2021). These include creating local training facilities and helping entrepreneurs to prepare business plans at affordable rates (Kazungu and Njau 2018). One recommendation is to reinforce individual artisans by making them aware of the importance of their abilities and by constantly educating them to upgrade their skills and product varieties. Another significant recommendation is to increase demand for the stone-made products and improve business ties. Business support and process innovations must also be provided to improve craftsmanship productivity and make it possible for artisans to generate more. In addition to its social and distributional implications and access to a better extension for stone-carving artisans, the government should develop policy measures to enhance the entrepreneurial ability of the artisans.

References

Bocchi S (2008) Exploring the stone-carving traditions of India. https://www.stoneworld.com/articles/85376-exploring-the-stone-carving-traditions-of-india

Brown J (2015) Making it local: what does this mean in the context of contemporary craft? Arts and Crafts Council, London. http://www.craftscouncil.org.uk/content/files/Crafts_Council_Local_Report_Web_SinglePages.pdf

Bruni A, Perrotta M (2014) Entrepreneuring together: his and her stories. Int J Entrep Behav Res 20 (2):108–127

Castro CJ (2004) Sustainable development: mainstream and critical perspectives. Organ Environ 17 (2):195–225

Dana L-P (1999) Preserving culture through small business: government support for artisans and craftsmen in Greece. J Small Bus Manag 37(1):90

Dana L-P (2000) Creating entrepreneurs in India. J Small Bus Manag 38(1):86–91

Dana L-P, Dana TE (2005) Expanding the scope of methodologies used in entrepreneurship research. Int J Entrep Small Bus 2(1):79–88

Dana LP, Salamzadeh A (2021) Why do artisans and arts entrepreneurs use social media platforms?: Evidence from an emerging economy. Nord J Media Manag 2(1)

Gangopadhyay A, Sen A (2019) Panchmura–The Terracotta Hub of Bengal: a contemporary socio-economic study of handicraft workers engaged in terracotta craft. Int J Hum Soc Sci Stud 5 (3):42–64

Ghosal I, Prasad B (2019) Inspiring digitalization of handicraft market: an empirical approach. Parikalpana KIIT J Manag 15(1/2):199–209

Ghosh BK (2014) Economics of eco-friendly terracotta products in Bankura District of West Bengal. J Econ 2(2):233–245

Groenland E, Dana L-P (2020) Qualitative methodologies & data collection methods: toward increased rigour in management research. World Scientific, London

Hazra KK (2017) Prospect of traditional craft in present economy: a study of earthen doll of Krishnagar, West Bengal. Int J Manag 8(4):75–81

Hazra KK, Barman A (2017) Survival of earthen doll products and the contemporary trade - an argument on potency of bengal pottery. Clear Int J Res Commer Manag 8(7)

Igwe PA, Madichie NO, Newbery R (2019) Determinants of livelihood choices and artisanal entrepreneurship in Nigeria. Int J Entrep Behav Res 24(4):674–679

Kabir MS, Hou X, Akther R, Wang J, Wang L (2012) Impact of small entrepreneurship on sustainable livelihood assets of rural poor women in Bangladesh. Int J Econ Financ 4 (3):265–280

Kazungu I, Njau J (2018) The artisans: livelihood sustainability in the context of handicraft micro and small enterprises in Moshi Tanzania. Int J Res Innov Soc Sci 2(12):357–364

Luckman S (2015) Craft and the creative economy. Palgrave Macmillan, New York, NY

Markwick MC (2001) Tourism and the development of handicraft production in the Maltese islands. Tour Geogr 3(1):29–51

Mukherjee S, Mukherjee M, Bhattacharya S (2016) Exploring the potentials of handicraft as a promotional tool for West Bengal tourism. Indian J Res 5(1):29–36

Pandey N, Garg AK, Malhotra R, Pandey DN (2007) Linking local knowledge to global markets: livelihoods improvement through woodcarving in India. World Dev:1–9

Pret T, Cogan A (2019) Artisan entrepreneurship: a systematic literature review and research agenda. Int J Entrep Behav Res 25(4):592–614

Ramadani V, Hisrich RD, Dana LP, Palalic R, Panthi L (2019) Beekeeping as a family artisan entrepreneurship business. Int J Entrep Behav Res 25(4):717–730

Sahoo PM, Joddar P, Biswas S, Sarkar B (2016) The significance of terracotta cottage industry in the socio-economic livelihood of people - a case study of bankura terracotta craft hub. Int J Curr Res 8(01):25800–25806

Solanki SS (2008) Unorganized sector of workers: rural artisans. India, science and technology

Swanson KK, Timothy DJ (2012) Souvenirs: icons of meaning, commercialisation and commoditization. Tour Manag 33(3):489–499

Tregear A (2005) Lifestyle growth or community involvement? The balance of goals of artisan food producers. Entrep Reg Dev 17(1):1–15

Yin RK (1984) Case study research: design and methods. Sage, Newbury Park

Websites

Get Bengal (2020, June 13) The dying art of exquisite stone carving of Susunia in Bankura. https://www.getbengal.com/details/the-dying-art-of-exquisite-stone-carving-of-susunia-in-bankura, Accessed on 09.02.2021

India-Craft (n.d) Upstone [online]. http://www.india-crafts.com/stone_products/upstone.html. Accessed on 09.02.2021

Official Website of Bankura District, Govt of West Bengal. http://www.bankura.gov.in/stone-carving.htm. Accessed on 24.01.2021

Stone Crafts of Susunia, Debasis Roy. https://artsusunia.com/about-us/. Accessed on 24.01.2021

The Craft and Artisans (2010) [online]. http://www.craftandartisans.com/stone-carving-of-west-bengal.html. Accessed on 09.02.2021

West Bengal Khadi and Village Industries Board. https://www.wbkvib.org.in/index.php/village-industries-m/cluster-development-m/424-stone-carving-project-at-bankura. Accessed on 24.01.2021

Sriparna Guha is a Research Scholar in the Department of Management at Brainware University, West Bengal. She has done her Post Graduation in the field of economics from Rabindra Bharati University and has completed Post Graduate Diploma in Applied Economics and Information Management from Globsyn Business School, Kolkata, India. She has authored seven research papers in national and international journals of repute. She has also attended different national and international workshops and conferences.

Anirban Mandal is currently working as an Associate Professor and Director Research in the Department of School of Management and Commerce at Brainware University, Kolkata, India. He has done his PhD from KIIT University, Bhubaneswar, India. He has more than 15 years of teaching experience in different renowned colleges and institutions of West Bengal and also a Visiting Faculty in Pelita Harapan University, Jakarta, Indonesia. He has presented many research papers in different areas of management in different national and international seminars and conferences. He has authored 20 research papers in national and international journals of repute.

Pranam Dhar is working as a Professor at West Bengal State University, Barasat, Kolkata, India, and has teaching experience of 22 years. He has authored 42 books and 226 research articles published in different regional, national, and international journals. He has supervised 20 MPhil dissertations and 7 PhD dissertations. He also has 23 national and international awards.

Sandeep Poddar is a Professor and Deputy Vice Chancellor (Research and Innovation) of Lincoln University College, Malaysia. He also served as Senior Research Director and Executive Editor (Publications), Lincoln University College, Adjunct Faculty (Honorary), Bharat Center, Canada. He has published more than 100 research papers (in reputed Scopus and Web of Science indexed journals and books, filed more than 15 patents, organized international conferences, and also edited books in Malaysia, Australia, and India. He is serving as Guest editor of different reputed Scopus indexed journals of Elsevier, Inderscience, and Pertanika publishers etc..

Léo-Paul Dana is a Professor at Dalhousie University and holds titles of Professor at Montpellier Business School and Visiting Professor at Kingston University. He is associated with the Chaire ETI at Sorbonne Business School. A graduate of McGill University and HEC-Montreal, he has served as Marie Curie Fellow at Princeton University and Visiting Professor at INSEAD. He has published extensively in a variety of journals including *Entrepreneurship: Theory and Practice*, *International Business Review*, *International Small Business Journal*, *Journal of Business Research*, *Journal of Small Business Management*, *Journal of World Business*, *Small Business Economics*, and *Technological Forecasting & Social Change*.

Social Entrepreneurship Among Artisans

Gaitri Kumari and Ebikinei Stanley Eguruze

Abstract The present study examines the roles of social entrepreneurs in women empowerment and rural community development in India. It is a qualitative study that analysed cross-case studies of two social entrepreneurial ventures. Firstly, the present research identifies five roles of social entrepreneurs' self-efficacy for solving social issues like women empowerment and rural community development. Secondly, the study identified the diverse characteristics of social entrepreneurs in rural community development via socio-economic development and sustainable livelihood. Thirdly, the study also found that these roles are interlinked, but each role can also be independently functional, meaningful, and impactful. The application of social entrepreneurship techniques, skills, and knowledge was critical to the transformation of rural community development. Sharing this new addition is fundamentally an essential contribution to social entrepreneurship knowledge. The present study follows a qualitative method using a cross-case analysis with particular attention to social entrepreneurial ventures engaged in handicraft social enterprises. The study is based on in-depth interviews, focus group discussions, and participant observations, including photos taken and videos made of the location. Social entrepreneurs are acting as change agents for solving the prevalent social problems of society like women's empowerment and rural community development. It facilitates social mobility and uplifting aspirations, particularly for social entrepreneurs, and hopes for a region otherwise less developed. It may have social infrastructural development potentiality and social policymaking. It would be an essential source for policy decision-making, policy determination, economic planning tool, and a practical guide in addressing wide-ranging social issues like sustainability, socio-economic development, women empowerment, and social entrepreneurs' role in rural community development.

G. Kumari (✉)
Anthropology Department, University of Manitoba, Winnipeg, MB, Canada

E. S. Eguruze
American University for Leaders (AUL), London, UK

L.-P. Dana et al. (eds.), *Artisan and Handicraft Entrepreneurs*, Contributions to Management Science, https://doi.org/10.1007/978-3-030-82303-0_10

1 Introduction

New ideas and new efforts are crucial ways of bringing about development. The most exciting aspect of social entrepreneurship is that it does not concern itself only with innovation; it has to achieve this fundamental objective through social change. Social enterprises are boosting social welfare services (Milligan and Fyfe 2004). It is supported that social enterprises can empower the communities and improve the social, economic, and environmental conditions (DTI 2002, 2006; Social Enterprise UK 2011). Leading social enterprises are located in rural areas (Harding 2006). However, rural social enterprises are under-researched (Muñoz 2011) and limited records available within this theme (Clark et al. 2007; Zografos 2007). The research papers concerning rural communities are focused on addressing charities, voluntary organisations, and local community initiatives (Fyfe 2005; Randle and Dolnicar 2009). There are several reasons for the success of community productions. For example, rural communities render by the shared traditional rural strength incorporating mutual knowledge, a sense of community, and social cohesion (Shucksmith et al. 1996). Social enterprises create sustainable and entrepreneurial rural communities (Steinerowski and Steinerowska-Streb 2012). Social enterprises are known as community development actors (Eversole et al. 2013; Smith and McColl 2016), serving as the new provider of public services or act as social actors to innovate to support their agenda (Zografos 2007). The cultural characteristics of indigenous communities are conducive for social enterprises (Giovannini 2012). They cater social well-being of the local community through its social purpose (Perez 2013; Thompson and Doherty 2006).

India has a robust and rapidly growing economy, with a gross domestic product (GDP) of $2.9 trillion, which places India as the fifth with the largest economy, compared to $2.7 trillion and $2.6 trillion (UN 2017). Furthermore, in terms of population, India has 1.34 billion people, which ranks India as the second country with the highest population in the world. It is also estimated that India's entrepreneurship or small business sector contributes over 1.3 million employment opportunities annually, making entrepreneurship the second largest sector only after agriculture by contributing to the economy. Similarly, the number of small businesses or entrepreneurs in India is about 48 million compared to that of the United States (23 million) (Arora and Singh 2020). In their summary, Prahlad (2008) and Swetha and Rao (2013) stated that the history of small businesses, such as entrepreneur development, dates back to the Valley Civilization (3200–2600 BCE). It was followed by massive growth and a modernisation period for entrepreneurship, which was driven by WWII experiences. It reflected a period of massive needs for goods and services. In between these periods was the experience of the colonial era, which was similarly remarkable. After that, the post-independent period also experienced a large-scale entrepreneurship advancement, which continued until this contemporary time.

The entrepreneurship development in the region of Jharkhand in India also is part of this experience. Local people, including women and indigenous people, are part of this history. Their brave, creative, and innovative efforts were geared toward overcoming the social barriers and challenges of unemployment, low income or lack of income, poverty, and inequality. Therefore, there was a need to explore new ways of survival, so innovation became the vogue, which enables them to explore and exploit opportunities. This study shows that India's development would be more balanced and even more successful when the role of social entrepreneurs in women empowerment and rural community development entrepreneurial opportunities and potentiality across India is maximally explored and exploited. Thus, as Prahlad (2008) argues, policy support for innovation at the grassroots level across India is crucial.

In this study, the authors examine the social entrepreneurial self-efficacy approach in the realisation of women empowerment and rural community development. The aim is to critically examine the phenomenon of social entrepreneurial self-efficacy as it applies in women empowerment and rural community development. The authors discussed the study's aim and objectives, problem, and the gap and reviewed the relevant extant literature and case analysis to achieve the objective below. After that, the findings were also discussed and interpreted. In conclusion, the study findings were re-enforced in line with the objectives. In the end, suggestions for possible further research opportunities were highlighted.

2 Research Problem and Research Objectives

India is one of the youngest countries globally, with 64% of its population are in the working age group. If most of the most youthful population decides to become social entrepreneurs (Salamzadeh et al. 2013; Lacap et al. 2018), maximum social problems will be resolved. Jharkhand is one of the states of India that has young working populations. Moreover, the Jharkhand state has taken several initiatives with the help of Jharkhand State Khadi and Village Industries Board and Jharkhand Silk, Textile, and Handicraft Development Corporation (Jharcraft) for encouraging entrepreneurship in the state. Hence, there is scope and rationale behind investigating the applicability of social entrepreneurship in the Jharkhand region. The research aims to study the phenomena of social entrepreneurial self-efficacy among handicraft social enterprises. This research problem is premised on the need to enhance the comprehension of the phenomenon of social entrepreneurship as a critical tool for women empowerment and rural community advancement while committing to the following three specific objectives:

1. To critically examine the roles of social entrepreneurship in achieving women empowerment and rural community development.
2. To critically investigate and analyse how these roles are linked to their skills and experiences.
3. To propose a theoretical framework describing the roles of social entrepreneurial self-efficacy given women empowerment and rural community development.

3 Research Gap

Most of the literature available in social entrepreneurship, especially handicraft social entrepreneurship in eastern states of India, came from Assam, Meghalaya, Tripura, and Bihar. Despite several attempts by the state government to improve handicraft entrepreneurship in the Jharkhand, there is still little empirical work. Moreover, despite this critical knowledge-sharing opportunity concerning the research problem, social venture based on reviving the traditional crafts in women empowerment and community development is an under-researched phenomenon. It has led to a gap in comprehension and assimilation of the role social entrepreneurs play in rural development. The research gap, therefore, is driven by addressing the research questions. What is the role of social entrepreneurs in women empowerment and rural community development? Can social entrepreneurs contribute to the further advancement and sustainability of the rural-based handcraftsmanship industry and the artisanship vocational sector? Moreover, would a qualitative approach be applicable and relevant to this particular community-oriented study context (Sayer 1992 as cited in Yin 2009)?

4 Review of Literature on Social Entrepreneurship and Self-Efficacy

The linkage between innovation, creativity, social entrepreneurship, and social entrepreneurship self-efficacy is inevitably close. It is an integral part of the social entrepreneurship process through innovation that brings about new ideas and new product development. Whereas, on the other hand, creativity is more to do with engaging in that specific action of impacting the difference, social entrepreneurship is somewhere in between. There are broadly two categories of social enterprises. The first is categorised as nonprofit organisations (NPOs) that undertake a market-oriented approach (Defourny and Kim 2011). The second is classified as profit-making enterprises that call attention to two aspects: economic sustainability of the social venture and solutions to social problems (Dacin et al. 2011).

Entrepreneurial behaviour is guided by entrepreneurial intentions (Tiwari et al. 2017). There are a few identified social entrepreneurial purposes, i.e. empathy, moral judgement, perceived social support, and social entrepreneurial self-efficacy (Mair and Noboa 2006). Social entrepreneurial self-efficacy is defined as a "person's belief that individuals can contribute toward solving societal problems" (Hockerts 2017). Higher social entrepreneurial self-efficacy shows that the social entrepreneur is highly motivated and confident in addressing the social issue (Sequeira et al. 2007). Moreover, self-efficacy through the social entrepreneurship process helps entrepreneurs develop the skills that made them different from managers (Chen et al. 1998).

It suggests that in the context of this social entrepreneurship discourse, self-efficacy means that the degree to which a person believes in themselves is fundamentally critical in measuring self-efficacy. To this, Dana (2000), in his study relating to creating entrepreneurship in India, added that even "giving youth (the necessary) self-confidence (in order) to become higher flyers" is a typical example of promoting self-efficacy. Further, Dana (2000) highlighted that factors that could boost self-efficacy might include extending cultural values, diligence, government regulations, provision of relevant resources that people need, and changing the artistic mindset of people regarding entrepreneurship (Dana 2000). It is critical because India is a multicultural society with massive, diverse ethnic nationalities and a considerable population base to identify potential entrepreneurial stars (Dana 2000). As with Dana (ibid), importantly, that is why, as the authors believe, undertaking this study as an opportunity of learning more about how to boost self-efficacy concerning women empowerment and rural community development is crucial.

Similarly, in this present study, as with Dana (2000), giving self-confidence and self-efficacy to women and rural community development could advance India's global competitiveness through women empowerment and rural community development. In an earlier study, Dana (1999) highlighted the culture preservation through small businesses in Greece. Dana (1999) argues that government support for artisans and craftsmen, removal of task burdens, and reducing bureaucracy were also necessary to enhance self-confidence among aspiring entrepreneurship development at targeted areas: regional development and promoting traditions and crafts overseas. Thus, the authors believe women empowerment and rural development processes may benefit from these lessons. Ultimately, India will gain through support for women entrepreneurs and rural community development.

The handicraft industry not only provides employment opportunities but also revives declining craft practices. The Jharkhand state has an abundance of minerals, metals, and woods. Also, there are famous crafts like terracotta, woodcrafts, jute crafts, tribal jewellery, bamboo crafts, indigenous tribal paintings, Dokra metal casting, and tribal weavings that are the primary livelihood of indigenous communities. Therefore, Jharkhand has become a popular destination for handicraft social entrepreneurs in the past decade which leads to potential sustainable employment opportunities for the local communities of Jharkhand.

Similarly, the grassroots drive to bringing about the potential revival of indigenous art forms such as Paitker painting through innovation in the Jharkhand region of India is no different. It is all about the role of social entrepreneurs and entrepreneurship to achieve women's empowerment and rural community development. The role of women in indigenous crafts revival has become evident to reap employment benefits along with their exposure in the public domain (Buckley 1998; Attfield and Kirkham 1989). It has motivated the present study. The current research is focused on highlighting the five key roles of social entrepreneurs in addressing the value of self-efficacy for solving social issues like women empowerment and rural community development. It might help trigger the rejuvenation handicraft industrial sector in the Jharkhand region of India, which has been overlooked as a potential tool of social entrepreneurial self-efficacy for many years. It is believed that sharing this new addition is fundamentally a critical contribution to the knowledge of handicraft social enterprises.

More specifically, social entrepreneurs are recognised as crucial players in delivering innovative and cost-effective social business models for resolving social issues and creating social values (Khanapuri and Khandelwal 2011; Zeyen et al. 2012). Moreover, social entrepreneurs focus on economic value and social value creation (Mair and Mart 2006). Self-efficacy is identified as an affecting antecedent in the field of social entrepreneurial research. The high self-efficacy of social entrepreneurs allows perceiving feasible social business models (Mair and Noboa 2006; Mair and Mart 2006). Several entrepreneurship scholars proved that self-efficacy helps to anticipate the opportunities; therefore it is suggested to study the significance of self-efficacy in social entrepreneurship phenomena (Krueger and Brazeal 1994; Mair and Noboa 2006; Mair and Mart 2006; Smith and Woodworth 2012; Hockerts 2010).

It is an underlying fact that the role of women is indispensable in local, national, and global development (Clark 2013). Even though they live in poor rural communities, they have participated in local economies. Their participation has positively fostered the work environment and facilitated them to enjoy a better status in their household and local communities (Coughlin and Thomas 2002). Regarding the context of social entrepreneurship, social enterprises "can sustain the empowerment of the weakest social sectors like indigenous women, who suffer a condition of double discrimination" (Giovannini 2012). It has been observed that patriarchal culture in indigenous communities obstructs women's empowerment. However, social enterprises have encouraged women's empowerment by giving them employment opportunities and controlling their income source (Maguirre et al. 2016). As always, the underlying factor that prompted social entrepreneurship is the ability to quest for opportunities to create social values, generate employment, and eradicate poverty and inequalities. Moreover, there is a need that created opportunities for entrepreneurs to innovate new ways of creating an equalitarian society.

This review of extant literature focuses on building on a theoretical framework underpinning this study's objectives, which aims to recreate the notion of the role of social entrepreneurs as a model. Entrepreneurs' self-efficacy plays mediating role between social capital and new venture creation (Kannadhasan et al. 2018). Social capital is defined as the extent of the availability of social networks and the quality of resources owned by an entrepreneur (Bourdieu 2011). Social capital is crucial for entrepreneurial phenomena as it facilitates the identification of business opportunities, knowledge acquisition, reputation building, networking, and performance improvement (Lechner and Dowling 2003; Shaw et al. 2008; Zhang et al. 2020). Accordingly, as we would notice, the social capital theory is used to construct the theoretical framework intended to examine the self-efficacy factors of social entrepreneurship in women empowerment and rural community development. The rate of social entrepreneurship indicates the social capital of the country (Perkins et al. 2002; Häuberer 2010; Estrin et al. 2013). A review of literature related to methodological process does highlight the fact that social entrepreneur and entrepreneurship are models that embed several vital characteristics and roles including social leadership (Dees 1998; Borins 2000; Wallace 1999; Cornwall 1998), as an influencer (Hodgson 2007; Oliver 1991), as a motivator, (Holland 1985), as an employer (Zahra et al. 2009), and a network architect (Adler and Kwon 2002; Lee et al. 2001).

5 Methodology

The present study follows a qualitative approach. Although literature relating to a qualitative approach involving social entrepreneurs' self-efficacy may have been scarce in connection with the handicraft social enterprises, we used the same methodology in this research. It is in reliance on the fact that a qualitative approach has been known to have been a valuable tool in gathering data in a wider rural setting (following Sayer 1992, cited in Yin 2009), on an exploratory basis. The research strategy used is the cross-case analysis between two social entrepreneurial ventures. Given that social entrepreneurship is a widespread phenomenon in social science literature, research on social enterprises has followed case studies (Anderson et al. 2006; Hockerts 2010). Case studies are suitable strategies as research in this subject area is usually impending and mainly in exploratory stages. Therefore, case studies allow generating a large amount of information with the help of in-depth investigation (Bhattacherjee 2012). The case study inquiry relies on collective evidence from various resources (Groenland and Dana 2019). The data collection instruments used in the present study are interviews, focus group discussions, and observation. The study incorporated 24 in-depth interviews, three focus group discussions, and participant observations. Also, field observation was conducted, including photos taken and videos made of the location as a backup.

The primary reason was to encourage deeper comprehension of the phenomenon being researched. The authors seek to understand the phenomenon under study by getting embedded in it and getting close to the participants as close and practically as possible. Previous scholars have successfully adopted similar methodological design preferences in their various qualitative study endeavours (Patton 1982; Dana and Dana 2005). It means this methodological framework has been supported. It is posited that "methodological mandate to be contextually sensitive, inductive, and naturalistic," which means that researchers must get close to the phenomenon under study (Dana and Dana 2005: 85–86). Earlier scholars also supported this methodology. They argue that in the qualitative methods attempts, they understand the setting under study through direct personal contact through physical proximity for some time and the development of closeness (Patton 1982: 10), also cited by Dana and Dana (2005). However, other scholars previously found in a qualitative study that not only variety of data sources can be relevant (Yin 1981, as also cited by Dana and Dana 2005), but that, significantly, the data are well documented, verifiable, and reliable (Yin 1981), as also cited in Dana and Dana (2005). Accordingly, these data from the present two case studies of *Pipal Tree* and *Maatighar* are similarly well documented for further verification and reliability where necessary, which helped enriched the outcome. It means that in this present study, the choice of qualitative design methodology was appropriate, as it has allowed added value to knowledge, which hitherto unnoticed or underutilised. The authors argue that this made a significant contribution to methods because it improved reliability.

The present study is based on two handicraft social enterprises, namely *Pipal Tree* and *Maatighar*. The *Pipal Tree* is engaged with the training of woodcraft skills to facilitate women empowerment and rural development. In comparison, the *Maatighar* is primarily working towards the revival of the indigenous craft of Jharkhand, namely, Paitker painting. It is one of the oldest indigenous art forms performed by the Chitrakar community of Jharkhand, India. However, the Paitker painting is usually performed by men of the Chitrakar community. However, *Maatighar* has taken the initiative to endow Paitker's skill to women to facilitate women's empowerment and rural indigenous community development. The research population is targeted because both are handicraft social enterprises working towards women empowerment and rural community development over 4 years and share the same social entrepreneurial attributes. So, their experiences and knowledge became relevant during the data collecting field exercise.

The research sample selection is based on the fact that Jharkhand is a forest-covered state of eastern India. The rich tribe culture is synonymous with ancient craft succession in Jharkhand. There are 30 Scheduled Tribes in Jharkhand. The endangered craft forms are still being practised in rural Jharkhand. However, these art forms are on the verge of extinction. However, the state government has come forward to rescue these heritage crafts of Jharkhand by incorporating marketing and retail platforms like *Jharcraft* and *Kusum*. Irrespective of government support, handicrafts of Jharkhand are struggling to survive in the market. To overcome such situations, social entrepreneurs who know the economic potential of this sector have come forward to support and sustain the craft culture of Jharkhand.

Utpal Shaw has founded *Pipal Tree*, which is a for-profit social entrepreneurial venture. It has been established in the year 2014 with a vision to enforce women's empowerment in the rural setting of Jharkhand. It was all started with the social entrepreneurial thrive of Utpal Shaw, who always wanted to do something for unprivileged and secluded women of the society. He started this venture at Ghatshila with a handful of around three to four women who suffered ostracism in their family and yet wanted to step forward to change their lives. He trained them and encouraged them to pursue woodcrafts as their livelihood. Other women also got inspired and reached out to *Pipal Tree* to learn woodcraft skills. Each woman artisan of *Pipal Tree* has an awe-inspiring story to tell. Most of them are single parents and ostracised by family. Few of them could not feed their children, but now they provide food and schooling facilities. Mr. Utpal took pride by quoting that "...these women have made it possible to achieve Pipal Tree whatever it is today." It has managed to get a decent market in no time. Earlier, we had no retail place. As soon as the craft got popular, we managed to open nine retail shops in the major cities of Jharkhand.

Virendra Kumar has founded *Maatighar*, a for-profit organisation that is working for the revival of Paitker painting with a vision to hoard the longstanding heritage of Jharkhand. He envisioned providing sustainable livelihood to the Chitrakar community of Jharkhand, known for performing an extinct art form called Paitker painting. It strongly focuses on the empowerment of the Chitrakar community of Jharkhand. Chitrakars or Painters is a community that habitat across the border of West Bengal and Jharkhand. Mr. Virendra Kumar envisioned *Maatighar* in 2017. He was on an excursion to Amadobi village where he accidentally met Bijoy Chitrakar. This village is also known as Painters' village because of the Chitrakar community that resides there. Bijoy Chitrakar has shown and narrated his Paitker painting to him. He got curious about the Paitker art and Chitrakar community. Bijoy Chitrakar averred that "...it is difficult to sell Paitker; therefore, Chitrakars have migrated to nearby cities in search of sustainable livelihoods." After listing the ordeal of Bijoy Chitrakar and exploring the milieu of Chitrakars, he was motivated to help these artisans and revive the Paitker painting. He formed his team and conceived the idea of *Maatighar*. He knew that the community is suffering from hardship due to a lack of support regarding training, marketing, and promotions. He propelled absconded Chitrakars to resume the Paitker art form. He also included women in the Paitker skill development training to empower women of the rural community. His altruism towards the Chitrakar community has helped them to get a sustainable livelihood. On asking about the Paitker painting, he said:

> Paitker painting is a traditional craft form of the Chitrakar community. The painting uses natural colors driven out of flowers, vegetables, and stones. The brush is also made up of natural materials like bamboo and hairs of goat and squirrel.

This research adopted an exploratory design to understudy the phenomenon more deeply through cross-case analysis following Yin (1998, 2003). The authors utilised mix-of-tools, including interviews, focus group discussions, and observation with social entrepreneurs and artisans. In these conversations, for example, authors used the telephone as well as personal interviews. Additionally, the authors took photos of these specially made pieces of handicrafts. Moreover, the authors took a collection of video documentaries.

Meanwhile, authors also attended life workshops and exhibition events. During that time, they made further direct critical observations, using sight and feeling and appreciating how these specially made handicraft materials were being designed and constructed life in action. Additionally, the authors also utilised open-ended questions to gather relevant data from participating social entrepreneurs and artisans during the visits. The questions included social and economic aspects emphasising social entrepreneurial self-efficacy towards women empowerment and rural community development. The empirical work for this study took place between 2016 and 2019. Altogether 24 respondents participated in the personal interview, including social entrepreneurs and women artisans. The authors selected interviewees based on their importance, visibility, expertise, and recommendation. The duration of the personal interview ranges from 45 min to 2 h. The authors conducted observation on the workshops of *Pipal Tree* and *Maatighar* collectively for 102 h. The transcript recorded were of 342 pages. Data triangulation is performed with the help of collective data collection instruments to validate information generation. The data

Table 1 Comparison of Pipal Tree and Maatighar

	Pipal Tree	Maatighar
Type of enterprise	Handicraft social enterprise	Handicraft social enterprise
Name of social entrepreneur	Mr. Utpal Shaw	Mr. Virendra Kumar
Year of establishment	2014	2017
Type of value creation	• Women empowerment • Skill development • Sustainable employment • Socio-economic development • Rural community development	• Revival of indigenous craft (Paitker painting) • Skill development • Women empowerment • Indigenous community development • Rural community development

was subsequently analysed and the outcome of which led to the formation of the insight.

The cross-case analysis followed the procedure of categorisation, abstraction, and comparison of *Pipal Tree* and *Maatighar* as shown below (see Table 1).

Since both the handicraft social enterprises are from the same state, each participant's view is not different from the other. The authors conducted focus group discussions to address the discrepancies that appeared in the personal interview. Data triangulation and informants from *Jharcraft* (Jharkhand government undertaking handicraft enterprise) contributed to verifying participants' views.

5.1 Case Analysis

According to Ketokivi and Choi (2014), "the premise in theory-generating case research is that in the context of the specific research question and empirical setting, explanation (theory) derives from exploration (analysis)." We commenced with the identification of themes that have been extracted from the verbatim of the field study. After this, we identified the constructs of the cases by discussing them in-depth. We not only (1) achieved the first objective of the study in this analysis but also (2) processed the transcripts under the perceptions of the social entrepreneurs and converted same as meaningful as they can be, and then (3) the literature documentary evidence was analysed in which the significant findings were modelled as reflected in a framework as exhibited in Fig. 1. The framework exhibited in Fig. 1 is inspired by the study of Kumari (2020), where she explained the five key roles of social entrepreneurs in women empowerment and indigenous community development (Kumari 2020).

Further, a deeper analysis of the qualitative data was carried out, during which we arrived at an expected outcome based on social entrepreneurs' perceptions (Stake 2005). These analyses led us to believe the insight that roles of social entrepreneurs are not merely varied but valuable and helpful to a wide range of causes, including

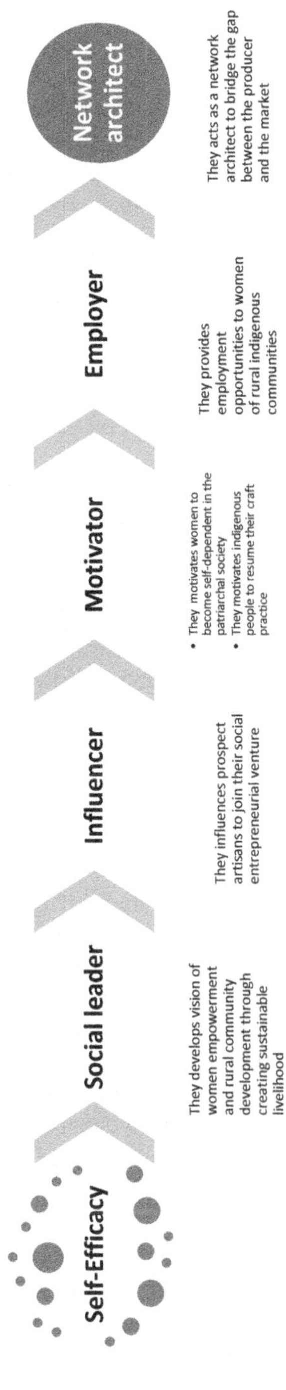

Fig. 1 Role of the social entrepreneur in women empowerment and rural community development

improvements in the welfare, wellness, and well-being of artisans as well as entire indigenous and rural communities (Kumari 2020). The cross-case approach led to astute findings that help to comprehend our knowledge and become the basis of the theory-building of this study.

Self-efficacy or trust in the effectiveness of social entrepreneurship ventures has been widely explored in women empowerment, rural community development, and many other fields (Kroeker 1995; Maton and Salem 1995; Perkins 1995; Perkins et al. 1996; Speer and Hughey 1995; Saegert et al. 2001). The confidence in building a successful business model results from high entrepreneurial self-efficacy (Sequeira et al. 2007). Moreover, in an emerging market, prospective social entrepreneurs exhibit high self-efficacy related to higher innovation, social impact, sustainability, and expandability of the venture (Urban 2015).

The definition of empowerment given by Rappaport (1987) is defined as an action through which people achieve the power to secure their lives and communities. It denotes a new perspective to social capital by emphasising the cognitive attributions and motivating forces that encourage community members to earn sustainable development. It also addresses the well-being of the individual and community level and the community's empowerment (Douglas et al. 2002). The concept of social capital is defined as the gain of potential resources with the help of perceived reputation, social network, and personal contacts with investors and prospective customers (Chia and Liang 2016). Moreover, social capital is crucial for the acquisition of significant knowledge for the newer firms (Yli-Renko et al. 2001), especially when social entrepreneurs seek to gain the knowledge of market demands and needs considering social value creation (Austin et al. 2006).

6 Findings and Discussion

The paper established advancement in the study of Kumari (2020) with the effectiveness of social entrepreneurial self-efficacy for women empowerment and rural community development. Kumari (2020) proposed five primary functions relating to social entrepreneurs for tackling societal challenges, including women empowerment and rural community advancement. The excerpts of two community-oriented cases were modelled as social entrepreneurship ventures where one was engaged in female equality and inequality and skill development. In contrast, the other was involved in the revival of indigenous craft, women empowerment, and rural community support. At the same time, both cases proved that social entrepreneurs are indeed fundamentally critical agents for indigenous and rural community advancement.

Notably, the paper highlighted the essence and inherent values in the role of social entrepreneurs, not only in promoting women empowerment and rural community development in particular but also towards reviving indigenous crafts and facilitating the sustainability of the indigenous community, which has been lacking over the years. To be specific, the social entrepreneur's self-efficacy demonstrates the role of social leader, influencer, motivator, employer, and network architect (see Fig. 1).

In Fig. 1, the researcher highlights the role of social entrepreneurial self-efficacy in women empowerment and rural community development.

Self-Efficacy Both social entrepreneurs were determined to address the social issue of women empowerment and rural community development. However, their approach is different. Utpal Shaw was explicitly focused on endowing woodcraft skill development training for women empowerment of the rural community. Virendra Kumar was focused explicitly on reviving the indigenous craft of Paitker painting to facilitate the development of the Chitrakar community of Jharkhand. Social entrepreneurs are also seen as problem-solvers; these models unravelled the complex social problems by creating an impact on their communities (Zahra et al. 2009). Indigenous heritage could be established by the amalgamation of several elements like tradition, custom, creativity, and innovation. Artists and artisans play a significant role in creating, renewing, and transmitting indigenous heritage, reviving the cultural practices (Varutti 2015). Several factors can enable indigenous businesses that include operational business aspects like access to capital, supply, and a skilled workforce, with proper education and training (Whitford and Ruhanen 2010). Paitker is one of the oldest paintings of Jharkhand. It is more than 500 years old. As a social entrepreneur, Virendra is working to revive this art practice. *Maatighar* has three primary operations, i.e. research and development, product development, and artisans.

Social Leader Based on these two case studies, both social entrepreneurs became apparent as social leaders. On the one hand, Utpal Shaw strived for women empowerment through employability using the endowment of woodcraft skills. On the other hand, Virendra Kumar illustrated his astonishment at the rare practice of the indigenous craft of Paitker painting. He observed the conditions of Paitker artisans very closely and decided to support the heritage art. He formed a team of experts and artisans to provide a marketable platform for the Paitker painting. Both cases show that social leaders and followers have contributed to the epoch-making effect on social development. In light of their perspectives, we further submit that Utpal Shaw and Virendra Kumar were equally exemplary inspirational and pragmatic social entrepreneurs in engendering female equality advocacy on the one hand and in indigenous and rural community advancement challenges on the other hand. Moreover, both social entrepreneurs do share a wide range of attributes and capabilities: rendering leadership (Dees 1998); originality, self-respect, resourcefulness, and inspiration (Borins 2000); uplifting disadvantaged and vulnerable indigenous and rural communities (Wallace 1999); exemplary community-oriented self-help leadership (Cornwall 1998); tackling practical issues for the needy (Hibbert et al. 2001); and pragmatic implementers of a vision (Haven-Tang and Jones 2012).

Influencer Both social entrepreneurs have acted as influential factors in addressing two different social issues. *Pipal Tree* helped the women artisans realise their skill potential, whereas the *Maatighar* helped the indigenous community protect and preserve their heritage craft. Meanwhile, both social entrepreneurial ventures have enhanced the performance of the handicraft industry of Jharkhand. The major influential factors identified in both the social entrepreneurial ventures are their capabilities to enhance employment opportunities, socio-economic development of artisanal communities (women and indigenous), and improvement of the handicraft market (woodcraft and Paitker painting). Sociological scholars argue that the institutionalised patterns of behaviour and individual practices can be influenced by mutual dependence (Oliver 1991; Hodgson 2007). It can be modified, or even renewed, through the commitment of influential individuals or well-regulated groups (Martin 2000). Entrepreneurs act as change agents to convince their group members to collaborate and help achieve their desired objectives (Dorado 2005; Sotarauta 2009). So these change agents influence the behaviour of others owning to their network-based leadership and their interpretative power (Leca et al. 2008; Sotarauta and Pulkkinen 2011).

Motivator Both social entrepreneurial ventures are perceived as drivers for indigenous and rural community advancement. Also, they have encouraged and motivated rural communities, especially women, to work in the handicraft clusters of Jharkhand. On the one hand, *Pipal Tree* has motivated the reluctant women of the indigenous rural community to learn woodcraft. In contrast, *Maatighar* has urged the destitute Chitrakars to continue their heritage craft. It was not easy to convince women to learn craft skills due to the setbacks of family and society.

Moreover, due to the decline of Paitker painting, many artisans from the Chitrakar community had left the craft practice. Virendra Kumar's motivation helped many artisans learn and improve the craft as per the standard market demand. Scholars interpreted motivation differently in the context of social entrepreneurship: SEs are drivers for success (Holland 1985) or enablers, facilitators, and innovators (Stettner 2003). They encourage their employees to offer innovative ideas and, if needed, delegate responsibilities to them (Stettner 2003) or reward or recognise success (Bundaleska 2007). The entrepreneur should award if the employee has successfully implemented the idea (Bundaleska 2007).

Employer Both social entrepreneurial ventures successfully employ their targeted segment, whether tribal women artisans or rural communities. However, both social entrepreneurial ventures have different business models. *Pipal Tree* has evolved over the years. Initially, the business model was simple, as fewer artisans were working for social entrepreneurial ventures. It all started in 2014 with the commencement of induction programs in nearby rural areas of Ghatshila. Utpal Shaw visited two to three women with his team to encourage more women to learn woodcraft skills and earn a better livelihood. Once women showed their interest, he started their training. After training, they were ready to work on the site or at home as per their comfort. Women were given the designs and raw materials which they carve at their home or the workshop. After cutting techniques, it is delivered to the workshop, where master artisans assemble these designed pieces. After assembling, the woodcrafts are packed and delivered to the destination retails of *Pipal Tree*. They encourage their customers to get involved either through woodcraft design or feedback.

However, the business model evolved in 2018 as the number of skilled artisans increased and demand increased. The advanced business model of *Pipal Tree* is connected to different villages via village coordinators. Each village coordinator is responsible for ten artisans. The respective village coordinators get the requisition of woodcrafts from the Ranchi production centre. Archana is in charge of the Ranchi production centre. She knows pretty well which village coordinator is good in which woodcraft. At Ranchi production centre, Malti analyses the inventory and stock of raw materials and finished products. She has been told to put requisition of woodcraft items if three items from a box have been sold.

The administration team of *Pipal Tree* has a total of seven trainers and three production managers. The trainers are looking after the Khunti and Godda districts of Jharkhand. The trainers are responsible for the endowment of woodcraft skills under corporate social responsibility and government training programs. Along with training, they also monitor the progress of artisans. Also, out of three production managers, one is looking after Jamshedpur city, and two are taking care of Patratu (Ramgarh) town of Jharkhand.

The prime intention of *Maatighar* is to revive the Paitker painting. Therefore, their long-term measures are to aware customers about Paitker, encourage skill development for reluctant Paitker artisans, and induce standard production. They have no retail space, but they are freelancing for Jharcraft and *Pipal Tree* organisations. However, recently, they have started working with Amazon to sell their craft on e-tailing. The measurement of the internal process is the operational indicators of productivity and quality, measured constantly. The longer view entails the learning and growth, the profitability of the firm now and in the future.

Network Architect These social entrepreneurial ventures have acted as network architects by connecting the artisans to the desired segment of the market. *Pipal Tree* had started with its retail platforms, but later on, they have approached Jharkhand government and e-commerce platforms. The Jharkhand government has given them retail spaces at all the tourist places of Jharkhand. They have also created their website from where the artisans get orders and sell without the interference of intermediaries. *Maatighar* has no big team, and their skilled artisans are also few; therefore, they have not launched their retail and online platform. However, they are using their network to sell the Paitker craft. Earlier, Paitker artisans were not aware of modern marketing and retail media. Still, *Maatighar* has linked them to various e-commerce platforms from where they get their orders without the interference of intermediaries. They have approached online shopping platforms like amazon.in and Flipkart.in for selling the Paitker painting. They have started it with small orders as they lack skilled artisans. According to social capital theory, external networks help firms gain access to resources that may be responsible for their business performance and survival (Adler and Kwon 2002). Interaction of entrepreneurial intention with external connections helps enhance social entrepreneurial ventures' performance (Lee et al. 2001). Networks that connect entrepreneurs to capital, suppliers, employees, partners, and customers are the principal constituent for ease of the ongoing process of the social entrepreneurial ventures (Kline and Milburn 2010).

The study identified the most significant roles of social entrepreneurs' self-efficacy: social leadership, influencing and motivating rural communities to create value creation vis-a-vis generating employment for the local community, especially women, and building strategic networks and collaboration with significant others. The social enterprises helped the indigenous rural community to participate in the skill development training programs, thereby extending sustainable livelihood. Moreover, it helped to enhance the self-dependency of women by making them breadwinners of the family. Also, women are financially running the family, thereby experiencing a reduced rate of domestic violence in their homes and thereby gaining more acknowledgement and recognition of women in society. They have moreover improved access to better educational opportunities and facilities for their children. Crucially, the research also observed remarkable gains being made in such areas; evidence of the sustainability of the crucial Paitker painting sector would be a positive and constructive step towards advancement of the craftsmanship market and broader connections to the target market of the product.

Notably, the research also revealed how these roles are linked to their skills and experiences. They have persuaded government policymakers to provide marketing facilities such as building space for organising exhibitions, and training programs have enabled additional work such as freelancing in Paitker artisanship. Also, they have managed to gain teaching consultancy jobs with reputable schools in Jamshedpur, where they practise teaching Paitker artisanship to students more directly in their hobby classes. Moreover, quantitatively the numbers of Paitker artists have increased from just 2 to over 15. Also, there has been increased interest in painting woodcrafts.

Moreover, there is also the promotion of cultural products and services through the Internet platform. The launching of websites encouraged and enabled customers to observe live workshops while the exhibition allows customers to place customised orders online and more. The use of online facilities has also enabled taking website service of the hot jar in attracting potential consumers through their websites, which has improved the knowledge of customers' buying behaviours of woodcrafts and Paitker painting. Moreover, offering the crafts trade with strategic support radicalised the handicraft sector. Also, it helped with the sustainability of the Paitker painting within the indigenous rural community which was critically analysed.

The researchers also identify areas of barriers and challenges that are impacting on social entrepreneurial efforts. While there are improvements in the condition of handicraft social enterprises due to social entrepreneurs' self-efficacy through innovative measures, deeper engagement, and participation in the revival of the indigenous crafts and sustainability of the woodcrafts sector, at the same time, the combination of challenges are detrimental: lack of access to finance, as they are primarily self-funding, negligence of administration, illiteracy, meeting quality standards, productivity constraints, marketing channels, outlets, and unskilled artisans.

7 Conclusion

The two cases have reinforced that social entrepreneurs are catalysts for women's empowerment and indigenous and rural community advancement. Rural community advancement, including improvement in the welfare, wellness, and well-being of the indigenous communities that have suffered multidimensional disadvantages, was critical. Progress in living conditions of the indigenous people and rural communities could be best learned sufficiently, according to the Human Development Index (HDI) (Bannerjee 2018). Furthermore, the "capability approach to development" is considered a more "people-centric" strategy towards eliminating impoverishment in a needy society (Sen 1993). It is fundamentally critical to encourage, motivate, and support social entrepreneurs and indigenous and rural communities to embrace "employment security" as well as "security "through employability," both of which phenomena are equally useful and relevant sustainable approaches to learning. There is also a need to acknowledge resources and capabilities while still appreciating their crucial differences (Subramanian et al. 2013). The significant strengths of artisans may include the ability the sustenance craftsmanship, revenue creating, self-employment, as well as employment creation and commitment/dedication to entrepreneurship, all of which collectively work together towards the achievement of indigenous community regeneration and rural economic growth in general (Ahamed and Karim 2019). Eliminating improvement, including other barriers such as education, may stimulate societal progress in general (Bannerjee 2018).

Further, this study advanced insightful depth concerning the roles of social entrepreneurs' self-efficacy in collective terms, particularly in connection with women empowerment and indigenous and rural community development in the Jharkhand region of India. Nevertheless, there is a greater scope of research in different situations with different types of social entrepreneurs. Crucially, the study advocated the positive and constructive changes of social enterprises in the handicraft industry, which is helpful in indigenous and rural community survival and the sustainability of the entire nation: in the micro-, meso-, and macro-development sense of the perception.

Similarly, the paper reinforced that social entrepreneurs are particularly resourceful in keeping handicraft entrepreneurship alive and motivating and encouraging skill development, critical to the indigenous and rural community, thereby contributing positively and constructively towards poverty eradication through access to local, national, and international marketing platforms.

Besides the above outcomes, the paper also identified some limitations, including critical areas for further research, which may interest readers. Firstly, this is a methodological development research paper, and as such, literature is purposively limited to only the theoretical framework underpinning this study. Secondly, this study utilised two social entrepreneurial ventures: great contrasts, they are similar in several ways. Nevertheless, the underlying challenges are more alike than different. Thirdly, the study highlighted five functions of social entrepreneurs in the context of the Jharkhand region of India. There might be more roles potentially elsewhere. Furthermore, there may be a possibility that continuing research may uncover novel functions that social entrepreneurs need to engage in to enrich our understanding of the theory of social entrepreneurs, which has hitherto been missing. Therefore, as this study was centred around the Jharkhand region, it automatically opens up further research opportunities for similar research in other areas across India and other developing countries.

References

Adler P, Kwon S (2002) Social capital: prospects for a new concept. Acad Manag Rev 27:17–40
Ahamed DM, Karim R (2019 June) Impact of rural tourism product on the socio-economic condition of Artisans in Birbhum District: a case study on Kantha Stitch handicraft. Research Directions, Special Issue-June, pp 153-162
Anderson RB, Dana LP, Dana TE (2006) Indigenous land rights, entrepreneurship, and economic development in Canada: "opting-in" to the global economy. J World Bus 41(1):45–55
Arora N, Singh B (2020) Corporate governance and underpricing of small and medium enterprises IPOs in India. Corp Gov Int J Bus Soc
Attfield J, Kirkham P (1989) A view from the interior: feminism, women, and design, vol 8. Women's Press, London
Austin J, Stevenson H, Wei-Skillern J (2006) Social and commercial entrepreneurship: same, different, or both? Entrep Theory Pract 30(1):1–22
Bannerjee A (2018) A Micro level study of socio-economic and health status of great Andamanese and Onges of Andaman Island. Orient Anthropol:19–29
Bhattacherjee, A. (2012). Social science research: principles, methods, and practices
Borins S (2000) Loose cannons and rule breakers, or enterprising leaders? Some evidence about innovative public managers. Public Adm Rev 60:498–507
Bourdieu P (2011) The forms of capital (1986). In: Cultural theory: an anthology, vol 1, pp 81–93
Buckley C (1998) On the margins: theorising the history and significance of making and designing clothes at home. J Des Hist 11(2):157–171
Bundaleska E (2007) Motivation of employees in entrepreneurship. Entrepreneurship – problems, dilemmas, and perspectives, pp 197–200
Chen CC, Greene PG, Crick A (1998) Does entrepreneurial self-efficacy distinguish entrepreneurs from managers? J Bus Ventur 13(4):295–316
Chia C-C, Liang C (2016) Influence of creativity and social capital on the entrepreneurial intention of tourism students. J Entrep Manag Innov 12(2):151–168
Clark S (2013) Wind beneath my wings: policies promoting high-growth oriented women entrepreneurs. Int J Gend Entrep 5(1):36–59
Clark D, Southern R, Beer J (2007) Rural governance, community empowerment and the new institutionalism: a case study of the Isle of Wight. J Rural Stud 23(2):254–266
Cornwall J (1998) The entrepreneur as building block for community. J Dev Entrep 3(2):141–148
Coughlin JH, Thomas AR (2002) The rise of women entrepreneurs: people, processes and global trends. Quorum Books, Westport
Dacin MT, Dacin PA, Tracey P (2011) Social entrepreneurship: a critique and future directions. Organ Sci 22(5):1203–1213
Dana LP (1999) Preserving culture through small business: government support for artisans and craftsmen in Greece. J Small Bus Manag 37(1):90
Dana LP (2000) Creating entrepreneurs in India. J Small Bus Manag 38(1):86

Dana LP, Dana TE (2005) Expanding the scope of methodologies used in entrepreneurship research. Int J Entrep Small Bus 2(1):79–88
Dees JG (1998) Enterprising nonprofits. Harvard Business Review, January–February, pp 55–67
Defourny J, Kim SY (2011) Emerging models of social enterprise in Eastern Asia: a cross-country analysis. Soc Enterp J 7(1):86–111
Dorado S (2005) Institutional entrepreneurship, partaking, and convening. Organ Stud 26 (3):385–414
Douglas DP, Hughey J, Speer PW (2002) Community psychology perspectives on social capital theory and community development practice. Community Dev 33(1):33–52
DTI (2002) Social enterprise: a strategy for success. DTI, London
DTI (2006) A social enterprise strategy for scotland: a consultation. DTI, London
Estrin S, Mickiewicz T, Stephan U (2013) Entrepreneurship, social capital, and institutions: social and commercial entrepreneurship across nations. Entrep Theory Pract 37:479–504
Eversole R, McNeish JA, Cimadamore AD (eds) (2013) Indigenous peoples and poverty: an international perspective. Zed Books
Fyfe NR (2005) Making space for "neo-communitarianism"? The third sector, state and civil society in the UK. Antipode 37(3):536–557
Giovannini M (2012) Social enterprises for development as buen vivir. J Enterp Commun People Places Global Econ 6(3):284–299
Groenland E, Dana LP (2019) Qualitative methodologies and data collection methods: toward increased rigour in management research, vol 1. World Scientific
Harding S (2006) Science and social inequality: feminist and postcolonial issues. University of Illinois Press
Häuberer J (2010) Social capital theory. s.l.:Research
Haven-Tang C, Jones E (2012) Local leadership for rural tourism development: a case study of Adventa, Monmouthshire, UK. Tour Manag Perspect 4:28–35
Hibbert SA, Hogg G, Quinn T (2001) Consumer response to social entrepreneurship: The case of the big issue in Scotland. Int J Nonprofit Volunt Sect Mark 7:288–301
Hockerts K (2010) Social entrepreneurship between market and mission. Int Rev Entrep 8 (2):177–198
Hockerts K (2017) Determinants of social entrepreneurial intentions. Entrep Theory Pract 41 (1):105–130
Hodgson GM (2007) Institutions and individuals: interaction and evolution. Organ Stud 28 (1):95–116
Holland JL (1985) Making vocational choices. Prentice-Hall, Englewood Cliffs, NJ
Kannadhasan M, Charan P, Singh P, Sivasankaran N (2018) Relationships among social capital, self-efficacy, and new venture creations. Manag Decis
Ketokivi M, Choi T (2014) Renaissance of case research as a scientific method. J Oper Manag 32 (5):232–240
Khanapuri VB, Khandelwal MR (2011) Scope for fair trade and social entrepreneurship in India. Business Strategy Series 12(4):209–215
Kline C, Milburn LA (2010) Ten categories of entrepreneurial climate to encourage rural tourism development. Ann Leisure Res 13:320–348
Kroeker CJ (1995) Individual organizational, and societal empowerment: a study of the processes in a Nicaraguan agricultural cooperative. Am J Commun Psychol 23:749–764
Krueger NF, Brazeal DV (1994) Entrepreneurial potential and potential entrepreneurs. Entrep Theory Pract 18:91–91
Kumari G (2020) Role of social entrepreneurs in women empowerment and indigenous people development: a cross-case analysis. J Asia Entrep Sustain 16(2):106–161
Lacap JPG, Mulyaningsih HD, Ramadani V (2018) The mediating effects of social entrepreneurial antecedents on the relationship between prior experience and social entrepreneurial intent: the case of Filipino and Indonesian university students. J Sci Technol Policy Manag 9(3):329–346
Leca B, Battilana J, Boxenbaum E (2008) Agency and institutions: a review of institutional entrepreneurship

Lechner C, Dowling M (2003) Firm networks: external relationships as sources for the growth and competitiveness of entrepreneurial firms. Entrep Reg Dev 15(1):1–26
Lee C, Lee K, Pennings J (2001) Internal capabilities, external networks, and performance: a study of technology-based networks. Strateg Manag J 22:615–640
Maguirre MV, Ruelas GC, TORRE CGDL (2016) Women empowerment through social innovation in indigenous social enterprises. RAM Revista de Administração Mackenzie 17(6):164–190
Mair J, Mart I (2006) Social entrepreneurship research: a source of explanation, prediction, and delight. J World Bus 41(1):36–44
Mair J, Noboa E (2006) Social entrepreneurship: how intentions to create a social venture are formed. In: Mair J, Robinson J, Hockerts KN (eds) Social entrepreneurship. Palgrave Macmillan, Basingstoke, pp 121–135
Martin R (2000) Institutional approaches in economic geography. Blackwell, Oxford
Maton KI, Salem DA (1995) Organizational characteristics of empowering community settings: a multiple case study approach. Am J Community Psychol 23:631–656
Milligan C, Fyfe NR (2004) Putting the voluntary sector in its place: geographical perspectives on voluntary activity and social welfare in Glasgow. J Soc Policy 33(1):73–93
Muñoz SA (2011) Health service provision through social enterprise: opportunities and barriers identified by social entrepreneurs and procurement professionals in the UK. Int J Entrep Innov 12(1):39–53
Oliver C (1991) Strategic responses to institutional processes. Acad Manag Rev 16(1):145–179
Patton MQ (1982) Qualitative methods and approaches: what are they? New Dir Inst Res 1982 (34):3–15
Perez JC (2013) Social enterprise in the development agenda. Opening a new road map or just a new vehicle to travel the same route. Soc Enterp J 9(3):247–268
Perkins DD (1995) Speaking truth to power: Empowerment ideology as social intervention and policy. Am J Commun Psychol 23:765–794
Perkins DD, Brown BB, Taylor RB (1996) The ecology of empowerment: Predicting participation in community organizations. J Soc Issues 52:85–110
Perkins DD, Hughey J, Speer PW (2002) Community psychology perspectives on social capital theory and community development practice. Community Dev 33(1):33–52
Prahlad C. K., Entrepreneurs to explore domestic opportunities, 2008
Randle M, Dolnicar S (2009) Not just any volunteers: segmenting the market to attract the high contributors. J Nonprofit Publ Sect Market 21(3):271–282
Rappaport J (1987) Terms of empowerment/exemplars of prevention: Toward a theory for community psychology. Am J Community Psychol 15:121–148
Saegert S, Thompson JP, Warren MR (2001) Social capital and poor communities. Russell Sage Foundation, New York
Salamzadeh A, Azimi MA, Kirby DA (2013) Social entrepreneurship education in higher education: insights from a developing country. Int J Entrep Small Bus 20(1):17–34
Sayer A (1992) Method in social science: a realist approach. Routledge, London
Sen A (1993) Capability and well-being. In: s.l.:s.n
Sequeira J, Mueller SL, McGee JE (2007) The influence of social ties and self-efficacy in forming entrepreneurial intentions and motivating nascent behavior. J Dev Entrep 12(3):275–293
Shaw E, Lam W, Carter S (2008) The role of entrepreneurial capital in building service reputation. Serv Ind J 28(7):899–917
Shucksmith M, Chapman P, Clark GM, Black S, Conway E (1996) Rural Scotland today: the best of both worlds? Avebury
Smith AM, McColl J (2016) Contextual influences on social enterprise management in rural and urban communities. Local Econ 31(5):572–588
Smith IH, Woodworth WP (2012) Developing social entrepreneurs and social innovators: a social identity and self-efficacy approach. Acad Manag Learn Edu 11(3):390–407
Social Enterprise, UK (2011). http://www.socialenterprise.or-g.uk/press-releases.php

Sotarauta M (2009) Power and influence tactics in the promotion of regional development: an empirical analysis of the work of finnish regional development officers. Geoforum 40 (5):895–905

Sotarauta M, Pulkkinen R (2011) Institutional entrepreneurship for knowledge regions: in search of a fresh set of questions for regional innovation studies. Environ Plann 29(1):96–112

Speer PW, Hughey J (1995) Community organizing: an ecological route to empowerment and power. Am J Community Psychol 23:729–748

Stake RE (2005) Multiple case study analysis. Guilford Press, New York

Steinerowski AA, Steinerowska-Streb I (2012) Can social enterprise contribute to creating sustainable rural communities? Using the lens of structuration theory to analyse the emergence of rural social enterprise. Local Econ 27(2):167–182

Stettner M (2003) The new managers handbook. CWL Publishing Enterprises, Madison

Subramanian D, Verd JM, Vero J, Zimmermann B (2013) Bringing Sen's capability approach to work and human resource practices. Int J Manpow 34(4):292–304

Swetha T, Rao KV (2013) Entrepreneurship in India. Int J Soc Sci Interdiscip Res 2(7):1–13

Thompson J, Doherty B (2006) The diverse world of social enterprise. A collection of social enterprise stories. Int J Soc Econ 33(5/6):361–375

Tiwari P, Bhat AK, Tikoria J (2017) The role of emotional intelligence and self-efficacy on social entrepreneurial attitudes and social entrepreneurial intentions. J Soc Entrep 8(2):165–185

United Nations Permanent Forum on Indigenous Issues (2017) Indigenous peoples, indigenous voice factsheet

Urban B (2015) Evaluation of social enterprise outcomes and self-efficacy. Int J Soc Econ 42 (2):163–178

Varutti M (2015) Crafting heritage: artisans and the making of Indigenous heritage in contemporary Taiwan. Int J Herit Stud 21(10):1036–1049

Wallace SL (1999) Social entrepreneurship: The role of social purpose enterprises in facilitating community economic development. J Dev Entrep 4:153–174

Whitford M, Ruhanen L (2010) Indigenous tourism businesses in queensland: criteria for success. In: CRC for sustainable tourism. Gold Coast

Yin RK (1981) The case study crisis: some answers. Adm Sci Q 26(1):58–65

Yin RK (1998) The abridged version of case study research: design and method. In: Handbook of applied social research methods. Sage, pp 229–259

Yin RK (2003) Designing case studies. In: Maruster L, Gijsenberg MJ (eds) Qualitative research methods. Sage, London, pp 359–386

Yin R (2009) Case Study research: design and methods. Thousand Oaks, CA, Sage

Yli-Renko H, Autio E, Sapienza HJ (2001) Social capital, knowledge acquisition, and knowledge exploitation in young technology-based firms. Strateg Manag J 22(6–7):587–613

Zahra SA, Gedajlovic E, Neubaum DO, Shulman JM (2009) A typology of social entrepreneurs: motives, search processes and ethical challenges. J Bus Ventur 24:519–532

Zeyen A, Beckmann M, Susan M, Gregory Dees J, Khanin D, Krueger N, Patrick J. Murphy, et al. (2012) Social entrepreneurship and broader theories: shedding new light on the 'bigger picture'. J Soc Entrep 2015:1–20

Zhang W, Zhao W, Gao Y, Xiao Z (2020) How do managerial ties influence the effectuation and causation of entrepreneurship in China? The role of entrepreneurs' cognitive bias. Asia Pac Bus Rev 26(5):613–641

Zografos C (2007) Rurality discourses and the role of the social enterprise in regenerating rural Scotland. J Rural Stud 23(1):38–51

Gaitri Kumari has more than 10 years of academic experience in the course of Management. She is working as an Associate Postdoctoral Fellow in the Anthropology Department of the University of Manitoba. She has completed a Ph.D. in Management from Birla Institute of Technology, Ranchi, India. She has authored several scholarly works, including research papers and book chapters. She is actively serving as a reviewer for reputed journals. She is also acting as a Managing Editor of the Journal of Youth & Community Development.

Ebikinei Stanley Eguruze is an Associate Professor in Marketing, American University for Leaders (AUL), London, UK. He received his PhD in Marketing from Cardiff Metropolitan University, UK, on Tackling Poverty, using Social Marketing Techniques. He was formerly of the School of Marketing, Niger Delta University, Bayelsa State, Nigeria. He has authored books *Tackling Poverty* (2016) and *Strategy for Tackling Poverty in Nigeria* (2017). He is also acting as a Chief Editor of the Journal of Youth and Community Development.

Part III
Toward the Future: Social Media, Technology and Obstacles

Social Media Use by Artisans

Saurabh Singh, Robert Hisrich, and Xiaowei Guo

Abstract Social media, in general, is a form of communication that enables users to share content and messages utilizing information technology-enabled applications such as Facebook, Instagram, and Twitter. According to the popular social media marketing service provider Hootsuite.com, the very first social media platform called sixdegrees.com started in 1997. The platform provided users with features such as sending messages to other users and creating personal profiles. Over the last decade, the number of social media platforms, as well as users of these platforms, has increased substantially. The high rate of adopting such platforms can be attributed to relatively higher access to high-speed Internet, availability of affordable smartphones, and attractiveness of numerous functions offered by the latest social media platforms ranging from video calls to online shopping.

1 Introduction

The high rate of adoption of social media platforms by artisans has impacted them in numerous ways around the world. Artisans can now sell their products directly to consumers by listing their products on websites such as Etsy.com. Not only are the artisans selling their products online themselves, they are also actively showcasing their skills and art on social media platforms. This progress has enabled the development of a closer relationship between consumers and artisans due to content sharing and communication abilities afforded to the artisans by social media platforms. These latest developments had a major impact on the arts and crafts industry as new opportunities and paradigms are available to the artisans. In this chapter, we discuss the importance of social media use by artisans and how they use this tool to their benefit.

S. Singh (✉) · R. Hisrich · X. Guo
Kent State University, Kent, OH, USA
e-mail: ssingh34@kent.edu; rhisric1@kent.edu; xguo15@kent.edu

L.-P. Dana et al. (eds.), *Artisan and Handicraft Entrepreneurs*, Contributions to Management Science, https://doi.org/10.1007/978-3-030-82303-0_11

2 The Age of Social Media

The popularity of social media has been growing exponentially over the last few decades. Based on 2019 Pew Research Center survey, about 72% of Americans used some type of social media. Another 2021 survey from Statista.com indicated that the Facebook family applications consisting of Facebook, Instagram, WhatsApp, and Facebook messenger have a total of 7.2 billion users worldwide as of February 2021. An interesting fact about social media is that the number of hours spent per day on these platforms in developing countries is much higher than in developed countries. Based on a 2018 Global Digital report, users in the Philippines, Brazil, and Indonesia spend the highest number of hours per day on social media platforms.

3 Strategic Implications of Artisan's Social Media Use

Presence on social media platforms provides significant opportunities to artisans. Historically artisans have relied on artisan markets to sell their products. They also have exploited the opportunity to sell their products to brands worldwide that market the goods produced by such artisans under their name brand (Dana and Salamzadeh 2021). The advent of social media has allowed artisans an unparalleled opportunity to market their products themselves. One of the key advantages of showcasing their products with their artisans' profiles is the break from traditional brands and interaction with the person who is crafting the products.

When the artisans sell their products to brands, it is a possibility that the brands would use digital advertising to persuade the consumers. However, it is different when the artisans are showcasing their products themselves on social media. Consumers can engage with artisans and get information about the products. Such digital communication can be beneficial for artisans. Digital communication is a very important emerging tool that firms utilize to generate engagement with consumers (Colicev et al. 2018). Not all digital communication is beneficial; some consumers may judge certain digital communication as digital advertising (Wu 2016). In such instances, it is essential for artisans to utilize marketing techniques such as quick wit. Quick wit is the practice of sharing a message which is humorous and is not bound by anticipation (Brant 1948). Researchers have found that the incorporation of quick wit enables firms to achieve higher levels of virality and firm value (Borah et al. 2020). The virality of the social message content is also beneficial for the consumers; by sharing the content, social media users can signal to people their higher relative social capital by demonstrating the fact that they are "in the know" (Akpinar and Berger 2017).

Engagement with consumers through social media platforms has many benefits for artisans and numerous objectives accomplished by using these activities over time. Drummond et al. (2020) conceptualized four layers of social media marketing capabilities that are applicable to artisan's presence on social media platforms. The layers are connect, engage, coordinate, and collaborate. Presence on social media platforms allows artisans to connect and engage with a potential individual or institutional customers. The connections and engagement also help the artisans generate awareness about the creativity and uniqueness of their products. Coordination and collaboration are facilitated by social media platforms where potential customers can coordinate and collaborate with the artisans to get customized products to their liking.

Artisans might also use their social media presence to solidify their relationship with customers. Social customer relationship management is the activity where businesses utilize social media platforms to improve their relationships with consumers (Malthouse et al. 2013; Palalic et al. 2020). Artisans frequently share attractive content on their social media profiles. Researchers have found that content generated by businesses has the highest impact on consumers when these consumers are experienced, tech-savvy, and social media prone (Kumar et al. 2016). Consumers follow artisans on social media platforms and are tech-savvy; experienced consumers might be more influenced by the deliberate customer relationship practices by the artisans.

Artisans can present themselves on social media as a brand or person. The communication style of the artisan on social media platforms is critical. The communication style might have an impact on trust vested by consumers in the artisans. For unfamiliar brands, an informal communication style has a higher positive relationship with brand trust, and the reverse is true for familiar brands (Gretry et al. 2017).

One of the key objectives of artisan's social media presence is to promote persuasion among potential consumers. Persuasion is an attempt by a party to deliberately alter another party's perceptions and future actions by utilizing expressions that are reasonable (Lee and Xia 2011). For a message or an expression to be persuasive, the communication of benefits to the receiver is a must (Lee et al. 2010). Based on the elaboration likelihood model, persuasion among people might be achieved by utilizing the peripheral or central route (Petty and Cacioppo 1986). The central route of persuasion relies on communication of benefits directly to the consumer, whereas the peripheral routes rely on achieving persuasion by delivery of cues of benefits. On social media platforms such as Facebook and Instagram, the consumers have the option to like and share posts from other parties. Such options can enable consumers to shape perceptions about the source and content of the post. Posts that are popular and have a high number of likes and shares directly affect consumer's preferences through the central route of the persuasion model (Sinclair et al. 2010).

Artisans can share content on their social media profiles and interact with consumers directly. A similar interaction is also achievable on certain e-commerce platforms that specialize in providing advertising and online selling opportunity to artisans. Etsy.com is an excellent example of such platforms. Based on a 2021 survey by Statista.com, Etsy's annual revenue was 1.7 billion US dollars in 2020. The same survey reflects that the platform has about 4.36 million active sellers from across the world and about 81.9 million active buyers in 2020. Of all the sellers on

Etsy, about 81% identified as women. The classification of Etsy as an e-commerce platform does not do it justice. The platform is more accurately a social commerce platform. A social commerce platform is a type of e-commerce platform that enables the social interactions between the seller and the buyer as well as information sharing between various buyers (Zhang and Benyoucef 2016). Information sharing between buyers occurs by leaving product reviews and images for future buyers to consider before making a purchase. Facebook marketplace is another example of social commerce platform. This feature of Facebook allows the consumers to directly buy from other users on Facebook. The sellers utilize their commercial profiles and provide information to prospective buyers by interacting with them utilizing the instant message service offered by Facebook.

Social media use by artisans is not a one-time activity. Artisans regularly engage in social media activities such a posting attractive content and interacting with consumers. Over the course of time, the artisans might develop social ties with the consumers. Such social ties will have varying levels of strength; in the context of social media platforms, the strength is the level of mutual understanding between users of social media platforms driven by frequency of daily interaction (Yang and Tong 2020). Intuitively, such strong ties between actors might lead to higher levels of mutual trust (Moorman et al. 1993). Researchers have also found that buyers who have stronger social ties with sellers are more likely to complete purchases as compared to similar buyer with weak social ties (Yang and Tong 2020).

4 Impact on Artisans

Artisans are present in every part of the world, and the usage of social media impacts differently in different regions based on numerous economic and sociological variables. The adoption of social media by artisans has had a tremendous impact on the lives of artisans in developing countries. In India, non-farm labor constitutes about 40–50% of the rural population and is composed of artisans like potters; carpenters compose the skilled category of such non-farm labor (Banik and Bhaumik 2015). Based on a 2021 Statista.com survey, the export of handicrafts from India rose from 0.48 billion US dollars in 2011 to about 1.77 billion in 2020. There are several explanations for the growth of handicraft export from India; one explanation is the increase in technological and social capital available to Indian artisans in the last few years (Dana et al. 2021). The impact of social media on artisans is ever more important as some researchers believe that networks of social relations, which are directly influenced by technological and social capital, have the capability to positively impact economic behavior (Granovetter 1995).

Artisans can either be self-made or practice producing goods from skills that were handed down from one generation to another generation. There are certain communities of artists in some parts of the world that have been producing the same handicrafts for hundreds of years. For example, the artists in the Murano islands of Italy have been producing Murano glass artifacts since the thirteenth century. The marble inlay artists in India have been crafting inlay of semi-precious stones in marble for centuries, with the most prominent work visible in the present-day monument of the Taj Mahal. Over the course of time, such communities of artisans abandon many of the sociological restrictions such as race, caste system, and social class to form a guild or a trade union and can be best classified as a new system of industry (Mukerjee 1937). Such new systems of industries might get new wings with the popularity and accessibility of social media platforms among these communities. Such communities can showcase their arts and skills on social media and sell their products directly to customers worldwide, which was not possible without information technology-based social media applications.

Artisans have historically not focused on maximizing the growth of their business but instead focused on independent, manual production; this mindset did not cause much conflict for the artisans in the past (Keh et al. 2002). Some researchers refer to artisans who do not have intentions to grow their business as artisan entrepreneurs (Solomon and Mathias 2020). However, despite their resistance to growth, such ventures are growing, in part because these entrepreneurs feel that they can still maintain their identity and freedom by serving the interests of stakeholders (Solomon and Mathias 2020). Parts of these advancements are due, at least in part, to the rise of pro-artisan movements and technological advancements, which have enabled the artisan entrepreneurs to achieve growth rates like never before (Pret and Cogan 2019).

5 Fair Labor Practices and Social Media

Worldwide, the arts and crafts industry employ artisans who come from a variety of demographic backgrounds. The rise in global trade coupled with transparency in working conditions and lives of artisans has uncovered some unsettling facts about the arts and handicraft industry. One of these facts is the widespread employment of child labor in developing countries. According to a 2020 US department of labor report, about 152 million children are victims of child labor worldwide. A fraction of such child labor is employed as artisans by companies that are involved in the arts and crafts business. The same survey highlights products produced by child labor across the world. For example, children work in the production of footwear and garments in Bangladesh. In India, children work in gems, jewelry, silk, brassware, and numerous other arts and crafts industries. Countries across the world have put in place legislation and enforcement to end child labor. Sadly, the practice persists. The United States has been a leader in advocating an end to child labor practices. To curb the practice, US Congress established the Iqbal Masih award in 2008. Iqbal Masih was a 4-year-old boy from Pakistan sold into child labor. He escaped the situation of weaving carpets and started to advocate the end of child labor. Sadly, Iqbal was killed in 1995 at the age of 14. Iqbal is not the only child forced into labor and who fought for his rights. There are hundreds of thousands of children who face the sting of child labor and do not have the means of escaping such dire situations.

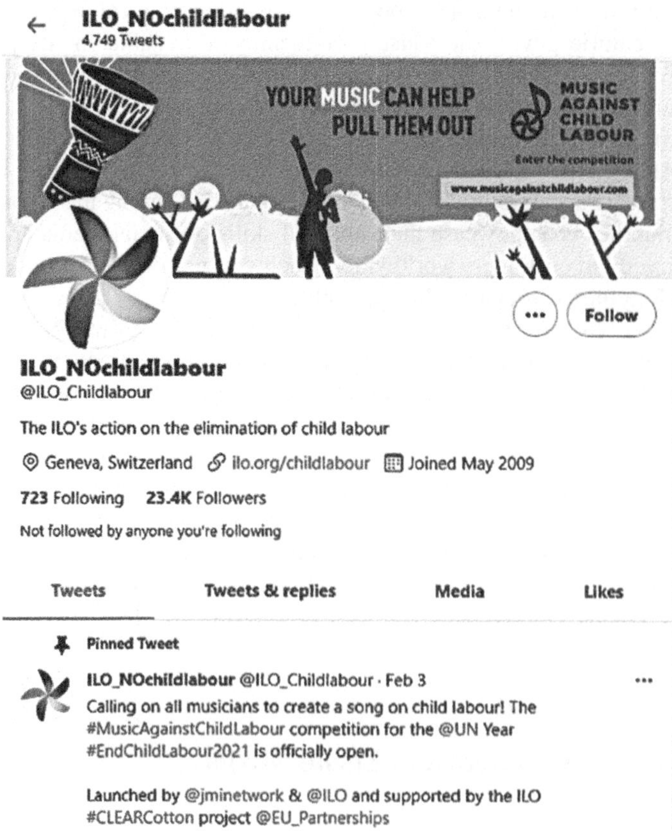

Traditional mechanisms to combat child labor have helped lower the cases of child labor, yet the most important tool afforded to victims of child labor is information technology (IT). IT offers its users the power of information, visibility, communication, and transparency. One of the applications of IT is social media platforms. Social media platforms allow their users the possibility to reach out to people across the world. The platforms afford their users the possibility to directly communicate with other users irrespective of location. The information shared by users is not restricted to certain topics if it does not violate the general policies of the platforms. The power of access to the Internet and social media help reduce the cases of child labor around the world. The International Labor Organization supports awareness of child labor by utilizing social media platforms such as Twitter. The organization has a page on Twitter by the name of "ILO_NOchildlabour." The page is an excellent tool for potential victims to share their concerns or obtain resources about overcoming potential barriers to combat child labor.

The popular social media platform Instagram also offers its users the opportunity to share content based on hashtags. A popular hashtag on Instagram to generate awareness against child labor is #nochildlabour. Any user can share their voice about possible child labor by using the hashtag, and the content would be accessible to users around the world instantly.

6 Women Artisans and Social Media

Women artisans are an integral part of the arts and crafts industry. Based on a 2020 Statista.com survey, 81% of all sellers on popular crafts shopping website Etsy.com identify themselves as women. The number is a representation of women who have avoided the traditional channels of selling their crafts and have entered the online marketplace. Part of the women artisan's success in the online marketplace is through the support from individual designers who showcase the works of women artisans on their social media pages. The practice helps designers and women artisans by generating awareness about who the people are behind specific arts and crafts.

Women artisans also set up their own entrepreneurial ventures and utilize social media to market their art and products. An example of such a venture is Okhai from Gujarat region in India. Based on the website of the venture, about 2300 rural tribal women artisans make products for the brand and derive financial benefit by actively engaging with Okhai.

Ventures like Okhai are an excellent tool for women artisans to have better recognition for their work, get better wages, and stay in tune with the trends in the industry. Ventures like Okhai also receive support from corporations who help the cause of promoting gender equality and better work conditions for artisans. Based on information from the company's website, Okhai has support from corporations such as Tata Chemicals, who help the artisans achieve modern handicraft production skills.

7 Fair Trade and Transparency

Consumers love buying arts and crafts from around the world but are not aware whether the artisans who made the products are treated fairly. Consumers might also have concerns about child labor, as discussed earlier. The consumer in today's information technology-driven age demands answers and prefers transparency. For example, a 2015 cone communication study on millennials found that 87% of millennials would prefer to purchase a product which has a social or environmental benefit. The same survey also reported that nine out of ten millennials would switch brands if offered a choice that supports a cause. The statistics for other age groups are not that drastically different. Consumers wish to choose brands that support a cause and are ethical in their practices.

Brands have utilized the "Fair Trade" label on their products to justify their product sourcing practices as ethical. Based on Fair Trade USA website, "Fair trade is a global movement made up of a diverse network of producers, companies, consumers, advocates, and organizations putting people and planet first." As a result, the brand can get their products as Fair Trade Certified, enabling them to assure their consumers that they responsibly support their workers and environment. In addition, popular online selling platforms for artisans such as Novica.com ensure their consumers that they incorporate fair trade practices in their operations.

Some consumers are not satisfied by fair trade certificate alone. They also want to know the exact person who made their product. The drive to achieve more transparency has enabled the hashtag movements such as #WhoMadeMyClothes. The movement has significant conversations on popular social media platforms such as Twitter and Instagram. Movements like these are an excellent tool for consumers as well as artisans to connect and share information with each other, which might build trust and communication.

References

Akpinar E, Berger J (2017) Valuable virality. J Mark Res 54(2):318–330

Banik & Bhaumik (2015) A brand-new game. Retrieved 14 March 2021 from https://www.economist.com/business/2015/08/27/a-brand-new-game

Borah A, Banerjee S, Lin Y, Jain A, Eisingerich A (2020) Improvised marketing interventions in social media. J Mark 84:69–91

Brant CS (1948) On joking relationships. Am Anthropol 50(1):160–162

Colicev A, Malshe A, Pauwels K, O'Connor P (2018) Improving consumer mindset metrics and shareholder value through social media: the different roles of owned and earned media. J Mark 82(1):37–56

Dana LP, Salamzadeh A (2021) Why do artisans and arts entrepreneurs use social media platforms?: Evidence from an emerging economy. Nord J Media Manag 2(1)

Dana LP, Salamzadeh A, Ramadani V, Palalic R (2021) Understanding contexts of business in Western Asia: land of bazaars and high-tech booms. World Scientific, Singapore

Demographics of Social Media Users and Adoption in the United States (2019) Retrieved 9 March 2021 from https://www.pewresearch.org/internet/fact-sheet/social-media/

Digital in 2018: World's internet users pass the 4 billion mark - we are social (2018) Retrieved 9 March 2021, from https://wearesocial.com/blog/2018/01/global-digital-report-2018

Drummond C, O'Toole T, Mcgrath H (2020) Digital engagement strategies and tactics in social media marketing. Eur J Market

Etsy (2021) Retrieved 14 March 2021, from https://www.statista.com/topics/2501/etsy/

Granovetter M (1995) Getting a job: a study of contacts and careers. University of Chicago Press, Chicago

Gretry A, Horváth C, Belei N, Riel AV (2017) "Don't pretend to be my friend!" When an informal brand communication style backfires on social media. J Bus Res 74:77–89

India: value of handicrafts exports 2020 | Statista (2021) Retrieved 14 March 2021 from https://www.statista.com/statistics/624202/export-value-of-handicrafts-india/

Keh HT, Der Foo M, Lim BC (2002) Opportunity evaluation under risky conditions: the cognitive processes of entrepreneurs. Entrep Theory Pract 27(2):125–148

Kumar A, Bezawada R, Rishika R, Janakiraman R, Kannan PK (2016) From social to sale: the effects of firm-generated content in social media on customer behavior. J Mark 80:25–27

Lee G, Xia W (2011) A longitudinal experimental study on the interaction effects of persuasion quality, user training, and first-hand use on user perceptions of new information technology. Inf Manag 48(7):288–295

Lee AY, Keller PA, Sternthal B (2010) Value from regulatory construal fit: the persuasive impact of fit between consumer goals and message concreteness. J Consum Res 36(5):735–747
Malthouse EC, Haenlein M, Skiera B, Wege E, Zhang M (2013) Managing customer relationships in the social media era: introducing the social CRM house. J Interact Mark 27(10):270–280
Moorman C, Deshpande R, Zaltman G (1993) Factors affecting trust in marketing relationships. J Mark 57(1):81–101
Most used social media 2020 | Statista (2021) Retrieved 9 March 2021 from https://www.statista.com/statistics/272014/global-social-networks-ranked-by-number-of-users/
Mukerjee R (1937) Caste and social change in India. Am J Sociol 43(3):377–390. Retrieved March 14, 2021, from http://www.jstor.org/stable/2768625
Palalic R, Ramadani V, Mariam Gilani S, Gërguri-Rashiti S, Dana LP (2020) Social media and consumer buying behavior decision: what entrepreneurs should know? Manag Decis
Petty R, Cacioppo J (1986) The elaboration likelihood model of persuasion. Adv Exp Soc Psychol 19:123–205
Pret T, Cogan A (2019) Artisan entrepreneurship: a systematic literature review and research agenda. *Int J Entrep Behav Res* 25(4):592–614
Sinclair RC, Moore SE, Mark MM, Soldat AS, Lavis CA (2010) Incidental moods, source likeability, and persuasion: liking motivates message elaboration in happy people. Cognit Emot 24(6):940–961
Solomon S, Mathias B (2020) The artisans' dilemma: Artisan entrepreneurship and the challenge of firm growth. J Bus Ventur 35:106044
Wu T (2016) The attention merchants. Penguin, New York
Yang R, Tong C (2020) Do social ties matter for purchase frequency? The role of buyers' attitude towards social media marketing. Comput Hum Behav 110:106376
Zhang KZK, Benyoucef M (2016) Consumer behavior in social commerce: a literature review. Decis Support Syst 86:95–108

Saurabh Singh is pursuing his PhD in Marketing at Kent State University and is research assistant of Dr. Robert Hisrich. He earned an MBA in Marketing from Illinois State University in 2017. Mobi is an enthusiast of marketing and entrepreneurship. He hails from New Delhi, India, where he started multiple artisan jewelry and furniture businesses. Mobi has a knack for entrepreneurship and in future wishes to engage in research related to artisan entrepreneurs. The rise of female artisans in entrepreneurship interests him, and he wishes to start a business in the future that empowers women artisans.

Robert Hisrich is the Bridgestone Professor of International Marketing and Entrepreneurship and Director of the Global Management Center at Kent State University (2015–present). He previously held the Garvin Chair of Entrepreneurship and Director of the Walker Center of Global Entrepreneurship at Thunderbird Graduate School of Management (2005–2015). He has received Honorary Degrees from Chuvash State University (Russia) and from Miskolc University (Hungary) as well as two Fulbright Fellowships. Author of 46 books, one of which, *Entrepreneurship*, is in 14 languages, and over 350 articles. Dr. Hisrich is on the faculty of universities around the world.

Xiaowei Guo is a PhD student at Kent State University. Prior to enrolling at Kent State University, Xiaowei received her Masters of Art in Accounting in 2016 from Arizona State University. She is an enthusiast of research and academia. She has 2 years of experience teaching Fundamental and English accounting. She enjoyed her responsibilities of curriculum design, course coordination, and instruction during her teaching endeavors. Xiaowei is passionate about research in the field of consumer behavior encompassing decision-making, attitudes, and emotions.

Artisans and Social Media: Cases from Kosovo

Nora Sadiku-Dushi, Afërina Skeja, and Veland Ramadani

Abstract It is hard to imagine today's world without social networks. About half of the total world population are active social media users. This high number of users was seen by businesses as a good opportunity for their promotion and rising the number of potential customers. These advantages have been exploited especially by small businesses who usually lack marketing expertise and large personal networks and therefore have used the opportunity offered by social media to increase the visibility of their business. Artisans fall into the category of small businesses that face many challenges when it comes to promoting their work. The purpose of this chapter is to explore how these artisans use social media to promote their work and communicate with their customers and to learn whether the use of social media has influenced the survival of artisans in Kosovo. To achieve this objective, we have purposefully chosen five cases of filigree artisans from the city of Prizren in Kosovo who still keep alive the tradition of handicrafts and proudly continue to survive the difficulties of modern times.

1 Introduction

Social networks have become an inevitable means of communication today, both for individuals and businesses. Today, approximately 3.6 billion people are using social media worldwide, a number projected to increase to almost 4.41 billion in 2025 (Statista 2021). Even though there is no agreed definition of social media, they are usually described as web-based services that allow users to create public or semi-public profiles as well as create a list of other users and communicate or share different contents with them (Ellison 2007). According to Kaplan and Haenlein

N. Sadiku-Dushi · A. Skeja
University for Business and Technology, Pristina, Kosovo
e-mail: nora.sadiku@ubt-uni.net; aferina.skeja@ubt-uni.net

V. Ramadani (✉)
Max van der Stoel Institute, South-East European University, Tetovo, North Macedonia
e-mail: v.ramadani@seeu.edu.mk

L.-P. Dana et al. (eds.), *Artisan and Handicraft Entrepreneurs*, Contributions to Management Science, https://doi.org/10.1007/978-3-030-82303-0_12

(2010), social networking sites allow users to create personal information profiles and invite other people to access those profiles where they can exchange messages and other contents. In a practical sense, social media offer the participating community the ability to post photos and videos, to message, tag, comment, review, like, dislike, follow, and many other options. This popularity of the media did not go unnoticed by various companies who realised that this tremendous usage of social media by a large number of people could be turned into a business advantage. Thus, based on the popularity and spread of their use, these social media were seen as a good opportunity that can be used as an important marketing tool by various companies. Being that social media marketing is a type of entrepreneurial marketing makes it suitable especially for SMEs, which, due to their limited resources, must rely on unsophisticated and creative marketing tactics (Sadiku-Dushi et al. 2019). Limited financial resources and lack of expertise are just some of the main challenges that SMEs face when trying to promote their businesses; therefore, social media is considered a potential solution to these challenges (Hassan et al. 2015; Dana and Salamzadeh 2021). Artisans also fall into the category of small businesses, and being small makes them face many challenges when it comes to promoting their work. According to Au and Anthony (2016), the artisans usually work at home and rarely interact personally with their clients. Instead, they use social media such as Facebook, Twitter, and Instagram as the main communication tools with their clients.

The purpose of this chapter is to understand whether social media has influenced the survival of artisans in Kosovo and how artisans use these tools to promote their work. In that order, this study was conducted to provide answers to the following research questions:

RQ1: Do artisans use social media to promote their work?
RQ2: What are the opportunities that social networks have offered them in promoting their work?
RQ3: Do artisans believe that social networks are helping their crafts to survive the time?

By the purposeful sampling, the filigree artisans from the city of Prizren in Kosovo are chosen. The reason why filigree artisans are selected as a sample for this study is that they represent one of the few surviving artisans who still fanatically preserve the tradition of this handicraft, also known outside the borders of Kosovo.

2 Literature Review

2.1 The Artisan Concept

In everyday life, when we refer to an artisan and artisanship, one often thinks of a craftsman and that their work is called craftsmanship. According to the Cambridge dictionary, the word "artisan" is defined as "someone who does skilled work with

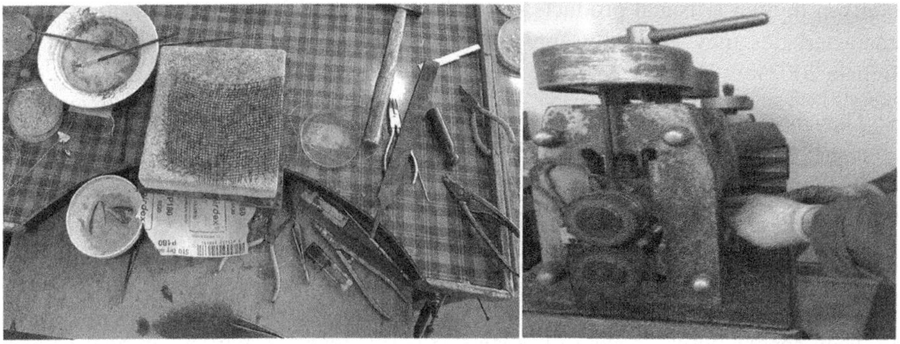

Fig. 1 Tools used in a filigree artisan, Prizren Photo © Afërina Skeja

their hands". Even though there is no unified definition, many authors have made explanations of what is considered artisan. According to Baldacchino and Cutajar (2011), artisan is defined "as a skilled person who creates objects of aesthetic and/or functional value, mainly by manual labor, using traditional craft techniques and/or materials" (Baldacchino and Cutajar 2011, p 21). On the other side, Hobsbawm (1984) states that the "word artisan or its equivalent, used without qualification, is automatically taken to mean something like an independent craftsman or small master, or someone who hopes to become one" (Hobsbawm 1984, p 356). The World Intellectual Property Organization (WIPO) defines artisans as people who make products manually and work individually or can be helped by people that they are in close personal contacts such as a friend, family members, apprentices, or even a small number of workers who offer a sense of community as well as create an attachment to the craft (Idris and Belisle 2003). If we look closely at all the definitions, we see that skills are what they have in common, making us realise that the most important thing that an artisan is supposed to have is a skill.

Artisan is work made in a workshop by the craftsmen himself or with the help of assistants or apprentices (Fig. 1). Artisan products are typically produced one at a time, with individual variations often based on requirements from particular consumers. As in pre-industrial and post-industrial society, people worked as artisans to meet their own and society's needs. This is the reason why artisans may be found in all economic sectors. Potters, shoemakers, bakers, weavers, and blacksmiths are just some of the old crafts. The shift from the traditional to a modern economy, and change of tastes, has caused some of the old artisans to disappear. However, over time different new artisans such as car mechanics, electricians, photographers, and artistic and decorative crafts have emerged and will have growing markets (Inkster 1991).

To create artisan products, a traditional artisan must possess the skill and tools as well as must engage the mental and physical efforts in the work process, which will offer him pleasure and pride. In addition to pleasure and pride, artisanship also offers the opportunity to survive and become stronger, especially for those who have no other access to cash (Agrawal and Agrawal 2019).

Even though artisanal products still have no commonly agreed definition, some characteristics may generally apply to a wide range of craft products (Idris and Belisle 2003):

- They are usually produced by hand or by mechanical means but where the contribution of the craftsman's hand remains the most important part of the final product.
- There are no restrictions on the production quantity.
- Even when artisan may produce many products, none of them are completely identical.
- They are made from raw materials produced in a sustainable way.
- Their special nature stems from their distinctive features, which can be practical, artistic, aesthetic, creative, cultural, functional, traditional, religious, social, and significant.

Handicraft products can be grouped into six broad categories that are mainly based on the material used or the combination of material and technique used, such as basket/knitting/vegetable fibre works, leather metal, ceramics, textiles, and wood. Other categories may contain the various animal, mineral, or vegetable materials used in handicraft production that is rare, hard to work with, or specific to a particular country or region, such as stone, glass, bones, horns, ivory, shells, seashells, or pearls. There are also additional categories created when different techniques and materials are used at the same time (Idris and Belisle 2003).

Being an attractive and important field for every society, this field has attracted the attention of many authors who have studied different aspects of it. Some studies address different perspectives of the artisans, such as their contributions to the economy and society (Ramadani et al. 2019; Luckman 2015) or even their impacts on tourism development and regional competitiveness (Bakas et al. 2019; Ferreira et al. 2019; Ratten et al. 2019; Teixeira and Ferreira 2019; Thomas et al. 2013).

2.2 The History of Artisans in Kosovo

The Republic of Kosovo (Fig. 2) has an area of 10,905.25 km^2. The country is located in the south-eastern part of Europe, bordered by Albania to the southwest, Montenegro northwest, Serbia northeast, and Macedonia to the south, with a total border length of 743.5 km (Kosovo Agency of Statistic 2020a). The approximate population in Kosovo is 1.78 million (Kosovo Agency of Statistics 2020b). The capital of Kosovo is Pristina containing more than 15% of the total population. Currently, there are 38 municipalities with 1469 settlements organised under the laws of the country.

Kosovar citizens are the poorest in Europe, second only to Moldova. The GDP per capita in 2016 (PPP) was only $10,400. The unemployment rate in 2017 was 30.5%, whereas the youth unemployment rate is estimated to be 49.5%. Such a high unemployment rate leads to emigration and informal or unreported economy (The

Fig. 2 Map of Kosovo. Source: United Nations (2021). Map No. 4069 Rev. 7 Jul 2020 available on https://www.un.org/Depts/Cartographic/map/profile/kosovo.pdf

World Factbook 2021). In addition to the low employment rate in Kosovo, 18.8% of employed people work in unstable jobs. Workers with unstable jobs are either self-employed people without employees or those who work unpaid in family businesses. These two groups of workers are less likely to have a formal employment agreement compared to paid workers. In the category of unstable employment, 19.4% are in the

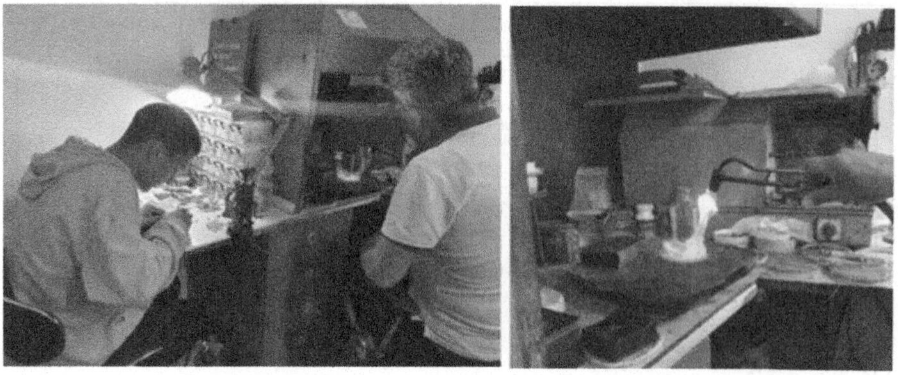

Fig. 3 "Ustah" Nrec Gjini and his son Gjon Gjini during the work process, Prizren. Photo © Afërina Skeja

artisan sector as self-employed, whereas there are 15% unpaid family workers (Kosovo Agency of Statistics 2020c).

The organisation of economic life in Kosovo until half a century ago was based mainly on households and the patriarchal organisation of the family. The family economy was focused, among other things, on handicrafts dominated mostly by natural production and simple artisans. From the old artisans, we can distinguish tailors, weavers, blacksmiths, silk workers, carpenters, saddlers, bakers, confectioners, potters, silversmiths, barbers, etc. The artisan's products and services represented an exceptional segment of the development of small and medium enterprises. Based on the data from 1986, there were 113 active craft activities in Kosovo. Today, more than half of the artisans practising in Kosovo could be found in mostly 15 handicraft activities (Ministry of Environment and Spatial Planning 2004).

The artisan development initiated the creation of groups of craftsmen called Esnafs, who dealt with the organisation and regulation of artisanship as a specific sector of the economy as well as the promotion of their artistic work. Becoming an artisan in Kosovo was not an easy task because one had to go through four stages to become a master. These stages could last up to 10 years, and one had to pass two exams conducted by *esnaf* which was the highest body of artisan. The first phase begins with the apprenticeship (called *çirak*). The second phase is the *shegërt* degree. After passing the exam, the shegërt qualifies as a *kallf*. A master known as *ustah* is the last phase of specialisation in craftwork (Fig. 3) (Municipality of Pejë 2016).

Mostly, handicrafts have been passed forward through generations. The social developments and developments in industry and trade affected the suffering and disappearance of many of these crafts by making it very difficult to find a market for them.

Artisanship was spread in all municipalities of Kosovo. However, some cities were more known for this kind of work. The most distinguished cities for artisanship

Fig. 4 Old Stone Bridge, Prizren Photo © Afërina Skeja

were Prizren (Fig. 4), Prishtina, Peja, Gjakova, and Vushtrri. In these cities, some streets were named based on the handicrafts that were produced there. Even though each of the above-mentioned cities has its unique artisan characteristics, this chapter will focus only on Prizren filigree artisans. Prizren Municipality lies in the area of 627 km^2 and is located in southwest of Kosovo. The municipality has 76 settlements with 177,781 inhabitants (Municipality of Prizren 2021).

Throughout history, the development of Prizren was closely related to developments in terms of handicrafts, trade, and the road network, and as such, it was appraised as one of the most eminent craft centres of the Balkans. The number of artisans increased gradually, from century to century. In the second part of the nineteenth century, Prizren had reached its peak with 124 types of artisans operating in over 1384 workshops. For centuries, the Prizren artisans have been engaged in metal, leather, textiles, wood, food, and service activities. In the nineteenth century, Prizren was the second most important economic and trade centre within Albanian territories having approximately 1500 workshops.

However, technology development gave rise to a decline in artisan manufacturing by causing some of these artisans to disappear. Nevertheless, Prizren still has masters who create different types of crafts that are used in everyday life or sold as souvenirs (Fig. 5) (Municipality of Prizren 2012).

Prizren is still considered the city of crafts. Today although the handicrafts such as coppersmith, tailor crafts, weaving handicraft, and embroidery of Prizren textile still exist and are perfect, other crafts remain in line with the traditional ones, e.g., filigree is still worked with discipline and fervent love as well as handmade works with different samples of silver lace (Municipality of Prizren 2012).

Fig. 5 Different artisanal products that can be bought as souvenirs, Prizren. Photo © Afërina Skeja

Even though Kosovo does not have direct access to the sea, its mountainous terrain, favourable climate, and numerous natural, cultural, and historical resources make this country attractive for tourism (Ministry of Trade and Industry 2014). Fanatically preserved culture and artisans make the city of Prizren one of the most attractive tourist destinations for both local and foreign visitors, ranking it among one of the three most visited destinations in Kosovo (Kosovo Agency of Statistics 2020d). Although there is no accurate data on overnight visitors, according to some estimates of tourism actors in this municipality, their number is around 150,000–200,000. The highest number of visitors is from the neighbouring country Albania. As European countries are concerned, the Turkish and the German tourists dominate. In the last 2 years, the number of Asians has also increased significantly (Municipality of Prizren 2019).

Prizren can be described as a city of culture and tourism. There are many reasons why Prizren is one of the most popular places for foreign visitors. Both by its natural beauty and its special architecture, Prizren makes an inevitable city (Fig. 6).

The artisans also add to the beauty of this city. In many countries, old crafts contribute greatly to a destination's culture and travel experience. Crafts can be an important contributor to a country's economy, employing people and preserving cultural heritage. The tourism industry offers an important export market for a variety of artisanal products. Tourists often spend part of their budget to buy various artisanal products and take them home as souvenirs (Municipality of Prizren 2015).

a. b.

Fig. 6 (**a**) Sinan Pasha Mosque, Ottoman architecture, 1615. (**b**) League of Prizren, first built in 1878. This is its last rebuilt version after it was burned during the Kosovo war, Prizren. Photo © Afërina Skeja

2.3 *Artisans that Survived the Time*

As mentioned before, Prizren used to be the city of crafts and handicrafts, and these traces can still be seen today. In Prizren, the most distinguished crafts were the crafts of the gunsmith, silversmith, cutlers, scissor-makers, coppersmith, and tinsmith; the crafts of tanners and saddlers; the crafts of white woollen cap makers, tailors, and silk processors; the crafts of quilt makers, woollen gown makers, and woollen rug-makers; the craft of watchmakers; the craft of pottery; etc. (Siqeca 2011). Various technological developments have caused some of these handicrafts to disappear. This disappearance has also been influenced by the change of peoples' lifestyles and the decrease of interest in some types of artisanal products. But, even despite these changes and many difficulties, there is a surviving artisan: the filigree artisan. Filigree is continuing to proudly distinguish Prizren as one of the most famous places for this type of crafts.

The biggest part of the jewellery craft products in Prizren in the nineteenth and early twentieth century consisted of gold and silver washed with gold, while others were made of copper and bronze. The eighteenth and the nineteenth century was characterised by the production of bracelets with several rows of chains and some belts called "pafta". The end of the nineteenth and beginning of the twentieth century was known for pocket watch chains for men, head ornaments called "takëmi me aski" (meaning table-sets with straps), rings, and bracelets made of one or more parts and mirror frames. The latest works, from the beginning of the twentieth century, are men's chains; earrings; women's necklaces; one-piece, two-piece, and multipiece

Fig. 7 Filigree works, Prizren, Photo © Afërina Skeja

closed-type bracelets; brooches; silver filigree belts; bracelets and belts called "fishekli"; etc. (Siqeca 2011).

Without a doubt, as mentioned before, the artisan that makes Prizren and Kosovo proud of is a filigree artisan (locally known as *filigran*) (Fig. 7). This fine work is created with thin threads of silver or gold. The origin of filigree is believed to begin in Egypt. However, it is supposed that filigree has been present in Kosovo since the fifteenth century (Municipality of Prizren 2019).

The filigree craft is the most widespread, the most popular, and almost the only one that has continued to survive to this day, also remaining as one of the most attractive and useful crafts in Prizren. The ancient filigree masters or silversmiths are among the most famous craftsmen of Prizren. These craftsmen, working with hand tools and twisting and curling with filigree technique artefacts of gold, silver, copper, amber, and precious stones, made the ancient city of Prizren known worldwide. The filigree bazaar where the goldsmiths of Prizren operated was considered the home of filigree and has been known since ancient times outside the Balkan Peninsula because of its high creative values (Filigrani 2021).

Many Prizren filigree products have been sold abroad and are exhibited in various exhibitions and museums around the world. Today, silversmith crafts can be found in more than 50 private shops. In these shops, old products made 50–60 years before may be only seen because most of them are not for sale (Fig. 8). Now, the filigree artisans make new models of gold and silver, customising them according to their customers' requirements. In addition to private shops, jewellery products are produced in the company "Filigran" which was founded in 1946 with over 150 local craftsmen. The number of craftsmen in this company decreased to ten artisans who

a. b.

Fig. 8 (**a**) Filigree cigarette case box crafted by Nexhmedin Pasuli in 1960. (**b**) Filigree bracelet crafted by Mark Gjini in 1970. The products are not for sale. Prizren. Photo© Afërina Skeja

continue to produce works of art in the original building. They produce yataghans, razors, fruit, candlesticks, jewellery, vases, glass, and other motifs based on customer requests. Prizren jewellery products have special historical and ethnological values. They bring the image of a perfect artistic mastery, specimens of which to this day are counted among the rare antiques, with particular importance (Siqeca 2011).

The importance of this fine artisanal work is also acknowledged by the mayor of the city of Prizren, who said that: "The craft of filigree is the most famous art of our city in the world because in the past these ornaments made by the hands of our masters have been sold in all Mediterranean cities" (PrizrenPress 2018).

After the 1990s, many political, social, and economic conditions in the country made most of the active filigrees of the city of Prizren move to neighbouring countries in search of a better working environment. The most prominent masters settled along the Adriatic coast, on the tourist areas of Croatia, Slovenia, and Montenegro. On one side, this caused the fading of this craft in Prizren, but on the other side, it has also marked the spread of working techniques and recognition of their values internationally.

Being aware of the importance it has for the city and in order to preserve and keep this artisan alive, the local NGO, "EC Ma Ndryshe", has launched the implementation of the "Filigree beyond the Craft" project, funded by the project "Dialogue among Communities through Comprehensive Preservation of Cultural Heritage", implemented by UNDP and funded by the European Union Instrument for Stability and Peace Contribution (IcSP). The purpose of this project was to contribute to the preservation of filigree craft by documenting, promoting, and transferring knowledge and skills to women and youth of different ethnicities from the Prizren region (six municipalities) leading to increased employability. The project specifically targets the Filigran Enterprise in Prizren in order to develop it into a sustainable entity that provides education, maintains craft and production, and improves its market indicators (Ec Ma Ndryshe 2021).

The Municipality of Prizren has also supported this project by providing space where some of the project activities have taken place, including filigree training workshops and internship programs. Additionally, the NGO "EC Ma Ndryshe" organised a Filigree Fair in 2019 which was held in "Kino Lumbardhi" – the old cinema of Prizren. According to the NGO, the aim of this fair was to promote filigree, build public awareness about it, and provide a way of local development via maintenance and promotion of this craft. This NGO also organised a panel named "Filigree: a potential for development" where except local craftsmen many craftsmen from Albania, North Macedonia, and Montenegro participated.

2.4 Social Media Usage in Kosovo

There is no doubt that today the use of social networks has become an integral part of everyone's life. In 2020, over 3.6 billion people were using social media worldwide and those numbers are projected to increase to almost 4.41 billion by 2025 ("Number of social media users 2025 | Statista", 2021).

These global trends have not left Kosovo aside either. A national quantitative research done by the Kosovo Association of Information and Communication Technology (STIKK and KANTAR 2019) revealed that 96% of Kosovo households have an Internet connection. Almost every person in Kosovo uses the Internet (96%) at least on some occasion, while 81% are considered to be active Internet users. As social media are concerned, Facebook is the leading platform used by 67%, followed by Instagram as the second most used social media platform. High Internet penetration was used by companies who took advantage of the opportunities offered by these social media by turning them into a place where they promote their businesses. Today, it is almost impossible to do a simple search for any company name that one may think of and having no results on at least one of the social media platforms. Beqiri (2017), in a study regarding the marketing of the companies through social media conducted with 120 companies in Kosovo, found that companies use social networks extensively for marketing purposes. Facebook is the most used platform for marketing with 98.33% followed by Instagram with 41.67% and YouTube with 33.33%. It is worth mentioning that all these companies own a business page that is frequently updated. The other important finding is that promoting their activities through videos has proven to be very effective and sufficient to capture the attention of a certain number of audiences. The main reasons why companies use social media for their marketing strategy are to understand the needs and requirements of customers (73%) and to launch promotional offers and products. Companies in Kosovo consider that marketing through the social media platform revealed to have an advantage compared to traditional marketing in generating sales, although they still dedicate higher financial investments in traditional marketing forms. Similarly, Sadiku-Dushi (2017), through observation methodology with the sample of 50 randomly selected companies, found that 90% had FB business pages, but not all of them were using the opportunities that offer business pages properly, resulting in a low number of people following them. The main reason for the low number of followers was the poor maintenance or very rare posts on their profiles. There is no doubt that social media offer many opportunities in exchange for the time and effort that companies should invest in them. Keeping customers informed is not an easy task and requires a new way of thinking (Kaplan and Haenlein 2010). Therefore, companies need to understand that creating a business profile on social media is not enough for success. The profile will not work alone, and that is why sometimes it is better not to have a business page at all than to have one and not use it properly. Also, if businesses want to keep in trend with the globalised world, they need to advertise not only in their native language but also in foreign languages as well (Gashi and Ahmeti 2021).

When found that in social media, except investing time and effort, companies should be prepared for positive and negative comments and reviews and should be very careful in presenting their business and meeting customer expectations. Small companies that lack experience and resources should learn from their competitors and other companies that have a large number of page followers.

It can be concluded that social media have a crucial role in the promotion of small businesses because they give the chance to reach a wide audience. Therefore, small businesses and especially artisans need to devote their time and effort to appropriately and efficiently use all the benefits that social media offer in expanding their network and make their work visible regardless of their "smallness".

3 Methodology

Given that the number of artisans is limited and they are geographically spread in different locations made it difficult to undertake a quantitative study. Moreover, bearing in mind that there are no previous studies on this subject matter, a qualitative approach was considered as the logical way to accomplish this research. The qualitative approach is considered to be very suitable because it allows gaining understanding from direct contact with the research subjects, thus avoiding any potential mistakes such as asking the wrong question or solving the wrong problem (Dana and Dana 2005). In addition, to better understand the research subject, the approach of multiple case study was used. According to Yin (2013), "the case study method allows investigators to retain the holistic and meaningful characteristics of real-life events" (Yin 2013, p. 4). Bearing in mind that the goal of the research was to gain knowledge on the use of social media by artisans, the purposeful case selection was seen as the right choice, based on Polkinghorne's (2005) suggestion that purposeful sampling is very suitable in qualitative research because the collection of right and rich data is more important than the number of the subjects used in a study. Considering that artisans are scattered throughout the country and are often difficult to find because they usually operate in the premises of their own home, we have decided for logistical reasons and proximity to researchers to choose the filigree artisan cases in the town of Prizren. This selection is also made because the Prizren filigree artisans are very well known in the country and are considered as the most popular and almost the only artisans that have survived to the time. We initially identified six cases that we contacted to arrange meetings with them. One of them refused to participate in the research; therefore, we decided to do our research based on five case studies. In this type of research, this sample size is considered sufficient as it also complies with the Yin (2013) recommendations according to whom the replication logic requirement calls for a literal replication of three to four cases or six to eight cases.

Considering that interviews are the most common method of data collection in qualitative studies (Donalek 2005), we opted for semi-structured in-depth face-to-face interviews. This method allows the participants the necessary time and space to tell their stories. The interviews were designed carefully to answer the research questions of the study and to avoid eventual "yes" or "no" questions (Yin 2013). Also, to make participants feel more at ease during this time, they were asked to state anything they considered that was important for the research, which made the interview more interesting and at the same time enriching the study with additional information. The interviews were conducted from 12 to 20 May 2021. It took 8 days from the identification of cases to completion of interviews. For the participants to feel better and for us to see their work closely, the interviews were conducted at their workplaces. The interview time ranged from 17 to 29 min, with an average time of 20.8 min per interview. The oldest case was a 50-year-old man, whereas the youngest was 23 years old. Before the beginning of the interviews, the participants were asked if they mind recording the interview, but we noticed that they all hesitated, and to make the atmosphere more relaxing, we decided to take notes and photos instead of recording. At the end of the interview, every participant has signed the post-interview confidentiality form (Kaiser 2009), with which they stated which of the data we might publish in the study. Seeing this research as an opportunity for promotion even outside the borders of Kosovo, four of the cases agreed that we could use all their data without any amendments, whereas one participant asked us to refer to him as a Filigran.

Based on Thomas's (2006) suggestion, the notes taken during the interview were analysed using a general inductive approach. According to this approach, the raw data were grouped into summary by then removing all the unnecessary items from the analysis. The remaining data were grouped to match the research questions. Similar approaches were also used in other qualitative studies (Abdullah 2020; Ramadani et al. 2018; Sadiku-Dushi 2019).

4 Introducing the Cases

Since the interviewees initially did not understand why they were part of the research, the purpose of this study was initially explained to you. In order to feel more reclaimed, they were initially asked about more general things about themselves and their work. The cases are presented below.

Case 1 (Nrec Gjini) A gentleman in his early 50s. We visited Mr. Gjini in his workshop, which was a medium-sized space in which various work tools, silver wires, and works that were in progress were seen. He told us that the artisan was inherited from his father Mark Gjini. He started his first steps in this craft at the age of 10–12 and now has 40 years of experience. When his son Nue Gjini was 14 years old, Mr. Gjini started teaching him the art of filigree as well. Today, his son Nue is a master with 13 years of work experience. Even the second son of Mr. Gjini, Gjon Gjini (17 years old), is interested in filigree and works close to him to learn and become a master one day. He told us that also his daughters are very interested in the filigree artisan, but they are more concerned with the design of the works.

Case 2 (Durim Haxhifazliu) Durim is only 23 years old. We visited him in his store located in a shopping centre in Prizren, a small modern store arranged with a lot of taste, in which his filigree works and other silver ornaments were exposed. During the interview, he told us that he had started the artisan of filigree when he was only 9 years old. He had no ancestor in this craft, but out of the desire to take any craft, he accidentally met the filigree, and according to him, he "felt in love with it". He told us that it took him 7 years of hard work full of effort to reach the professional level in this craft.

Case 3 (Berat Pasuli) We visited Berat, an agile 28-year-old boy, in his store located in the centre of Prizren. His mastery in this artisan was inherited from his grandfather Nexhmedin Pasuli then his father, Abdullah Pasuli. His first steps in this artisan were at the age of 7. Today, he is a master with 21 years of experience in this craft. Both Berat and his older brother are active in this craft. During the conversation, he proudly told us that his grandfather was the chief in Filigran and his father was the employee supervisor. There were a lot of artworks exhibited in his store, but he told us that not all the crafts are for sale, because some are the works of his predecessors, and he preserves them with a lot of fanaticism. He also told us that he shares the workshop with his brother while they both have separate stores.

Case 4 (Refki Gjini) Refki Gjini is a guy under 30 who welcomed us to his shop in the centre of Prizren, a small shop in which various filigree works were exhibited with great finesse. Refki also inherited the artisan from his father and started learning it at the age of 16. Today Refki is a master with 12 years of experience in this work. At the moment, he is the only one in a family in this artisan.

Case 5 (Nickname: Filigran) The last case we visited was the Filigran company. This enterprise was founded in 2007 with the initiative of ten masters of filigree, most of whom have more than 30 years of work experience. We talked to the manager who asked us to refer to him as Filigran, kindly asking us not to use his real name. The gentleman was in his 50s. Out of the ten founders who were in the beginning, there were now seven left as three of them had passed away (two of them from the COVID-19 pandemic). He told us that the purpose of this enterprise is to preserve the tradition of filigree. To help them, the municipality offered them to use the building in which the workshop was located. He told us that they often organise filigree trainings that last from 6 to 8 months so that young people and people who want to learn this craft have the opportunity to learn and continue the filigree tradition.

5 Findings and Discussion

Since the nature of the research was qualitative, the interview questions were posed in such a way as to answer the research objectives. The responses were initially grouped based on the research questions, then we have identified the similarities and differences between the cases, and finally, the results are presented.

RQ1: Do artisans use social media to promote their work?

Based on the fact that, nowadays, social media is seen as a great tool for business promotion, and especially for small and medium enterprises, the first objective of this research was to understand whether artisans use social media to promote their work.

All the cases that were a part of this research confirmed that they use social media (Table 1). Four cases use Facebook and Instagram platforms, whereas only one case uses Facebook only (Fig. 9).

What is interesting to mention is that three of the cases expressed that they do not post their unique products due to the theft of their ideas. This is evident from the quotes below:

Table 1 The use of social media platforms by research cases

Cases	Facebook	Instagram
Nrec Gjini	Yes	Yes
Durim Haxhifazliu	Yes	Yes
Berat Pasuli	Yes	Yes
Refki Gjini	Yes	Yes
Filigran	Yes	No

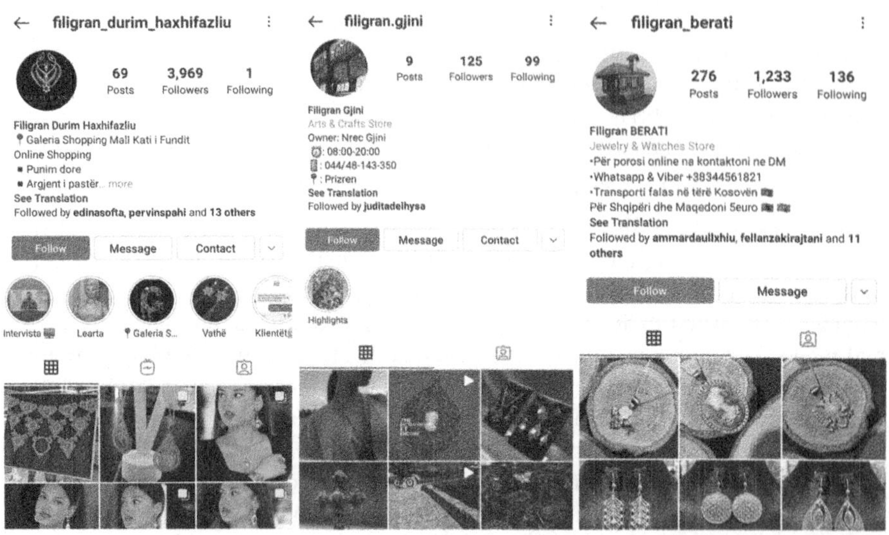

Fig. 9 Screenshots from the social media (Instagram) profiles of some of the interviewed artisans

I have Facebook and Instagram accounts which I use for promotion and not for sale. I rarely post on social networks due to theft of the ideas of my works. (Nrec Gjini)

I am using Instagram and Facebook. I post more silver products and I rarely post filigree works. Even when I do, I only post those works that are classic (which can be found also in other stores), whereas the special and unique works that I have, I usually do not post them on social networks due to theft of work. (Refki Gjini)

A similar answer was also received from the Filigran:

We are using Facebook. Lately we do not post our unique works due to theft of work (we have previously posted unique works) but we post works that are classic (which is available to everyone). (Filigran)

The younger cases do not seem to have the same fear as the previous cases; they told us that they are not afraid of the posts they make on social networks.

I'm using Facebook and Instagram. I actively used both accounts, so every day I make posts of my new work. (Berat Pasuli)

Yes, I use Facebook and Instagram and post my filigree works. Within the week I post about 2-3 new works as well as make reposts. (Durim Haxhifazliu)

It is obvious from the responses that all the cases use social media, even though some of them have their own doubts when it comes to posting their unique products due to the fear of copying their work by other artisans.

RQ2: What are the opportunities that social networks have offered them in promoting their work?

Being that artisans are usually individual businesses and mostly act locally, they are unable to have a large base of customers. Witnessing the popularity of social media, we wanted to know if they see social media as an opportunity to promote their work. All respondents said that they had an increase in consumers due to their promotion on social networks. They all use these networks to promote products and communicate with consumers, whereas they use them less to make sales through them. This can be seen in the statement of Durim, who told us:

Social networks have helped me in terms of marketing, where I have also made numerous investments in social networks. But I also encountered many obstacles in social networks because there are many scams in social networks and this has affected the distrust of consumers in the product (selling fake products through social networks. But, still through social media I have costumers from other countries. (Durim Haxhifazliu)

Similar answer was given by Filigran, who said:

We had one project that funded a website for us, but we had more benefits from Facebook than from the website. We do not accept online orders. Earlier we had attempted to deliver outside Kosovo but we did not have the opportunity to do the shipments. Inside Kosovo we did not want (Filigran)

Other cases also stated that the use of social networks had increased the number of clients. They said that even customers from other countries found them through social media.

We have had customers from America who have seen us on social media. (Nrec Gjini)

Yes, we had orders from Macedonia (Skopje, Tetovo), Albania, and Kosovo. (Berat Pasuli)

RQ3: Do artisans believe that social networks are helping their crafts to survive the time?

As mentioned before, the number of artisans has decreased over time due to the advancements in technology as well as people's habits and tastes. Filigree artisan is considered as one of the artisans that is still surviving. The final objective of this research was to understand if social media impacted the survival of filigree artisan. All the cases claimed that social media had an impact on their promotion, but they do not agree that it was the social media that prevented the filigree from disappearing.

I can say for growth yes, but not for survival because we have inherited consumer. (Nrec Gjini)

Not for survival, but as a marketing tool very much. (Durim Haxhifazliu)

The answers to this question of all cases were short. None of them thinks that social media had some great impact on the survival of this artisan. During the conversation with them, it can be noted how passionately they love this job, and they all believe that the filigree artisan will always live and will be passed down from generation to generation.

6 Limitations and Future Research Directions

One of the main limitations of this paper is that only one type of artisan is involved and that the research took place in only one city, so the findings cannot be generalised. This restriction provides opportunities for further research in this field by including different types of artisans which are also found in different parts of Kosovo. Also, research on comparing opinions of different artisans regarding the role of social media could lead to valuable results.

Note: For cases 1, 2, 3, and 4, we have used their real names with their permission, while the name of case 5 has been changed based on his request.

References

Abdullah NM (2020) Family entrepreneurship and banking support in Kuwait: conventional vs Islamic banks. J Family Bus Manag

Agrawal A, Agrawal A (2019) A study on problems faced by Indian handicraft industry & suggestions for growth with special focus on digital marketing. Int J Account Financ Econ 1 (2):1–10

Au A, Anthony PJ (2016) Social media communication in the artisan economy. Int J Mobile Comput Multimedia Commun 7(3):32–41

Bakas FE, Duxbury N, de Castro TV (2019) Creative tourism: catalysing artisan entrepreneur networks in rural Portugal. Int J Entrep Behav Res 25(4):731–752

Baldacchino L, Cutajar C (2011) The artisan: a sustainable entrepreneur. In: Rizzo S (ed) Green jobs from a small state perspective: case studies from Malta. The Green European Foundation, Brussels

Beqiri G (2017) Marketingu i ndërmarrjeve në Kosovë përmes aplikimit të mediave sociale (Ph.D.). Universitetit Europian të Tiranës

Dana L-P, Dana TE (2005) Expanding the scope of methodologies used in entrepreneurship research. Int J Entrep Small Bus 2(1):79–88

Dana LP, Salamzadeh A (2021) Why do artisans and arts entrepreneurs use social media platforms?: Evidence from an emerging economy. Nordic J Media Manag 2(1)

Donalek JG (2005) The interview in qualitative research. Urol Nurs 25(2):124–125

Ec Ma Ndryshe, Filigree Beyond Craft. Retrieved 9 May 2021., from https://www.ecmandryshe.org/?page=2,33,594#.YKmjdqgzbIU

Ellison NB (2007) Social network sites: definition, history, and scholarship. J Comput-Mediat Commun 13(1):210–230

Ferreira J, Sousa BM, Gonçalves F (2019) Encouraging the subsistence artisan entrepreneurship in handicraft and creative contexts. J Enterp Commun People Places Global Econ 13(1/2):64–83

Filigrani, About Us. Retrieved 13 May 2021., from https://www.filigrani-pz.com/en/about-us

Gashi R, Ahmeti HG (2021) Impact of social media on the development of new products, marketing and customer relationship management in Kosovo. Emerg Sci J 5(2):125–138

Hassan S, Nadzim SZA, Shiratuddin N (2015) Strategic use of social media for small business based on the AIDA model. Procedia Soc Behav Sci 172(1):262–269

Hobsbawm EJ (1984) Artisan or labour aristocrat? Econ Hist Rev:355–372

Idris K, Belisle D (2003) Marketing crafts and visual arts: the role of intellectual property

Inkster I (1991) Science and technology in history: an approach to industrial development. Macmillan International Higher Education, London

Kaiser K (2009) Protecting respondent confidentiality in qualitative research. Qual Health Res 19 (11):1632–1641

Kaplan AM, Haenlein M (2010) Users of the world, unite! The challenges and opportunities of Social Media. Bus Horiz 53(1):59–68

Kosovo Agency of Statistic (2020a). Kosovo in figures, 2019. Retrieved 3 May 2021 from https://ask.rks-gov.net/media/5821/kosovo-in-figures-2019.pdf

Kosovo Agency of Statistic. (2020b). Estimation Kosovo population in 2019. Retrieved 3 May 2021 from https://ask.rks-gov.net/media/5537/vlersimi-i-popullsise-2019-angisht.pdf

Kosovo Agency of Statistic (2020c). Labour force survey, 2019. Retrieved 3 May 2021 from https://ask.rks-gov.net/media/5412/labour-force-survey-2019.pdf

Kosovo Agency of Statistic (2020d). Hotel statistics. Retrieved 3 May 2021, from https://ask.rks-gov.net/media/5384/hotel-statistics-q4-2019.pdf

Luckman S (2015) Craft and the creative economy. Palgrave Macmillan, New York, NY

Ministry of Environment and Spatial Planning (2004) Parku Kombëtar 'Sharri'. Retrieved 3 May 2021 from http://www.ammk-rks.net/repository/docs/PHPK_Sharri_shq.pdf

Ministry of Trade and Industry (2014) Profili i Sektorit të Turizmit. Ministry of Trade and Industry. This report is funded by the Finnish Ministry of Foreign Affairs within the framework of commitments through the Trade Assistance project, implemented by the United Nations Development Program (UNDP). Retrieved 3 May 2021 from https://kiesa.rks-gov.net/desk/inc/media/86E95F79-EEF6-4B2B-B1CC-A0317678A3AD.pdf

Municipality of Pejë (2016) Revitalization of Old Bazaars and Artisanship of Western Kosovo, An EU funded project managed by The European Union Office in Kosovo. Retrieved 3 May 2021, from http://www.phm-west.org/pdf/KataloguANG.pdf

Municipality of Prizren (2012) Prizren Venue of Civilizations. Retrieved 3 May 2021 from https://www.ecmandryshe.org/repository/docs/PRIZRENI-VENDTAKIM_I_CIVILIZIMEVE_eng.pdf

Municipality of Prizren (2015) Dokumenti Strategjik për Zhvillimin e Turizimit dhe Planet E Veprimit. Retrieved 3 May 2021 from https://kk.rks-gov.net/prizren/wp-content/uploads/sites/26/20220224.pdf

Municipality of Prizren (2019) Strategjia e Zhvillimit të Turizmit Retrieved 3 May 2021 from https://kk.rks-gov.net/prizren/wp-content/uploads/sites/26/2019/03/Draft-Strategjia-per-Zhvillimin-e-Turizmit_Komuna-e-Prizrenit_2019-2023.pdf

Municipality of Prizren (2021) Numri i Banorëve. Retrieved 3 May 2021 from https://kk.rks-gov.net/prizren/qyteti/numri-i-banoreve/

Polkinghorne DE (2005) Language and meaning: data collection in qualitative research. J Couns Psychol 52(2):137–150

PrizrenPress, Prizren: Filigrani, në shërbim të turizmit dhe ruajtjes së zejeve të moçme, 2018. Retrieved 12 May 2021, from https://prizrenpress.com/prizren-filigrani-ne-sherbim-te-turizmit-dhe-ruajtjes-se-zejeve-te-mocme/

Ramadani V, Ademi L, Ratten V, Palalic R, Krueger N (2018) Knowledge creation and relationship marketing in family businesses: a case-study approach. In: Ratten V, Braga V, Marques CS (eds) Knowledge, learning and innovation. Springer, Cham, pp 123–157

Ramadani V, Hisrich RD, Dana LP, Palalic R, Panthi L (2019) Beekeeping as a family artisan entrepreneurship business. Int J Entrep Behav Res 25(4):717–730

Ratten V, Costa C, Bogers M (2019) Artisan, cultural and tourism entrepreneurship. Int J Entrep Behav Res 25(4):582–591

Sadiku-Dushi N (2017) Getting noticed! Social media as a free tool for small business promotion. Knowl Int J 20(1):219–223

Sadiku-Dushi N (2019) Survival or willing? Informal ethnic entrepreneurship among ethnic serbs in Kosovo. In: Ramadani V, Dana L-P, Ratten V, Bexheti A (eds) Informal ethnic entrepreneurship future research paradigms for creating innovative business activity. Springer, Cham, pp 115–131

Sadiku-Dushi N, Dana LP, Ramadani V (2019) Entrepreneurial marketing dimensions and SMEs performance. J Bus Res 100(7):86–99

Siqeca S (2011) Artistic crafts' of prizren, rahovec and suhareka. CHWB, Prizren

Statista (2021) Number of social media users 2025. Retrieved 4 May 2021 from https://www.statista.com/statistics/278414/number-of-worldwide-social-network-users/

STIKK and KANTAR (2019) Internet penetration and usage in Kosovo. STIKK KANTAR, Prishtine

Teixeira SJ, Ferreira JJ (2019) Entrepreneurial artisan products as regional tourism competitiveness. Int J Entrep Behav Res 25(4):652–673

The World Factbook (2021) Kosovo. Retrieved 3 May 2021 from https://www.cia.gov/the-world-factbook/countries/kosovo/

Thomas DR (2006) A general inductive approach for analyzing qualitative evaluation data. Am J Eval 27(2):237–246

Thomas NJ, Harvey DC, Hawkins H (2013) Crafting the region: creative industries and practices of regional space. Reg Stud 47(1):75–88

United Nations (2021) Map of Kosovo, Map No. 4069 Rev. 7 Jul 2020. Retrieved from https://www.un.org/Depts/Cartographic/map/profile/kosovo.pdf. Accessed 01 May 2021

Yin RK (2013) Case study research: design and methods. Sage, Thousand Oaks, CA

Nora Sadiku-Dushi is a D.Sc in Business Administration. Her research interests include marketing, entrepreneurial marketing, entrepreneurship, small business management, family business management, management information systems, etc. She has authored and co-authored research articles in journals such as *Journal of Business Research* (JBR), *Journal of Enterprising Culture* (JEC), *European Journal of Management and Marketing Studies*, *Studia Universitatis Babes-Bolyai*, and *Oeconomica* and book chapters in books published by Springer as well as has attended several conferences. She acted as a committee member at USAID-Young Entrepreneurs Program/YEP and as a mentor in a Global Mentoring Walk Kosova. Currently, she is Assistant Professor at University for Business and Technology, Pristina, Kosovo.

Afërina Skeja holds a PhD in Business Administration from Trakya University. She completed her undergraduate studies in Computer Science at University of Prizren and her Master's studies in Business Management and Organization at Istanbul University. She is soon getting her second Master's degree in Informatics from University of Tetovo. Currently, she is a lecturer at University for Business and Technology, Pristina, Kosovo.

Veland Ramadani is a Professor of Entrepreneurship and Family Business at Faculty of Business and Economics, South East European University, North Macedonia. His research interests include entrepreneurship, small business management, and family businesses. He authored or co-authored around 140 research articles, 11 textbooks, and 18 edited books. He has published in *Journal of Business Research*, *International Entrepreneurship and Management Journal*, *International Journal of Entrepreneurial Behavior and Research*, and *Technological Forecasting and Social Change*, among others. Dr. Ramadani has recently published the co-edited book *Organizational Mindset of Entrepreneurship* (Springer). Dr. Ramadani is co-Editor-in-Chief of *Journal of Enterprising Communities* (JEC). He has received the Award for Excellence 2016 — Outstanding Paper by Emerald Group Publishing. In addition, Dr. Ramadani was invited as a keynote speaker in several international conferences and as a guest lecturer by President University, Indonesia, and Telkom University, Indonesia. In 2017, he was appointed as a member of Supervisory Board of Development Bank of North Macedonia, where for 10 months he served as an acting Chief Operating Officer (COO) as well.

Social Media and Digital Technologies Among Pottery Makers and in the Sewing Sector

Aidin Salamzadeh, Samira Sadat Mortazavi, and Morteza Hadizadeh

Abstract Creative industries are one of the most important areas of the global economy in the twenty-first century. Since the 1990s, they have been recognised as one of the fastest-growing sectors of industry and are now recognised as a key factor in the success of most developing and advanced economies. In today's world, creative industries are considered from an entrepreneurial point of view. With the development of the digital age, cultural and creative products have influenced most aspects of people's lives. These products are a combination of advanced business culture and excellent traditional culture. It is essential to pay attention to the creative cultural products due to their capacity for public acceptance, thanks to the cultural heritage of traditions and the need of communities to use those products in daily life, and they will face high economic capacity. To increase productivity in these industries, combining the dimension of innovation and technology with the application of digital technologies and social media to develop the sales market and introduce as many products as possible can be considered effective. This chapter introduces the creative industries and examines relevant issues in cultural and artistic products focusing on the pottery, ceramics, and sewing industries. It also analyses the digital technologies and social media to promote these products. The spatial domain of this research is Iran, which was conducted to investigate the current situation and the research issue in this geographical area.

A. Salamzadeh (✉)
Faculty of Management, University of Tehran, Tehran, Iran
e-mail: salamzadeh@ut.ac.ir

S. S. Mortazavi
Islamic Azad University, Ghazvin, Iran

M. Hadizadeh
Shahid Beheshti University, Tehran, Iran

L.-P. Dana et al. (eds.), *Artisan and Handicraft Entrepreneurs*, Contributions to Management Science, https://doi.org/10.1007/978-3-030-82303-0_13

1 Introduction

The creative economy can be considered the science governing the economic rules related to the creative industries, culture, and art economy. Creative industries are at the heart of the creative economy, and art and culture are at the heart of cultural and artistic industries. The combination of these two issues leads to the emergence of creative culture and artistic industries. Using the tools of innovation and creativity leads to market development. One of the most important examples of this development can be examined in using social media and digital technologies to preserve and expand the interests of creative culture and artistic industries. Cultural and creative industries (henceforth CCIs) are defined as "industries that are rooted in creativity, individual skill and talent and have the potential for creation of wealth and job". These industries are increasingly recognised as crucial for social and economic development (Landoni et al. 2020). Creative industries are associated with intensive knowledge activities, where ideas or knowledge acts as commodities. The creative process is often described in terms of cognitive processes such as generating, selecting, evaluating, describing, and transforming ideas.

Technological advances, knowledge creation, and innovation are at the core of their activities, and the four types of twenty-first-century digital skills (information, critical thinking, creativity, and problem-solving skills) are essential assets for experts working in the creative industries (van Laar et al. 2020). The creative industry's main components are population, technology and culture, and the most important of them, the use of technology in this industry (Fardani et al. 2021). At the beginning of the digital age, social media is an appropriate tool for creative businesses and consumers for business transactions without time and space constraints, so social media has great contrition to market creative economy products. It is expected that central and regional government and banking institutions be able to develop creative economic activities (Romdonny and Maulany 2020). Social media use to develop marketing strategies makes businesses more attractive and helps them promote their products in target markets, thanks to social networks' viral power (Nyagadza 2020). The evolution of art markets through digital development has changed the content of the art industry and the way art is traded, consumed, and valued (Arora and Vermeylen 2013). Various socio-cultural areas act as mechanisms to activate art markets (Komarova and Velthuis 2018). The emergence of digitalisation with changing cultural and economic relations has significantly impacted the art market and its institutions. In this chapter, we focus on the market of ceramic, pottery, and sewing arts to explain the trend of market changes in these industries, emphasising the Iranian market.

Given the expansion and development of digital technologies and social media, this chapter reviews the research literature in the area of creative cultural industries such as ceramics, pottery, and sewing to identify new entrepreneurial opportunities in the area of creative cultural and artistic industries. Besides having ancient values that reflect societies' history and culture, these industries are widely used as a style of life in daily relationships, so it has played an essential role in the economic market, and this market has changed due to technology development. Identification of these changes more accurately can lead to increased economic productivity in art markets. Given what was stated above, this chapter has studied different areas of artistic entrepreneurship, including creative economy, entrepreneurship of creative cultural industries, and social media and digital technologies in the creative economy. This study also examines the status of the creative economy and creative industries such as ceramics, pottery, and sewing in Iran.

2 Creative Economy, Art Markets, and Art Galleries of Iran

2.1 Creative Economy

"Creative economy" is an evolving concept created based on potential creative assets, production, and economic development. The creative economy encompasses a set of interconnected industries and includes knowledge-based industries, cultural industries, and creative industries, where ideas are the main driver of the creative economy. These industries produce tangible and intangible goods and services that are created, produced, and traded (Gouvea et al. 2020). The idea of the creative economy focuses on creative assets and culture-rich national resources. Creative industries that use these resources provide conditions for the emergence of countries' unique cultural identities and contribute to economic growth and increase their global economy participation (Parshukova and Riazantseva 2021). Considering innovation as part of a creative economy opens up broader perspectives on sustainable development goals since it creates new opportunities and markets. Initial estimates suggest that the market size be 12 trillion USD by 2030 (President 2020). Governments still consider entrepreneurship, innovation, and the creative economy at all levels, the business sector, society, and international organisations in general (Dana 2011). Emphasis on large-scale operations (commonly referred to as industrial scale), manufacturing, mining, agriculture, retail, etc. is constantly being replaced by a different view on the economy, economic growth and development, material prosperity, and economic well-being (Gouvea et al. 2020). A creative economy is a type of economy that has a form of economic-economic relations created in the production, distribution, exchange, and consumption of goods based on human talents and non-standard, non-traditional ideas, strategies, and actions. New knowledge will provide more effective solutions to socio-economic problems (Iarmosh et al. 2021). A creative economy can increase income for society and create jobs and economic value from export activities. It also promotes the diversity of social culture and human resources development (Asriati et al. 2021). The vision and mission of the creative economy in 2025 can be achieved by increasing the foundations and actors as elements of the model of building a creative economy. The five main components that need to be strengthened in the development of creative industries are as follows: (1) industry, that is, a set of enterprises operating in the creative industry, (2) technology, that is, a possibility for the realisation of individual creativity in the form of real works, (3) resources, that is, input other than creativity and individual knowledge that is necessary in the creative process, for example, natural resources, land, (4) institution, that is, social order (norms, values, and laws) including industry associations, professional associations, and other creative societies, and (5) financial intermediary, that is, financial intermediary institutions.

The main actors involved in the development of a creative economy can be divided into the following categories:

1. *Intellectuals*—people who are seeking for gaining satisfaction in the cultivation of art and science and are willing to use knowledge and transfer it
2. *Business*—that is business actors who are able to turn creativity into economic value
3. Government—as catalyst and advocacy, regulator, consumers, investors and entrepreneurs, urban planners, who can enable the creative industry to grow and develop

A creative economy is a sector of a populist industry that has the potential to develop in an effort to support the growth of the national economy. The industry has a broader market and is growing in line with current development and can foster creativity and innovation and create value-added to its business activists. A creative economy can increase income and help distribute public welfare (Romdonny and Maulany 2020). The creative economy, as one of the fastest-growing economic sectors in today's global economy, promotes human progress, social expansion, and cultural diversity; stimulates entrepreneurship; attracts high-quality labour in terms of income generation, job creation, and export income; and paves the way for economic success (Toma et al. 2018).

2.2 Art Market

The art market acts as a collective mediating structure and creates a multilateral agency that includes financial, economic, educational, political, and social sectors (Baia Curioni et al. 2020). In general, art markets intersect culture and economy and play a key role in shaping our views of artwork, increasing their value (Dana 1999). Art markets' role is crucial even to artists, as they generate income from this market, thereby supporting their livelihoods and continuing their activities. Almost all the artworks displayed in museums were first traded in art markets based on economic trade, and today, some are displayed in an art museum as masterpieces (Grigoroudis et al. 2021). The art market often reflects economic developments and trends that generate wealth (McAndrew 2020). It has been evident since the beginning of the millennium, as wealth has spread in the global economy around the world (Vermeylen 2015, p. 31). Working capital and liquidity in the art markets can increase, which depends on the situation in which markets are valued correctly. A person who can determine the value and organise the relationship between buyer and seller can encourage more transactions. In markets where the creators of artworks are accepted in the absence of the evaluator and only the market is defined as an intermediary market, direct contact to determine the transaction price is required, resulting in a process that causes a negative impact on the evaluation of works (Aerne 2020). Artists are defined as one of the most critical components in the art markets. They are considered as distinguished, individual, creative people who have freedom of action. They are considered unique and transcendent in comparison to other professions. Moreover, artists seem to be flexible and neoliberal in creating works. In general, they have to constantly discuss a hierarchical art system, conditions, and possible fluctuations, and given the nature of the artwork as an internal process, they do it alone and through strategies such as branding (Ramadani et al. 2019). Collective practices and behaviours for artists in an organised and valuable art market seem to create individual value for the artist (Sooudi 2020). Thus, some valuable structures and even intermediaries take the responsibility of facilitating the marketing and selling of artists' works. Hence, they will play a key role in reducing sales operations, improving the artist's status, enhancing the nature of the artworks, and increasing the financial share of this market.

2.3 *Art Galleries*

In a modern definition, art galleries refer to private places where art is displayed, priced (its economic value is assessed), and sold (Moulin 1995). Galleries can act as a market agent and represent specific artists who sell their work through exhibitions, catalogues, events, and advertisements. They are often defined as a trusted advisor to artists' work. A gallery's definition includes institutions that are very different in terms of size, centrality, and financial and organisational capacity. Their sustainability is based on a combination of short-term operations (selling artworks for the initial financing of an enterprise) and long-term and medium-term operations (maintaining, controlling, and increasing the value and status of artists) (Baia Curioni et al. 2020). It is thought that increasing financial value is the main driver for galleries. However, creating customer value is more important in art galleries (Williams et al. 2020). Art galleries play a primary role for both art intermediary and evaluation (Komarova and Velthuis 2018). Art galleries are the most critical intermediary in the contemporary art market. They form a relationship between artists and buyers (supply and demand) and link other factors that help increase market value (Maguire and Matthews 2012). Value in art galleries refers to all aspects of artistic value beyond financial credit. For example, celebrating artworks is an aesthetic experience created socially in a complicated manner. The role of artworks cannot be reduced to the transfer of services because art galleries themselves do not generate value. They need the participation of the viewer. However, organisations can indirectly influence value creation. The guidelines provided by the gallery influence art value. In the cultural sector, especially in public art galleries, there is significant potential for developing marketing measures and market research (Williams et al. 2020).

2.4 Art-Based Social Enterprise

Social enterprises are concepts that have more drawn the attention of media, politicians and public people, as well as the academic and scientific community in recent decades. They mainly focus on promoting social change by providing new and transformative solutions to eradicate poverty, solve environmental problems, increase social inclusion, and increase political participation or welfare of society (Pinheiro et al. 2021). Based on existing definitions of social enterprises, they mainly include two distinct characteristics. They follow a social mission to obtain business income (Beaton and Dowin Kennedy 2021). Also, social enterprises can play a crucial role in reducing the negative effects of major crises (Farhoud 2021). Social enterprises promise art to maintain independence in a global economic system, which allocates a creative activity to social and economic goals (McQuilten et al. 2015). Art-based social enterprises tend to emerge in the areas of textiles, handicrafts, exhibitions, and sales in the gallery. The artistic and economic aspects of art-based enterprises are related to the social area. For example, creative practices such as art, handcrafts, and design have a unique ability to generate social capacity for deprived people and communities, including effects such as job creation, skills training, and individual capacity building (McQuilten et al. 2015). Art-based social enterprises (ASEs) aim to create positive social benefits for young people who experience some forms of marginalisation. They offer creative products or services to help them accomplish this mission. The growth of ASEs reflects a growing interest in the ways of art support of social and economic development and new ways of generating employment outside the labour market. They expand opportunities for more people to participate in art markets and challenge the dominant models of the cultural production and consumption market (McQuilten et al. 2020).

2.5 The Creative Economy of Iran

In Iran, creative industries are defined as industries in which the three components, culture, technology, and society, play a significant role. In other words, attention to the creative economy by the Iranian government requires paying attention to these three components, and creative industries will not exist unless these components are studied and localised with a convergent approach. Based on studies conducted by CISAC (The International Confederation of Societies of Authors and Composers), 2.250 trillion USD, or about 3% of the world's gross domestic product, is allocated to the creative economy at present. Creative industries around the world have also created about 30 million jobs, which is about 1% of the world's active population. In this regard, Asia and Oceania, with a 743 billion USD creative economy, have created about 12.7 million jobs and are ranked first in this area. Europe follows them with 709 billion USD and 7.7 million jobs, North America with 620 billion USD and 4.7 million jobs, Africa and the Middle East with 58 billion USD and 2.4 million jobs, and Latin America with 124 billion USD and 1.9 million jobs, respectively. The diversity of Iranian ethnic groups and the cultural and artistic background of Iranians are two issues that can help the growth of creative industries in Iran before any other issue. Also, Iranian ethnic groups such as Turkmen, Kurds, Lors, and Baluchs have their own culture that this culture can be studied and commercialised as the origin of the production of creative industrial products. Moreover, Iranian people have always been known as people with rich culture and art around the world for centuries. Historical works of previous periods in the form of architecture, handicrafts, decorative accessories, and so on are evidence in this regard. Handicrafts are one of the excellent capacities of the creative industry in Iran, but no significant macro-policies have been made on them, unfortunately. It can be stated that those handicrafts that can be considered as Iranian creative industries are mainly made by traditional and home workshops. Although this issue has maintained the quality of the Iranian creative industry, low level of products has caused that a major part of these products to be consumed inside the country and there is no opportunity to offer them in international markets.

In addition to these capacities, it can be stated that many areas of the Iranian creative industry remain pristine. For example, the industry of making computer games and animation is among the areas in which Iran is the only consumer. Besides, the Iranian creative industry has not been exposed to any of the media areas such as magazines, cinema, Internet, and television, while the income of developed countries of the world from this field is about 90 billion USD. In this regard, the lack of related educational infrastructure is one of the main reasons for ignoring these areas. Iranian society is transitioning from a traditional to modern society, and many aspects of technology and communication have neglected. Thus, there are no government facilities to strengthen the skills related to these areas in the interested people. Given what was stated above, the development of the Iranian creative industry needs much work. Given the economic sanctions imposed and the existence of large competitors to the creative industries globally, commercialising the ideas of the creative industry in Iran to export them in the mid-term seems to be impossible. However, this movement has started a few years ago and is gradually continuing. Sanctions have limited communication between the Iranian art market and the international art network. Galleries try to overcome these limitations through online marketing and exhibitions. Therefore, these sanctions affect the form of marketing applied by the sellers and directly affect the type of art production. Such changes are also transforming the art market in Arab countries. The transition from tangible to intangible assets has become a strategy for the regional market to neutralise the sanctions and develop and trade with global institutions (Rafiei Vardanjani 2020).

3 Craft Entrepreneurship in Iran

3.1 Cultural Creative Product

Creativity is one of the essential concepts in psychology to explain and measure. People have ideas in the face of issues and events that can be considered creative, but only a few can describe the factors that create creativity in the subject matter. Creativity can be described by focusing on the product and the observed behaviour. Creative product criteria include performance, novelty, aesthetics, product executability, and product value (Varol 2018). Cultural and creative products are among the most basic everyday needs, which are a combination of "cultural elements" and "creative elements" (Varol 2018). In recent economic literature, the concept of "creativity" has found increasingly important in happiness, motivation, and life satisfaction. The effects and creative activities on consumer welfare in relation to cultural, sociological, psychological, and educational aspects have also been analysed. Policymakers and international institutions (e.g., UNCTAD/UNESCO Report on the Creative Economy, 2010, 2013, and 2016) have recently considered these concepts. Moreover, there is no clear analytical definition of these goods and activities and research on their specific characteristics compared to other types of products and activities in economic literature (Sanfilippo and Bariletti 2017). Creative products are the result of creative ideas that can be defined as objects, technology, or new ideas and can be used to solve problems in real life (Suyidno et al. 2020). In the era of the Internet + (plus), cultural and creative products have the most application in social life and have influenced all aspects of people's lives. Cultural and creative products are a combination of advanced business culture and excellent traditional culture (Zhu 2020). A creative cultural product can be defined as the result of design activities in which cultural resources and elements are creatively transformed into new products (Lee and Lin 2019).

3.2 Creative Goods and Services

For any sector of the economy, a growth perspective or outlook is required with the availability of human capital and related expertise. This is especially important in the case of creative industries because creative talent is a determining characteristic of the creative industries (Bakhshi et al. 2013). In terms of enterprises' business participation, participation in global value chains means enterprises' demand for intermediary goods and services that enter domestic production and consumption or are exported for foreign production and consumption. A variety of regulations governs creative service businesses around the world. These regulations vary widely in different geographical areas. There is also significant heterogeneity among the creative sectors. In terms of export flows, creative IT-based industries have had more exports (Di Novo et al. 2020). Digital products and an increase in intangible capital cause disorder in business institutions based on social structures. It provides an in-depth insight into this technical and social development and progress in creative professions (Hearn and McCutcheon 2020).

Creative goods and services based on UNCTAD classification are as follows (UNCTAD 2018) (Fig. 1).

3.3 Ceramics and Pottery Industry

Nowadays, the creative economy and related creative industries have received more attention, and also handicrafts are an important part of these creative industries. Today's definition of handicraft products has a symbolic and aesthetic content, and their creativity has been inspired by creative designs, new forms, and specific materials (Bathelt and Boggs 2003; Lash and Urry 1994; Luckman 2013). Examining advertising provides a deeper understanding of the relationship between production and demand. Due to the change in the business nature of products in pottery and ceramics, we see a transition from a traditional market in which manufacturers played a major role to a skilful market with different complexities and angles (Fig. 2). Therefore, the need for market development research in the ceramic sector has found increasing importance. In this skilful market, manufacturers and traders are more involved in the process of meeting consumer's demand and, most importantly, the need to respond to market demand. Therefore, paying attention to this issue highlights the importance of investigating consumption from a sales perspective (Ewins 2020). Attention to competition and innovation in ceramic manufacturers in the EU is mainly made by medium-sized enterprises that respond quickly to changing demand and new opportunities. Automation and environmental

Creative Goods (7 groups, 25 subgroups)		
Art crafts	**Design**	**Audiovisuals**
Carpets Celebration Other art crafts Paperware Wickerware Yarn	Architecture Fashion Glassware Interior Jewellery Toys	Film CDs, DVDs, tapes **Visual arts** Antiques Painting Photography Sculpture
New media	**Performing arts**	**Publishing**
Recorded media Video games	Musical instruments Printed music	Books Newspaper Other printed matter

Creative Services (8 items)	
Advertising, market research and public opinion polling	Computer services
Research and Development	Information services
Architectural, engineering and other technical services	Franchises and similar rights
Audiovisual and related services	Other royalties and license fees

Fig. 1 UNCTAD classification of creative goods and services (UNCTAD 2018)

Fig. 2 Ceramics gallery in Iran-Qazvin © Photo by Morteza Hadizadeh

technologies are widely used. Clusters cause innovation and increase competition. Innovations include specialised exposure of industry to value-added products, access to new markets in emerging economies, and its ability to provide services according to market needs. This sector is increasing research and development in the area of technical ceramics, smart materials, laser use, process automation, and labelling (European Commission 2020). The focus of this industry in the east is mainly on villages or less developed cities. Pottery is discussed as a kind of artisan entrepreneurship. Artisan networks and innovative and entrepreneurial behaviours play a key role in some rural artisan enterprises' growth. Innovation can reinforce rural industry through networks and entrepreneurship. The value of innovations and networks are recognised as key elements in the entrepreneurship of rural artisans. However, rural entrepreneurship is an emerging field of study, and it is becoming one of the most significant ways to promote rural development by relying on creative start-up enterprises (Marques 2019).

Strategies for developing the pottery and ceramics industry in less developed countries:

1. Many potters leave their job due to inconsistency in supply and demand, and new generations are unwilling to be a potter. Entrepreneurial opportunities in this industry need to be discovered and obtain information on members of the potters' families.

2. Many potters cannot expand their business due to the financial constraints they face. Government agencies can provide special financial assistance to the pottery sector.
3. For many potters, there are no educational facilities at the local level, making it more difficult for women from distant places to receive the necessary training. Government agencies should organise regular training programs.
4. Most potters use traditional equipment to produce pottery, which is costly and time-consuming. They need modern equipment to increase production rate and improve product quality.
5. The ICT sector should support the digital market by training and providing appropriate platforms in the area of e-commerce and marketing. It can lead to adopting an effective approach in receiving and delivering orders from rural areas for entrepreneurs.
6. The Export Promotion *Bureau* (EPB), the SME Foundation, and the local government should hold product exhibitions inside and outside the country. Besides, they can set up public awareness programs that highlight the negative effects of plastic products on the environment and encourage people to buy bio-friendly products such as various pottery products (Muzahidul et al. 2020).

3.4 Sewers

With the increasing growth and development of information and communication technologies and industrial production processes, the conditions for producing creative symbolic goods with cultural themes have been provided. Innovative ideas and thoughts presented in a specific socio-cultural context, which previously appeared uniquely due to lack of possibilities for reproduction and dissemination in the form of individual products, have now found the opportunity to be widely spread locally, nationally, regionally, and globally in various formats as cultural and creative industries. The fashion industry, as one of the most popular and profitable cultural industries in the modern world, plays a serious role in transmitting innovative ideas influenced by the underlying and fundamental layers of the cultural identity of a society, so that social thinkers have discussed it as a window opened to identity, social class, and social change. Also, cultural theorists have focused on fashion to reflect symbolic meaning and social ideals.

Fashion has also been investigated as a phenomenon representing modernity's key characteristics (Hemphill and Suk 2009). The fashion industry is a 1.3 trillion USD business that employs more than 300 million people worldwide. It is a significant economic force and stimulus for global GDP. This industry operates in a competitive market dominated by global brands. Despite the last decade's financial crisis, the fashion industry has grown rapidly and has undergone extensive changes. With a global increase in people's age, the fashion industry has nowadays found an opportunity to serve both the young and old generations simultaneously (Gazzola et al. 2020). The fashion industry is associated with the digital world more than ever.

Fig. 3 Sewers gallery and knitting workshop Iran-Qazvin © Photo by Samira Mortazavi

With the development of e-commerce, digital operating systems and digital marketing strategies have become popular in the fashion market, and many new brands emerged, allowing enterprises to engage with customers through the virtual world (Lee 2017a, b). The fashion industry follows a linear model consisting of three main stages of collecting (collecting of raw materials), fabrication (production of clothes), and waste (subsequent wearing and disposal of clothing) (Brydges 2021). The role of fashion entrepreneurs has changed throughout history. In the late nineteenth century, the role of a fashion designer was introduced. Before that time, these people were known as sewers or tailors, and they were designing clothes, making models and templates, and then sewing the final clothes together. The aristocracy primarily dictated fashion at that time. Models were more standard, but fabric selection was critical, so textiles were often the main priority in design. In the late nineteenth century, the role of the tailor evolved to become a fashion designer. They have established their businesses as arts entrepreneurs (Fig. 3). It becomes similar to an artist. In the late twentieth century, the consumer was given more importance, and the rapid response to consumer needs was economically very profitable. In the twenty-first century, sustainability and social responsibility are two critical issues, and consumers now have ethical demands that were not previously considered in the industry. Consumers are now more critical so that they can influence fashion. In a volatile world, it can be stated that a successful fashion entrepreneur is someone who can respond to changing demands. In fact, by understanding today's world and the change in the industry, a tailor's role can be changed into a producer of creative artist clothes with creative imagination (Brandstrup 2021).

3.5 Case of Iran

Economic areas, which welcome creativity, generate significantly more wealth and will be more stable in future. Governments can develop business investment strategies and shift excess industries or constraints to future industries. The current national policy, which requires all local governments in Iran to promote creative industries in their regions, seems to be ineffective. The creative industry is influenced by the economic dynamics of the real estate market and by government interventions and an increase in personal value held by enterprises, workers, and citizens (Liu 2015). In general, creative industries in Iran's cities, including Isfahan, should be encouraged by using particular policies and development strategies. Lack of communication with other creative urban communities creates a social barrier that jeopardises its status as a creative city. Promoting handicrafts helps increase a city's attractiveness and indirectly supports service industries, such as tourism. Thus, urban management in Isfahan, considered as one of the important bases in the area of creative industries in Iran, should revive the tourism sector by presenting its local cultural products in international markets. However, cultural planning should focus on evaluating the cultural needs of an area to determine the methods of creating it (Ghazi and Goede 2019). As another example of an Iranian city, we can refer to Lalejin, a city that has been a place of ceramics and pottery for at least 200 years. Despite occasional successes, for example, being selected as "World Pottery Capital" in 2016, it faces declining demand by consumer products in this industry. Innovation is a key to survival and sustainability, but the capacity for innovation is low. For experts, understanding the evolution of the ecosystem and the cultural foundation of observations will help design an accurate and sustainable ecosystem renewal program. Linking cultural characteristics, ecosystem evolution, and results is an appropriate and fruitful way of research (Salamzadeh and Kawamorita 2017; Ghazinoory et al. 2020).

Based on the studies, the Iranian pottery galleries in this industry have faced nine significant problems (Fig. 4), as follows (Afrakhteh et al. 2016): (1) problems related to equipping the required resources and raw materials, (2) technical and technological problems, (3) structural and infrastructural problems, (4) problems related to advertising and information, (5) legal problems, (6) executive and management problems, (7) financial and credit problems, (8) educational problems, promotion and research, and (9) problems related to the supply and marketing system.

Investigating the current situation of different stages of the fashion cycle in Iran suggests that the endogenous clothing fashion process is not formed based on the principles of unity of indigenous culture in Iran. In the current situation, there is no systematic and coordinated activity among components of different stages of the

Fig. 4 Pottery gallery in Iran-Qazvin © Photo by Samira Mortazavi

fashion cycle in Iran, and if there is coordination, it is imitated from the best-selling imported patterns and in line with the flow and demand from other non-indigenous brands (primarily European) that are influential in global markets. Thus, the lack of indigenous influential and identity-forming brands is essential in the lack of proper formation of the indigenous fashion cycle. Among the issues and problems of the fashion cycle, especially those derived from content analysis to explain the relationship between the concepts, the problem of "lack of forming influential indigenous factors" is considered as the most crucial problem, which ultimately leads to the non-formation of the endogenous process of Iranian Islamic fashion (Afrough and Mehrbanifar 2018).

4 Social Media and Digital Technologies in the Creative Economy of Iran

4.1 Innovation Ecosystem

The literature on innovation topics focuses on the innovation ecosystem. The innovation network and the digital innovation ecosystem have attracted academics and industries' attention (Yin et al. 2020). The term "innovation ecosystem" (IE) has attracted the attention of many organisations in recent years (Oh et al. 2016; Salamzadeh et al. 2017). The work structure in innovation ecosystems consists of three main approaches: platform-based ecosystem or digital ecosystem, regional/local ecosystem, and industrial ecosystem (Salamzadeh 2018). In the digital ecosystem, a multi-faceted platform is made of at least two prominent faces. The first case enables stakeholders and actors to design and develop innovative products and services. The second case facilitates the management, sale, or gaining income from new products and services between operating system shareholders and users or customers. Both of them use data to benefit in the course of evolution in customer behaviour and performance. They continuously improve the products and services of the digital platform. Thus, digital operating systems create complex and dynamic interactions and automated transactions between various actors (customers, developers, users, and suppliers) (Boyer 2020). Digital innovation is changing the way businesses and governments operate. It is nowadays the driving force of the growth of business and economy. The emergence of digital innovation is increasingly essential for managers and policymakers (Chae 2019). Despite the role that creative and cultural firms (CCFs) play in industrialised countries' economic development, they tend to remain small and often fail due to specific constraints and stresses of industry such as lack of management skills, growing complexity, and limited value chain. However, there is relatively limited scientific interest in the specific conditions and processes that enable CCFs to meet these obligations and extend the business models they have adopted throughout their life cycle for their survival. Using the BMI concept creates a structure for resetting the CCF operating system, creates and presents value, and makes it possible to exploit entrepreneurial opportunities over time. CCFs should use their symbolic, relational, and cultural assets to develop customer relationships and expand their business. They reveal the importance of using different resources in the enterprise ecosystem to create and present value through BMI. Shortage of tangible assets in entrepreneurial jobs is not necessarily a factor to impose constraints but rather a stimulus to reorganise the enterprise's activities and increase the relative value created and captured. It also contributes to emerging studies of the interaction between digital transformation and BM and shows how enterprises are taking advantage of new opportunities offered by digital technologies to grow. However, digital technologies are ambivalent since they can foster shorter and modular value chains on the one hand, but they may create new barriers and resources that maintain control of critical complementary assets on the other hand (Landoni et al. 2020).

4.2 Social Media

Social media allows people to interact freely with others and offers marketers different ways to reach and interact with consumers. Not surprisingly, marketers have embraced social media as a marketing channel since it has very high and potential audiences, who spend many hours of the day using social media on different operating systems. Academically, social media has also been welcomed, and extensive studies have been conducted on social media marketing and related topics, word of mouth (WOM) marketing on online networks. These media have culturally created a dominant form of communication used as primary media by enterprises for advertising and other communication forms. They have geopolitical implications that have increased these networks' importance (Appel et al. 2020). Global influence and penetration of social media reached about 54% in 2020. They have the greatest influence in Northern and Western Europe, followed by North and South America. Social media are constantly expanding, evolving, and growing globally. The total number of social media users is expected to reach more than 4.4 billion by 2025, which will be almost half of the world's population. Social media started as an entertainment tool and became a powerful marketing tool. Social media play a key role in establishing the relationship between marketers and customers (Palalic et al. 2020). Social media marketing is on the rise since this type of media becomes vital in the industry and shows further development potential. Investment in social advertising worldwide is predicted to increase from about 32 billion USD in 2017 to approximately 48 billion USD in 2021. The United States is the world's largest social media advertising market, with more than 14.8 billion USD (Statista 2020). The large volume of data generated on the Internet has reached unprecedented numbers, enabling new data-driven methods to study art and its markets. However, this type of data-driven research has created many methodological constraints on art market researchers, particularly due to information asymmetries, e-commerce operating systems, and online sale platforms, which involve potential innovation (Van Miegroet et al. 2019). For example, two digital operating systems, namely, Artsy and Artnet, provided media coverage, as two activities that have traditionally operated in the visual arts world, such as selling and writing artwork. Media production is different from a traditional art magazine (Salamzadeh 2020). In fact, art critics are perceived as key actors in the process of legitimising art, as they argue for the aesthetics that contribute to its artistic and economic value. The expansion of the art market is predictable only if potential customers have the knowledge to assess the artistic and economic value of the work (Sirois 2021; Dana and Salamzadeh 2021). Users express their opinions and feelings about almost everything on social media. This online behaviour has led to a number of applications that use social media data to assess public opinion (Foka 2018). Using this capability, the Instagram social network advertises itself as a platform where galleries and sellers increasingly advertise their work and interact with many audiences (Repo and Matschoss 2020).

4.3 *Digital Technologies*

At the age of the Fourth Industrial Revolution, digital technologies' development and adoption have become common in academic and professional areas (Sahut et al. 2020). The term "digital technologies" refers to the set and pattern of intelligent and innovative technologies in the age of industry 4.0, such as big data analyses, IoT, and cloud computing that realise connectivity, communication, and automation. Digital technologies bring opportunities and challenges for the sustainable development of manufacturing enterprises (Li et al. 2020). With the integration of digital technologies in the manufacturing industry, a digital transformation has been created, which has created changes in traditional production methods and operations management and offered the potential to improve product development, production efficiency, and customer service (Neuhofer et al. 2015). Digital technologies activate business models of the circular economy. Digital technologies enable small enterprises to improve their resource flow and create and absorb value and innovate in the business model to improve society's welfare. Circular economics is a concept that creates an opportunity for enterprises to move from linear to cyclical thinking in the supply chain and from product-driven to value-driven services in relation to their customers (Ranta et al. 2021). With the global expansion of the Internet and the advent of digital technologies, developments in digital entrepreneurship have accelerated.

Digital entrepreneurship is a type of entrepreneurship that can be achieved by creating innovative products and services by many segments of society, and the sale of these emerging products and services in many operating systems is realised in light of developments and advances that occur by the growth of technology. New software and applications, social networks, easier access to the Internet, and information technology growth have provided many new opportunities for entrepreneurs. Thanks to these advances, digital entrepreneurship has emerged as a new form of entrepreneurship. Digital entrepreneurship can be considered as the realisation of entrepreneurship in digital contexts. These activities have resulted in flexibility, speed, cost, quality, meeting different demands and needs, and innovations that have created some new demands and needs in the consumer. Digital entrepreneurship also provides job opportunities for manufacturers and small business owners to sell their products and services easily in digital markets. Social networks, easy and cheap access to the Internet, software and mobile applications, and the new generation of information technologies have brought many new opportunities for entrepreneurs, including art entrepreneurs (Balli 2020). Digitisation of activities is an important condition for establishing a sustainable competitive advantage in the market. Digitalisation is a basis for a leadership position in a competitive market. The process of digitalisation of all processes of human life will increase undoubtedly in future. Industry owners need to combine different competitive methods to achieve their strategic goal for development. Digital technology is one of these methods that increases the competitive advantage in the retail sector. There are common classes of products for sale in the retail market, including durable goods, daily consumption of food, and art, significantly affecting these markets' performance (Borisova et al. 2020).

5 Conclusion

Creative industries are rooted in cultural and artistic industries. Cultural industries produce creative tangible and intangible artistic products and can reproduce income and wealth through using cultural assets and producing both traditional and contemporary knowledge-based goods and services. A common characteristic of cultural industries in this definition is the use of the creativity of cultural knowledge and intellectual property to produce products and services with social and cultural content. An essential aspect of cultural industries is that they are very important in terms of promoting and protecting cultural diversity and ensuring democratic access to culture. This dual nature of the combination of cultural and economic aspects gives a different appurtenance to cultural industries. The advent of social media and digital technologies has brought many changes to today's world. In the global economy, we live in an age of digital technologies and social media, in which new technologies and mass media and virtual networks are an integral part of the lives of audiences of these technologies. With the increasing growth and development of new technologies and communication and development of industrial production processes, we move towards producing creative and cultural goods.

Digital technologies in the manufacturing industry and digital transformation result in product efficiency, production, and increased customer service quality. Paying attention to digital technologies and social media in today's society improves the performance of small industries. The use of digital technologies and social media also creates new opportunities for entrepreneurs in the cultural and artistic areas, and they can easily present their products and services in digital markets. Finally, it can be stated that the application of digital technologies and social media in the economy, including the creative economy, brings social welfare and economic development. Paying attention to the Iranian government's creative economy requires considering three components, namely, culture, technology, and society, and these components should be studied and localised with a convergent approach. The diversity of Iranian ethnic groups and the cultural and artistic background of Iranians are considered potential advantages for the growth of Iran's creative industries.

Unfortunately, no significant macro-policy has been made in these industries. Iranian pottery and ceramics industries, which can be considered as Iranian creative industries, are mainly made by traditional and home workshops. Although this issue has maintained the quality of the Iranian creative industry, a low production level has caused Iran, as a country with the high cultural potential to present products in international markets, to not be able to meet the domestic needs and even import these works. In the sewing industry sector, the domestic and endogenous clothing fashion process based on the unifying principles of indigenous culture has not been formed in the country. In the current situation, there is no systematic activity among the components of different stages of the fashion cycle in Iran, and if there are coordination and harmony among them, it imitates from the best-selling imported models and in line with the flow and demand from other influential brands (mostly European) in global markets across the borders. After reviewing the literature on entrepreneurship in the area of creative cultural and artistic industries, the researcher concluded that by using digital technologies and increasing the level of communication, using social networks and content production to introduce the products of art markets in social media, art markets can be expanded and more share of consumer markets can be obtained. This increased share in domestic markets by marketing, focusing, and encouraging the use of more works, and in foreign markets, in light of cultural advantages and affinities and with the plan of dialogue of civilisations enables Iran to market its creative cultural products and create its share of almost pristine markets.

References

Aerne A (2020) The creation of a global market for Colombian contemporary art through valuation and match-making. Poetics 86:101525

Afrakhteh H, Armand M, Athari Z (2016) Analysis of challenges facing the pottery industry in Lalejin using grounded theory. J Geogr Reg Dev

Afrough E, Mehrbanifar H (2018) A study of the fashion cycle of clothing in Iranian society. Women Cult Arts 10(1):1–27

Appel G, Grewal L, Hadi R, Stephen AT (2020) The future of social media in marketing. J Acad Mark Sci 48(1):79–95

Arora P, Vermeylen F (2013) Art markets. In Handbook on the digital creative economy. Edward Elgar Publishing

Asriati N, Thoharudin M, Budiman J (2021) Education of entrepreneurship and creative economy in women independence based on the center of community learning activities program. Elementary Educ Online 20(1):738–749

Baia Curioni S, Equi Pierazzini M, Forti L (2020) Philosophic money. The contemporary art system as a market and cultural agent. In: Arts, vol 9(4). Multidisciplinary Digital Publishing Institute, p 110

Bakhshi H, Hargreaves I, Mateos-Garcia J (2013) A manifesto for the creative economy. Nesta, London

Balli A (2020) Digital entrepreneurship and digital entrepreneurship approach in turkey: ankara case. İşletme Araştırmaları Dergisi 12(2):1058–1071

Bathelt H, Boggs JS (2003) Toward a reconceptualisation of regional development paths: Is Leipzig's media cluster a continuation of or a rupture with the past? Econ Geogr 79(3):265–293

Beaton EE, Dowin Kennedy E (2021) Responding to failure: the promise of market mending for social enterprise. Public Manag Rev 23(5):641–664

Borisova VV, Panfilova EE, Raza H (2020) Labor market transformation in the context of the digitalization of the economy. In: International Online Forum named after A Ya. Kibanov "Innovative personnel management". Springer, Cham, pp. 265–274

Boyer J (2020) Toward an evolutionary and sustainability perspective of the innovation ecosystem: revisiting the panarchy model. Sustainability 12(8):3232

Brandstrup M (2021) Entrepreneurs in the fashion industry. In World encyclopedia of entrepreneurship. Edward Elgar

Brydges T (2021) Closing the loop on take, make, waste: Investigating circular economy practices in the Swedish fashion industry. J Clean Prod 293:126245

Chae BK (2019) A general framework for studying the evolution of the digital innovation ecosystem: the case of big data. Int J Inf Manag 45:83–94

Dana LP (1999) Preserving culture through small business: government support for artisans and craftsmen in Greece. J Small Bus Manag 37(1):90

Dana LP (2011) World encyclopedia of entrepreneurship. Edward Elgar

Dana LP, Salamzadeh A (2021) Why do artisans and arts entrepreneurs use social media platforms?: Evidence from an emerging economy. Nord J Media Manag 2(1)
Di Novo, S., Fazio, G., & Vermeulen, W. N. (2020). 12 facts about the UK's international trade in creative goods and services. Creative Industries Policy and Evidence Centre. https://pec.ac.uk/research-reports/12-facts-about-the-uks-international-trade-in-creative-goods-and-services
European Commission (2020). https://ec.europa.eu/growth/sectors/raw-materials/industries/non-metals/ceramics_en
Ewins N (2020). Variations in American marketing practices of early 19th-century ceramic importers and dealers, reflecting culture and identity. J Hist Res Market
Fardani I, Agustina IH, Yuliandra MAD (2021) Development of creative economy geospatial database using an open source GIS program. In IOP conference series: materials science and engineering, vol 1098(3). IOP Publishing, p 032002
Farhoud M, Shah S, Stenholm P, Kibler E, Renko M, Terjesen S (2021) Social enterprise crowdfunding in an acute crisis. J Bus Ventur Insights 15:e00211
Foka AF (2018) An artist ranking system based on social media mining. Inform Retrieval J 21 (5):410–448
Gazzola P, Pavione E, Pezzetti R, Grechi D (2020) Trends in the fashion industry. The perception of sustainability and circular economy: a gender/generation quantitative approach. Sustainability 12(7):2809
Ghazi EL, Goede M (2019) Creative industries: a case study of Isfahan, Iran. Int J Soc Econ 46 (2):271–287
Ghazinoory S, Sarkissian A, Farhanchi M, Saghafi F (2020) Renewing a dysfunctional innovation ecosystem: the case of the Lalejin ceramics and pottery. Technovation 96:102122
Gouvea R, Kapelianis D, Montoya MJR, Vora G (2020) The creative economy, innovation and entrepreneurship: an empirical examination. Creat Indust J 14:1–40
Grigoroudis E, Noël L, Galariotis E, Zopounidis C (2021) An ordinal regression approach for analysing consumer preferences in the art market. Eur J Oper Res 290(2):718–733
Hearn G, McCutcheon M (2020) The creative economy: the rise and risks of intangible capital and the future of creative work. In The future of creative work. Edward Elgar Publishing
Hemphill CS, Suk J (2009) The law, culture, and economics of fashion. Stanford Law Rev 61 (5):1147–1199
Iarmosh O, Prokhorova V, Shcherbyna I, Kashaba O, Slastianykova K (2021) Innovativeness of the creative economy as a component of the Ukrainian and the world sustainable development strategy. In IOP conference series: earth and environmental science, vol 628(1). IOP Publishing, pp 012035
Komarova N, Velthuis O (2018) Local contexts as activation mechanisms of market development: contemporary art in emerging markets. Consum Mark Cult 21(1):1–21
Landoni P, Dell'era C, Frattini F, Petruzzelli AM, Verganti R, Manelli L (2020) Business model innovation in cultural and creative industries: Insights from three leading mobile gaming firms. Technovation 92:102084
Lash S, Urry J (1994) Economy of signs and space. University of London
Lee I (2017a) The internet of things in the modern business environment. Hershey, PA, IGI Global
Lee I (2017b) The internet of things in the modern business environment. IGI Global, Hershey, PA
Lee YC, Lin CY (2019) Developing a design process model for cultural creative product: case study of a table lamp
Li Y, Dai J, Cui L (2020) The impact of digital technologies on economic and environmental performance in the context of industry 4.0: a moderated mediation model. Int J Prod Econ 229:107777
Liu H (2015) Creative industries and Urban spatial structure: agent-based modelling of the dynamics in Nanjing. Advances in Asian Human-Environmental Research. Springer
Luckman S (2013) The aura of the analogue in a digital age: women's crafts, creative markets and home-based labour after Etsy. Cult Stud Rev 19(1):249
Maguire JS, Matthews J (2012) Are we all cultural intermediaries now? An introduction to cultural intermediaries in context

McAndrew, C. (2020). The art market 2020. Art Basel & UBS Report. Basel: Art Basel & UBS [Google Scholar]
Marques CS, Santos G, Ratten V, Barros AB (2019) Innovation as a booster of rural artisan entrepreneurship: a case study of black pottery. Int J Entrep Behav Res 25(4):753–772
McQuilten G, White A, Neville B, Dembek K (2015) Impact and sustainability in art based social enterprises. The University of Melbourne, Melbourne
McQuilten G, Warr D, Humphery K, Spiers A (2020) Ambivalent entrepreneurs: arts-based social enterprise in a neoliberal world. Soc Enterp J
Moulin R (1995) The museum and the marketplace: the constitution of value in contemporary art. Int J Polit Econ 25(2):33–62
Muzahidul M, Akter L, Pervez AK, Nabi MN, Uddin MM, Arifin Z (2020) Application of combined SWOT and AHP for strategy development: evidence from pottery industry of Bangladesh. Asian J Agric Rural dev 10(1):81–94
Neuhofer B, Buhalis D, Ladkin A (2015) Smart technologies for personalised experiences: a case study in the hospitality domain. Electron Mark 25(3):243–254
Nyagadza B (2020) Search engine marketing and social media marketing predictive trends. J Digital Media Policy
Oh DS, Phillips F, Park S, Lee E (2016) Innovation ecosystems: a critical examination. Technovation 54:1–6
Palalic R, Ramadani V, Mariam Gilani S, Gërguri-Rashiti S, Dana LP (2020) Social media and consumer buying behavior decision: what entrepreneurs should know? Manag Decis
Parshukova GB, Riazantseva IV (2021) Creative economy: regional government tasks. In SHS web of conferences, vol 94. EDP Sciences
Pinheiro P, Daniel A, Moreira A (2021) Social enterprise performance: the role of market and social entrepreneurship orientations. VOLUNTAS: Int J Volunt Nonprofit Org 32(1):45–60
President (2020). www.president.gov.ua/documents
Rafiei Vardanjani A (2020) United States economic sanctions on iran and their impacts on the middle eastern art market. In: Arts, vol 9(4). Multidisciplinary Digital Publishing Institute, p 132
Ramadani V, Hisrich RD, Dana LP, Palalic R, Panthi L (2019) Beekeeping as a family artisan entrepreneurship business. Int J Entrep Behav Res 25(4):717–730
Ranta V, Aarikka-Stenroos L, Väisänen JM (2021) Digital technologies catalysing business model innovation for circular economy—multiple case study. Resour Conserv Recycl 164:105155
Repo P, Matschoss K (2020) Social innovation for sustainability challenges. Sustainability 12 (1):319
Romdonny J, Maulany S (2020, March) Contribution of social media in increasing marketing of creative economy product. In 1st international conference on accounting, management and entrepreneurship (ICAMER 2019) (pp 87–90). Atlantis Press
Sahut JM, Dana LP, Laroche M (2020) Digital innovations, impacts on marketing, value chain and business models: an introduction. Can J Admin Sci/Revue Canadienne des Sciences de l'Administration 37(1):61–67
Salamzadeh A (2018) Start-up boom in an emerging market: a niche market approach. In Competitiveness in emerging markets (pp 233–243). Springer, Cham
Salamzadeh A (2020) How artisans and arts entrepreneurs use social media platforms. J Organ Cult Commun Confl 25(2):1–2
Salamzadeh A, Kawamorita H (2017) The enterprising communities and startup ecosystem in Iran. J Enterp Commun 11(4):456–479
Salamzadeh A, Arasti Z, Elyasi GM (2017) Creation of ICT-based social start-ups in Iran: a multiple case study. J Enterp Cult 25(01):97–122
Sanfilippo E, Bariletti A (2017) At the origin of the notion of creative goods in economics: Scitovsky and Hawtrey. At the origin of the notion of creative goods in economics: Scitovsky and Hawtrey, pp 5–34
Sirois G (2021) Digital media in the visual art world: a renewed relationship with the market. In: Rethinking cultural criticism (pp 163–184). Palgrave Macmillan, Singapore
Sooudi OK (2020, December). Alternative spaces and artist agency in the art market. In: Arts, vol 9 (4). Multidisciplinary Digital Publishing Institute, p 116

Statista (2020). www.statista.com
Suyidno S, Susilowati E, Arifuddin M, Sunarti T, Siswanto J, Rohman A (2020, March) Barriers to scientific creativity of physics teacher in practicing creative product design. In: Journal of Physics: Conference Series, vol 1491(1). IOP Publishing, p 012048
Toma SG, Peptenatu D, Andronache I, Ahammer H, Pintilii RD, Drăghici CC, Simion AG (2018) The creative economy in Romania, a key factor of economic integration in the European Union. In: Doing business in Europe (pp 329–350). Springer, Cham
UNCTAD (2018) Creative economy outlook. Trends in international trade in creative industries, 2002–2015
van Laar E, van Deursen AJ, van Dijk JA, de Haan J (2020) Measuring the levels of 21st-century digital skills among professionals working within the creative industries: a performance-based approach. Poetics 81:101434
Van Miegroet HJ, Alexander KP, Leunissen F (2019, September) Imperfect data, art markets and internet research. In: Arts, vol 8(3). Multidisciplinary Digital Publishing Institute, p 76
Varol E (2018) Opinions on the criteria of a creative product in fashion design. İdil Sanat ve Dil Dergisi 7(44):355–364
Vermeylen F (2015) The India Art Fair and the market for visual arts in the Global South. Cosmopolitan canvases: The globalisation of markets for contemporary art, pp 31–54
Williams M, Biggemann S, Tóth Z (2020) Value creation in art galleries: a service logic analysis. Australas Mark J 28(1):47–56
Yin D, Ming X, Zhang X (2020) Sustainable and smart product innovation ecosystem: an integrative status review and future perspectives. J Clean Prod 274:123005
Zhu E (2020) The digitalized development approach of creative product design in internet. In: Proceedings of the 3rd international conference on economy development and social sciences research (EDSSR 2020), Qingdao, China

Aidin Salamzadeh is an assistant professor at the University of Tehran. His interests are start-ups, new venture creation, and entrepreneurship. Aidin serves as an associate editor for *Revista de Gestão* and *Innovation & Management Review* (Emerald), as well as an editorial advisory in *The Bottom Line* (Emerald). Besides, he is the cofounder of the Innovation and Entrepreneurship Research Lab (UK) and a reviewer in numerous distinguished international journals. Aidin is a member of the European SPES Forum, the Asian Academy of Management, the Institute of Economic Sciences, and Ondokuz Mayis University.

Samira Sadat Mortazavi received the PhD degree in the field of entrepreneurship-technology from Islamic Azad University, Qazvin, Iran. Her research and teaching interests include entrepreneurial learning, small business management, and formulation of a business plan. Recently, her research focuses on the impact of entrepreneurship education on creativity.

Morteza Hadizadeh received the MSc degree in entrepreneurship-organisational field from Shahid Beheshti University, Tehran, Iran. He has earned a degree in BSc in the field of computer engineering from Imam Khomeini International University, Qazvin, Iran. His research interests include entrepreneurship in social networks and entrepreneurial learning. Recently, his research focuses on analysis and data mining of complex networks with the help of artificial intelligence to develop the future of entrepreneurship in social networks.

Technology Innovation Among Handicraft Artisans in Lesotho

Tšepiso A. Rantšo

Abstract The establishment of handicraft centres in Lesotho dates far back in history, before and after independence. However, handicraft centres received more attention from the government and other stakeholders during the post-independence era. Most of the craft centres were supported by government and international organisations during the initial years of independence. Some acquired technologies were more relevant at that time, while others use manual labour for the production of different goods. The findings of this study reveal that the situation of handicraft centres in Lesotho has not changed since their establishment. They still use technologies that were acquired during their establishment, while some are still using manual labour. Therefore, handicraft artisans produce traditional goods that are targeted mainly at the tourist market. They use raw materials obtained from the local suppliers, while some get raw materials such as grass freely from the surrounding areas. The use of simple and outdated technologies has restricted handicraft centres in Lesotho to expand into new and modern product lines that can attract local as well as foreign retail shops. It is in this regard that this book chapter recommends that the Lesotho government should assist artisanal entrepreneurs with the procurement of modern machinery that can produce modern fashionable goods.

1 Introduction

This book chapter investigates the use of technology among artisanal entrepreneurs in Lesotho. The use of technology by entrepreneurs cannot be detached from skills acquisition, both formal and non-formal. Therefore, it is important to look at the different types of skill development/acquisition among entrepreneurs. It is also important to study the sources of raw materials and the products that are manufactured by the artisans in Lesotho. This is because the type of raw materials informs the type of technology that is used by entrepreneurs and the kind of items

T. A. Rantšo (✉)
Department of Development Studies, National University of Lesotho, Rome, Kingdom of Lesotho

L.-P. Dana et al. (eds.), *Artisan and Handicraft Entrepreneurs*, Contributions to Management Science, https://doi.org/10.1007/978-3-030-82303-0_14

produced. In this case, this chapter investigates the use of technology, skill development, and type of raw materials and goods produced by cottage industries/craft businesses in Lesotho. The chapter is divided into four major sections. The first part is about the introduction, which studies cottage industries and particularly artisanal entrepreneurs. The second section looks at the methodologies used in the study. The third part is about the analysis of field data on artisanal entrepreneurs in Lesotho. And the last section provides a conclusion and recommendation.

Small-scale artisanal manufacturing enterprises can be traced far back in some European countries before the 1500, where entrepreneurs produced handicraft goods in cottage industries. Evidence shows that peasants participated in traditional handicraft making to supplement agricultural incomes (Houston and Snell 1984). The activities in the cottage industries included mainly the weaving of different types of items for sale in both local and regional markets. And many cottage industries used old-fashioned technologies for the production of goods. The output was mainly consumed in the domestic market (Ogilvie and Cerman 1996).

There were major developments in cottage industries between the fifteenth and nineteenth centuries. Many of them were owned by merchant capitalists (Butlin 1986). Cottage industries then started to follow the capitalist way of production, which included the division of labour and profit maximisation (Bythell 1983). Therefore, cottage industries expanded their scale of production by adopting new techniques of production (Houston and Snell 1984). The industrial phase that marked the transition from using out-dated methods of production to improved ones was termed proto-industrialisation (Ogilvie and Cerman 1996). The market opportunities for goods produced by artisans expanded beyond the local markets during the proto-industrialisation era. The use of improved technologies by artisans enabled the massive production of goods that were marketed internationally (Bythell 1983).

According to Herman (1956), cottage industries in developing countries are mostly family business enterprises generating part-time employment to produce goods for the household and village market. In this regard, goods produced by cottage industries are not meant for the large market or wider national consumption. Sometimes a family or group of families is hired by an entrepreneur or businessman who is not a community member. The businessman/woman supplies cottage industries with raw materials and then collects finished products and sells them at a profit (Herman 1956; Ramadani et al. 2019).

Research shows that hat-making artisanal entrepreneurs in north Sierra Peru depend on family labour. According to Portocarro et al. (2006), hat making is a labour-intensive activity that needs more labour power for weaving. Therefore, artisans depend on unremunerated family labour to speed up production (Portocarro et al. 2006). Although hat-weaving artisans in Peru relied mainly on family labour, some studies elsewhere show a different scenario. For instance, some cottage industries in Ethiopia created employment for farmers during the off-peak season in agriculture and also generate employment opportunities for other local people. For instance, about 599 cottage industries were established at around 1997 in Ethiopia, and each industry absorbed about five people for weaving and spinning of different items (Woldehanna 2002). Although it is common practice for small-scale businesses to be owned and operated by local people, research in the Lao People's Democratic Republic presents a different scenario. According to Dana (1995), most businesses in Lao are owned by foreign nationals (especially of Chinese origin).

It is also common for cottage industries in many countries to use locally sourced/manufactured forms of technology. According to Mukhopadhyay (1985), Meyer (1992), and Durham and Littrell (2000), small-scale artisanal entrepreneurs use modest craft technology as against industrial technology. As a result, most activities of artisanal enterprises are labour intensive (Chuta and Liedholm 1979; Owusu et al. 2010) and generate more employment per unit of capital than large-scale enterprises (Lanjouw 1999). For example, a study undertaken in Taiwan shows that small-scale artisanal enterprises use labour-intensive technologies that are home-produced. The use of indigenous technology in handicraft industries is also observed by Bhattacharya (1996) in Pakistan. Bhattacharya (1996) points out that artisanal enterprises in Pakistan use rudimentary technology that ensures productive employment to the growing labour force. The use of simple technologies makes small-scale artisanal enterprises able to absorb both unskilled and semi-skilled labour (Mcdade and Malecki 1997; Duncombe and Heeks 2002).

The use of craft technologies in cottage industries is further commended for assuring readily available capital inputs, including human capital and rudimentary means of production (Sahley 1995; Dana and Salamzadeh 2021). This makes artisanal enterprises to have a comparative advantage as far as access to the source of raw materials is concerned. This is because they exploit locally available natural resources for the production of goods (Saith 2001). Moreover, the use of readily available resources by artisanal enterprises promotes import-substitution industrialisation, which was once preferred by many developing countries.

The sources of raw materials for craft businesses are from local and foreign suppliers. In this case, evidence shows that artisans in the northern Sierra of Peru import straw from Ecuador for weaving hats, but the market for finished products (hats) is local within the community (Portocarro et al. 2006). It is also reported that the marketing of woven hats in urban areas is a major challenge due to urban consumer preference. Urban people do not prefer traditional hats, but modern western-style hats (Portocarro et al. 2006).

The use of technology among small-scale artisanal enterprises is often determined by location (McPherson et al. 1994). This is a case with artisanal enterprises in Kenya where the use of technology differs between enterprises located in homesteads and the ones in marketplaces. On the one hand, businesses situated in homesteads use simple technologies and small capital inputs, and many of them specialise in wood, reed products, and basket making (Norcliffe and Miles 1984). On the other hand, enterprises located in the market areas use better and more advanced technologies and specialise in activities such as brewing, construction, and transport (Norcliffe and Miles 1984).

The use of different types of simple technologies in artisanal enterprises is very important for the less educated people because it's easy for them to adopt simple technologies. This is because many people employed in artisanal enterprises lack formal education (Tellegen 1997; Beyene 2008). Therefore, they learn production techniques by looking at other workers who have acquired production skills before or elsewhere. In most cases, production skills acquired in artisanal enterprises are out of formal education but from in-house apprenticeship.

1.1 Government Support for Small-Scale Artisan Entrepreneurs

Different governments from both developed and developing countries played a major role in assisting small-scale artisans with capital, machinery, and other infrastructural services (Lanjouw and Feder 2001). It is pointed out by Dana (1999) that Greek government supported handicraft cooperatives with funding. The funds were channelled to artisans through Hellenic Organisation for Medium and Small-Size Enterprises and Handicrafts. This non-governmental organisation provided services such as handicraft training seminars to artisans for improving their production skills (Dana 1999).

Government assistance to small-scale entrepreneurs is also common in some developing countries. The Botswana government established Rural Innovation Centre to develop appropriate technologies for small-scale producers (Browne 1982). Similarly, Khadi and Village Industries Commission was the Indian government's initiative to upgrade the use of simple technologies to power-driven machines among small-scale entrepreneurs (Roy and Banerjee 2007).

1.2 The Advent of Globalisation and Cottage Industries in Developing Countries

The 1990s marked the period of accelerated globalisation where some factors of production moved freely across the national boundaries, and these are mainly capital and labour (Rantšo 2014). The movement of capital was in the form of multinational companies (MNCs) from developed to developing countries. It is stated that MNCs are found in different sectors of developing countries, mainly agriculture, food processing/manufacturing, mining, and many others. These foreign companies bring with them new technological inventions and sophisticated ways of production. However, they create stiff competition for small-scale local producers in poor countries (Kristiansen 2004).

According to Saith (2001), the main aim of capitalist industrialisation is to incorporate pre-capitalist modes of production through competition. In the capitalist world, competition counts; firms must be competitive, adopt new technologies, and exploit labour in order to accumulate more profits. And this is not the case with rural industries that are characterised by cottage industries and household-based techniques and forms of production (Saith 2001). Small-scale artisanal enterprises are often outcompeted by their modern industrial counterparts in the market. This is because large-scale industries employ sophisticated forms of technologies in the production process, whereas small-scale rural enterprises use simple technologies. It is further stated that when small businesses are outcompeted by the large ones in the market, workers lose their jobs. Therefore, they become proletarians who only have cheap (raw) labour power to offer to the large capitalist firms. When the process of outcompeting the small-scale traditional enterprises in the market is over, most of them try to find new niche markets in the urban areas (Saith 2001).

Saith (2001) argues that the modern capitalist economy and process leave no room for the survival of pre-capitalist forms of businesses that small artisanal enterprises resemble. This argument was once raised by Lewis (1954), who stated that small-scale enterprises often closed down businesses due to the movement of unskilled labour into urban areas in search of employment opportunities in the capitalist firms.

One other challenge that faces small-scale artisanal businesses is the lack of division of labour and relative specialisation. Saith (2001) argues that lack of specialisation and division of labour in artisanal enterprises cause businesses to be incompetent. As a result, many of them are overtaken and displaced by large capitalist firms. Therefore, artisanal enterprises have little chance of survival during the globalisation era (Saith 2001). When artisanal enterprises are dissolved by modern capitalist industries, unemployment and poverty persist.

Stiff competition between large-scale industries and small-scale artisanal enterprises producing the same goods has forced the latter to be innovative to survive. For instance, the All India Handicrafts Board worked together with artisans to come up with new products that combine both tradition and modern-day use (Bendi and Pany 2018). Shift in the use of traditional technologies to intermediate or modern ones is observed in some handicraft businesses such as weaving (Bendi and Pany 2018).

1.3 The Changing Use of Technology

It can be realised from the available literature that cottage industries originated in the rural areas, providing part-time employment mainly to peasants. Many cottage industries produced goods for the readily available local markets using unskilled family labour and simple technologies. However, with the advent of globalisation and liberalisation of trade, in particular, cottage industries had to respond to the changing global environment in order to be competitive. Therefore, many cottage industries in developing countries responded to the consequences of globalisation in different ways.

It is stated by Saith (2001) that the traditional or pre-capitalist industries that use outdated and primitive technologies have no room and role to play in the modern capitalist world. Furthermore, the use of obsolete technologies has affected the performance of many handicraft industries (Ghouse 2012). As a result, the modern capitalist industries have displaced traditional industries out of the market through competition because they (modern industries) use sophisticated, advanced, and modern technologies.

Some handicraft enterprises responded to the challenges of globalisation by adopting new forms of technology. According to Mishra (2015), some weaving handicraft businesses have shifted away from using spinning wheels to spinning mills to produce yarn. In addition, the use of handlooms/foot-power looms is now replaced by electricity-powered looms. The use of handlooms/foot-powered looms is laborious and time-consuming. It takes a handloom 5–6 days to weave a single shawl but some few hours for an electricity-powered loom to produce a large number of shawls (Mishra 2015). Therefore, technological change from the use of handlooms/foot-power looms to electricity power-driven looms signifies advancement in the weaving industry to produce different types of home furnishing fabrics such as bed spreads, pillows, pillow cases, carpets, and many others. However, it is reported that electricity-powered looms are very expensive and unaffordable to poor entrepreneurs (Mishra 2015).

It is not easy for artisanal entrepreneurs to acquire technology in some countries. Many entrepreneurs fail to adopt new forms of technologies without the assistance of government or non-governmental organisations. The challenge associated with failure to get modern technologies has been solved by networking of businesses (Scorsone 2002). The social networks are important for facilitating the diffusion of new technologies, product lines, and possible market opportunities.

1.4 Formation of Social Networks

Cottage industries are faced with many challenges that hinder their performance. Some of the problems could be solved through the establishment of a network of industries or clusters. When defining an industrial cluster, Bernat (1999) says 'is a group of establishments in the same or closely related industry, located in close proximity to each other, whether or not they are connected in the sense of forming a net wok'. Although the concept of networking among industries is not a new phenomenon in development literature, many cottage industries in Africa and some other developing countries work in isolation from each other (Kristiansen and Mbwambo 2003). Evidence shows that many cottage industries in developing countries are scattered in the rural areas of developing countries. As a result, it is difficult for the state or any social service provider to reach them with some important infrastructural services such as water, electricity, access to markets, training workshops, and lowering of transport costs (Shan-Shan and Hui-Ying 2007). Therefore, the challenge that is related to the lack of important social services and technologies is often solved by forming a cluster or a network. Businesses in a cluster operate from one region or location to make it easy for service providers to reach them. Cluster or network of industries also facilitates technological spill-over among industries (Scorsone 2002). It is stated that when industries operate in close proximity to each other, it is easy for technological transfer to take place. For instance, industries that have adopted new inventions can pass them on to other businesses in the network.

1.5 Research Methods

This research was based on the qualitative research approach to collect and analyse data. The qualitative data was obtained from the different secondary sources of information such as books, journals, and other Internet resources. The secondary source of information was obtained from the government policy document, Five Year Development Plan. The Five Year Development Plan was Lesotho's first policy document that provided strategies and programmes to improve different sectors of the economy. In addition to the use of the Five Year Development Plan, secondary data was obtained from books and journals. The Internet also provided useful information about the use of technologies in artisanal cottage industries in Lesotho. The qualitative data was also collected from the key informants, managers of the handicraft centres. In-depth face to face interviews were conducted in the three handicraft centres found in the three districts of Lesotho, Mafeteng, Maseru, and Leribe. The source of primary data was the three managers of Malealea Handicraft Centre, Lesotho Cooperatives Handicrafts, and Leribe Handicraft Centre, respectively. The data obtained from the respondents are analysed qualitatively.

1.6 Handicraft Cooperatives in Lesotho

According to the Fourth Year Development Plan, handicraft industries in Lesotho were encouraged because they are labour-intensive, utilise local raw materials (mainly grass and clay), provide exports, and generate income for many people in the rural areas (Kingdom of Lesotho 1987). According to the plan, the handicraft industry in Lesotho was made up of 30 cooperatives and 10 informal handicraft associations (Kingdom of Lesotho 1987). The plan reveals that the most tradable goods from the handicraft industries included tapestries and grass baskets. However, the market deteriorated due to a decline in tourism in the country (Kingdom of Lesotho 1987).

Handicraft businesses in Lesotho are not immune from the challenges brought by globalisation and trade liberalisation in particular. This has forced many small artisanal enterprises to be innovative so that they can be relevant in business. The handicraft businesses received support from the government to improve the entrepreneurial skills of workers and increase innovativeness to overcome the challenges associated with foreign competition. As a response to the challenges brought by globalisation and trade liberalisation, the Lesotho government improved handicraft enterprises in different ways to ensure their competitiveness in local and international trade.

First, Basotho Enterprise Development Corporation (BEDCO) was tasked with the responsibility of providing small-scale handicraft entrepreneurs with management training and counselling services (Kingdom of Lesotho 1997). Training was done by introducing technical (vocational training) courses at the secondary level of education for the introduction of entrepreneurship to students (Kingdom of Lesotho 1997). Second, BEDCO provided physical infrastructure to handicraft businesses. Third, the Central and Lesotho Bank provided credit to local entrepreneurs, and the plan was to include other financial institutions in this development (Kingdom of Lesotho 1997).

Although it was a plan for the Lesotho government to provide credit to handicraft entrepreneurs, this initiative never materialised. This is because the Lesotho government is too dependent on foreign sources for its expenditure (budget). Most government revenues come from the Southern African Customs Union (SACU) and foreign assistance. With the decline of SACU revenues to Lesotho and Swaziland, the country is still faced with financial problems. Many small-scale handicraft businesses continue to be faced with problems related to a lack of credit and infrastructure. Skill development is often provided by BEDCO, but it focuses on enterprises located in urban areas and neglects those in rural areas (Rantšo 2014).

2 Results and Discussions

2.1 The Type of Products Produced by the Handicraft Businesses

Many weaving handicraft cooperatives in Lesotho produce some traditional goods from wool and mohair using simple technology for the tourist market. There has been a slight change since the 1970s and 1980s in the operation of handicraft centres in Lesotho. However, many of them are still producing handwoven products using wool, mohair, and local grass. There are also some handicraft businesses that specialise in the production of other handmade goods such as clay pots, leather bags, fridge stickers, baskets, and some other goods. These goods are mainly targeted at tourist markets instead of the broader local market. Manufacturing traditional goods is one way of preserving and promoting Basotho culture. This is also a case with handicraft cooperatives in Greece that produce traditional goods to preserve culture (Dana 1999). As a way of preserving culture and satisfying the current market demands, handicraft centres in India produce goods combining both tradition and modern fashion (Bendi and Pany 2018).

However there are some handicraft centres that produce goods from other raw materials other than wool and mohair. The research findings suggest that wool and mohair products are the major dominant goods produced by businesses. For instance, woollen products such as tapestries, wall hangings, jerseys, and table mats are produced mainly by Leribe Craft Centre and Lesotho Cooperative Handicrafts. It is easy to produce these types of goods in Lesotho due to easy access to wool and mohair that is produced by local farmers. In addition, it is very cold in Lesotho during winter seasons, and this exerts a demand for warm wool and mohair products. The coarse wool and mohair fabrics are preferred in most cold countries around the world (Wang et al. 1999).

Hall hangings. Source: field data

Clay pots produced by artisans. Source: own study

It can further be noted from Table 1 that the three handicraft centres specialise in the production of different goods. There is no cooperative that is specialising in one product line. This is very important for diversifying the market opportunities. Specialising in many products attracts consumers locally and internationally. Specialising in different product lines is commended for increasing output and assuring efficiency in industries. Specialisation makes businesses to be competitive in the market with others that produce similar products. This is also a case in some Indian handicraft centres that specialise in the production of different items to satisfy different demands and tastes (Bendi and Pany 2018).

Table 1 Type of products produced by handicraft centres

Handicraft centre	Type of products
Malealea Cooperative Handicrafts	Baskets, necklaces, handbags, brooms, hats, cups, pots, fridge stickers, dolls
Lesotho Cooperative Handicrafts	Tapestries, table runners, floor rugs, wall hangings, yarn, table mats, bags
Leribe Craft Centre	Jackets, shawls, scarfs, ponchos, jerseys, bags, wallets, cushion covers, coasters, hats

Source: field data

Despite the importance of specialising in different product lines, the research findings reveal that shortage of labour hinders businesses to engage in this activity wholly. This is because handicraft centres employ few workers, which makes it impossible to produce an assortment of items. For instance, handicraft centres operate with ten workers and fewer. In the case of weaving handicraft products, workers participate in all different activities from classing, teasing, combing, scouring, and spinning of wool and mohair to the weaving of final products.

Production of different handicraft items is determined by access to raw materials. In this case, some handicraft centres are located in close proximity to the sources of raw materials, while others are found far from the sources in towns. Among the three handicraft centres interviewed, Malealea Handicraft Centre is the only one that is located in a rural area. This cooperative handicraft business is located in the rugged mountains of the Mafeteng District adjacent to the Malealea Lodge. It is stated by Dana (1997) that many Basotho farmers keep livestock such as sheep and goats for their social value in society. The livestock is not traded but kept for wool and mohair that are traded locally and internationally. Although Malealea Handicraft Centre is located in the rural areas where wool and mohair farmers are mostly found, the enterprise is not producing wool and mohair items. Instead, they specialise in the production of hats, mats, and brooms using grass found in the area.

Handwoven items from the use of local grass. Source: field data

2.2 *Types and Sources of Raw Materials for Handicraft Centres*

Leribe Craft Centre and Maseru Cooperative Handicrafts use mainly wool and mohair for the production of goods. These businesses purchase raw materials from the local farmers. However, it was mentioned that wool and mohair sourced from the local farmers are not of good quality; they are not clean. Workers spent more time cleaning them manually due to the lack of scouring facilities in the country. They use water from rivers, sinks, and washing basins to clean dirty wool and mohair. Despite the challenges associated with the use of raw wool and mohair, some studies in China reveal that about 80% of traditional knitwears are made out of mohair fibres (Wang et al. 1999). It is further reported by the authors that traditional yarn is coarse and produce heavy traditional cold-weather fabrics. However, with changing and increasing consumer preference of modern fabrics, the traditional mohair knitwear is in low demand nowadays (Wang et al. 1999).

The grass used to weave grass hats, baskets, and brooms. Source: field data

There are different sources of raw materials used in handicraft industries. Some handicraft centres obtain raw materials from local farmers. For handicraft businesses that specialise in the weaving of woollen items, the supply of raw materials is from local sheep and goat farmers who do not trade wool and mohair on the international market. However, farmers who are selling wool and mohair to local handicraft centres are few in number. This is because selling wool and mohair locally is not profitable compared to marketing them on the international market. The low supply of wool and mohair to local handicraft centres has forced them (handicraft entrepreneurs) to purchase raw wool and mohair from the wool and mohair traders who export to South Africa. Some of the wool and mohair traders are located far away from the handicraft centres, thus increasing the transport costs for them. It was mentioned that these traders sell low-quality wool and mohair to handicraft centres. The locally sourced raw materials produce coarse fibre that affects the quality of woven items.

There are some weaving handicraft businesses that import scoured wool and mohair from Port Elizabeth in South Africa. Although scoured wool and mohair produce fine and quality products, these imported raw materials are too expensive and unaffordable to many handicraft businesses. In addition to importing scoured wool and mohair from South Africa, the handicraft centres also purchase cotton and dye from neighbouring South Africa. Importing of raw materials is also common in some developing countries. For instance, some craft artisans in Peru import straw from neighbouring Ecuador to weave hats (Portocarro et al. 2006). These research findings show that free trade solves some challenges associated with the scarcity of raw materials in craft businesses.

Warming water for washing/cleaning of wool and mohair by one handicraft business. Source: field data

2.3 *Skill Acquisition and Transfer Among Artisanal Entrepreneurs*

Skill is about the art of doing/performing different entrepreneurial activities. Therefore, relevant skills are important for producing marketable and quality goods. Different sources of skill acquisition are important for imparting knowledge for the production of quality goods in handicraft centres. Diffusion of relevant and appropriate skills to workers also facilitates specialisation in marketable products by handicraft businesses. There are different sources of skill acquisition or transfer among artisanal entrepreneurs, and these are formal and informal trainings. However, formal training is considered the most important source of skills in production.

Education is considered a pre-requisite for the development of many countries in the world. This is because educated people easily adopt and acquire new information easily compared to the less educated ones. For instance, information dissemination is mainly through the use of the Internet and other electronic sources in the globalised world. The level of education is considered an important factor in handicraft centres. This is because the level of education determines the ability of an individual to adopt and apply new technologies. In this regard, the results of the study indicate that many artisanal entrepreneurs in Lesotho have no formal education, while others have primary education. These results suggest that it is not easy for handicraft artisans to have skill transfer from books and other electronic sources of information such as the Internet. This is because skills transfer can be obtained through studying relevant sources of information such as books.

Vocational education/training is an important part of formal/non-formal education that is important for skill acquisition and transfer among handicraft enterprises. In this respect, vocational training from both formal and non-formal education equips people with modern techniques of production. These can include, among others, new product designs, product finishing, and modern fashions. It was mentioned by entrepreneurs that lack of training in requisite skills impacts negatively on the production of handicraft items. For instance, it was highlighted by one artisanal entrepreneur with no vocational training that the challenge is to come up with new product designs that can attract customers. Although handicraft centres in Lesotho are characterised by artisans without education or a low level of education, there are some craft businesses that have employed people with vocational and technical training.

Despite the importance of formal education in skills transfer among artisanal handicraft entrepreneurs, non-formal education is also a significant source of skills transfer. The sources of non-formal skills transfer are training workshops and in-house apprenticeship. Artisans who learned production skills through in-house apprenticeship did not join the handicraft businesses during their initial establishment period but later. This is because some handicraft centres such as Leribe Craft Centre were established a long time back in the early twentieth century. The research findings also show that training and skills transfer to entrepreneurs were done by the foreign expertise from some developed countries that are advanced in the weaving of handicraft items. For instance, the skill of producing clay pots by Malealea Handicraft Centre artisans was diffused by the foreign expertise. This is the case with many handicraft businesses in Lesotho since their establishment in 1800.

Training through workshops is meant to enhance the production skills of artisans and the management of the businesses. The qualitative data reveals that training is only possible through support from agents of development partners, government ministries, and other entities. Some non-governmental organisations (NGOs), bilateral institutions, parastatals, and private business entrepreneurs have trained handicraft artisans in the production of yarn, scarfs, felting, book-keeping, tax paying, pricing, and costing. Although artisans received training from various production skills and business management, there was a concern that training was obtained long time back. In addition, there is lack of training in some essential business area such as development of business plans.

Skills transfer also occurred through social networks in craft businesses. For instance, one pottery entrepreneur at Malealea Handicraft Centre learned moulding skills from his foreign friend, who has established the pottery business in the area. The results of the study further revealed that some skilled and experienced members of craft centres train members of other cooperatives in spinning mohair and production of yarn. Skills transfer also occurred through trainings by donors.

2.4 Different Types of Technology Used by Crafts Artisans

Most of the technologies used by craft entrepreneurs are labour-intensive and depend on the use of manual labour. Artisans use their hands to weave hats and brooms using the local grass. Weaving of traditional hats and brooms and moulding of clay to produce pots and cups do not need the use of a specified or particular form of equipment. Entrepreneurs only apply their skills in producing these different items. In addition, manual labour is used to produce fridge stickers and dolls. However, there are some goods that are produced using some simple technologies. Artisans use crotches to knit jerseys and woollen hats. This shows that technologies used in craft enterprises do not need money to purchase (especially in the weaving of hats and brooms using the local grass), while some require little capital to purchase. For instance, crotches are not too expensive to purchase.

There are some simple and labour-intensive machines used by weaving handicraft enterprises. The cooperatives use labour-intensive foot-power looms to produce jerseys, scarfs, ponchos, hats, shawls, and other items listed in Table 1. The use of simple and labour-intensive technologies may be seen, on the one hand, as an advantage in that it creates more job opportunities in Lesotho. On the other hand, simple technologies, especially spinning wheels and foot-power looms, delay production and require much energy to operate. These types of technologies are also not cost-efficient and effective and are known to escalate the price of products. For instance, it takes the whole day to produce two rolls of yarn using a labour-intensive spinning wheel and many days to weave a shawl using foot-power loom. The manual power-driven machines delay production and affect the quantity and quality of goods produced. This has subjected goods produced by artisans to stiff competition in the market from goods produced by a large firm that uses modern types of machinery. Although handicraft enterprises still use outdated foot-power looms in Lesotho, their Indian counterparts use electrically powered looms to produce goods (Mishra 2015).

Foot-power loom used to produce shawls by artisans. Source: own study

The results of the study further reveal that there has not been innovation in the weaving handicraft centres since their advent in Lesotho in 1800. The enterprises still use the old-fashioned technologies that have been bought during the establishment of the craft centres. On the contrary, research on India shows that weaving handicraft businesses adopted the use of modern weaving machineries, electric power mills to spin yarn, and electric power looms to weave finished items. Although weaving handicraft centres in Lesotho still use traditional machines, there is one entrepreneur from the Malealea Handicraft Centre who uses electric-powered machine (Cowboy CB3200) for sewing leather bags. The following is the electric-powered loom used by artisans in some countries such as India.

The modern weaving electric power loom. Source: Internet

2.5 Acquisition of Technology

Technological innovation and diffusion are the most imperative processes in the production of handicraft goods. Some industries invent their own technologies, while others acquire technologies from outside. With the exception of the leather bag-producing entrepreneur from Malealea Handicraft Centre, the research findings show that technologies used by handicraft weaving businesses were acquired many years ago during the establishment of the businesses. These technologies were diffused by donors during the initial years of crafts' establishment. The machines are not replaced when not operating, and there are no new machines bought since then. In this regard, the machines are not functioning due to a lack of maintenance and replacement.

Diffusion of new technologies is a major determinant in the production of quality products in any handicraft business. However, the technological transfer is not a free process; craft businesses have to purchase new technologies. Lack of funds was mentioned as the major hindrance in technological transfer. As a result, technology is often transferred through the funding process. However, donor countries often diffuse obsolete technologies that fail to produce quality goods. This is the case with the hand and foot-power looms that are donated by some international NGOs.

3 Conclusion and Recommendation

Technology and skill development are very important for the performance of business enterprises. This is because many craft businesses find it very difficult to compete with the large industries that produce the same goods in the market. Adherence to the use of traditional or simple technologies by small-scale artisan entrepreneurs is said to be the major challenge in Lesotho. In this regard, research findings show that some handicraft enterprises in countries such as India have adopted modern technologies for the production of modern-fashioned goods. These goods target both local and international markets. This is not the case with small-scale handicraft businesses in Lesotho. Crafts artisans in Lesotho specialise in the production of traditional goods such as tapestries, wall hangings, rugs, and others that target the tourism market. Although production of traditional items with the use of simple technologies dominates most handicraft businesses, there are some enterprises that produce modern goods such as ponchos, scarfs, shawls, jackets, and others. However, these handicraft businesses use simple technologies such as spinning wheels and foot-power looms that delay production. In addition, these technologies are outdated and cannot keep pace with the ones used by large foreign industries, especially multi-national corporations (MNCs). In this case, the handicraft businesses fail to target the large market besides the tourist market. There are some artisanal entrepreneurs who use manual labour to produce goods such as hats, mats, and brooms using the local grass. These labour-intensive technologies impact negatively on production. This is because manual work delays production and escalates the price of products.

In the light of the above challenges that are faced by the handicraft businesses in Lesotho, this research recommends that the Lesotho Government, through the Ministry of Small Business Development, Cooperatives and Marketing, should assist small-scale, artisanal entrepreneurs with procurement of modern technologies that are powered by electricity. For instance, instead of using washing basins to clean raw wool and mohair, a scouring plant should be built in the country. The use of modern technologies will help entrepreneurs to produce quality goods that can attract both local and international consumers. This will make it easy for handicraft businesses to shift away from specialising in the production of traditional crafts that target mainly the tourist market. This is because the tourist market has since declined with the spread of the COVID-19 pandemic. Restriction on both local and international movements has caused the handicraft businesses to close down operations. The diffusion of modern technologies into the handicraft centres can assist them to produce modern-fashioned goods that can be competitive in both local and foreign markets.

References

Bendi S, Pany T (2018) Rural entrepreneurship through handicrafts of Odisha. International Journal of Advanced Technology and Engineering Research 1:122–126

Bernat G (1999) Industry clusters and rural labor markets. South Rural Sociol 15(1):170–187

Beyene A (2008) Determinants of off-farm participation decision of farm households in Ethiopia. Agrekon 47(1):140–161

Bhattacharya D (1996) The emerging pattern of rural non-farm sector in bangladesh: A review of micro evidence. Bangladesh Dev Stud 24(3–4):143–180

Browne A (1982) Rural development in Botswana: The role of small-scale industries. Geography 67(3):255–258

Butlin R (1986) Early industrialization in Europe: Concepts and problems. Geogr J 152(1):1–8

Bythell D (1983) Cottage industry and the factory system. History Today

Chuta E, Liedholm C (1979) Rural non-farm employment: A review of the state of the art. Michigan State University, Michigan

Dana L (1995) Small business in a non-entrepreneurial society: The case of the Lao People's Democratic Republic (LAOS). *Journal of Small Business Management* 33(3):95–102

Dana L (1997) Voluntarily socialist culture and small business in the Kingdom of Lesotho. Journal of Small Business Management 35(4):83–87

Dana L (1999) Preserving culture through small business: Government support for artisans and craftsmen in Greece. J Small Bus Manag 37(1):90–92

Dana LP, Salamzadeh A (2021) Why do Artisans and arts entrepreneurs use social media platforms?: Evidence from an emerging economy. Nordic Journal of Media Management 2(1)

Duncombe R, Heeks R (2002) Enterprise across the digital divide: Information systems and rural microenterprise in Botswana. J Int Dev 14(1):61–74

Durham D, Littrell M (2000) Performance factors of peace corps handicraft enterprises as indicators of income generation and sustainability. Cloth Text Res J 18(4):260–272

Ghouse S (2012) Indian handicraft industry: Problems and strategies. International Journal of Management Research and Review 2(7):1183–1199
Herman T (1956) The role of cottage and small-scale industries in Asian economic development. Econ Dev Cult Chang 4(4):356–370
Houston R, Snell K (1984) Proto-industrialization? Cottage industry, social change, and industrial revolution. Hist J 27(2):473–492
Kingdom of Lesotho (1987) Fourth five year development plan (1986/87–1990/91). Maseru
Kingdom of Lesotho (1997) Sixth five year development plan (1996/97–1998/99). Maseru
Kristiansen S (2004) Liberalisation, information and innovation: Cottage garment industries in Tanzania. Eur J Dev Res 16(2):375–395
Kristiansen S, Mbwambo A (2003) Survival of cottage industries in Africa: The case of clustering and social networks in Tanzanian garment industries. J Contemp Afr Stud 21(3):365–382
Lanjouw P (1999) Rural non-agricultural employment and poverty in ecuador. Econ Dev Cult Chang 48(1):91–122
Lanjouw P, Feder G (2001) Rural non-farm activities and rural development: From experience towards strategy. Rural strategy background paper no. 4: The world bank rural development family
Lewis A (1954) Economic Development with unlimited supply of labour. The Manchaster School 22(2):139–191
Mcdade B, Malecki E (1997) Entrepreneurial networking: Industrial estates in Ghana. Tijdschr Econ Soc Geogr 88(3):262–272
McPherson M, Chuta E, Liedholm C (1994) Small enterprise employment growth in rural Africa. Am J Agric Econ 76(5):1177–1182
Meyer R (1992) Supporting rural non-farm enterprises: What can be learned from donor. *Journal of Philippine Development Number 35* XIX(2):113–141
Mishra R (2015) Use of power looms in kashmir shawl industry. International Journal of Textile and Fashion Technology 5(1):29–32
Mukhopadhyay S (1985) Rural non-farm sector in Asia: A characterization. Econ Polit Wkly 20(22):966–968
Norcliffe G, Miles N (1984) An economic typology of small-scale rural enterprises in central Province, Kenya. Transactions of the Institute of British Geographers, New Series 9(2):211–229
Ogilvie S, Cerman M (1996) The theories of proto-industrialization. In: Ogilvie S, Cerman M (eds) European proto-industrialization. Cambridge University Press, Cambridge
Owusu V, Abdulai A, Abdul-Rahman S (2010) Non-farm work and food security among farm households in Northern Ghana. Food Policy 36:108–118
Portocarro J, Young T, Colman D (2006) Non-farm rural activities in a peasant economy: The case of the North Peruvian Sierra. J Int Dev 18(2):207–221
Ramadani V, Hisrich RD, Dana LP, Palalic R, Panthi L (2019) Beekeeping as a family artisan entrepreneurship business. Int J Entrep Behav Res 25(4):717–730
Rantšo T (2014) The role of the non-farm sector in rural development in Lesotho. PhD thesis, University of the Free State
Roy S, Banerjee P (2007) Developing regional clusters in India: The role of national laboratories. Int J Technol Manag Sustain Dev 6(3):193–210
Sahley C (1995) Strengthening the capacity of NGOs: Cases of small enterprise development agencies in Africa. INTRAC, Oxford
Saith A (2001) From village artisans to industrial clusters: Agendas and policy gaps in Indian rural industrialisation. J Agrar Chang 1(1):81–123
Scorsone E (2002) Industrial clusters: Enhancing rural economies through business linkages. Southern Rural Development Centre 23:1–8

Shan-Shan M, Hui-Ying W (2007) Solutions to small and medium-sized enterprise services of China. China-USA Business Review 3(6):79–81
Tellegen N (1997) Rural enterprises in Malawi: Necessity or opportunity. Ashagate, Hampshire
Wang X, Curiskis J, Zhou J (1999) Australian Mohair: Processing Performance and fabric properties. Rural Industries Research and Development Corporation, Kingston
Woldehanna T (2002) Rural Farm/non-farm income linkages in Northern Ethiopia. In: Davis B, Reardon T, Stamoulis K, Winters P (eds) Promoting farm/non-farm linkages for rural development. Food and Agriculture Organization of the United Nations, Rome, pp 121–144

Tšepiso A. Rantšo is Associate Professor of Development Studies at the National University of Lesotho. He obtained BA Development Studies and Human Geography at the National University of Lesotho, Masters of Development Studies at the University of Natal, and PhD in Development Studies at the University of the Free State in South Africa. He has presented academic papers in both local and international conferences. In addition, he has researched and published in different areas such as agriculture and rural development, rural non-farm sector, small-scale enterprises, foreign direct investment, youth unemployment, climate change, and food security.

Women Artisans Facing Obstacles

Shaista Noor, Chaudhry Shoaib Akhtar, Shaheryar Naveed, and Filzah Md Isa

Abstract Pakistan is a developing country with a population exceeding 200 million in 2021. Women comprise half of the population and are facing various social, economic, and cultural challenges in Pakistani society. Recent estimates show that more than three-fourths of employed women in urban areas are in non-governmental employment. Hence, the representation of women in the public sector is less than 2%. However, most women work in the informal sector, such as cottage and small-scale industries. Women artisan entrepreneurs have attained various fields such from fabric, material, and embroidery to jewellery, carving, mirror work, and other handicraft items. These women artisan entrepreneurs are striving hard with their lesser income to stand up in the male-dominated society. Hence, the business environment for women artisan entrepreneurs show the complicated interplay of various factors like social, cultural, traditional, and religious which mutually demonstrated a lower status of women in Pakistan. Women artisans may play a dual role in the country's economic development by keeping the cultural heritage alive for upcoming generations. Due to the lack of researches on women artisan entrepreneurs in developing countries, the present study explores the issues and challenges of women artisan entrepreneurs in Pakistan. A qualitative research strategy and a semi-structured interview technique are used for data collection. The present study's target population comprises of 20 women artisan entrepreneurs from Punjab zone rural areas. The findings revealed that women artisan entrepreneurs face various challenges such as poor infrastructure, power supply issue, power breakdown, no direct

S. Noor (✉)
Faculty of Business and Law, Taylor's University, Subang Jaya, Malaysia

Department of Public Administration, Fatima Jinnah Women University, The Mall Rawalpindi, Rawalpindi, Pakistan

C. S. Akhtar · S. Naveed
Department of Public Administration, Fatima Jinnah Women University, The Mall Rawalpindi, Rawalpindi, Pakistan

F. M. Isa
Faculty of Business and Law, Taylor's University, Subang Jaya, Malaysia
e-mail: filzah.mdIsa@taylors.edu.my

L.-P. Dana et al. (eds.), *Artisan and Handicraft Entrepreneurs*, Contributions to Management Science, https://doi.org/10.1007/978-3-030-82303-0_15

contact with the supplier, exploitation by middleman, limited marketing avenues, no direct customer contact, fewer finances, less familial support, and less profit. The results show that the younger generation is unwilling to continue their ancestors' profession due to confronted obstacles. This study will help policymakers formulate policies related to education and training facilities for women artisan entrepreneurs to keep this sector alive.

1 Introduction

Artisan and cultural entrepreneurship have gained significant attention for tourism and have played a vital role in regional development in recent decades. Artisan entrepreneurship entails creating and promoting artisan items and services that include handicrafts, paintings, garments, artwork, and truck art (Solomon and Mathias 2020). Artisan entrepreneurship is considered a key pillar of development that enhances the employment ratio and encourages investors to invest in local businesses while also preserving the heritage and culture. According to Bislimi (2020), the artisan industry supports the economy and contributes to a country's gross domestic product (GDP). Previous studies revealed that growing interest in the artisan industry globally has expanded the creative businesses and increased the creativity of handmade goods due to the competitive environment (Solomon and Mathias 2020). The artisan industry also witnesses the diversity to incorporate the culture and heritage at the same time (Kumar and Praveenkumar 2020). Entrepreneurs intensely rely and depend on relational learning by employing strong association in work and their working groups. In developing countries where the governments are unstable, and business environments are not too supportive, individuals' creativity helps to develop more unique ideas in their work. Informal learning is also a vital feature of an artisan entrepreneur's life to continue a successful business (Le Loarne-Lemaire et al. 2020; Ramadani et al. 2013).

Pakistan has an enriched culture and strong heritage that occupies a particular position in the traditional artisan industry compared to other industries. Skilled artisan entrepreneurs help to keep the local cultural identity alive. Women entrepreneurs play a significant role in artisan work, contributing to economic, social, and cultural development. The artisan industry has a massive labour force, especially in Pakistan's rural areas, that adds the traditional values in their artwork. However, due to globalisation, industrialisation, and the boom of social media, the artisan industry faces many problems that limit a country's development. There are many factors which Pakistani artisan industry is facing, such as frequent power supply breakdowns, lack of upgraded machines, lack of government interest, increased production costs, limited resources, lack of use of technology, lack of training to prepare coming generations, lack of market strategy, lack of investment in artisan business, and hurdles of accessing mainstream markets (Ahmed et al. 2020). The rise of the online market and technology has intensely changed the growing opportunities accessible to artisan entrepreneurs. No doubt, social media has provided new channels to display traditional work to target a bigger audience, as the statistics show that the handicraft industry contributes 14.60% to the country's economy; however, that is still not a satisfying percentage (Rashid and Ratten 2020; Palalic et al. 2020; Dana and Salamzadeh 2021). Most of the Pakistani population is illiterate, which means a significant chunk of the population is unaware of technology and social media use as a productive tool to gain more profit and take more orders within less time. According to Shafi et al. (2020), community businesses are essential for the sustainable local economy that generate income, improve living standards, support their families, and provide additional employment opportunities to local communities, especially women in rural and urban areas in Pakistan. Furthermore, machine-made products are commonly available in a wide range that is less expensive than traditional handicrafts, are less time-consuming to produce, and use more technology (Shrivastava and Kumar Dwivedi 2020).

Globally, scholars admitted that buyers had shifted their focus on product price to a product's quality that adds the product value commercially (Shafi et al. 2020). Artisan business can create new opportunities and help establish new markets and enhance additional income sources (Muhammad et al. 2021). The artisan business is facing lots of challenges in Pakistan, and the foremost is the lack of government support in devising policies and infrastructure for the development of artisans (Babar 2019). Lack of institutional framework hinders entrepreneurship's overall growth in the country (Nasir et al. 2019). Hence, there is a need to revive the artisan industry, give trainings to the national level, and promote our own Pakistani culture and heritage worldwide. Artisan entrepreneurship requires creating goods and services, which are handcrafted, to sell to others (Ferreira et al. 2019). It primarily originates from cultural traditions (Ramadani et al. 2019) that create a personal identity of the artisan crafting the product. Ratten et al. (2019) also pointed out that artisan entrepreneurship requires product use of uniqueness and creativity with a distinctive cultural component. Artisan entrepreneurship has significantly increased interest in the past few years (Pret and Cogan 2019). This increased interest can be seen because people are now more focused on culture-based businesses that keep the traditions alive and create a distinctive identity (Hoyte 2019). These artisan entrepreneurs can be seen in areas such as organic farming, handmade clothes, traditional food, beekeeping, etc. that are linked to the cultural heritage of the local area or region and have a direct bearing on the socio-economic development of the area (Porfírio et al. 2016; Ratten and Ferreira 2017; Tregear 2005). The chapter is structured as follows: We begin with women's artisan entrepreneurship background. Next, women entrepreneurial spirit in artisan entrepreneurship is presented, followed by women artisan entrepreneurship in Pakistan. The chapter is concluded with implications to government and non-profit organisations for the education and training of women artisan entrepreneurs and future research directions.

2 Women Artisan Entrepreneurship

Entrepreneurship refers to innovation and creativity along with profit maximisation or the start of a new business (Palalic et al. 2017). It helps boost economic growth, facilitates employment generation, contributes towards an increase in national income, and supports innovation (Aftab and Naveed 2018; Ramadani et al. 2017). In Pakistan, entrepreneurship activities have remained very limited. Compared with other developing countries such as India, Bangladesh, Sri Lanka, and other Asian countries, entrepreneurial activities have remained far lesser in Pakistan. According to The World Bank Annual Report 2007 and GEM 2012 Global Report (Shabbir et al. 2018), less attention is being paid to entrepreneurship culture in Pakistan as compared to other developing countries such as Bangladesh, Algeria, Sri Lanka, Malaysia, etc. (Ali et al. 2012; Noor and Isa 2020a). Artisan entrepreneurship is not a new phenomenon in Pakistan. Artisans or traditional entrepreneurs have existed in Pakistan for a long time. These entrepreneurs have been engaged with the traditional handicraft industry that includes furniture, clothes, shoes, toys, pottery, and fashion accessories such as handmade bangles, necklaces, etc. The artisan entrepreneurs are rich in diversity depicting varied cultural traditions across Pakistan. According to the Government of Pakistan, crafts and related trade work employ 14.4% of the female workforce (ESP 2019) and have a total of 255 million USD (Babar 2019). However, most artisan entrepreneurship is in the informal sector of Pakistan without having a proper institutional framework. Because of the non-existent framework, artisan entrepreneurship in Pakistan is finding itself in troubled waters. Shafi et al. (2020) have also pointed out that Pakistan's traditional handicraft industry is finding it hard to sustain itself in the wake of non-existent governmental patronage. It is somehow inevitable to mention that exposure to more challenges may lower the intention of being an entrepreneur as in the Pakistani context; many environmental and contextual factors discourage the establishment of entrepreneurial businesses (Ahmed et al. 2017). Nasir et al. (2019) have also identified that socio-cultural and environmental factors affect the growth of Pakistan's entrepreneurial businesses. There is a dire need to focus on infrastructure development if entrepreneurship is to flourish in Pakistan and ease of financial availability (Soomro et al. 2020).

2.1 *Obstacles*

Some of the many challenges faced by entrepreneurs are their limited resources, lack of supportive government regulations, and limited expertise in making and marketing their products (Arias and Cruz 2019; Muhammad et al. 2017a, b). The new entrepreneurs need to seek help from the ones who have already worked and have an in-depth knowledge of the potential challenges which a new entrepreneur may have to face during his/her initial phase of business, but the new ones may have to face the social barriers where experienced entrepreneurs may not be willing to share their success or failure stories with the new entrepreneurs (Hameed and Irfan 2019). Indulging in entrepreneurial business is more challenging in societies where entrepreneurial businesses are not very common. The first and foremost challenge is convincing their families not to continue to choose what their previous generations were choosing to do for sustainable livelihood. Facing society is another challenge when they treated them differently for not choosing any of the conventional occupations. Technological challenges are also a challenge when they regularly update their technical knowledge to stay in the global market. Financial challenge is also crucial when hardly anyone trusts and chooses enough to lend them the money they need to invest in entrepreneurial business. Then, there are also policy challenges as the government may change the policy regulations now and then, which may significantly affect business affairs (Jayadatta 2017; Isa et al. 2021a).

Many barriers negatively impact the growth of women's entrepreneurial businesses. The absence of a supportive regulatory environment and lack of family support will not help the business to flourish. Cultural beliefs and gender discrimination will also impact entrepreneurship's progress (Noor et al. 2020). Social values of the patriarchal system gender roles associated with traditional patriarchal systems lower female entrepreneurship's value (Faisal et al. 2017). Yaqoob (2020) has also pointed out that due to predominantly male dominance, Pakistani females have fewer opportunities to become entrepreneurs; however, they can become successful entrepreneurs with the right family support (Noor and Isa 2020a). In Pakistan's case, several factors discourage the growth of entrepreneurial activities and economic development, such as culture, society, economic and religious traditions, and settings (Muhammad et al. 2017a, b; Nasir et al. 2019). Elahi and Malik (2021) have also concluded that social norms, inadequate infrastructure, lack of access to markets, and lack of access to finance are major hurdles towards women entrepreneurs' success. If artisan entrepreneurship is taken into account, then lack of government support, lack of institutional framework, non-existent international networking, lack of design and skill facilities, and, above all, lack of any credit facilities from banks and other financial institutions are hindering the growth of artisans and their meaningful contribution towards economic development (Babar 2019; Yousfani et al. 2019). Rashid and Ratten (2020) have also highlighted a need for government to initiate policies that help artisan entrepreneurs in their efforts to sustain themselves. Further highlighting, the authors also point out that lack of finances is also one reason that artisan entrepreneurs shy away from establishing businesses.

2.2 *Contributing Factors*

The increased interest has been seen globally in artisan entrepreneurship which refers to homemade goods and services due to the evolution of creative industries and growing focus on the goods and services which have a cultural component (Ratten et al. 2019). Besides cultural and traditional components, being passionate about the business is also a key factor for artisan entrepreneurship business to be successful (Ramadani et al. 2019). The innovation of the products is also an essential factor of artisan entrepreneurship, which is beneficial for regional development (Hoyte 2019). Zeb and Ihsan (2020) have pointed out that women entrepreneurs tackle hurdles by engaging in innovative behaviours and taking risks for success despite a healthy male-dominant society. Some essential characteristics of artisan entrepreneurs are the passion of the artisan entrepreneur, the entrepreneur's personality, creativity in the product or service of the entrepreneur, culture, and heritage, which the entrepreneur's product portrays (Le Loarne-Lemaire et al. 2020).

Moreover, necessity can be a significant contributing factor in initiating an entrepreneurial venture (Pret and Cogan 2019). Rashid and Ratten (2020) have argued that if artisan entrepreneurs have to succeed, they need to scan their environment for opportunities and have the right kind of information and relational capital needs to be translated into social and professional networking. Shafi et al. (2020) have also indicated that developing networks can enhance the survival of artisan entrepreneurs and develop policy initiatives that include labour laws. Muhammad et al. (2021) have also argued for developing strong networks to help artisan females succeed. In this regard, the authors have pointed out that the best network is the artisan's family that help not only in terms of raising finances but also in marketing the products. Similar views have also been expressed by Dana et al. (2020) that point out towards use of healthy family and ethnic capital for the survival and development of ethnic communities engaged in entrepreneurship. Yaqoob (2020) has also argued on the same lines that family support and continuous learning can help women entrepreneurs to be successful.

3 Women Entrepreneurial Spirit in Artisan Entrepreneurship

Most of the work in artisan entrepreneurship is done by women, but they are less appreciated for their work (Marques et al. 2019). They use their hands to produce their unique products to put their passion, values, feelings, and creativity in making and promoting their products. Women artisan entrepreneurs have skills, talents, traditions, and passions that they utilise to produce limited quantities of their products and services, but they believe in themselves to realise the goals (Dana et al. 2020; Ferreira et al. 2019). It has been reported that good management skills are essential for the entrepreneurial success of women along with their honest reputation and hard work, which are contributing factors for the success of their business. However, they may have to face many challenges in order to succeed. Government regulations are significant barriers to their business success (Zhu et al. 2019). It is evident from research that women entrepreneurship is necessity-driven in many countries and mostly in growing economies (Ferdousi and Mahmud 2019; Isa et al. 2021b). Significant contributions are made to the economy by women artisan entrepreneurs (Pret and Cogan 2019).

Hence, entrepreneurship is being considered a vital tool for the growth of any country's economy. It has become the engine for economic, social, and cultural processes worldwide with the emergence of globalisation (Hoyte 2019). Entrepreneurship has played a significant role in empowering women around the world. It has become an essential source of income generation and employment creation (Din 2017; Noor and Isa 2020b). Women's entrepreneurial businesses are proliferating worldwide, which contribute to the social, economic, and political development of the countries and play an essential role in the empowerment of women so that they can achieve their goals (Faisal et al. 2017). Women may face difficulty in establishing entrepreneurial ventures because of cultural barriers. They might also have to face gender discrimination, fewer legal rights, and restrictions such as not being allowed to work outside the home or locality or country (Cavada et al. 2018). In the countries where patriarchy prevails, the environment for women entrepreneurs is not so encouraging. Even though the number of women entrepreneurs is increasing rapidly, the number of motivated women, who make a difference, is significantly less (Amrita et al. 2018). Women have limited social networks, which hinders the idea generation through collaboration and affects financial capital access. Furthermore, government regulations also do not support access to loans from banks. It becomes challenging for women entrepreneurs to scale up their businesses when facing financial, social, cultural, and legal barriers all at once (Faisal et al. 2017).

4 Women Artisan Entrepreneurship in Pakistan

The contribution of Pakistani women in government, politics, and business has been increased. Similarly, the number of female entrepreneurs can also increase rapidly, yet they face challenges to accomplish their dreams of being successful entrepreneurs (Yunis et al. 2018). Pakistan has a rich culture, and the products produced by the artisan entrepreneurs of Pakistan are exported worldwide. With the advent of globalisation, Pakistani artisans have also been allowed to showcase their international market products. This way, they not only create the opportunities to help themselves to earn their livelihood but also help to contribute towards the economy of the country. Governmental changes are putting much support in encouraging local artisans to take their products to the international market. However, the circumstances are not favourable for women artisan entrepreneurs as it is a solid custom to teach the girl child craftwork (Makhdoom 2016) as women are good at craft art in Pakistan. However, women's artisan talent remains unrecognized as most of them belong to underdeveloped areas. Women have the same right to be acknowledged in performing art as anyone else in society. They are playing a catalytic role in maintaining the distinctiveness of cultural heritage by keeping alive the dying craft for coming generations (Babar 2019); however, they need to learn new techniques for contemporary to the mainstream market shifting. Many government-level initiatives have been taken where artisan entrepreneurs can learn new skills and equip themselves with modern technologies (Rashid and Ratten 2020).

In Pakistan's context, an essential factor for women artisan entrepreneurs' success is family support (Atiq et al. 2018). The number of women artisan entrepreneurs is increasing rapidly in Pakistan, but they have to face far more challenges due to gender biasedness as patriarchy dominates in Pakistani culture (Amrita et al. 2018). In Pakistan, women are considered house-makers and are not generally accepted as breadwinners of the family. Contrary to men, women entrepreneurs have to face the conflict between family and business life, which originates from gender stereotype beliefs prevailing in society. While making an effort to balance work and family life, women entrepreneurs miss the opportunity to learn and plan their business matters. This factor is also a cause of dissatisfaction of women entrepreneurs as business owners (Faisal et al. 2017).

Noor et al. (2021) have also pointed out that women entrepreneurs are better at decision-making than housewives. However, women entrepreneurs face hurdles, especially in combating the cultural and conservative traditions of Pakistani society. Unfortunately, in Pakistan, entrepreneurship is generally viewed as gendered with a heavy emphasis on masculinity, due to which artisan women entrepreneurs are not empowered to engage directly in the market. The family institution has a critical role in explaining women's entrepreneurial activity (Elahi and Malik 2021). Further, Yunis and Hashim (2020) believe that with educational advancements, the family and societal mindset is slowly changing, helping to promote women artisan entrepreneurial activities, especially in the clothing, crafting, and traditional food sectors.

5 Key Objective

The main objective of the present study explores the issues and challenges confronted by Pakistani Women Artisan Entrepreneurs. It provides a snapshot of Pakistani Women Artisan Entrepreneur and associated challenges.

6 Methodology

The research design plays a vital role by providing the guideline to the researcher for hypothesis development and answering the research question (Dana and Dana 2005) and appears like a blueprint of research (Styles 1998). It comprises three main components: philosophical view, way to inquire, and the methodology adopted by the researcher (Creswell 2008). The methodology discusses the research design, process, and approaches used in the investigation (Miles and Huberman 1994). Qualitative research methodology has been used for the present study to investigate Women Artisan Entrepreneurs' current scenario in developing Asia (Pakistan) as the study is exploratory. Naturalistic inquiry is utilised to illustrate a specific group of people's experiences to get a detailed immersion of certain phenomena (Creswell and Poth 2012; Dana 1988, 1990). This approach helps to get an in-depth knowledge

Table 1 Interview questions

Sr. no	Interview question
1	How is your experience being an artisan entrepreneur?
2	What is the most challenging experience you encountered when you started your business as women artisan entrepreneur?
3	What strategies are you following to manage the artisan business?
4	What do you think are the main issues and challenges confronted by Pakistani Women Artisan Entrepreneurs?
5	What are your recommendations for the government and ministries that deal with the artisan industry?

of human experience from the participants' perspective (Dana and Dana 2005; Merriam and Merriam 2009; Patton 2002). The case study approach is a systematic inquiry of events or a set of events. Hence, the case study approach deals with single or multiple cases to answer the questions "why and how" (Alvarez et al. 1990; Yin 1994). For the present study, the explanatory research design is more appropriate as the study is exploratory (Easterby-Smith and Jackson 2008). The data collection was done through a semi-structured interview technique conducted with 20 women artisan entrepreneurs in well-known rural areas of the Province of Punjab, Pakistan. The participants' selection refers to Creswell and Poth (2012), with 5–25 participants enough for phenomena-based studies. A qualitative approach is a flexible approach, and it plays a catalytic role in the formulation of the relationship between an entrepreneur and the environment (Dana and Dana 2005). The semi-structured face-to-face interviews were conducted between March 2019 and September 2019. The span of interviews equal to 1–1.5 h. The interview question grid is prepared in the local language (Urdu) and transcribed later in the English language. A simple language was used, and technical terms were avoided (Covin and Wales 2018) in the interview question to thoroughly understand the meaning of the asked question and the research objective. Further, to achieve quality in the present study, validity, credibility, transferability, dependability, and data saturation are applied (Houghton et al. 2013). Table 1 shows the interview questions asked to the women artisan entrepreneurs in well-known villages of Province Punjab, Pakistan, such as (1) Boharwala/District Bahawalpur, (2) Jhok Mehar Shah/Bhakkar District, (3) Akhori/Attock District, (4) Chikkar, (5) Daokham/Jhelum District, (6) Basti Mundhe, (7) Bakhri Ahmad Khan/Layyah District, (8) Kheewa, (9) Maroof/District Gujrat, (10) Kot Manan, (11) Mundair Kalan/Sialkot District.

Tables 2 and 3 summarises the women entrepreneur's personal and business background regarding age, marital status, education level, year of establishment, business type, monthly expense, primary income source, etc.

Table 2 Demographics characteristics

Sr. no	Variable		WAE1	WAE2	WAE3	WAE4	WAE5	WAE6	WAE7	WAE8	WAE9	WAE10
1	Age	20–25 years	×	×	×	×	×	×	×	×	×	×
		26–31 years	√	×	×	√	×	√	√	×	√	√
		31-onward	×	√	√	×	√	×	×	√	×	×
2	Marital status	Single	√	×	√	×	√	×	×	√	×	×
		Married	×	√	×	×	×	√	×	×	√	√
		Widow	×	×	×	√	×	×	√	×	×	×
3	Educational level	Secondary	√	×	×	√	√	×	√	×	√	×
		Primary	×	√	×	×	×	√	×	×	×	√
		Tertiary	×	×	×	×	×	×	×	×	×	×
		Vocational	×	×	√	×	×	×	×	√	×	×
4	Year of establishment	3–6 years	√	×	×	√	√	×	×	√	×	√
		7–10 years	×	√	√	×	×	×	√	×	×	×
		11 onwards	×	×	×	×	×	√	×	×	√	×
5	Nature of business	Jewellery Designer	√	×	×	√	√	×	√	×	×	√
		Embroidery	×	×	×	×	×	×	×	×	×	×
		Pottery	×	√	×	×	×	×	×	√	×	×
		Mirror work	×	×	×	×	×	×	×	×	√	×
		Boutique	×	×	√	×	×	√	×	×	×	×
6	No. of workers	3–5	×	×	√	×	×	×	√	×	×	√
		6–9	√	×	×	×	√	×	×	×	√	×
		9–12	×	√	×	√	×	√	×	√	×	×
7	Entrepreneurial experience	3–5 years	√	×	√	×	√	×	×	√	×	√
		6–9 years	×	√	×	×	×	×	√	×	√	×
		10 onwards	×	×	×	√	×	√	×	×	×	×

8	Main source of income	Artisan products	√	√	√	√	√	√	√	√	√	√
		Others	×	×	×	×	×	×	×	×	×	×
9	Government financial support	Yes (how much)	×	×	×	×	×	×	×	×	×	×
		No	√	√	√	√	√	√	√	√	√	√

Note: *WAE1* Women Artisan Entrepreneur 1

Table 3 Demographics characteristics

Sr. no	Variable		WAE11	WAE12	WAE13	WAE14	WAE15	WAE16	WAE17	WAE18	WAE19	WAE20
1	Age	20–25 years	√	×	×	√	×	√	×	√	×	×
		26–31 years	×	×	×	×	×	×	×	×	×	×
		31 onwards	×	√	√	×	√	×	√	×	√	√
2	Marital status	Single	×	×	√	×	×	×	√	×	×	×
		Married	×	×	×	√	√	×	×	×	√	×
		Widow	√	√	×	×	×	√	×	√	×	√
3	Educational level	Secondary	×	×	×	×	×	×	×	×	×	×
		Primary	×	√	×	×	√	×	√	×	√	√
		Tertiary	√	×	×	√	×	√	×	√	×	×
		Vocational	×	×	√	×	×	×	×	×	×	×
4	Year of establishment	3–6 years	×	×	√	×	×	×	√	×	×	×
		7–10 years	×	√	×	×	√	×	×	√	×	√
		11 onwards	√	×	×	√	×	√	×	×	√	×
5	Nature of business	Jewellery Designer	×	×	×	×	×	×	×	×	×	×
		Embroidery	√	×	√	×	×	×	×	×	×	×
		Pottery	×	×	×	×	×	×	×	×	×	×
		Mirror work	×	√	×	×	√	×	×	√	×	√
		Boutique	×	×	×	√	×	√	√	×	√	×
6	No. of workers	3–5	×	√	×	×	√	×	×	×	×	×
		6–9	√	×	√	×	×	√	×	×	√	×
		9–12	×	×	×	√	×	×	√	√	×	√
7	Entrepreneurial experience	3–5 years	×	√	×	×	×	×	×	×	×	×
		6–9 years	√	×	√	×	×	√	×	√	√	√
		10 onwards	×	×	×	√	√	×	√	×	×	×

8	Main source of income	Artisan products	√	√	√	√	√	√	√	√	√	√
		Others	×	×	×	×	×	×	×	×	×	×
9	Government financial support	Yes (how much)	×	×	×	×	×	×	×	×	×	×
		No	√	√	√	√	√	√	√	√	√	√

Note: *WAE11* Women Artisan Entrepreneur 11

7 Findings and Discussion

Table 4 summarises generated themes and sub-themes quoted by the participants—the similarities and differences of participants' views highlighted by cross-referencing of coded data. Thus, continuous evaluation results in fewer themes for a research question. So five broad themes and 50 sub-themes emerged (Crotty 1998).

7.1 *Experience as an Artisan Entrepreneur*

Concerning the findings related to experiences as an artisan entrepreneur, the participants expressed struggle (19), tolerance (14), demanding (13), tough (12), and patience (8) (Fig. 1). The findings relate to past literature as women entrepreneurs face a difficult time when they want to start a business due to various factors related to financing, culture, and environment (Ahmed et al. 2017; Bislimi 2020; Cavada et al. 2018; Hoyte 2019; Lemaire et al. 2017; Noor and Isa 2020a; Ratten and Dana 2017; Shabbir et al. 2018). The women are reserved for household chores, and men are treated as bread earners in Pakistani society and, especially in rural areas, due to lack of education and feudal system. Even then, to support their families, women artisan entrepreneurs are striving hard. The participants' verbatim responses are as follows:

> It was very tough to convince my husband and his family. I am good at embroidery, and due to a large family, I could not send my two kids to school. I decided to start a business to cover household expenses. I asked for help from my family for initial finances, but I failed. Then, with my husband's permission, I sold my jewellery, and I got only Rs 8000, and I initiated the business with that amount around 11 years back. I faced the most challenging time with my family, as they were not supportive at all. I have skills but no support to utilise my skills in the right way. (WAE 6)

> Due to my husband's death, I decided to take a step, although I faced various issues. But to take care of my children, I fought for my rights and asked my brother to help me. I am living in my brother's house since my parents passed away. I am earning less, but Alhamdulliha, I can take care of my children with these skills. Here, we want to do something, but we always snubbed by male family members. I know this is an art that our forefathers transferred us. I want my daughter will study and carry our work also. (WAE 4)

7.2 *Encountered Obstacles*

Concerning the findings of encountered obstacles, while running the business, the participants stated that the followings are the main factors: limited business knowledge (20), less earning due to middleman (20), less profit (20), no support from the government (20), middleman frauds (20), poor infrastructure (19), less access to market (19), bargaining with middleman (19), feudal system (18), conservative

Table 4 Generated themes

Broad themes	Sub-themes	Referred by no. of participants
Experience as artisan entrepreneur	Struggle	19
	Tolerance	14
	Demanding	13
	Tough	12
	Patience	8
Encountered obstacles	Limited business knowledge	20
	Limited earnings due to middleman	20
	Less profits	20
	No support from government	20
	Middleman frauds	20
	Poor infrastructure	19
	Less access to markets	19
	Bargaining with middleman	19
	Feudal system	18
	Conservative relatives	18
	Lack of financial capital	17
	No exposure	16
	Large families	11
Business strategies	Funds seeking	19
	Raw material information	19
	Direct marketing	17
	Trade fairs	15
	Team building	14
	Wholesale	13
	Trying to adapt modern tools of communication	11
Issues and challenges	Financial shortages	20
	Less access to market	20
	Less payment	20
	Less sale due to industrialisation	20
	No access to the raw material supplier	19
	Middleman exploitation	19
	Difficulty in business expansion	19
	Sale at low price	19
	Imported Chinese product	19
	Lack of knowledge about modern designs	19
	Weak logistic support	18
	No direct customer interaction	18
	Competitors (mills and organised units)	18
	No export of product	17
		17

(continued)

Table 4 (continued)

Broad themes	Sub-themes	Referred by no. of participants
	Unable to meet changing customer needs	
	No access to modern technologies	17
	No digital connection	17
Recommendations for policymakers and ministry	Loan facilities on special terms and conditions	20
	Innovative product development workshops	20
	Facilitation programme for women artisan entrepreneurs	20
	External funds for women artisan entrepreneurs	20
	Training and development programmes	19
	Marketing assistance programme	19
	Communication platforms to link artisan with potential buyers	19

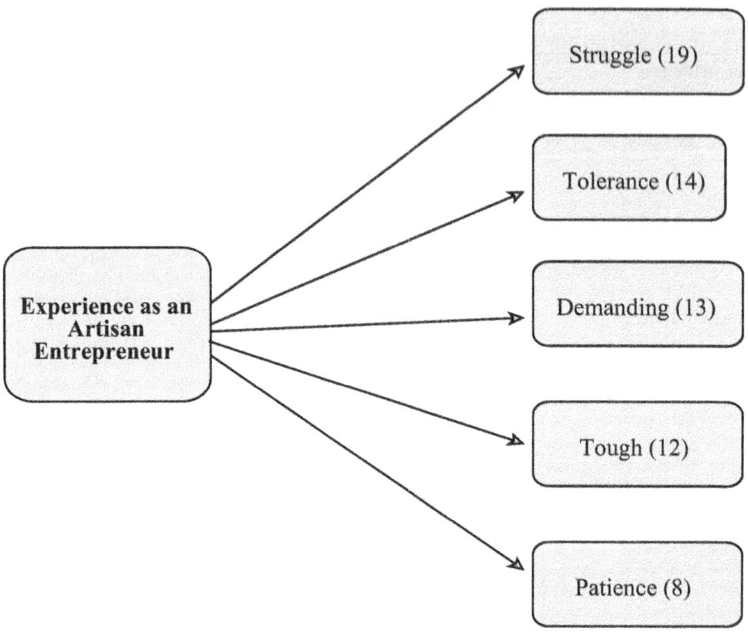

Fig. 1 Experience as an artisan entrepreneur

relatives (18), lack of financial capital (17), no exposure (16), and large families (11) (Fig. 2). The findings are in correspondence with past literature on women in entrepreneurship as women are deprived in various aspects such as finances,

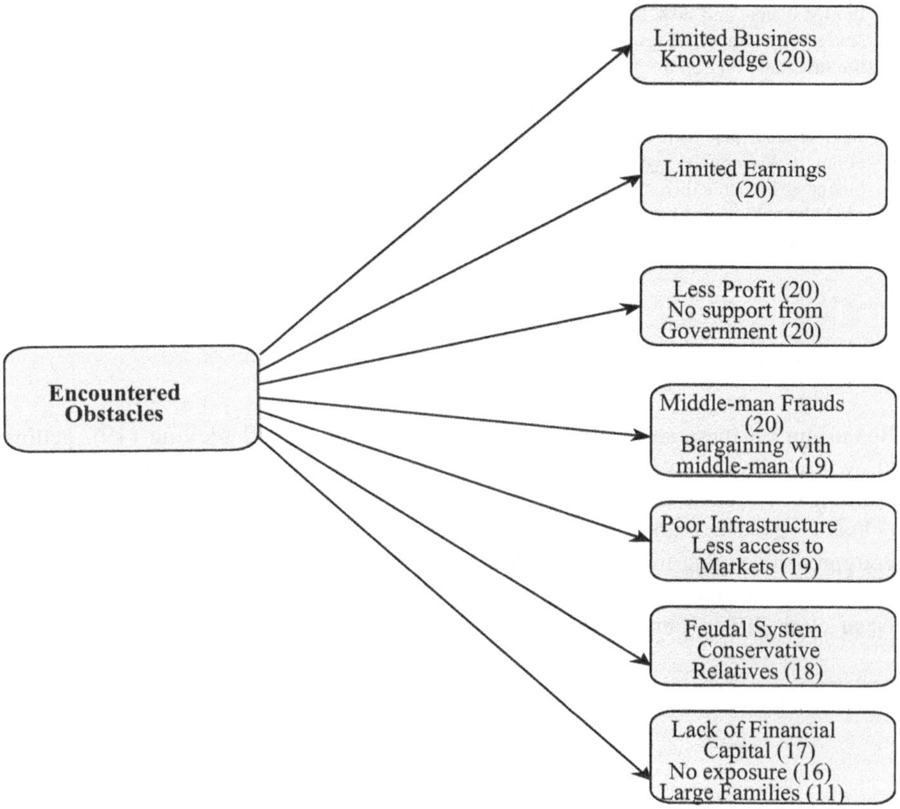

Fig. 2 Encountered obstacles

education, family, culture, male dominance, and no government support (Amrita et al. 2018; Babar 2019; Dana 1999; Faisal et al. 2017; Ferreira et al. 2019; Muhammad et al. 2017a, b; Noor et al. 2021) as these artisan women entrepreneurs are exploited by the middlemen who sell the products at the double price and give only 10% of that to women artisan. Thus, due to ignorance of the market system and procedures, these women artisan entrepreneurs accept the small portion of income, and the middleman enjoys the larger portion of income on every product by never telling them the true story of selling it out. The feedback of participants mentioned is below:

> We faced many obstacles as we prepare the product and pass it to the middle man who takes it as we cannot go on our own. I am unmarried and often requested my brothers to help me sell it so that we can get maximum profit. I wish my father was alive at this stage; then, he would have helped me out. So I have no choice except to rely on the middle-man. Now I am unable to take more orders as I have seven workers now, and I also know I am not getting the benefit that I should have. (WAE 8)

> We have no support from family and no support from the government. We want to work, but we are facing extreme issue due to a lack of education. My husband got a stroke due to

family issues, and now he is bedridden. No one in the family can support us. For the last seven years, I am managing the home. I argued a lot with the middle man about pricing and the raw material vendor. (WAE 15)

Due to an extended family system, we are answerable for everything we are doing. I started with scratch, just with Rs 5000. Pottery is our ancestors' work, and I am very passionate about it. Previously, we would make it for our family friends. When I adopted it as a business, I faced a difficult time from the relatives' side as their thinking is minimal. I wish I could be able to make this art successful not only in Pakistan but also abroad. This art is my specialty. (WAE 2)

7.3 Business Strategies

Regarding business strategies, participants highlighted fund seeking (19), getting know-how about raw material (19), direct marketing (17), trade fairs (15), team building (14), wholesale (13), and trying to adapt to modern tools of communication (11) (Fig. 3). The findings are in line with previous researches with women artisan entrepreneurs trying to streamline their business to overcome the obstacles (Alam et al. 2018; Elahi and Malik 2021; Isa et al. 2021a; Kumar and Praveenkumar 2020; Nasir et al. 2019; Ramadani et al. 2019). The participants stated that with limited

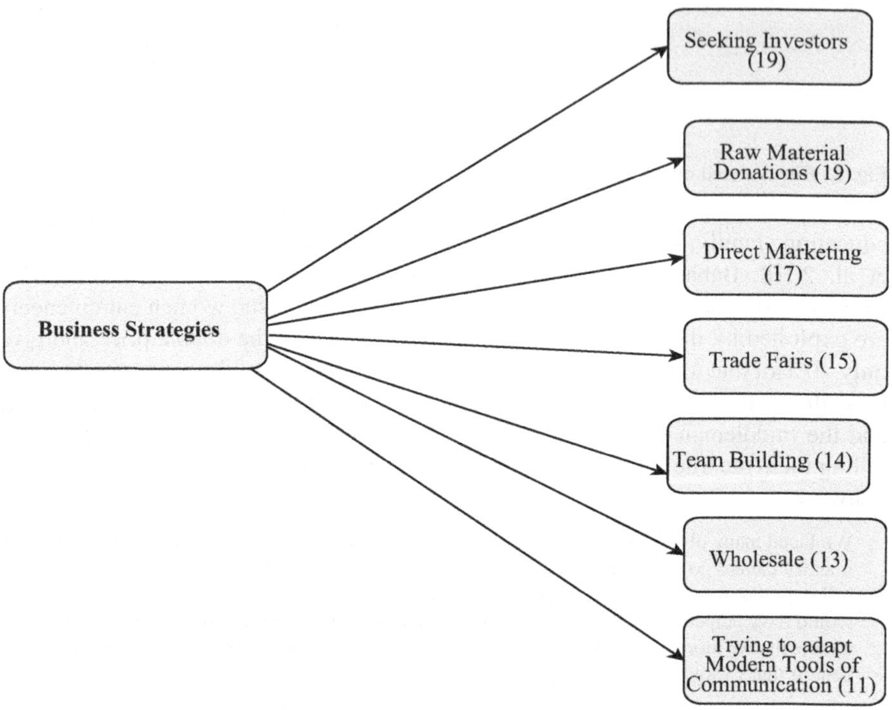

Fig. 3 Business strategies

resources, they seek investors who can finance and help them to get into direct with the customer in order to market products. Artisan women entrepreneurs' minds are changed, as they are eager to attend the trade fairs and are focused on building strong teams and trying their best within limited resources to learn modern communication tools. The women artisan entrepreneur must have a deeper understanding of internal weaknesses and strengths to resolve the associated challenges in operation, marketing, and management. The participant feedback is listed below:

> We are trying to get investor as due to shortage of finances, we cannot produce in bulk. If we want to excel we must do direct marketing, and for that a strong team is essential. We can excel with teamwork. (WAE 9)

> For us, it is essential that we attend the trade fairs and meet with the customer as we need direct marketing to save the amount we give to the middle man. Secondly, by direct marketing, we can retain customers and can make more new customers. (WAE 12)

7.4 *Issues and Challenges*

In findings related to issues and challenges, participants highlighted about financial shortages (20), less access to markets (20), less payment (20), less sale due to industrialisation (20), no access to supplier and raw material (19), middleman exploitation (19), difficulty in the business expansion (19), sale on low price (19), imported Chinese products (19), lack of knowledge about modern design (19), weak logistic support (18), no direct customer interaction (18), competitors (mills and organised unit) (18), no export of products (17), unable to meet customer needs (17), no access to modern technologies (17), and no digital connection (17). The findings correspond to previous literature as women entrepreneurship faced various issues and challenges related to individual, financial, environmental, and cultural factors (Ahmed et al. 2020; Noor and Isa 2020a; Rashid and Ratten 2020; Solomon and Mathias 2020; Yaqoob 2020). The feedback of the participants is stated below:

> We have no direct contact with customers, and therefore we have to sell our products at a low price or the price set by the middleman. So if we argue with the middleman situation, he does not work with us and lets another middle man help us as these middlemen are working in a group and are connected. Hence, we have no other way but to accept the price which they give us. Therefore, we are unable to get profit and are just working for bread and butter. (WAE 16)

> Due to Chinese product and industrialisation, people prefer to buy the product with a variety of designs, and I will say our sale is reducing day by day as we cannot cope with the changing needs of customers in terms of design and creativity. Secondly, due to poor infrastructure and inadequate logistic facilities, we cannot provide the product in time and thus show our bad impression. I feel like Artisan Art is being diminished very soon as there is no support for us. (WAE 13)

7.5 Recommendations

Regarding the recommendations to policymakers and ministry, the majority of the participants highlighted the need for loan facilities on special terms and conditions (20), innovative product development workshops (20), facilitation team (20), external funds (20), training and development programmes (19), marketing assistance programmes (19), and communication platforms to link artisan with potential buyers (19). The findings are in tandem with past literature of women entrepreneurs in other sectors such as SMEs, cottage industries, and enterprises which stress governmental support in terms of funding, training programmes, workshops, and facilitation programmes, especially for women entrepreneurs (Marques et al. 2019; Noor and Isa 2020b; Pret and Cogan 2019; Ratten and Ferreira 2017; Shafi et al. 2020). The verbatim responses from the participants are listed below:

> Facilitation centre is needed from the government side especially in villages. Middleman exploits us and we are not getting the right price for our efforts. To cut down the issues associated with finances, proper funding programs are needed from the government side on easy terms and conditions. Similarly, Artisan Entrepreneurs must be linked to potential buyers. (WAE 2)

> We need workshops to produce different styles and products as we are unaware of the customer needs from us. The changing trend has changed the customer needs and wants. Women Artisan Entrepreneurs must have workshops related to marketing, management, and design of the product. We have the skill, but we are not using it in the right direction. (WAE 19)

The findings depict that women artisan entrepreneurs face obstacles in terms of financing, family size, and environmental and cultural issues. Literature highlights that less than 25% of women in Pakistan avail the facility of microfinance as they are considered less trustworthy than their male counterparts (Muhammad et al. 2021; Nasir et al. 2019; Zeb and Ihsan 2020). Women face gender discrimination at the macro- and micro-level in Pakistani society as women comprise 50% of Pakistan's entire population and can play a constructive role in overall economic support and contribute to GDP. The artisan entrepreneurship sector has remarkable opportunities among the active women population. The artisan is specialised in their field as they possess the technical and practical skills, and their contribution may be enhanced by proper support from the government side. The findings highlight that appropriate socio-economic and cultural forces are essential for the progress and development of women artisan entrepreneurship in Pakistan. Most people are economically and culturally pressured due to the feudal system, and landlords subdue them. Thus, people have lesser rights, specifically women in rural areas, as they are much oppressed due to male dominance and the feudal system. Even then, women artisan entrepreneurs struggle with patience and courage despite middleman exploitation and no direct customer contact. The middleman does not want to break their monopoly as they are getting more profits by paying less to women artisan entrepreneurs. In other words, the middleman seeks their benefit and profit and is unwilling to facilitate them for community development.

Women artisan entrepreneurs' number is increasing in Pakistan's countryside; however, they face various challenges such as familial, cultural, technological, financial, operational, and government-related. Even then, they strive to generate extra income to support their family. Due to gender stereotypes, family support is less as men are considered bread earners and women are reserved for household chores. Women artisan entrepreneurs' continuous struggle, especially in the clothing, crafting, and food sector, helped in the promotion of women as artisan entrepreneurs (Amrita et al. 2018; Yunis and Hashim 2020) in the last few years. All across the globe, women constitute half of the population, so the half responsibility comes on the shoulder of women entrepreneurs for their country's progress and growth. The artisan sector may have tremendous potential, and mostly the women are involved in it, whereas the women are less appreciated and encouraged in this regard. Although they possess skills, creativity, and talent, they suffer from a lack of proper support in terms of funding, marketing, communication, training and development, and business expansion. More support for women artisan entrepreneurs may help them appear as a rising star for the country's economic development.

8 Theoretical Justification

The underpinning theory for the present study is liberal feminism focusing on gender discrimination as it describes the relationship between gender and sex in society. In women entrepreneurship, this particular theory stresses the discrimination-based disadvantages confronted by women entrepreneurs. Moreover, it also emphasises the need to discuss theories that define the differences between male and female socialisation and gender discrimination in entrepreneurship (Yadav and Unni 2016). The main aim of liberal feminism is to eliminate the barriers, which women are facing in society. Hence, there is a need to resolve the issues about women entrepreneurs and eliminate the barriers faced by women so that they can work in the society same as men, and it is considered as one of the main reasons for women's lesser participation in entrepreneurial activities (Morris et al. 2006). It is recognised that recent researches on women entrepreneurship are not according to feminist perceptive, but it can be viewed according to the feminist framework. As the entrepreneurship literature focuses on gender-related institutional and legal barriers, liberal feminism is a good fit.

9 Conclusion and Implications

The findings describe that artisan entrepreneurship plays a significant role in society and women artisan entrepreneurs are the custodian of creative industries that lead to the creative economy. The creative industries come up with the development of a sustainable community in every economy. Thus, women artisan entrepreneurs' work helped them to attain social value in the community by indulging in prosocial business practices associated with the creativity and traditional skills of artisan. The artisan entrepreneurs face familial, cultural, technological, financial, operational, and government-related issues. Even then, they are working with passion and are eager to help their families. Women artisan entrepreneurs may prove and excel as they are diligent and passionate; however, proper support, guidance, and facilitation are needed in this regard. Below mentioned are the implications for growth and women artisan entrepreneurs' success in the artisan industry. The women artisans need special attention from government and non-profit organisation.

1. The government may initiate a unique facilitation programme for these women artisan entrepreneurs based on training, funding, and facilitation to connect them with potential customers. Secondly, special training regarding technology usage is needed as most of the women artisan entrepreneurs in remote areas are illiterate or only pass middle school.
2. A standard policy may be developed for artisan entrepreneurs' welfare as heritage is dying due to ignorance and lack of facilitation.
3. The banking sector may initiate a particular loan programme for women artisan entrepreneurs on easy terms and conditions with proper facilitation as mostly the women artisan entrepreneurs are illiterate and unable to understand the complicated loan procedure.
4. The NGOs and private sector may participate in facilitation programmes by providing training and development programmes for prospective and existing women artisan entrepreneurs at regular intervals and with proper monitoring to ensure their presence.
5. There is a need for awareness camps in remote villages as mostly the women are unaware of the policies and programmes that have been initiated exclusively for women from the government side.
6. There is a dire need to provide women artisan entrepreneurs with a conducive working environment that enables them to utilise available resources effectively.

10 Limitations and Future Research Direction

The study findings may add to the existing body of knowledge on obstacles of women artisan entrepreneurship. The current research is limited to Pakistan (Punjab villages) due to time and cost constraints. Future research may cover other provinces of Pakistan such as Sindh, Balochistan, and Khyber Pakhtunkhwa remote areas by utilising the quantitative technique. Comparison of women artisan entrepreneurs province-wise is another promising area. Further to get a broader perspective, future researches may cover Asian countries such as India, Bangladesh, and others. Thus, the women artisan entrepreneur success may lead to the drastic economic growth of the country.

Acknowledgement This research will not be possible without the technical support from Fatima Jinnah Women University (FJWU), Rawalpindi Pakistan, and Taylor's University (TU) Malaysia. Therefore, we would like to express our gratitude to both FJWU and TU for giving us this meaningful research opportunity. The authors would like to express appreciation to the participants of this study (Punjab region, Pakistan) for their support and assistance with regard to this research.

References

Aftab M, Naveed TA (2018) Role of microfinance institutions in entrepreneurship development in district Gujrat, Pakistan. Journal of Asian Development 7(1):51–68

Ahmed T, Chandran VGR, Klobas J (2017) Specialised entrepreneurship education: Does it really matter? Fresh evidence from Pakistan. International Journal of Entrepreneurial Behaviour and Research 23(1):4–19

Ahmed I, Islam T, Usman A (2020) Predicting entrepreneurial intentions through self-efficacy, family support, and regret: A moderated mediation explanation. Journal of Entrepreneurship in Emerging Economies 13(1):26–38

Alam MN, Rakib SG, Hossain MM, Rahman SM (2018) Do competencies of entrepreneurs influence the performance of small and medium firms: A study on small and medium size poultry firms in Khulna city. Khulna University Business Review

Ali S, Lu W, Cheng C, Chaoge L (2012) Media inattention for entrepreneurship in Pakistan. European Journal of Business and Management 4(18):96–100

Alvarez M, Binkley E, Bivens J, Higher P, Poole C, Walker P (1990) Case-based instruction and learning: an interdisciplinary project. Proceedings of 34th annual conference. College Reading Association. Reprint, 2–18

Amrita K, Garg CP, Singh S (2018) Modelling the critical success factors of women entrepreneurship using fuzzy AHP framework. Journal of Entrepreneurship in Emerging Economies 10 (1):81–116

Arias RAC, Cruz AD (2019) Rethinking artisan entrepreneurship in a small island: A tale of two chocolatiers in Roatan, Honduras. International Journal of Entrepreneurial Behaviour and Research 25(4):633–651

Atiq M, Siddique M, Mufti O (2018). A stakeholder approach to social entrepreneurship: the case of Fascino Couture. Abasyn University Journal of Social Sciences, 1–15. https://search.ebscohost.com/login.aspx?direct=true&db=aph&AN=136487413&lang=pt-br&site=ehost-live

Babar W (July, 2019). Handicrafts industry can fight poverty. Daily Times. Retrieved from https://dailytimes.com.pk/425359/handicrafts-industry-can-fight-poverty/

Bislimi K (2020) Determinants of family entrepreneurship in the beekeeping sector. Journal of Family Business Management

Cavada MC, Bobek V, Skoko H, Maček A (2018) Cultural foundations of female entrepreneurship in Mexico: Challenges and opportunities. Naše Gospodarstvo/Our Economy 64(1):28–40

Covin JG, Wales WJ (2018) Crafting high-impact entrepreneurial orientation research: Some suggested guidelines. *Entrep Theory Pract* 43(1):3–18

Creswell JW (2008) Editorial: Mapping the field of mixed methods research. J Mixed Methods Res 3(2):95–108

Creswell JW, Poth CN (2012) Qualitative inquiry and research design: Choosing among five approaches. Retrieved from https://in.sagepub.com/en-in/sas/qualitative-inquiry-and-researchdesign/book246896

Crotty M (1998) The foundations of social research: Meaning and perspective in the research process. Sage, Thousand Oaks, CA

Dana L (1988) Kindling entrepreneurship: The Australian experience and what Canadians might learn from it. Journal of Small Business and Entrepreneurship, Fall 6:49–57

Dana L (1990) Saint Martin/Sint Maarten: A case study of the effects of politics and culture on economic development. Journal of Small Business Management 28:91–98

Dana LP (1999) Preserving culture through small business: government support for artisans and craftsmen in Greece. J Small Bus Manag 37(1):90–92

Dana LP, Dana TE (2005) Expanding the scope of methodologies used in entrepreneurship research. Int J Entrep Small Bus 2(1):79

Dana LP, Salamzadeh A (2021) Why do Artisans and arts entrepreneurs use social media platforms?: Evidence from an emerging economy. Nordic Journal of Media Management 2(1)

Dana LP, Gurau C, Light I, Muhammad N (2020) Family, community, and ethnic capital as entrepreneurial resources: Toward an integrated model. J Small Bus Manag 58(5):1003–1029

Din TMU (2017) Handicraft entrepreneurship: Tool for economic development in rural economy. Journal of Humanities and Social Sciences 3(1):1–4

Easterby-Smith TM, Jackson P (2008) Management research: An introduction, 3rd edn. Sage, London

Economic Survey of Pakistan (2019) Economic Survey of Pakistan 2018–19. Finance Division, Ministry of Finance, Government of Pakistan

Elahi N, Malik QA (2021) Assessing the environmental and social obstacles to women entrepreneurs: a case study of Pakistan. In Women Empowerment and Well-Being for Inclusive Economic Growth (pp 90–105). IGI Global

Faisal MN, Jabeen F, Katsioloudes MI (2017) Strategic interventions to improve women entrepreneurship in GCC countries: A relationship modeling approach. Journal of Entrepreneurship in Emerging Economies 9(2):161–180

Ferdousi F, Mahmud P (2019) Role of social business in women entrepreneurship development in Bangladesh: Perspectives from Nobin Udyokta projects of Grameen Telecom Trust. Journal of Global Entrepreneurship Research, 9(1)

Ferreira J, Sousa BM, Gonçalves F (2019) Encouraging the subsistence artisan entrepreneurship in handicraft and creative contexts. Journal of Enterprising Communities 13(1–2):64–83

Hameed I, Irfan Z (2019) Entrepreneurship education: A review of challenges, characteristics and opportunities. Entrepreneurship Education 2(3–4):135–148

Houghton C, Casey D, Shaw D, Murphy K (2013) Rigour in qualitative case study research. Nurse Res 20(4):12–17

Hoyte C (2019) Artisan entrepreneurship: A question of personality structure? International Journal of Entrepreneurial Behaviour and Research 25(4):615–632

Isa FM, Muhammad NM, Ahmad A, Noor S (2021a) Effect of ICT on women entrepreneur business performance: case of Malaysia

Isa F, Mohd Nor NA, Noor S (2021b) Leadership and decision-making style among women entrepreneurs: A case of Malaysia. International Review of Management and Business Research 10(1):68–79

Jayadatta S (2017) Major Challenges and Problems of Rural Entrepreneurship in India. IOSR Journal of Business and Management (IOSR-JBM) 19(9):35–44

Kumar SP, Praveenkumar S (2020) Factors influencing development of women entrepreneurship in unorganised sector in Madurai District. Article in International Journal of Psychosocial Rehabilitation 24:2020

Le Loarne-Lemaire S, Partouche-Sebban J, Razgallah M, Maalaoui A (2020) Antecedents of well-being for artisan entrepreneurship: A first exploratory study. Int J Entrep Small Bus 41 (1):96–114

Lemaire SL, Maalaoui A, Dana LP (2017) Social entrepreneurship, age and gender: Toward a model of social involvement in entrepreneurship. Int J Entrep Small Bus 31(3):363

Makhdoom T (2016) Women's home-based handicraft industry and economic wellbeing: a case study of Badin Pakistan. *The Women - Annual Research Journal of Gender Studies* 8:40–55

Marques CS, Santos G, Ratten V, Barros AB (2019) Innovation as a booster of rural artisan entrepreneurship: A case study of black pottery. International Journal of Entrepreneurial Behaviour and Research 25(4):753–772

Merriam SB, Merriam SB (2009) Qualitative research: A guide to design and implementation. Jossey-Bass

Miles MB, Huberman MA (1994) Qualitative analysis: An expanded sourcebook, 2nd edn. Sage, Thousand Oaks, CA

Morris MH, Miyasaki NN, Watters CE, Coombes SM (2006) The dilemma of growth: Understanding venture size choices of women entrepreneurs. J Small Bus Manag 44(2):221–244

Muhammad N, McElwee G, Dana LP (2017a) Barriers to the development and progress of entrepreneurship in rural Pakistan. Int J Entrep Behav Res 23(2):279–295

Muhammad N, McElwee G, Dana LP (2017b) Barriers to the development and progress of entrepreneurship in rural Pakistan. International Journal of Entrepreneurial Behaviour and Research 23(2):279–295

Muhammad S, Ximei K, Saqib SE, Ul Haq Z, Muhammad N, Bank, M (2021) The family network support and disparity among rural-urban women informal entrepreneurs: empirical evidences from Khyber Pakhtunkhwa Pakistan. Journal of Geography and Social Sciences 2(2):122–132. Retrieved from http://www.jgss.com.pk

Nasir M, Iqbal R, Akhtar CS (2019) Factors affecting the growth of women entrepreneurs in Pakistan. Pakistan Administrative Review 3(1):35–50

Noor S, Isa FM (2020a) Contributing factors of women entrepreneurs' business growth and failure in Pakistan. International Journal of Business and Globalisation 25(4):503

Noor S, Isa FM (2020b) Entrepreneurial opportunities for Malaysian women in ageing care industry. Social and Management Research Journal 17(2):83

Noor S, Isa FM, Mohd Nor L (2020) Ageing care centre women entrepreneur: a silver bullet for ageing tsunami in Malaysia. Sains Humanika 12(1)

Noor S, Isa FM, Nor LM (2021) Women empowerment through women entrepreneurship: A comparison between women entrepreneurs and fulltime housewife in Pakistan. Iranian Journal of Management Studies 14(2):347–363

Palalic R, Ramadani V, Dana LP (2017) Entrepreneurship in Bosnia and Herzegovina: Focus on gender. Eur Bus Rev 29(4):476–496

Palalic R, Ramadani V, Mariam Gilani S, Gërguri-Rashiti S, Dana L (2020) Social media and consumer buying behavior decision: what entrepreneurs should know? Manag Decis 59 (6):1249–1270

Patton MQ (2002) Qualitative research and evaluation methods. Sage

Porfírio JA, Carrilho T, Mónico LS (2016) Entrepreneurship in different contexts in cultural and creative industries. J Bus Res 69(11):5117–5123

Pret T, Cogan A (2019) Artisan entrepreneurship: A systematic literature review and research agenda. International Journal of Entrepreneurial Behaviour and Research 25(4):592–614

Ramadani V, Gërguri S, Dana LP, Tašaminova T (2013) Women entrepreneurs in the Republic of Macedonia: Waiting for directions. Int J Entrep Small Bus 19(1):95

Ramadani V, Dana L, Sadiku-Dushi N, Ratten V, Welsh DH (2017) Decision-making challenges of women entrepreneurship in family business succession process. Journal of Enterprising Culture 25(04):411–439

Ramadani V, Hisrich RD, Dana LP, Palalic R, Panthi L (2019) Beekeeping as a family artisan entrepreneurship business. International Journal of Entrepreneurial Behaviour and Research 25 (4):717–730

Rashid S, Ratten V (2020) Commodifying skills for survival among artisan entrepreneurs in Pakistan. Int Entrep Manag J:1–20

Ratten V, Dana L (2017) Gendered perspective of Indigenous entrepreneurship. Small Enterp Res 24(1):62–72

Ratten V, Ferreira J (2017) Future research direction for cultural entrepreneurship and regional innovation. International Journal of Entrepreneurship and Innovation 21(3):163–169

Ratten V, Costa C, Bogers M (2019) Artisan, cultural and tourism entrepreneurship. International Journal of Entrepreneurial Behaviour and Research 25(4):582–591

Shabbir MS, Shariff MNM, Alshaibani YH, Faisal M, Salman R (2018) Entrepreneurship and skills development for socioeconomic growth; Present landscape and future agenda for Pakistan. Acad Entrep J 24(3)
Shafi M, Yin L, Yuan Y, Zoya (2020) Revival of the traditional handicraft enterprising community in Pakistan. J Enterp Communities People Places Glob Econ 15(4):477–507
Shrivastava U, Kumar Dwivedi A (2020) Manifestations of rural entrepreneurship: The journey so far and future pathways. Manag Rev Q:1–29
Solomon JS, Mathias BD (2020) The artisans' dilemma: artisan entrepreneurship and the challenge of firm growth. J Bus Ventur 35(5):106044
Soomro BA, Almahdi HK, Shah N (2020) Perceptions of young entrepreneurial aspirants towards sustainable entrepreneurship in Pakistan. Kybernetes
Styles C (1998) Export performance measures in Australia and the United kingdom. J Int Mark 6 (3):12–36
Tregear A (2005) Lifestyle growth or community involvement? The balance of goals of artisan food producers. Entrep Reg Dev 17(1):1–15
Yadav V, Unni J (2016) Women entrepreneurship: Research review and future directions. J Glob Entrep Res 6(1):12
Yaqoob S (2020) Emerging trend of Women entrepreneurship in Pakistan. Journal of Arts and Social Sciences 7(2):217
Yin RK (1994) Case study research: Design and methods, 2nd edn. Sage, Newbury Park, CA
Yousfani K, Aslam Y, Mahar Q, Kazi H (2019) The impact of microfinance on growth of women entrepreneurship in Pakistan. Journal of Entrepreneurship, Business and Economics 7 (1):133–152
Yunis MS, Hashim H (2020) The gendering of context: A fresh perspective of women social enterprise in Pakistan. Business and Economic Review 12(1):25–48
Yunis MS, Hashim H, Anderson AR (2018) Enablers and constraints of female entrepreneurship in Khyber Pukhtunkhawa, Pakistan: institutional and feminist perspectives. Sustainability (Switzerland) 11(1)
Zeb A, Ihsan A (2020, March) Innovation and the entrepreneurial performance in women-owned small and medium-sized enterprises in Pakistan. Women's Stud Int Forum 79:102342
Zhu L, Kara O, Zhu X (2019) A comparative study of women entrepreneurship in transitional economies: The case of China and Vietnam. Journal of Entrepreneurship in Emerging Economies 11(1):66–80

Shaista Noor holds a Doctorate from Taylor's University Malaysia in the area of women entrepreneurship and ageing. Currently, affiliated with Fatima Jinnah Women University, Pakistan and published various research papers in entrepreneurship, commercialisation, leadership, management, marketing and ageing. Her work on 'Commercialisation of academic research in higher education institution in Pakistan' is acknowledged by the HEC Pakistan in 2015. She has proposed a recommendation plan for HEIs, industry and government, and a best practice model for technology transfer offices in Pakistani universities to follow. She has worked as a PhD output in the Malaysian Government Ageing Flagship Project and is currently involved in various projects. She is also an entrepreneur and provides mentorship to young startup.

Chaudhry Shoaib Akhtar is associated with Fatima Jinnah Women University as Assistant Professor in the Department of Public Administration. He received his PhD from Universiti Teknologi Malaysia, in Management. He has more than 15 years of teaching and research experience. He is also an entrepreneur and provides mentorship to young start-ups. He is widely published in international journals. His research interests include entrepreneurship, social capital, implementation science, and learning organization. He is currently heading the Office of Research, Innovation and Commercialization (ORIC) at Fatima Jinnah Women University Pakistan.

Shaheryar Naveed is PhD in Management with emphasis on organizational behaviour. He is an Assistant Professor, at Department of Public Administration Fatima Jinnah Women University, Rawalpindi, Pakistan. He has more than 15 years of teaching, research, and training experience at both national and international levels. He is also an entrepreneur working in apparel/fashion industry. He is well published and participates in international conferences. His research interests include organizational behaviour, leadership, social psychology, and social entrepreneurship. He is currently heading Centre for Learning at Fatima Jinnah Women University Pakistan.

Filzah Md Isa is Associate Professor at the Taylor's University, Malaysia. She has published numerous papers and is involved in several professional bodies. She was chosen as the first runner-up for the Best Entrepreneurship Mentor/Coach for Academia of Malaysia by the Ministry of Higher Education (MOHE) in December 2015. As an educator, she has vast experience in teaching and mentoring both undergraduate and postgraduate students and executives from various fields and industries. She is now serving as the Advisory Board Member at the Centre for Academic Learning Writing and Support Service (CALWASS) at Bharia University, Islamabad, Pakistan, starting May 2019.

The manufacturer's authorised representative in the EU is Springer Nature Customer Service Centre GmbH, Europaplatz 3, 69115 Heidelberg, Germany. If you have any concerns regarding our products, please contact ProductSafety@springernature.com

Printed and bound by CPI Group (UK) Ltd, Croydon, CR0 4YY
28/09/2026
02224089-0011